John Roberts

Accounting Principles

for Non-Accounting

Students

2nd edition

Design and Typesetting: Text4study

Proof reading: Susan Robertson

Printed and bound in Great Britain by: The Bath Press

2nd edition - February 2007

LIBRARY OF CONGRESS CATALOGING IN PUBLICATION DATA

Robertson, John

Accounting Principles for Non-Accounting Students

Included bibliographies and index

ISBN 9781 8731 8621 3

1. Financial accounting, Cost accounting, Management accounting

I. Title

Text4study

62 Kingsmead, Lechlade, Glos. GL7 3BW
Email: susan@text4study.com

Preface

This book has been written specifically with the non-accounting student in mind. Such students, we know from our experience, are following programmes where accounting is not a major element of the degree. Students simply require an appreciation of accounting both to understand its unique language and to use certain elements in their studies. With this in mind, we have constructed each chapter to provide a blend of explanation supported by examples. At the end of chapters 2 to 6 and 7 to 14 there are additional exercises with answers to the arithmentic components of each exercise at the end of the book.

The book is organised in the twelve chapters shown in the following illustration:

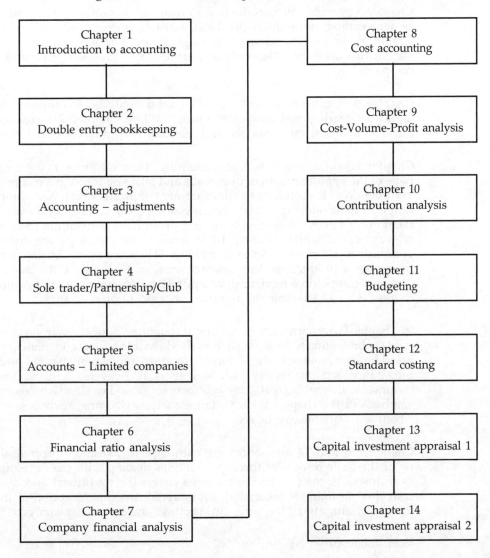

Chapter 1 Introduction to accounting	Chapter 8 Cost accounting
Chapter 2 Double entry bookkeeping	Chapter 9 Cost-Volume-Profit analysis
Chapter 3 Accounting – adjustments	Chapter 10 Contribution analysis
Chapter 4 Sole trader/Partnership/Club	Chapter 11 Budgeting
Chapter 5 Accounts – Limited companies	Chapter 12 Standard costing
Chapter 6 Financial ratio analysis	Chapter 13 Capital investment appraisal 1
Chapter 7 Company financial analysis	Chapter 14 Capital investment appraisal 2

Chapter 1 provides an introduction to the income statement, and the balance sheet. It assumes that you have had little formal exposure to the main financial statements used within an organisation and the rules and conventions used in drafting them. It will take you through these and the working capital cycle, quite gently.

Chapter 2 introduces you to double entry bookkeeping. A simple concept, i.e. that each transaction affects two accounts, hence the double entry. However, many students initially find this difficult to grasp. We would recommend – persistence; it will reward you in the end, since double entry bookkeeping is similar to the ABC of a language, it acts as a foundation to begin to understand accounting processes.

Chapter 3 provides an introduction to many of accounting 'adjustments' such as depreciation, revaluation, goodwill, accruals, prepayments. Chapters 4 and 5 build on the previous chapters through the preparation of the main financial statements used by sole traders, partnerships, club/societies and limited companies.

Chapter 6 is concerned with financial ratio analysis covering profitability, liquidity, gearing and employee ratios. While Chapter 7 introduces non-financial analysis, ratio models, and working with published accounts.

Chapter 8 is concerned with cost accounting. Here we focus on the contentious issue of the apportionment of overheads and take you through a comprehensive example. We also consider the development of product costs and complete the chapter by introducing activity based costing (ABC). Chapter 9 examines the relationships between cost, volume and profit (CVP), including the concept of relevant costs, while Chapter 10 contiunes and develops the contribution approach to short-term decision making. Here we cover closing a business (dropping a product/service), best use of scarce resources, the make or buy decision, competitive tendering, accept/reject a special order and complete the chapter with an example on marginal -v- absorption costing.

In Chapter 11 we introduce budgeting through the budget environment. Also a range of budgeting techniques such as fixed/flexible budgets, incremental or zero based budgets, rolling budgets, forecast/outturn and activity based budgets. The preparation and purpose of cash budgets is also covered. In Chapter 12 we continue with the 'budgets' for products/services, i.e. standard costing. The emphasis of the chapter is on variance analysis covering, revenues, materials, labour and variable overheads.

Chapters 13 and 14 are concerned with capital investment appraisal. They cover the basic principles through examples dealing with the development of cash flows. A comprehensive example covers the traditional and discounted cash flow techniques associated with capital investment appraisal including the use of annuity tables, inflation, taxation and sensitivity analysis.

John Robertson   February 2007

Contents

CHAPTER ONE

INTRODUCTION TO ACCOUNTING

When you have finished studying this chapter you should be able to:

❑ Understand the relationship between the income statement and the balance sheet;

❑ Understand the structure of a balance sheet both vertical and 'two sided', interpret and show the effect of single transactions;

❑ Prepare income statements, describe their relationship between the opening and closing balance sheets and comment on the differences between profit and cash;

❑ Describe the main components of the working capital cycle.

1.1   Introduction

The successful study of accounting and finance is dependent upon the assimilation of a number of basic principles. Rather than deal will all of these by way of a comprehensive introduction, in this chapter, we have selected only those needed for the earlier chapters of the book. In these earlier chapters, the particular focus of attention is upon the principles, content, layout and interpretation of the main financial statements.

This chapter provides an overview of accounting both for those with little or no background in the subject and for those with some background who wish to review some fundamental principles. Specific reference will be made to important terminology. To know what financial statements do not communicate is just as important as knowing what they do communicate.

Fundamental principles are discussed in this chapter without employing some of the specific accounting techniques (like double entry bookkeeping) and jargon (like debit and credit). It is directed at answering two important questions often asked by managers and other parties with an interest in an organisation: How well it did or will perform over a given time period? What is, or will be the financial position at a given point of time? The accountant answers these questions with two main financial statements which we shall consider at length in this chapter – the income statement and the balance sheet.

Our focus of attention in this chapter is directed at 'for-profit' organisations and, in particular, limited liability companies. Such organisations typically revolve around a similar, usually regular, cycle of economic activity. For example, retailers and most businesses buy goods and services then modify them by changing their form or by placing them in a convenient location, so that they can be sold at higher prices with the aim of producing a profit. The total amount of profit earned during a particular period heavily depends on the excess of the selling prices over the costs of the goods and services (the mark-up) and the speed of the operating cycle (the turnover).

Financial statements are used by organisations to summarise aspects of past, present and expected; likely or anticipated future performance. These financial statements are the result of applying certain principles, like double entry bookkeeping and some are reliant upon accounting conventions, a basic knowledge and understanding of which is essential in most of what follows.

An important part of this chapter is to cover the main components of the working capital cycle, i.e. inventory control, credit control and cash control. These will be discussed at pages 9 to 13, with additional explanations given in *Appendix A* to this chapter.

1.2   Introduction to balance sheet and income statement

Our discussion in this chapter will focus on:

1.   The balance sheet;

2.   The income statement;

3.   The working capital cycle.

In the rest of this section we will introduce the main components of the balance sheet and show its relationship to the income statement. In *Section 1.3* we will show the development of a balance sheet over a number of periods; this will include the relationship with the income statement. We will also describe the main components of the working captial cycle and show its relationship to the balance sheet.

1.   Balance sheet

The balance sheet is the financial statement used to illustrate an organisation's financial position. It can be likened to a snapshot because it is a static representation of an organisation's financial position in the form of its total assets and total liabilities at a particular point in time.

The balance sheet is reliant upon the following simple equation:

$$\textbf{TOTAL ASSETS} \ = \ \textbf{TOTAL LIABILITIES}$$

In developing this equation in this chapter, our focus of attention will be upon the assets and liabilities found in the balance sheet of a limited liability company. However, in principle, though not the terminology used, it is also applicable to most types of organisations. What are assets and liabilities?

Total assets

These are those resources obtained from the sources of finance which are expressed in monetary terms. Assets to be found in a company balance sheet are those in its possession, whether owned or controlled, and which are expected to yield future economic benefits. As shown in *Figure 1.1*, assets are usually referred to as being 'non-current' or 'current'. Non-current assets are those like land and buildings, machinery, vehicles, which are intended for use in the business and are not intended for sale as part of normal trading activity. Current assets form part of the working capital of a business and are instrumental in the generation of profit within the business. The main items of current assets include inventories, trade and other receivables and cash held for use within the business.

Figure 1.1 Total assets

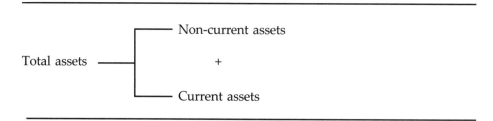

Total liabilities

These are monetary obligations arising from past events and can be thought of as being the sources of finance used by the business. They include 'liabilities' to the owners, known as shareholders' (owners') funds or equity, which is usually categorised as share capital and reserves (such as retained profit), and liabilities to external sources of finance in the form of long-term loans and short-term sources (current liabilities) like trade payables and bank overdrafts. The sources of finance and how they may be generally categorised is illustrated in *Figure 1.2.*

Figure 1.2 Total liabilities

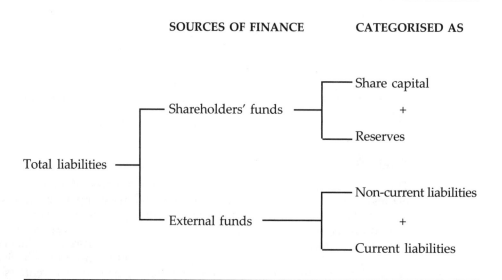

2. Income statement

The income statement summarises the revenue generated and the costs incurred in the trading period between two balance sheet dates. Where the revenue exceeds the cost there is a profit and where the costs exceeds the revenue a loss is incurred.

In a profitable environment the result of recording accounting transactions will be that the assets of the business will increase automatically. On a regular basis, at least annually for publication purposes, companies prepare income statements to determine the amount of profit generated by and retained in the business. The amount retained is added to the shareholders' fund under the sub-heading *retained earnings*, (please note that retained earnings in the balance sheet refers to the accumulated profits retained in the business over time, thereby increasing the total liabilities section). In this way the benefit to shareholders from profitable activity is recognised in the form of growth in the assets.

Profit that is retained in the business forms an important link between successive balance sheets. In *Figure 1.3* we show the relationship between the opening balance sheet, the income statement for the period and, the closing balance sheet at the end of the period (often a period will relate to one year).

Figure 1.3   Relationship between balance sheet and income statements

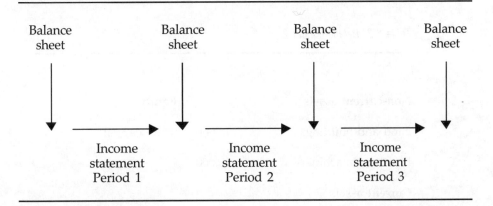

In *Figure 1.3*, moving from left to right we have:

❑   The opening balance sheet for period 1, the income statement for period 1 and, the closing balance sheet for period 1;

❑   The next day, the closing balance sheet for period 1 becomes the opening balance sheet for period 2 and the process repeats itself.

1.3   Example – Main financial statements

In the following example we will show 'snapshots' of a business by comparing two balance sheets. To start, we will invest £50,000 in our business. How will this be shown in our opening balance sheet?

Table 1.1 Balance sheet 1.

	£		£
Current assets		**Equity**	
Cash and cash equivalent	50,000	Share capital	50,000
	50,000		50,000

In balance sheet 1, we show the £50,000 cash under a subheading current assets; this is what the company owns. On the liabilities side of the balance sheet we show the £50,000 as share capital, i.e. owners capital or equity; this is what the company owes. If the company were to be liquidated, it would simply take the £50,000 cash and pay it back to the owners (shareholders).

Table 1.2 Balance sheet 2.

	£		£
Non-current assets		**Equity**	
Land and buildings	15,000	Share capital	50,000
Plant and machinery	10,000		
Current assets			
Cash and cash equivalent	25,000		
	50,000		50,000

It is now a game! Called 'spot the difference'. You are required to spot the difference between balance sheet 1 and balance sheet 2. Please note, these are the confidence builders!

In this case we can see that the company has bought land and buildings for £15,000 and, plant and machinery for £10,000. We can also see that the cash has reduced by the same amount, i.e. (£15,000 + £10,000). This is a good example of the principles of double entry book keeping; every transaction affects two accounts; in this case land and buildings and cash, and, plant and machinery and cash.

Table 1.3 Balance sheet 3.

	£		£
Non-current assets		**Equity**	
Land and buildings	15,000	Share capital	50,000
Plant and machinery	10,000		
Current assets			
Inventories	15,000		
Cash and cash equivalent	10,000		
	50,000		50,000

Still with the confidence builders! Now spot the difference between balance sheet 2 and balance sheet 3. Yes, we have bought stock and paid for it with cash. This is typical when companies commence trading since it is unlikely that they will be able to obtain stock on credit. Many small companies find themselves squeezed for cash flow by having to give credit to their customers while their suppliers are reluctant to extend similar credit to them.

Table 1.4 Balance sheet 4.

	£		£
Non-current assets		**Equity**	
Land and buildings	15,000	Share capital	50,000
Plant and machinery	10,000	Retained earnings	4,000
Current assets			
Inventories	7,000		
Trade and other receivables	20,000		
Cash and cash equivalent	2,000		
	54,000		54,000

Now this is more like it. The difference between balance sheet 3 and balance sheet 4 shows that some trading has taken place. This is evident by the figure for trade receivables. Trade receivables are our customers whom we have sold goods on credit. We can also see that there is a figure for profit for the year, i.e. we have 'made' a profit on the sale of the goods. Finally, the inventory and cash figures have also reduced.

Therefore, balance sheet 3 can be viewed as our opening balance sheet, we will construct an income statement to show the trading, while balance sheet 4 is our closing balance sheet for the period. We will now construct an income statement (which should explain all the changes from the two balance sheets).

Table 1.5 Income statement for the period ending xx/xx/xx

	£ Working	£ Final
Revenues (assume all credit)		20,000
less Materials	8,000	
less Wages and overheads	8,000	
Cost of sales		16,000
Profit for period		4,000

Why is profit shown as a liability? It is important to recognise that the physical profit is achieved through trading, i.e. when goods move from inventory and are sold to customers. The profit element is added at this point although it is not physically received until the customer pays for the goods. If we left it at that, the balance sheet would not balance. It would have more on the assets side of the balance sheet, i.e. retained profit. Therefore, we have to put a corresponding entry on the liabilities side of the balance sheet. Who owns the profit? The shareholders of the business. If the business was liquidated at this point and we obtained book values, the original share capital and the profit would be returned to the shareholders (owners).

We might ask at this point 'how successful is the company, so far'? In pure profit terms, profit as a percentage of sales £4,000 ÷ £20,000 x 100 = 20% would be considered very good in most cases. However, here we have an example of a company which is selling goods profitably but is running out of cash. Quite simply, it doesn't have enough cash to convert its remaining stock into a saleable condition. Furthermore, it is also unable to buy further stock. Is the position that the company finds itself in purely the result of selling goods on credit (i.e. its trade receivables) or are there other important messages here?

The position is similar to many start–up companies. In this case, we started the company with £50,000 in cash. This should have been sufficient funding until we achieved a foothold in our particular market. However, what did we do? We went out and purchased premises (land and buildings) and equipment (plant and machinery). This immediately took away half of our cash. What should we have done? Perhaps we should have rented our premises and, rented or leased our equipment. This would have conserved our cash which could then have been used in trading.

Table 1.6 Balance sheet 5.

Non-current assets	£	Equity	£
Land and buildings	15,000	Share capital	50,000
Plant and machinery	10,000	Retained profit	4,000
Current assets		**Current liabilities**	
Inventories	17,000	Trade and other payables	10,000
Trade and other receivables	20,000		
Cash and cash equivalent	2,000		
	64,000		64,000

The difference between balance sheet 4 and balance sheet 5 introduces trade and other payables. Trade payables are our suppliers who have supplied us goods on credit. In this case, our stock has increased by £10,000 and we now have trade payables with a £10,000 balance (owing).

We are now relying on our suppliers to supply us goods on credit and our customers to pay their bills.

At this point we will suspend this activity and consider the main components of the working capital cycle. In balance sheet 5 the working capital cycle is represented in the lower section, i.e. trade payables to inventory to trade receivables to cash to trade payables. We will now examine each of the components within the working capital cycle with the focus on internal control systems.

Working capital cycle

The working capital cycle helps to highlight the financial controls, i.e. stock control, credit control and cash control. There is no recognised control system for trade payables. The working capital cycle can be shown as follows:

Figure 1.4 Main components of the working capital cycle

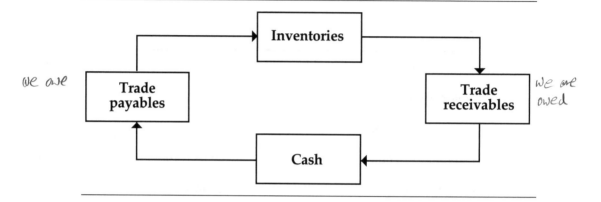

we owe (handwritten, left)   *we are owed* (handwritten, right)

A control system

What is a control system? and, What do we mean by control? In its simplest form, a control system will have three elements:

1. **Record**: to set a standard, limit or plan;

2. **Analyse**: to compare actual against standard, limit or plan and identify any deviation;

3. **Correct**: to take corrective action, if required. Sometimes referred to as feedback.

The following diagram shows a typical control system. Most business systems use feedback based on measuring the output.

Figure 1.5 Control system with feedback loop

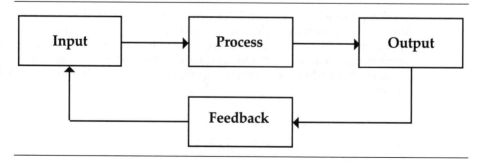

Pareto – a system of prioritising control

The Pareto curve, or more commonly referred to as the 80 : 20 rule suggests, for example that:

❐ 80% of a company's revenues comes from 20% of its customers;

❐ 80% of the value of inventory is held in 20% of the lines;

❐ Consultants can show a 80% return for a 20% effort;

❐ 80% of problems come from 20% of staff.

The 80 : 20 rule is a generic statement, it is not an exact measure. You may find that the actual figures range from 70 : 30 to 90 : 10.

Figure 1.6 The Pareto curve

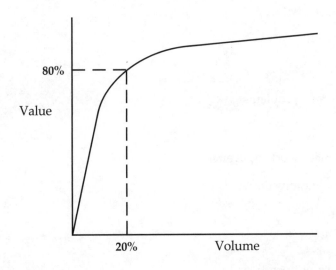

A B C analysis

The principle underpinning Pareto can be extended by the use of ABC analysis. Taking the previous example where 80% of the value (of inventory) was held by 20% of the volume. In ABC analysis we would list all inventory values in descending order. If we moved down the list until we had accounted for say 60% of the value, we might find that this represented 15% of the inventory held. This would become our A class inventory. Similar movements would be taken to determine B class inventory with the remainder being the C class inventory. This is shown in *Figure 1.7*.

Figure 1.7 Results from conducting an ABC analysis

	A	B	C
Volume %	15	25	60
Value %	60	25	15

Inventory control

Inventory control is, the process by which a company ensures that it has sufficient inventory to meet its operational requirements. A typical system of inventory control should include the following levels:

1. Maximum;

2. Reorder;

3. Minimum.

Inventory control - problems

Too high:

❏ Ties up limited working capital;

❏ Cost of holding inventory;

❏ Obsolescence.

Too low:

❏ Might interrupt operations.

Credit control

The aim of credit control is to minimise bad debts. A company will not be able to trade without experiencing a certain level of bad debts. What are the elements of a credit control system?

1. Credit control policies;

2. Credit rating;

3. Collection.

Credit control - problems

High trade receivable days:

❐ Ties up limited working capital;

❐ Shift in marginal trade receivables.

Low trade receivable days:

❐ Could lose customers.

Cash control

Many profitable companies go out of business because they run out of cash. An important element in the working capital cycle, the control of cash requires that a company prepares annual cash budgets together with daily, weekly or monthly cash flow forecasts.

The aim of cash control is to highlight:

1. **Cash surpluses**. To forward plan investments of cash for a short-term; benefit, interest received.

2. **Cash shortages**. To reduce the disasterous effects of running out of cash; the ability to modify our plans at an earlier date.

Trade payables

There is no recognised control for trade payables. It would seem that it requires the mirror treatment we give to trade receivables, i.e. do unto others. Trade payables are our suppliers, they supply us goods on credit, all they ask is that we pay their invoices on time. In times of expansion, suppliers will often provide a substantial portion of the financing requirements of a company. If a company had to go to the bank to obtain short-term financing, it would have to pay interest on the loan.

Therefore, the treatment for trade payables is similar to that of our trade receivables, i.e. obtain as much credit from our suppliers as we can afford – but pay their invoices on time. Prompt payment of the suppliers invoices will build up a good credit rating for our company.

Summary

You will find a fuller explanation to the three main financial controls, i.e. inventory, credit and stock control, in *Appendix A* to this chapter.

We will now continue with the company snapshots, with the difference(s) between balance sheets 5 and 6.

Table 1.7 Balance sheet 6.

	£		£
Non-current assets		**Equity**	
Land and buildings	15,000	Share capital	50,000
Plant and machinery	10,000	Retained earnings	4,000
Current assets		**Current liabilities**	
Inventories	17,000	Trade and other payables	10,000
Trade and other receivables	10,000		
Cash and cash equivalent	12,000		
	64,000		64,000

The difference between balance sheet 5 and balance sheet 6 shows that we have received £10,000 in cash from our trade receivables. Therefore, the trade receivables balance has reduced by £10,000 and the cash balance has increased by £10,000.

We now have the means (cash) to convert further stock for resale.

Table 1.8 Balance sheet 7.

	£		£
Non-current assets		**Equity**	
Land and buildings	15,000	Share capital	50,000
Plant and machinery	10,000	Retained earnings	4,000
Vehicles	5,000		
Current assets		**Current liabilities**	
Inventories	17,000	Trade and other payables	10,000
Trade and other receivables	10,000		
Cash and cash equivalent	7,000		
	64,000		64,000

The difference between balance sheet 6 and balance sheet 7 shows that we have spent £5,000 cash on a vehicle. At this point in our trading activities this does not seem to be a good idea. Balance sheet 7 clearly shows that we have taken £5,000 out of our working capital cycle and put it into non-current assets, i.e. vehicles. This often occurs when companies make capital investment decisions, either for new plant or vehicles or to acquire another business. In the short-term the company is vulnerable to the reductions in working capital.

The differences between balance sheet 7 and balance sheet 8 shows a number of movements; inventories, trade receivables, no cash, bank overdraft and profit. In fact we have completed another trading activity. Balance sheet 7 being the opening balance sheet, the trading in the form of an income statement (shown on page 16) and balance sheet 8 being the closing balance sheet, provide the important starting point, linkages and end point.

Table 1.9 Balance sheet 8.

	£		£
Non-current assets		**Equity**	
Land and buildings	15,000	Share capital	50,000
Plant and machinery	10,000	Retained earnings	11,000
Vehicles	5,000		
Current assets		**Current liabilities**	
Inventories	5,000	Trade and other payables	10,000
Trade and other receivables	40,000	Bank overdraft	4,000
	75,000		75,000

In this example, trade receivables have moved from £10,000 to £40,000 indicating a sale of £30,000 on credit. Inventories have reduced from £17,000 to £5,000 indicating usage of materials of £12,000. Cash has become an overdraft of £4,000, resulting in a spending of £11,000 on wages and overheads. Retained profit has increased from £4,000 to £11,000 indicating a profit on the transaction of £7,000. These movements can be seen in the income statement, *Table 1.10.*

Table 1.10   Income statement for the period ending xx/xx/xx

	£	£
Revenues		30,000
less Materials	12,000	
less Wages and overheads	11,000	
Cost of sales		23,000
Profit for period		7,000

Table 1.11   Balance sheet 9.

	£		£
Non-current assets		**Equity**	
Land and buildings	15,000	Share capital	50,000
Plant and machinery	10,000	Retained profit	8,000
Vehicles	5,000		
Current assets		**Current liabilities**	
Inventories	5,000	Trade and other payables	10,000
Trade and other receivables	40,000	Bank overdraft	4,000
		Dividend payable	3,000
	75,000		75,000

The difference between balance sheet 8 and balance sheet 9 shows that the (retained) profit has reduced from £11,000 to £8,000, while an entry for a (proposed) dividend payable of £3,000 is shown in the current liabilities section. We might be concerned with the possible future of this company. So much relies on collecting in the amounts owing from its customers. For example, £10,000 of the trade receivables figure is outstanding from the previous transaction. How can we obtain more stock from our suppliers? How can we convert stock for resale? How can we pay our trade payables? Are we concerned that we have a bank overdraft?

The fact is, this game has been a fairy story. And like all good fairy stories they all start off 'once upon a time' and finish 'they all lived happily ever after'. This is the case with this small company. Wish it were true in practice.

Table 1.12 Balance sheet 10.

	£		£
Non-current assets		**Equity**	
Land and buildings	15,000	Share capital	50,000
Plant and machinery	10,000	Retained earnings	8,000
Vehicles	5,000		
Current assets		**Current liabilities**	
Inventories	5,000	Trade and other payables	2,000
Trade and other receivables	15,000		
Cash and cash equivalent	10,000		
	60,000		60,000

We will leave you to make up your own minds regarding the fortunes of this company. What we have shown is the build-up of a balance sheet to show the main components. We have also shown the income statement and its relationship with the opening and closing balance sheets.

While the two sided balance sheet does have an appeal, i.e. total liabilities equals total assets, this is not the format used in published accounts throughout the UK and Europe. On the next page, we produce the final balance sheet (10), in one of the accepted UK formats. This is a vertical layout where the assets are followed by the liabilities rather than shown side by side and the two categories of working capital, current assets and current liabilities, are placed together within the first section.

Table 1.13 Balance sheet 10 – Vertical format.

	£	£
Non-current assets		
Land and buildings		15,000
Plant and machinery		10,000
Vehicles		5,000
Total non-current assets		30,000
Current assets		
Inventories	5,000	
Trade and other receivables	15,000	
Cash and cash equivalent	10,000	
	30,000	
Current liabilities		
Trade and other payables	2,000	
Net working capital		28,000
Total assets less current liabilities		58,000
Equity		
Share capital		50,000
Retained earnings		8,000
Total equity		58,000

1.4   Accounting concepts

The following provides an explanation of these generally accepted principles:

❏   **Entity:** An organisation is deemed to have a separate existence from its owners. This means that personal transactions are excluded from business accounts.

❏   **Going concern:** An organisation is assumed to continue in operational existence for the foreseeable future.

❏   **Money measurement:** Accounting only records those events that may be described and measured in money terms.

❏   **Timing of reports:** A time period is fixed as a basis for measurement of profit or loss.

❏   **Realisation:** Accounting recognises only those profits that have been realised in the accounting period. Other than in certain specific situations, profit is only accounted for when the earning process is virtually complete.

❏   **Consistency:** The accounting treatment of particular items should be the same from period to period; if changed, the difference should be revealed.

❏   **Prudence or conservatism:** Provision should be made for all potential costs whereas, as indicated, profits should not be accounted for until realised. This means that a far more conservative approach is adopted towards accounting for profit than is the case for costs.

❏   **Accruals/Matching:** Accounts have to ensure that costs are matched with their associated revenues.

❏   **Materiality:** Non standard usage in accounting practice is permissible if the effects are not material.

Appendix A - Working capital cycle

1. Inventory control

The financial objective of inventory control is to minimise the overall costs of holding stock while taking into account the various objectives of other functions within a company. For example, marketing might want to maintain a full range of merchandise, purchasing might want to concentrate on a reduced range but in greater volumes because they can obtain better prices and, finance might want to minimise the amount of working capital tied up in inventories. An effective system of inventory control seeks to optimise the needs of the various users.

Inventory control is achieved through implementing the following system, which involves:

❏ Setting inventory levels;

❏ Monitoring movements against stock levels;

❏ Taking corrective action.

Calculating inventories levels

A company should set maximum, minimum and reorder levels. Inventory levels should take account of historic and forecast volumes, lead times, cost of holding and, reorder size.

Monitor movements against inventory levels and corrective action

Once levels have been calculated for all inventory items, it is important to monitor movements and take the necessary corrective action. For example, if following a receipt of goods the inventory goes above the maximum level, any outstanding purchase orders should be cancelled. If it is forecast that the usage will reduce, then the company might consider a special offer or sale.

Similarly, following an issue of goods, if inventory reaches the reorder level, this should automatically trigger the preparation of a purchase order, where it would be anticipated that the goods would be received before inventory reached the minimum level. Should an issue of goods cause the inventory level to fall below minimum then outstanding purchase orders should be referred to the supplier to obtain delivery dates.

2. Credit control

The main objective of credit control is to minimise bad debts. This requires that a balance is achieved between the risk of granting credit to a customer and, the loss of profits through not trading with that customer.

It is not uncommon, when discussing credit control with a group of managers, for the first thoughts to be 'how quickly can we collect monies owed from customers?' What we need to bear in mind is, that this is a control system and will require the following:

❏   The establishment of a credit control policy;

❏   The vetting of new customers;

❏   The monitoring of the ageing of debts;

❏   The taking of corrective action.

Establishing a credit control policy

A credit control policy sets the general terms by which a company will offer credit. This will include the period of credit, for example 'net 30 days', and, the timings and actions which will take place should the credit period be extended by the customer. A good example of the actions taken is provided by the (UK) electricity, telephone, and gas companies. First there is a reminder, then usually two weeks later a final reminder, followed by a polite letter advising that your supply will be 'cut-off' if payment is not made within say, seven days. This is often followed up by a further letter advising that supply will be 'cut-off' from a specified date unless immediate payment is received.

When a company establishes its credit period it is important to take into account the competitive environment. For example, if other companies in the same industry are granting 60 days credit, a company offering 30 days would tend to lose customers to its competitors.

Vetting new customers

All new customers should be vetted to determine their creditworthiness and establish credit limits. This process takes many different forms but attempts to determine customers':

❏   **Ability to pay**. This should be relatively simple, requiring a review of a customers' financial position. This could be achieved through bank references, analysing the annual accounts, or by using a credit bureau.

❏   **Willingness to pay**. Assessing a company's willingness to pay by assessing their track record. For example, if individuals pay their household bills within the accepted time limits they would be deemed as showing a willingness to pay.

Establishing credit limits can take the form of making an allowance for an initial sum with regular reviews to increase the credit limit if required. Other systems involve complex models that take into account a number of variables or the use of a credit bureau.

Monitoring the ageing of debts

On the receipt of an order from an existing customer the credit department should check that:

❑   The new order would not make their outstanding balance exceed their credit limit; and,

❑   There are no outstanding debts on the account.

When the order has been fulfilled and an invoice sent to the customer there should be a continuous monitoring of the account. Regular reports should be produced to show the age of all outstanding amounts, for example, between one month to two months, two months to three months, and over three months. An ageing report can take the following format:

Table 1.14   Age classification of trade receivables

Invoice	Amount £	1 to 2 Months	2 to 3 Months	Over 3 Months	Remarks
MR 201	30,000			30,000	Court action
MR 209	15,000			15,000	Receiver
MR 245	60,000		60,000		Letter sent
MR 246	25,000		25,000		Cheque promised
MR 247	100,000	100,000			
MR 260	40,000	40,000			
	270,000	140,000	85,000	45,000	

Corrective action

It is important that corrective action is taken in accordance with the credit control policies of the company. If customers know that they can extend their credit periods without losing their rating then the 'marginally good payer' may move to being a 'marginally bad payer'. The forms of corrective action should include:

❏ A review of the credit limit of a customer;

❏ Reject orders due to poor creditworthiness. For example, when a customer attempts to extend the credit limit; or, a potential customer fails the creditworthiness checks;

❏ Send out regular statements, final reminder and, if necessary, final offer;

❏ Start court proceedings. This will often mean a lengthy procedure of claim and counter claim taking at least six months. Even if successful with a court action, there is no guarantee that the debt will be paid. A small company will often have to rely on the courts to recover the debt.

How to improve collection

One of the simplest methods of reducing the overall credit is to ensure that customers are invoiced promptly. In many cases this can reduce the payment period by anything up to two weeks.

Offering cash discounts for earlier payment can result in a significant improvement of cash flow. For example, if a company's credit terms were 'net 30 days', it might offer a cash discount of two percent for payment within 10 days.

Many small companies charge interest of up to 10% on overdue accounts in an effort to encourage prompt payment despite the competitive risk involved.

Some companies factor the collection of trade receivables to a debt collection agency. Depending upon the terms agreed, the agency will normally advance between 80 to 90 percent of a company's debts, the balance being paid less a percentage when they recover the debts. This is particularly useful to companies who cannot afford to set up and run their own credit control department.

3. Cash control

The main objective of a cash control system is to plan the expected operations of a company over a future period of time. Such a plan requires forecasts of future revenues and, cash expenditure covering purchases of materials, wages, equipment etc. Assumptions will also have to be made concerning the time delays from sales to receipts and, from purchases to payments. The following example shows the three main components of a cash budget:

i.   Forecast of revenues and cash receipts;

ii. Forecast of cash expenditure;

iii. Monthly net cash flow and cash balance.

i. Forecast of revenues and cash receipts

Revenue forecast for the six month period July to December, together with a forecast of 75% being credit sales.

Credit periods are expected to be 80% collected after one month and the remaining 20% after two months.

Table 1.15   Components of a cash budget

i. Forecast revenues and cash receipts

	May £m	Jun £m	Jul £m	Aug £m	Sept £m	Oct £m	Nov £m	Dec £m
Forecast revenues	40.0	44.0	68.0	80.0	64.0	32.0	24.0	44.0
Credit sales	*30.0*	*33.0*	*51.0*	*60.0*	*48.0*	*24.0*	*18.0*	*33.0*
Credit receipts								
1 month (80%)		*24.0*	*26.4*	*40.8*	*48.0*	*38.4*	*19.2*	*14.4*
2 months (20%)			*6.0*	*6.6*	*10.2*	*12.0*	*9.6*	*4.8*
Total credit receipts			*32.4*	*47.4*	*58.2*	*50.4*	*28.8*	*19.2*
Cash sales	10.0	11.0	17.0	20.0	16.0	8.0	6.0	11.0
Total cash receipts			49.4	67.4	74.2	58.4	34.8	30.2

Note: The above calculations show the variation in forecast revenues and the expected total cash receipts. For example, in October the forecast revenues are £32 million with expected total cash receipts of £58.4 million. In practice, a company would not prepare a forecast without making adjustments for bad debts.

ii. Forecast of cash expenditure

	Jun £m	Jul £m	Aug £m	Sept £m	Oct £m	Nov £m	Dec £m
Forecast purchases	26.4	40.8	48.0	38.4	19.2	14.4	26.4
Cash payments for purchases		26.4	40.8	48.0	38.4	19.2	14.4
Wages paid		5.6	5.6	5.6	5.6	5.6	5.6
Overheads and expenses paid	9.0	9.0	9.0	9.0	9.0	9.0	
Capital expenditure		15.0	15.0	0	0	15.0	0
Total cash expenditure		56.0	70.4	62.6	53.0	48.8	29.0

iii. Monthly net cash flow and cash balance

	Jul £m	Aug £m	Sept £m	Oct £m	Nov £m	Dec £m
Total cash receipts	49.4	67.4	74.2	58.4	34.8	30.2
Total cash expenditure	56.0	70.4	62.6	53.0	48.8	29.0
Net cash flow	–6.6	–3.0	11.6	5.4	–14.0	1.2
Opening cash balance	3.0	–3.6	–6.6	5.0	10.4	–3.6
Closing cash balance	–3.6	–6.6	5.0	10.4	–3.6	–2.4

CHAPTER TWO

DOUBLE ENTRY BOOKKEEPING

2.1   Introduction

In this chapter we will describe the double entry bookkeeping process through a number of examples. Should you wish to become proficient in this area we suggest that you work through the same examples until 'the penny drops'. Yes, while it is a simple process it often takes time before one becomes familiar with the system.

We will start by explaining the basic rules of double entry bookkeeping. A tip, do not try to bring your own logic into these rules – just follow them to the letter and you will succeed. From experience, we know that many students find it difficult to apply these rules without question, but if you continue to rework the same example you will eventually understand the rules/process.

The main aim of this chapter is to provide an example of the double entry bookkeeping process from initial transactions through to the preparation of a trial balance. In later chapters we will use a trial balance as the starting point to produce final accounts – these are the Trading account, the Income statement and the Balance sheet.

2.2   Rules

In accounting, each transaction affects two items (or accounts). The main rules used to determine the actual positions are as follows:

Figure 2.1 Rules - Double entry bookkeeping

Debit	Credit
IN	OUT
RECEIVER	GIVER

These two rules simply state,

Debit what comes in   Credit what goes out

and/or

Debit the receiver   Credit the giver

Please note, it is possible to mix and match the two basic rules.

2.3   Example 1

On the 1st January U.N. Welcome started a business, the initial transactions were:

Jan 1   Started a business with £1,000 cash;

Jan 2   Purchased goods £250 on credit from G.Ashley;

Jan 3   Bought display equipment and paid £200 cash;

Jan 5   Sold goods for cash £400.

Each transaction affects two accounts. Here we show the two accounts and apply the rules to the above transactions.

	Debit	Credit
1. Started a business with £1,000 cash	Cash	Capital
2. Purchased goods £250 on credit from G.Ashley	Purchases	G.Ashley
3. Bought display equipment and paid £200 cash	Equipment	Cash
4. Sold goods for cash £400	Cash	Revenues

1.   Jan 1   Started a business with £1,000 cash

The first transaction requires us to open two accounts. One for cash and the other for capital. Try to follow the posting. You will see that we have debited the cash account with £1,000. Notice we say capital, this refers to the other side of the transaction. In the capital account we have entered a credit of £1,000, this time it refers to the other side of the transaction which is cash. The posting to the accounts would be:

Cash

Dr.			Cr.
Jan 1 Capital (1)	1,000		

Capital

Dr.			Cr.
		Jan 1 Cash (1)	1,000

2.   **Jan 2**   **Purchased goods £250 on credit from G.Ashley**

In this transaction we debit what comes in, i.e. purchases and we credit the giver, i.e. G. Ashley. G. Ashley is a supplier of goods to the business on credit, therefore, a trade payable.

Purchases

Dr.					Cr.
Jan 2	*G. Ashley* (2)	250			

G. Ashley

Dr.					Cr.
			Jan 2	*Purchases* (2)	250

3.   **Jan 3**   **Bought display equipment and paid £200 cash**

In this transaction we debit what comes in, i.e. display equipment and we credit what goes out, i.e. cash. There is an assumption that the display equipment is for use within the business, i.e. an asset, therefore, not the goods in which the business trades.

Display Equipment

Dr.					Cr.
Jan 3	*Cash* (3)	200			

Cash

Dr.					Cr.
Jan 1	Capital (1)	1,000	*Jan 3*	*Equipment* (3)	200

4.   Jan 5   Sold goods for cash £400

In this transaction we debit what comes in, i.e. cash and we credit what goes out, i.e. sales. Revenues can either be for cash (as in this example) or sold on credit to a customer. Note that purchases (in transaction 2) has a debit balance while sales (below) has a credit balance; this will always be the case.

Cash

Dr.					Cr.
Jan 1	Capital (1)	1,000	Jan 3	Equipment (3)	200
Jan 5	*Revenues (4)*	*400*			

Revenues

Dr.					Cr.
			Jan 5	Cash (4)	400

Balancing off the accounts.

We will use the cash account to provide an example of balancing off the accounts. The balancing amounts are shown in italics.

Cash

Dr.					Cr.
Jan 1	Capital (1)	1,000	Jan 3	Equipment (3)	200
Jan 5	Revenues (4)	400	Jan 7	*Balance c/d*	*1,200*
		1,400			1,400
Jan 8	*Balance b/d*	*1,200*			

a. Check to see which side is greatest. In this case it is the debit side with £1,000 + £400 = £1,400.

b. Add the two entries on the debit side, then take the total across to become the total of the credit side, i.e. £1,400.

c. Deduct any amounts on the credit side from the total to obtain the balance, i.e. £1,400 - £200 = £1,200.

d. Finally, transfer the balance down to the debit side.

2.4   Example 2

In this example we have introduced a number of other transactions. We also show the two accounts for each transaction and the rule.

	200X	Transactions
1.	Aug 1	Started business depositing £20,000 into bank;
2.	Aug 3	Bought goods on credit from G. Marsh, £3,000;
3.	Aug 4	Withdrew £3,000 cash from bank;
4.	Aug 7	Bought motor van paying £2,000 cash;
5.	Aug 10	Sold goods on credit to T. Barr & Co, £500;
6.	Aug 21	Returned goods to G. Marsh, £400;
7.	Aug 28	T. Barr & Co. pays the amount owing by cheque;
8.	Aug 30	Bought furniture from B. Wise Ltd, £1,500;
9.	Aug 31	Paid £2,500 by cheque to G. Marsh.

We will now post each of the transactions, balance off the accounts and produce a trial balance. (Please note, we will show each initial posting in italics; postings already in the accounts will be in normal typeface).

1.   Aug 1   Started business depositing £20,000 into bank

Accounts	**Transaction rules**
Bank	Debit what comes in
Capital	Credit the giver

Bank

Dr.						Cr.
Aug 1	*Capital (1)*	*20,000*				

Capital

Dr.				Cr.
		Aug 1	Bank (1)	20,000

2.   Aug 3   Bought goods on credit from G. Marsh, £3,000

Accounts	**Transaction rules**
Purchases	Debit what comes in
G. Marsh	Credit the giver

Purchases

Dr.			Cr.
Aug 3	G. Marsh (2)	3,000	

G. Marsh

Dr.				Cr.
		Aug 3	Purchases (2)	3,000

3.   Aug 4   Withdrew £3,000 cash from bank

Accounts	**Transaction rules**
Cash	Debit what comes in
Bank	Credit what goes out

Cash

Dr.			Cr.
Aug 4	Bank (3)	3,000	

Bank

Dr.					Cr.
Aug 1	Capital (1)	20,000	Aug 4	Cash (3)	3,000

4.   Aug 7   **Bought motor van paying £2,000 cash**

Accounts   **Transaction rules**
Motor van   Debit what comes in
Cash   Credit what goes out

Motor van

Dr.					Cr.
Aug 7	*Cash (4)*	2,000			

Cash

Dr.					Cr.
Aug 4	Bank (3)	3,000	*Aug 7*	*Motor van (4)*	2,000

5.   Aug 10   **Sold goods on credit to T. Barr & Co, £500**

Accounts   **Transaction rules**
T. Barr & Co   Debit the receiver
Revenues   Credit what goes out

T. Barr & Co

Dr.					Cr.
Aug 10	*Revenues (5)*	500			

Revenues

Dr.					Cr.
			Aug 10	*T.Barr & Co (5)*	500

6.   Aug 21   Returned goods to G. Marsh, £400

Accounts   **Transaction rules**
G. Marsh   Debit the receiver
Returns out   Credit what goes out

G. Marsh

Dr.					Cr.
Aug 21	Returns out (6)	400	Aug 3	Purchases (2)	3,000

Returns outwards

Dr.				Cr.
		Aug 21	G. Marsh (6)	400

7.   Aug 28   T. Barr & Co pays the amount owing by cheque

Accounts   **Transaction rules**
Bank   Debit what comes in
T. Barr & Co   Credit the giver

Bank

Dr.					Cr.
Aug 1	Capital (1)	20,000	Aug 4	Cash (3)	3,000
Aug 28	T. Barr & Co (7)	500			

T. Barr & Co

Dr.					Cr.
Aug 10	Revenues (5)	500	Aug 28	Bank (7)	500

8. Aug 30 Bought furniture from B. Wise Ltd, £1,500

Accounts **Transaction rules**
Furniture   Debit what comes in
B. Wise Ltd   Credit the giver

Furniture

Dr.					Cr.
Aug 30	B. Wise Ltd (8)	1,500			

B. Wise Ltd

Dr.					Cr.
			Aug 30	Furniture (8)	1,500

9. Aug 31 Paid £2,500 by cheque to G. Marsh

Accounts **Transaction rules**
G. Marsh   Debit the receiver
Bank   Credit what goes out

G. Marsh

Dr.					Cr.
Aug 21	Returns out (6)	400	Aug 3	Purchases (2)	3,000
Aug 31	Bank (9)	2,500			

Bank

Dr.					Cr.
Aug 1	Capital (1)	20,000	Aug 4	Cash (3)	3,000
Aug 28	T. Barr & Co (7)	500	Aug 31	G. Marsh (9)	2,500

Trial balance as at 31st August 2000X

	Dr. £	Cr. £
Bank	15,000	
Cash	1,000	
Motor van	2,000	
Furniture	1,500	
Purchases	3,000	
Capital		20,000
B. Wise		1,500
Revenues		500
G. Marsh		100
Returns outwards		400
	22,500	22,500

In the above trial balance we have determined the balances on each of the accounts without going through the process of balancing off. We would suggest that you use pre-lined paper, write up each of the transactions, balance off the accounts and produce a trial balance.

2.5   Expenses

So far, we have concentrated on buying and selling goods mainly for resale. Another important element is the expenses incurred, or additional income received.

Expenses include rent, rates, heating, lighting, wages and salaries. They could also be grouped, for example, administration expenses, marketing and selling expenses. Additional income will include, for example, interest received, rent received, discounts received.

Figure 2.2 Alternative rule

Debit	Credit
Expenses	Cash or Bank or Creditor

2.6   Example 3

The following balances are brought forward from the previous period; Bank £14,000 Dr., Cash £1,000 Dr., Equipment £3,000 and Capital £18,000

1.   Jun 1   Paid rent £300 by cheque;

2.   Jun 4   Interest received on bank deposit, £500;

3.   Jun 8   Paid wages £2,500 by cash;

4.   Jun 9   Paid electricity bill by cheque, £65.

In this example there are starting balances brought forward from the previous period. Therefore, we now have to open up accounts for Bank, Cash, Equipment and Capital.

Bank

Dr.						Cr.
Jun 1	Balance b/d	14,000	Jun 1	Rent (1)		300
Jun 4	Interest received (2)	500	Jun 8	Cash (contra) (3a)		2,000
			Jun 9	Electricity (4)		65

Cash

Dr.					Cr.
Jun 1	Balance b/d	1,000	Jun 8	Wages (3b)	2,500
Jun 8	Bank (contra) (3a)	2,000			

Equipment

Dr.			Cr.
Jun 1	Balance b/d	3,000	

Capital

Dr.				Cr.
		Jun 1	Balance b/d	18,000

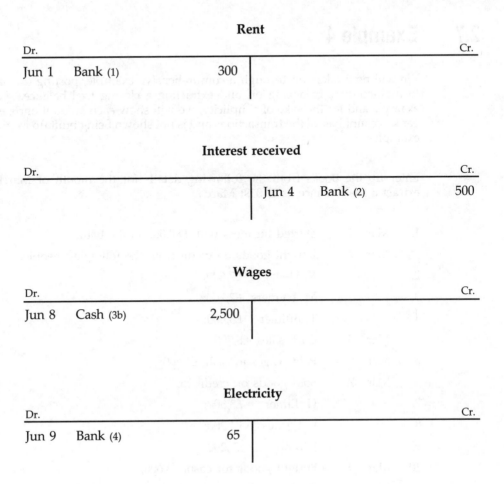

Rent

Dr.				Cr.
Jun 1	Bank (1)	300		

Interest received

Dr.				Cr.
			Jun 4 Bank (2)	500

Wages

Dr.				Cr.
Jun 8	Cash (3b)	2,500		

Electricity

Dr.				Cr.
Jun 9	Bank (4)	65		

In each of the above transactions we have debited the expense account, i.e. rent, wages, electricity and either credited bank or cash. In the case of interest received, we credited the income account and debited (in this case) bank.

For the payment of wages, there was insufficient cash. Typically, a cheque would be made out to cash and presented to the bank. The accounting transaction is debit (what comes in), i.e. cash and credit (what goes out), i.e. bank, this is known as a contra entry; see transaction (3a) 8th June. We can then pay the wages from cash; see transaction (3b).

In the *Example 4*, we will balance off all the accounts and produce a trial balance.

2.7   Example 4

We will now take you through a comprehensive example, posting transactions to the accounts, balancing off and extracting a closing trial balance. For this example and for the sake of simplicity, we will show each account once, e.g. the bank account has all the transactions and is not shown being built up as previous examples.

Enter up the books from the following details for the month of March, and extract a trial balance as at 31st March.

1.	Mar	1	Started business with £80,000 in the bank;
	Mar	2	Bought goods on credit from the following people:
2.			K. Henry £7,600;
3.			M. Hymers £2,700;
4.			T. Bulmer £5,600;
5.	Mar	5	Cash sales, £8,700;
6.	Mar	6	Paid wages in cash, £1,400;
	Mar	7	Sold goods on credit to:
7.			H. Elmer £3,500;
8.			L. Locke £4,200;
9.			J. Tenor £7,200;
10.	Mar	9	Bought goods for cash, £4,600;
	Mar	10	Paid the following by cheque:
11.			M. Hymers £2,400: Cash discount £300;
12.			T. Bulmer £5,200: Cash discount £400;
13.	Mar	12	Paid wages in cash, £1,400
	Mar	13	The following customers paid by cheque:
14.			L. Locke £4,000: Cash discount £200;
15.			J. Tenor £5,000: Cash discount £200;
16.	Mar	15	Bought shop fixtures on credit from Betta-Build, £5,000;
17.	Mar	18	Returned goods to K. Henry, £2,000;
18.	Mar	21	Paid Betta-Build a cheque for £5,000;
19.	Mar	27	Goods returned by H. Elmer, £500;
20.	Mar	30	J. Dent lent us £6,000 by cash;
21.	Mar	31	Bought a motor van paying by cheque, £12,000.

Work through the example then repeat a number of times, only referring to the answer when in difficulty.

Balancing the accounts is shown in italics. Initially, you should ignore this until you have worked through all the transactions. We have balanced off each account for completeness. Check each of the balances against the listing in the trial balance (at the end of the example). You will notice that some of the accounts don't have any balance; therefore, they are not shown in the trial balance.

Bank

Dr.					Cr.
Mar 1	Capital (1)	80,000	Mar 10	M. Hymers (11a)	2,400
Mar 13	L. Locke (14)	4,000	Mar 10	T. Bulmer (12a)	5,200
Mar 13	J. Tenor (15)	5,000	Mar 21	Betta-Build (18)	5,000
			Mar 31	Motor van (21)	12,000
			Mar 31	*Balance c/d*	*64,400*
		89,000			*89,000*
Apr 1	*Balance b/d*	*64,400*			

Capital

Dr.					Cr.
Mar 31	*Balance c/d*	*80,000*	Mar 1	Bank (1)	80,000
		80,000			*80,000*
			Apr 1	*Balance b/d*	*80,000*

Purchases

Dr.					Cr.
Mar 2	K. Henry (2)	7,600	*Mar 31*	*Balance c/d*	*20,500*
Mar 2	M. Hymers (3)	2,700			
Mar 2	T. Bulmer (4)	5,600			
Mar 9	Cash (10)	4,600			
		20,500			*20,500*
Apr 1	*Balance b/d*	*20,500*			

K. Henry

Dr.					Cr.
Mar 18	Returns out (17)	2,000	Mar 2	Purchases (2)	7,600
Mar 31	*Balance c/d*	5,600			
		7,600			7,600
			Apr 1	*Balance b/d*	5,600

M. Hymers

Dr.					Cr.
Mar 10	Bank (11a)	2,400	Mar 2	Purchases (3)	2,700
Mar 10	Disc. received (11b)	300			
		2,700			2,700

T. Bulmer

Dr.					Cr.
Mar 10	Bank (12a)	5,200	Mar 2	Purchases (4)	5,600
Mar 10	Disc. received (12b)	400			
		5,600			5,600

Cash

Dr.					Cr.
Mar 5	Revenues (5)	8,700	Mar 6	Wages (6)	1,400
Mar 30	J. Dent (20)	6,000	Mar 9	Purchases (10)	4,600
			Mar 12	Wages (13)	1,400
			Mar 31	*Balance c/d*	7,300
		14,700			14,700
Apr 1	*Balance b/d*	7,300			

Wages

Dr.						Cr.
Mar 6	Cash (6)	1,400		Mar 31	Balance c/d	2,800
Mar 12	Cash (13)	1,400				
		2,800				2,800
Apr 1	Balance b/d	2,800				

Revenues

Dr.						Cr.
Mar 31	Balance c/d	23,600		Mar 5	Cash (5)	8,700
				Mar 7	H. Elmer (7)	3,500
				Mar 7	L. Locke (8)	4,200
				Mar 7	J. Tenor (9)	7,200
		23,600				23,600
				Apr 1	Balance b/d	23,600

H. Elmer

Dr.						Cr.
Mar 7	Revenues (7)	3,500		Mar 27	Returns in (19)	500
				Mar 31	Balance c/d	3,000
		3,500				3,500
Apr 1	Balance b/d	3,000				

L. Locke

Dr.						Cr.
Mar 7	Revenues (8)	4,200		Mar 13	Bank (14a)	4,000
				Mar 13	Disc. allowed (14b)	200
		4,200				4,200

J. Tenor

Dr.						Cr.
Mar 7	Revenues (9)	7,200	Mar 13	Bank (15a)		5,000
			Mar 13	Disc. allowed (15b)		200
			Mar 31	Balance c/d		2,000
		7,200				7,200
Apr 1	Balance b/d	2,000				

Discount received

Dr.					Cr.
Mar 31	Balance c/d	700	Mar 10	M. Hymers (11b)	300
			Mar 10	T. Bulmer (12b)	400
		700			700
			Apr 1	Balance b/d	700

Discount allowed

Dr.					Cr.
Mar 13	L. Locke (14b)	200	Mar 31	Balance c/d	400
Mar 13	J. Tenor (15b)	200			
		400			400
Apr 1	Balance b/d	400			

Shop fixtures

Dr.					Cr.
Mar 15	Betta-Build (16)	5,000	Mar 31	Balance c/d	5,000
		5,000			5,000
Apr 1	Balance b/d	5,000			

Betta-Build

Dr.					Cr.
Mar 21	Bank (18)	5,000	Mar 15	Shop fixtures (16)	5,000
		5,000			5,000

Returns outwards

Dr.					Cr.
Mar 31	*Balance c/d*	2,000	Mar 18	K. Henry (17)	2,000
		2,000			2,000
			Apr 1	*Balance b/d*	2,000

Returns inwards

Dr.					Cr.
Mar 27	H. Elmer (19)	500	*Mar 31*	*Balance c/d*	500
		500			500
Apr 1	*Balance b/d*	500			

J. Dent (Loan account)

Dr.					Cr.
Mar 31	*Balance c/d*	6,000	Mar 30	Cash (20)	6,000
		6,000			6,000
			Apr 1	*Balance b/d*	6,000

Motor van

Dr.					Cr.
Mar 31	Bank (21)	12,000	*Mar 31*	*Balance c/d*	12,000
		12,000			12,000
Apr 1	*Balance b/d*	12,000			

Selected Transactions (mainly transaction 11)

M. Hymers

Dr.				Cr.
Mar 10 Bank (11a)	2,400	Mar 2	Purchases (3)	2,700
Mar 10 Disc. received (11b)	300			
	2,700			2,700

We bought goods from M. Hymers on 2nd March worth £2,700. M. Hymers has a credit balance on the account of £2,700.

On 10th March, we pay M. Hymer £2,400 (bank transaction (11a)). This still leaves a credit balance of £300 which is transferred to a discount received account (transaction (11b)). The £300 is a 'cash discount' (i.e. that £300 less cash is spent to clear the debt owing to M. Hymers) that M. Hymers has allowed for prompt payment.

Transaction (12) follows the same process, while transactions (14) and (15) are cash discounts that we give to our customers, i.e. discount allowed (to Locke and Tenor).

Please note that we open separate accounts for discount received, discount allowed, returns inwards and returns outwards. If at a later date, we want to net these accounts then we can do so; we cannot do the reverse, e.g. having netted off say returns into one account it is difficult to find out the level of returns inwards and returns outwards.

Trial balance

In order to explain the purpose of a trial balance it is necessary to take a few steps back. The basic data of any accounting system relies on recording initial transactions, e.g. paid wages, or purchased goods for sale. In the first case we would debit wages and credit either bank or cash.

Throughout a year many hundreds or thousands of transactions will be recorded. The trial balance is simply a listing of all the accounts that will have a debit or credit balance. The result should be that the total debits equal the total credits. It is possible that the total of the debits equals the total of the credits but does not reveal errors, e.g. posting to the wrong account.

Therefore, the trial balance is a check on the accuracy of the accounts and forms the basis for the preparation of the main financial statements.

We now show the trial balance as at the end of March.

Trial balance as at 31st March 200X

	Dr.	Cr.
	£	£
Bank	64,400	
Purchases	20,500	
Cash	7,300	
Wages	2,800	
H. Elmer	3,000	
J. Tenor	2,000	
Discount allowed	400	
Shop fixtures	5,000	
Returns inwards	500	
Motor van	12,000	
Capital		80,000
K. Henry		5,600
Revenues		23,600
Discount received		700
Returns outwards		2,000
J. Dent (Loan account)		6,000
	117,900	117,900

Exercise 2.1

On the 1st March B.E.Good started a business, the initial transactions were:

Mar 1   Started a business with £10,000 cash;

Mar 6   Purchased goods £2,500 on credit from *R.Matthew & Sons*;

Mar 7   Bought equipment and paid £3,500 cash;

Mar 9   Sold goods for cash, £3,000.

Exercise 2.2

On the 1st October P. Green started a business, the initial transactions were:

Oct 1   Started a business depositing £20,000 cheque into bank;

Oct 2   Purchased goods £3,200 on credit from *F.Ewart & Co*;

Oct 5   Bought motor van and paid £2,500 by cheque;

Oct 8   Returned goods to *F.Ewart & Co* worth, £300.

Exercise 2.3

On the 1st May R.E. Joyce started a business, the initial transactions were:

May 1   Started business depositing £3,000 into bank;

May 4   Bought goods on credit from *DottyCom Ltd*, £3,000;

May 5   Withdrew £500 cash from bank;

May 8   Bought motor van paying £1,500 by cheque;

May 11   Sold goods on credit to U. Candoit, £2,500;

May 14   Returned goods to *DottyCom Ltd*, £500;

May 15   U. Candoit pays the amount owing by cheque;

May 22   Bought furniture on credit from *B. Wise Ltd*, £1,500;

May 31   Paid £2,000 by cheque to *DottyCom & Co*.

Exercise 2.4

On the 1st May R.E. Joyce started a business, the initial transactions were:

Aug 1   Started business depositing £8,000 into bank;

Aug 3   Bought goods on credit from *I.T.Digital & Co*, £6,000;

Aug 4   Withdrew £2,000 cash from bank;

Aug 7   Bought furniture paying £1,500 cash;

Aug 10   Sold goods on credit to *M.Istaken Ltd*, £4,500;

Aug 21   Returned goods to *I.T.Digital & Co*, £300;

Aug 28   *M. Istaken Ltd* pays the amount owing by cheque;

Aug 30   Bought goods on credit from *U.N.Wise Ltd*, £1,500;

Aug 31   Paid £4,000 by cheque to *I.T.Digital & Co*.

Exercise 2.5

The following balances are brought forward from the previous period; Bank £20,000 Dr., Cash £2,000 Dr., Motor van £6,000 and Capital £28,000

Nov 1   Paid rent £800 from cash;

Nov 5   Interest received on bank deposit, £450;

Nov 13   Paid wages £1,400 by cash;

Nov 16   Paid insurance policy by cheque, £1,200.

Exercise 2.6

The following balances are brought forward from the previous period; Bank £8,000 Dr., Cash £1,400 Dr., Motor Van £7,000 and Capital £16,400

Aug 1   Paid wages £600 from cash;

Aug 3   Rent received by cash, £300;

Aug 6   Paid motor expenses £500 by cash;

Aug 10   Paid telephone bills by cheque, £300.

Exercise 2.7

Enter up the books from the following transactions for the month of August, and extract a trial balance as at 31st August.

Aug. 1   Started business with £50,000 in the bank;

Aug. 2   Bought goods on credit from the following people:

         R.E.Turn Ltd.   £30,000;

         L.Last Ltd   £12,000;

         C.Cooke & Co   £22,000;

Aug. 5   Cash sales, £32,000;

Aug. 6   Paid wages in cash, £4,400;

Aug. 7   Sold goods on credit to:

         Sid Spice   £14,000;

         K. Krankie   £19,000;

         N. Nettle   £30,000;

Aug. 9   Bought goods for cash, £18,000;

Aug. 10   Paid the following by cheque:

         L.Last Ltd   £11,400:   Cash discount   £600;

         C.Cooke & Co   £20,900:   Cash discount   £1,100;

Aug. 13   Paid wages in cash, £4,400;

Aug. 14   The following customers paid by cheque:

         K. Krankie   £18,500:   Cash discount   £500;

         N. Nettle   £25,000:   Cash discount   £800;

Aug. 15   Bought shop fixtures on credit from *Betta-Build*, £8,000;

Aug. 18   Returned goods to *R.E.Turn Ltd.*, £5,000;

Aug. 21   Paid *Betta-Build* a cheque for, £8,000;

Aug. 27   Goods returned by Sid Spice, £1,200;

Aug. 30   J. Jones lent us £12,000 by cash;

Aug. 31   Bought a motor van paying by cheque, £15,000.

Exercise 2.8

Enter up the books from the following transactions for the month of June and extract a trial balance as at 30th June.

June 1   Started business with £60,000 in the bank, and £5,000 cash in hand;

June 2   Bought goods on credit from D. Duval, £50,000;

June 3   Credit sales to the following:

T. Woods	£6,600;
F. Couples	£2,500;
P. Mickleson	£4,300;

June 4   Goods bought for cash, £2,300;

June 5   Bought motor van paying by cheque £8,000;

June 7   Paid motor expenses by cheque, £120;

June 9   Credit sales to the following:

C. Montgomerie	£2,400;
L. Westwood	£2,600;
D. Clarke	£6,500;

June 11   Goods bought on credit from the following:

N. Price	£24,000;
E. Els	£6,200;
G. Norman	£4,600;

June 13   Goods returned to N. Price, £2,500;

June 15   Paid motor expenses by cash, £50;

June 19   Goods returned by F. Couples, £1,100;

June 20   Cash taken for own use (drawings), £1,000;

June 21   Paid the following suppliers by cheque:

E. Els	£5,500:	Cash discount	£700;
G. Norman	£4,000:	Cash discount	£600;

June 23   T. Woods paid account in cash, £6,200: Cash discount, £400;

June 25   P. Mickleson paid by cheque, £4,300;

June 26   Cash sales, £3,400;

June 27   Cash taken for own use, £2,400;

June 28   Goods returned to N. Price, £4,200;

June 29   Paid for postage stamps by cash, £40;

June 30   Credit sales to the following:

F. Couples	£4,300;
P. Mickleson	£6,700;
L. Westwood	£4,500;

CHAPTER THREE

FINANCIAL ACCOUNTING – ADJUSTMENTS

LEARNING OBJECTIVES

When you have finished studying this chapter and completed the exercises, you should be able to:

❑   Understand the adjustments made to non-current assets and their affect on the income statement and balance sheet, e.g. depreciation, disposal, revaluation;

❑   Describe the main components of current assets including inventory (valuation), trade receivables (bad debts written off, provision for doubtful debts) and prepayments;

❑   Describe the main sources of long-term financing.

3.1 Introduction

In *Chapter 1,* we introduced the balance sheet from the start-up of a business through a number of transactions. Our aim was to provide an easy entry into the terminology of accounting and, show the main sections of the balance sheet together with its interrelationship with the income statement.

In this chapter we intend to use the balance sheet as our structure. We will take each section and explain the adjustments that have to be made (e.g. depreciation, bad debts, provision for doubtful debts, accruals, prepayments) and, how they are treated in the accounts. We will also explain some of the other items that find their way onto the balance sheet (e.g. share premium, revaluation reserve).

In Appendix A to this chapter we have included the bookkeeping entries for depreciation, bad debts, provision for doubtful debts, accruals and prepayments.

Please note, that we will continue to use a two sided balance sheet throughout this chapter, showing the assets on the left hand side and the liabilities on the right hand side, hence, the balance sheet equation: *total assets equals total liabilities.* Once you become familiar with this layout you will find it easier to cope with balance sheets using vertical layouts.

Table 3.1   Outline balance sheet

Non-current assets	**Equity**
Land and buildings	Issued share capital
less Depreciation	Share premium
Plant and machinery	Revaluation reserve
less Depreciation	Retained earnings
Vehicles	
less Depreciation	
Other non-current assets	
Investments	Long-term loans
Current assets	**Current liabilities**
Inventories	Trade and other payables
Trade and other receivables	Accruals
less Provision for doubtful debts	Bank overdraft
Prepayments	Taxation
Short-term investments	Dividend
Cash/Bank	

3.2 Non-current assets and adjustments

We saw in *Chapter 1*, that non-current assets were those assets that had a life greater than one year. These are the assets that a company acquires before it can begin trading. They consist of land and buildings, plant and machinery, equipment, vehicles, furniture, and others. There are a number of adjustments required when accounting for non-current assets, these are:

❑ Depreciation. Since the assets extend over an accounting period (normally one year) we have to find a method of attaching a portion of their cost to each accounting period; this is referred to as depreciation, i.e. the wearing down of an asset.

❑ Disposal. We also have to recognise that assets will be sold, either at the end of their useful life or part way through their useful lives.

❑ Trade investments. Another asset in the non-current assets section of the balance sheet. Trade investments normally consist of a portfolio of shares held, of companies in the same line of business, major suppliers or major customers. These differ from short-term investments since we cannot say with any certainty that we will be able to sell trade investments (i.e. shares) at the time we might wish to.

We will now deal with:

1. each of the main classes of non-current assets and the adjustments for depreciation;

2. the disposal of non-current assets; and,

3. trade investments.

1. Depreciation

The purchases a company makes can fall into two categories. The first is as an expense (or cost), for example wages, telephone, electricity. These items are written off in the income statement for the period in which they are incurred. The second is when an asset is bought for use in the business and has an estimated useful life exceeding one year. There is an 'unexpired' part of the cost, which is reflected in the balance sheet as a non-current asset. These assets are written off in future income statements over their estimated useful life by a process known as depreciation.

Depreciation is a measure of the wearing out, consumption or other loss of value of a non-current asset whether arising from use, passage of time or obsolescence through technology and market changes.

The most common methods of depreciation are, (i) **straight line,** where a fixed amount is taken to the income statement each year; (ii) **reducing balance,** where a fixed percentage is applied to the remaining balance, in this case the amount taken to the income statement will start higher than the straight line method but will reduce each year.

The annual figure for depreciation is treated as a deduction of profit in the income statement (thereby reducing the profit for the period), while the accumulated figure for depreciation is shown in the balance sheet as a deduction from the asset.

Depreciation methods

We will now use the following example to demonstrate the straight line, the reducing balance, and the sum of the digits methods. The last of these is less common but you may encounter it.

Example

A vehicle bought for £20,000 with an estimated useful life of four years and an estimated residual value £2,592.

a. The straight line method

The formula for calculating the annual depreciation provision under the straight line method is as follows:

$$\text{Annual depreciation provision} = \frac{(\text{Cost of asset} - \text{estimated residual value})}{\text{Expected useful life in years}}$$

$$= \frac{(£20,000 - £2,592)}{4}$$

$$= £4,352$$

The straight line method allocates the net cost equally against the income statement, for each year of the estimated useful life of an asset. It is a simple method to apply and understand. However, it takes no account of the fact that an asset will tend to 'lose' a larger proportion of its value in the earlier years.

b. Reducing balance method

With the reducing (or diminishing) balance method, a fixed percentage is deducted from the annual balance that exists at the beginning of the accounting period, i.e. cost of asset less any accumulated depreciation. How this approach works can be readily seen using the same example where it is assumed that the relevant rate to apply is 40%.

The depreciation for the first year would be £8,000, in the second year it would be (£20,000 – £8,000) x 40% = £4,800, and in the third year it would be (£20,000 – £8,000 – £4,800) x 40% = £2,880. This process would continue for one more year, that is until the end of the estimated useful life of the asset. In this fourth and final year, the depreciation charge would be £1,728, leaving a balance remaining of £2,592 which is the estimated residual value.

The formula used to calculate the percentage to be applied is as follows:

$$r = 1 - \sqrt[n]{\frac{s}{c}}$$

where

r = rate of depreciation

n = estimated useful life in years

s = estimated residual value

c = cost of asset

By applying the formula to the information relating to the example, we can see how the rate of 40% is determined.

$$= \quad 1 \ - \ 0.6$$

$$= \quad 0.4 \quad \text{or} \quad 40\%$$

The reducing balance method allocates a higher proportion of the cost of an asset to the earlier years. In the above example, £8,000 was allocated for the first year while only £1,728 was allocated in the fourth and final year.

c. Sum of the digits

This method is called the 'sum of the digits', or the 'sum of the years digits'. It can be compared to a reducing or diminishing balance method in that it allocates a higher proportion of the cost of an asset to the earlier years. Using the data in the same example, the annual depreciation charge is calculated as follows:

Table 3.2 Calculation of sum of digits depreciation

Year 1	4	4/10	6,963
Year 2	3	3/10	5,222
Year 3	2	2/10	3,482
Year 4	1	1/10	1,741
	10	10/10	£17,408

The basis for determining the annual depreciation charge is found simply by reversing the order of the years, so that for year 1 the depreciation charge is determined from the last year (4 in this case) which is expressed as a fraction of the sum of the digits of the years (4+3+2+1 in this case). Thus, 4/10 of the net depreciation charge of £17,408 (i.e. £20,000 – £2,592), is charged against year 1, and so on for subsequent years.

Table 3.3   Comparison of depreciation methods – sum charged each year

	Straight line £	Reducing balance £	Sum of the digits £
Year 1	4,352	8,000	6,963
Year 2	4,352	4,800	5,222
Year 3	4,352	2,880	3,482
Year 4	4,352	1,728	1,741
Total	17,408	17,408	17,408

UK companies are able to choose any method of depreciation, or even a range of methods, for different categories of assets. While most use the straight line method, care needs to be exercised when making inter-firm comparisons since the use of different methods will affect the reported profits.

Accounting treatment for depreciation

Companies must state the method used to calculate depreciation for each major class of non-current asset. This can be found in the accounting principles section of the published accounts. The accounting treatment for depreciation of a non-current asset is as follows:

1. Calculate the depreciation provision for each asset. For example, land and buildings are normally depreciated over 50 years or for the estimated life of the building if less than 50 years. 'Hire equipment is depreciated at rates between 3 to 15 years straight line, while non-hire equipment at rates between 25% to 45% per annum' (*Speedy Hire plc* 2006 report).

2. The annual provision for depreciation is taken into the income statement. This has the result of reducing both the taxable and retained profits for the year and, ultimately, the income statement balance in the liabilities section of the balance sheet. (please note that the depreciation written into the income statement and the depreciation 'allowed' for taxation purposes can be substantially different in amount).

3. The final adjustment is on the assets side of the balance sheet. Non-current assets are held at cost or realisable value with annual depreciation accumulating over the life of an asset. In published accounts you will typically find a single figure for tangible non-current assets; in a note to the accounts you will find a full page in tabular format providing all the information required, i.e. opening balance, additions, disposals together with annual and accumulated depreciation by each major class of non-current asset.

Example – Depreciation of non-current assets

We will now show an example of the depreciation of a non-current asset. Assume that a company has non-current assets of £300,000. They have been replaced at the beginning of the year and are due to be depreciated, straight line over five years, i.e. £60,000 per year. On the liabilities side of the opening balance sheet, the company has issued share capital of £100,000 and retained earnings, i.e. accumulated profits of £200,000. For the purpose of this example, we will assume that the current assets equals the current liabilities at £600,000 each.

We will also assume that the company has a revenues (sales) of £2,000,000, cost of sales of £1,500,000, and, administration and distribution costs of £300,000.

The opening balance sheet, income statement and closing balance sheet for the first year are shown in *Table 3.4*.

Table 3.4 Opening balance sheet, income statement and closing balance sheet

OPENING BALANCE SHEET

ASSETS	£	LIABILITIES	£
Non-current assets	300,000	Issued share capital	100,000
less Depreciation	0	Other reserves	0
Net book value (NBV)	300,000	Retained earnings	200,000
			300,000
Current assets	600,000	Current liabilities	600,000
	900,000		900,000

INCOME STATEMENT

	£	
Revenues	2,000,000	
less Cost of sales	1,500,000	(assume all cash items)
Operating profit	500,000	
less Admin and distribution	300,000	(assume all cash items)
Net profit before taxation	200,000	

CLOSING BALANCE SHEET

ASSETS	£	LIABILITIES	£
Non-current assets	300,000	Issued share capital	100,000
less Depreciation	0	Other reserves	0
Net book value (NBV)	300,000	Retained earnings	400,000
			500,000
Current assets	800,000	Current liabilities	600,000
	1,100,000		1,100,000

If we now assume that at the year-end the company decides to provide for depreciation on its non-current assets over 5 years straight line. The annual depreciation provision would be £60,000.

In *Table 3.5*, we now show the opening balance sheet, the income statement and closing balance sheet with depreciation included (ignore taxation and dividend). You will notice that the annual charge for depreciation is added into the cost of sales (i.e. 1,500,000 + 60,000) which reduces the retained profit. This would result in the liabilities side of the closing balance sheet being £60,000 less than the assets side of the balance sheet. To correct this, we deduct the depreciation charge from the non-current asset (i.e. 300,000 – 60,000).

Table 3.5   Opening balance sheet, income statement and closing balance sheet

OPENING BALANCE SHEET

ASSETS	£	LIABILITIES	£
Non-current assets	300,000	Issued share capital	100,000
less Depreciation	0	Other reserves	0
Net book value (NBV)	300,000	Retained earnings	200,000
			300,000
Current assets	600,000	Current liabilities	600,000
	900,000		900,000

INCOME STATEMENT

	£
Revenues	2,000,000
less Cost of sales *	1,560,000
Operating profit	440,000
less Admin and distribution	300,000
Net profit before taxation	140,000

* In Chapter 1, we gave a simplified view of cost of sales. In practice, it represents a large number of items including, for example, depreciation.

CLOSING BALANCE SHEET

ASSETS	£	LIABILITIES	£
Non-current assets	300,000	Issued share capital	100,000
less Depreciation	60,000	Other reserves	0
Net book value (NBV)	240,000	Retained earnings	340,000
			440,000
Current assets	800,000	Current liabilities	600,000
	1,040,000		1,040,000

Finally, we will show the provision for depreciation for a second year. We will assume that the company has achieved the same turnover, and other costs from the previous year. The closing balance sheet (above), now becomes the opening balance sheet for this period; we will show the income statement for the period and the closing balance sheet in *Table 3.6*.

Table 3.6   Income statement and closing balance sheet (end of second year)

INCOME STATEMENT

	£
Revenues	2,000,000
less Cost of sales	1,560,000
Operating profit	440,000
less Admin and distribution	300,000
Net profit before taxation	140,000

CLOSING BALANCE SHEET

ASSETS	£	LIABILITIES	£
Non-current assets	300,000	Issued share capital	100,000
less Depreciation	120,000	Other reserves	0
Net book value (NBV)	180,000	Retained earnings	480,000
			580,000
Current assets	1,000,000	Current liabilities	600,000
	1,180,000		1,180,000

2. Disposal of assets

It is important to note, that estimates of the rate of depreciation to be applied, the useful life of the asset, and its disposal value, may be nothing more than guesswork. The actual outcome may be very different from the estimates and how we deal with differences is explained below.

Example 1 – Disposal of a non-current asset

A company purchased a non-current asset on 1st January 2003 for £47,000. It had an estimated economic life of seven years and an expected disposal value of £5,000. The asset was sold on the 31st December 2006 for £15,000.

The company used the straight line method for depreciation such that the annual depreciation charge would be found as follows:

$$\text{Straight line depreciation} = \frac{(£47,000 - £5,000)}{7 \text{ years}}$$

$$= £6,000 \text{ per annum}$$

Any loss on the disposal of the asset would be included in the income statement and would result in a reduction of the profit for the period. (Similarly, any profit on the disposal of an asset would result in an increase in the profit for the period).

Had the company known that disposal would take place after four years rather than seven years, with proceeds of £15,000, its annual depreciation charge would have been:

$$\text{Straight line depreciation} = \frac{(£47,000 - £15,000)}{4 \text{ years}}$$

$$= £8,000 \text{ per annum}$$

In other words, by depreciating the asset at £6,000 over four years, now, given perfect knowledge, i.e. the life, 4 years and the disposal value £15,000, we can see that the company has undercharged depreciation over the actual life of the asset. Four years at £2,000 per year has not been written off against profit which otherwise would have been. Upon the disposal, any profit or loss needs to be calculated as shown in *Table 3.7*.

Table 3.7   Profit or loss on disposal of asset

	£	£
Sale price		15,000
Cost of asset at 1st January 2003	47,000	
less Accumulated depreciation	24,000	
Net book value at 31st December 2006		23,000
Profit or loss on disposal of asset		–8,000

Accounting treatment for the disposal of an asset

The acquisition and disposal of assets becomes a regular activity within most companies. The acquisition of assets is straightforward since it only requires one transaction, i.e. opening an account for the asset and reducing the cash/bank balance for the payment. The disposal of an asset requires additional transactions, the aim being to clear out from the accounts all evidence relating to that asset. A typical process would be to:

1. Transfer the cost of the asset being sold into an asset disposals account – which clears the asset out of the accounts;

2. Transfer the accumulated depreciation into an asset disposals account – which clears the accumulated depreciation for the asset out of the accounts;

3. Post the remittance received from the sale of the asset. This has the effect of increasing the cash or bank balance. The other entry in the accounts would be in the asset disposals account;

4. Transfer the balance (i.e. the difference) on the asset disposal account to the income statement:

   ❑ If the net balance on the disposal account is greater than the remittance received there is a loss on the sale of the asset and this is taken into the income statement as a cost;

   ❑ If the net balance on the disposal account is less than the remittance received there is a profit on the sale of the asset and this is taken into the income statement as an income.

Example 2 – Disposal of a non-current asset

We will continue with the example used in the previous section on depreciation, i.e. *Table 3.6*. If we assume that at the end of the second year the company disposed of £100,000 of non-current assets and received a cheque for £50,000. The profit or loss on the disposal would be as follows:

Table 3.8   Profit or loss on disposal of asset

	£	£
Sale price		50,000
Cost of asset (at beginning of first year)	100,000	
less Accumulated depreciation	40,000	
Net book value (at end of second year)		60,000
Profit or loss on disposal of asset		−10,000

The income statement and balance sheet after the disposal would be as shown in *Table 3.9* – (please note, this is *Table 3.6* adjusted for the disposal).

Table 3.9   Income statement and closing balance sheet after disposal (end of second year)

Income Statement

	£
Revenues	2,000,000
less Cost of sales	1,560,000
Operating profit	440,000
less Admin and distribution	300,000
less Loss on disposal of asset	10,000
Net profit before taxation	130,000

Closing Balance Sheet

Assets	£	Liabilities	£
Non-current assets	200,000	Issued share capital	100,000
less Depreciation	80,000	Other reserves	0
Net book value (NBV)	120,000	Retained earnings	470,000
			570,000
Current assets	1,050,000	Current liabilities	600,000
	1,170,000		1,170,000

Notes to explain the movements following the disposal.

1. We have shown the loss on the disposal of the non-current asset as a separate item in the income statement, i.e. £10,000. This has the effect of reducing the profit before taxation by £10,000 to £130,000.

2. In the liabilities section of the balance sheet, we show £130,000 being added to the retained earnings (balance) to give £470,000.

3. In the non-current assets section of the balance sheet, we deduct £100,000 from the (cost) of the non-current assets and £40,000 from the (accumulated) depreciation. This leaves a net book value, for non-current assets of £120,000.

4. In the current assets section of the balance sheet, we add the £50,000 received in payment for the non-current asset.

The balance sheet now balances at £1,170,000 total assets (i.e. non-current assets £120,000 plus current assets £1,050,000); £1,170,000 total liabilities (i.e. issued share capital £100,000 plus retained earnigns £470,000 plus current liabilities £600,000).

3.   Revaluation of assets

Not all assets are depreciated. Land, for example often increases in value and such revaluations are commonly seen in the balance sheets of UK companies.

Given that a professional revaluation has been undertaken on the assets of our example company, which has had the effect of increasing the total value from £200,000 to £500,000. This is shown in the balance sheet both as an increase in the non-current asset value from £200,000 to £500,000 and, at the same time, increasing the reserves (under the heading 'revaluation reserve') by £300,000; thus keeping the balance sheet in balance. Unlike depreciation, however, such revaluations have no impact either on the income statement (since they do not involve an increase in profits from trading) or, the cash flow statement (since they do not involve movements of cash).

Table 3.10 shows the impact of a revaluation of non-current assets on the balance sheet of our example company.

Table 3.10 Balance sheet – Impact of revaluation

Balance Sheet (without revaluation)

Assets	£	Liabilities	£
Non-current assets	200,000	Issued share capital	100,000
less Depreciation	80,000	Other reserves	0
Net book value (NBV)	120,000	Retained earnigs	470,000
			570,000
Current assets	1,050,000	Current liabilities	600,000
	1,170,000		1,170,000

Closing Balance Sheet (with revaluation)

Assets	£	Liabilities	£
Non-current assets	500,000	Issued share capital	100,000
less Depreciation	80,000	Revaluation reserve	300,000
Net book value (NBV)	420,000	Retained earnings	470,000
			870,000
Current assets	1,050,000	Current liabilities	600,000
	1,470,000		1,470,000

Many companies now revalue their non-current assets on a regular basis. The outcome is a stronger balance sheet that reflects the current value of the assets, and at the same time provides an increase in the equity of the business.

One potential advantage to the company, of including current values of assets through revaluations on a regular basis, is that it should make the cost of acquiring the company greater should a takeover be considered. The assumption for listed companies is that the revaluation will be incorporated by the market in the company's share price. Revaluations may also improve the ability of the company to borrow funds because the ability to borrow, without recourse to the shareholders, is usually limited to a percentage of assets. Anything that increases the assets should increase borrowing power.

3.3   Current asset adjustments

In this section, we will concentrate our discussion on two of the main elements which form part of the current assets section of the balance sheet. These are:

1. Inventory, including methods of valuation and the effect on the income statement;

2. Trade and other receivables, including debtor age analysis, the treatment of bad debts, provision for doubtful debts and, prepayments.

1. Inventory

The term inventory is used to describe goods available for sale in the normal course of a business. In a manufacturing company it will also include work-in-progress and raw materials. A single value for inventories is shown in the current assets section of the balance sheet with a breakdown (if necessary) shown in a note to the accounts. This value represents the closing inventories of the business at the end of the accounting period. By default, the closing inventories then becomes the opening inventories for the next accounting period.

Perhaps the single most contentious issue with inventory is the valuation. We will describe a number of the commonly used methods and, show the impact a change in the valuation of inventory has on the 'apparent' profits of a business. The following methods of valuation will be covered:

1. **First in first out (FIFO)**. Using this method inventory is issued at the oldest price. This means that any closing inventory will be valued at the latest prices;

2. **Last in first out (LIFO)**. Using this method inventory is issued at the latest price. This means that any closing inventory will be valued at the earliest prices;

3. **Average price**. Using this method inventory is issued at an average price which will normally be recalculated each time a consignment of goods is received. Average price will tend to value closing inventory at latest prices since the 'changing' average will 'drop' earliest prices.

Example – Inventory valuation methods

A company is considering the method they will use for inventory valuation. The following data has been collected:

Revenues for the year £116,250

Purchases in   January   2,000 units at £16.00 per unit

             June   2,600 units at £20.00 per unit

             November   1,200 units at £21.00 per unit

There was no opening inventory

Closing inventory 1,550 units

Table 3.11   *Comparison of inventory valuation methods*

	FIFO		Average		LIFO	
	£	£	£	£	£	£
Revenues for period		116,250		116,250		116,250
Opening inventory	0		0		0	
+ Purchases (i)	109,200		109,200		109,200	
	109,200		109,200		109,200	
– Closing inventory (ii)	32,200		29,187		24,800	
= Cost of sales		77,000		80,014		84,400
Gross profit		39,250		36,237		31,850

(i)   Purchases for the period are calculated as follows:

    (2,000 x £16) + (2,600 x £20) + (1,200 x £21) = **£109,200**

(ii)   Closing inventory at the end of the period is calculated as follows:

    FIFO   Latest purchase   1,200 x £21.00 = £25,200

                   Next latest purchase   350 x £20.00 = £7,000 = **£32,200**

    Average cost £109,200 ÷ 5,800 units = £18.83 x 1,550 units   = **£29,187**

    LIFO   Opening inventory   0   0   0

                   Next latest purchase   1,550 x £16.00   £24,800 = **£24,800**

2. Trade and other receivables

Trading with customers and allowing credit transactions will inevitably lead to a number of bad debts. However, an effective system of credit control will help to minimise bad debts. In this section we will cover the following:

a. Preparation of an age analysis of trade receivables;

b. The accounting treatment for writing off bad debts;

c. The accounting treatment for making a provision for doubtful debts.

a. Age analysis of trade receivables

The assessment and control of bad and doubtful debts is an integral part of a credit control system. On a regular basis, and as a routine, trade receivable balances are assessed against the number of days outstanding. This means allocating the whole or part of the balance of a trade receivable account into specific time periods. It is then possible to determine, for example, those accounts over a certain time period with a view to take immediate action. An example is shown in *Table 3.12*.

Table 3.12 Age analysis of trade receivables

	Total	31 – 60	61 – 90	over 90	Action
	£	£	£	£	
A. Able	60,000				
Acorn Partnership	20,000		20,000		Review credit
B. Ball and Co.	150,000	20,000	40,000	30,000	Review credit
Bottle Ltd	10,000			10,000	Court action pending
Bunce Plc	350,000	100,000	100,000		
Calder and Sons	25,000				
Candy Stores Ltd	10,000				
Cookside B.C.	30,000		20,000		Review credit
....					
....					
Total	6,200,000	3,200,000	500,000	140,000	

From the totals above and the comments it might be thought prudent to make a provision of 2.25% of trade receivables, i.e. £140,000 ÷ £6,200,000 x 100.

b. Bad debts written off

A debt is bad and will be written off when a company considers that it is unlikely to receive payment against the debt. The procedure is as follows:

i.   Clear out any outstanding balance on individual trade receivable accounts into a bad debts account. This process will continue throughout the year as trade receivable accounts are closed and transferred into the bad debts account. Should the debt be recovered, this process will be reversed;

ii.   At the end of the accounting period the balance on the bad debts account is transferred, as a cost, to the income statement; the effect being to reduce the profit for the period;

iii. Also, at the year end, it may be necessary to write off further bad debts. In this case, we would have to increase the amount being written-off in the income statement and deduct the additional bad debts from the trade and other receivables balance in the closing balance sheet.

c. Provision for doubtful debts

Throughout the year an assessment is made of each trade receivable's account to consider the actions which must be taken to ensure prompt and timely payment on each account.

At the end of an accounting period an assessment is made of each trade receivable account to consider the collectability of the remaining balances. A provision for doubtful debts simply recognises the fact that not all trade receivable balances offer the same opportunity for payment. The provision takes a conservative view of all trade receivable balances and recognises the accounting principle of prudence.

The provision for doubtful debts will change each year depending on the collectability of the remaining balances and the economic environment, for example, if the economy is booming then there is less likelihood of default from payment of a debt.

Once the amount of the provision has been determined, the increase (or decrease) in the provision (from the previous year) will be taken into the income statement, thereby reducing (or increasing) the profit for the period. The new provision will be deducted from the trade and other receivables figure in the current assets section of the balance sheet.

3. Prepayments (paid in advance)

Prepayments, i.e. amounts paid in advance, relate to expenditure incurred on goods or services for future benefit, which is to be charged to future operating periods. Examples include; fire insurance, rent/rates, vehicle taxes paid in advance, payment for goods in advance. At the end of the accounting period prepayments are in effect sundry debtors; they owe the company a product or service which will not be 'received' until (usually) the next accounting period.

Prepayments are deducted from the expense/cost in the income statement and added into the current asset section of the balance sheet at the end of the period in which they are determined.

Example – Prepayment of insurance

The fire insurance account shows an opening balance of £210, representing fire insurance paid in advance and covering the period 1st Jan 2006 to 31st March 2006. Further payments were made for fire insurance in advance covering six monthly periods as follows, 1st April £480 and 1st October £500.

In this example we have an opening balance, i.e. at the end of the previous year £210 had been paid for a future period. Similarly, at the end of this period £500 of fire insurance has been paid for the period 1st October 2006 to 31st March 2007. Therefore, taking an equal amount, £250 relates to this period while the remaining £250 relates to a future period, i.e. 1st January 2007 to 31st March 2007.

From the fire insurance account we would transfer (£210 + £480 + £500 – £250) £940 into the income statement representing the fire insurance for the period. In the fire insurance account there would be a balance remaining of £250, i.e. at the end of the period, the fire insurance company was a sundry debtor to the company for three months of fire insurance.

The net result would mean that the cost of fire insurance would be reduced in the income statement thereby increasing the retained profit. It would also mean that the current assets section of the balance sheet would be greater by the £250 reduction in the cost of fire insurance. We would have to include an item in the current assets section of the balance sheet as a sundry debtor to record the prepayment of fire insurance.

3.4   Long-term financing

Share capital

Share capital relates to various classes of shares that can be offered by a company. Those subscribing to the shares, or buying them on the open market, are referred to as shareholders. The various classes of shares can be described as follows:

Ordinary shares

Ordinary shares are the most common method of shareholder financing. At any given time, a company will have a maximum limit of authorised share capital that the directors can issue. This can be increased following approval at a company's annual general meeting.

Issued share capital relates to the number of shares that have been issued; a monetary value is placed on the share capital by multiplying the number of shares issued times their nominal or par value. Nominal value is the price at which shares were originally issued.

Preference shares

Preference shares normally carry an entitlement to dividend at a fixed rate per annum. Cumulative preference shares relate to an entitlement to have the dividend cumulate until the company is able to pay out a dividend on the shares. Convertible preference shares relate to an entitlement to covert the shares into ordinary shares, usually within a given time period and at an agreed conversion. It is possible to have convertible cumulative preference shares. Preference shares may or may not have voting rights. At the time of liquidation of a company the preference shareholders will receive payment before the ordinary shareholders.

Rights issues

Rights issues are normally associated with companies who feel they can raise additional share capital from their existing shareholders. The terms of the issue might be that existing shareholders can apply for additional shares, say three shares for every eight held; the offer price will usually be attractive, set at a price that is less than the market price. A rights issue is not available to the general public.

Bonus, script or capitalisation issues

Bonus, script or capitalisation issues are normally associated with a restructuring of the capital of a business. If a business has been successful and built up reserves through profitable trading, revaluation of assets or simply through acquiring an additional premium on shares, the directors might be advised to restructure the share capital. A bonus/script/capitalisation issue are free shares offered to existing shareholders, say one bonus share for every share held. An example might be that a company's shares are trading at £4.00. If a shareholder currently held 100 shares they would be worth £400. When a one to one bonus issue is made the shareholder will now have 200 shares but the value of the share will reduce to £2.00 per share, therefore, 200 shares at £2.00 per share – still worth £400. The reality is that the reduction in the share price might not be to £2.00, it might be £2.20; also, more trading tends to be carried out when share prices are lower, therefore, the £2.00 share price should increase at a faster rate than the previous £4.00 share price.

This is not the only reason for bonus issues. Perhaps the more pressing reason is the restructuring of the shareholder's fund. By offering a bonus issue (free issue) to existing shareholders, the company can transfer amounts from accumulated profits, share premium or revaluations into share capital.

Share premium

Share premium is the difference between the amount paid for a share and its nominal value. If a company has been successful it will not issue new shares at the nominal (or par) value. It would expect to obtain a premium on the issue. Company law requires that issued share capital is shown at its nominal value and any excess is taken into a share premium account. The share premium account is a capital reserve that cannot be readily distributed to shareholders.

Please note, we are not referring here to cash. This side of the balance sheet is the source of funds not the funds themselves. For example, if a company wanted to issue further shares the following might be observed:

Issue 100,000 shares at £3.00; Market value is £3.50; Nominal value is £1.00.

The company would receive £300,000 cash (ignoring any issue expenses).

On the liabilities side of the balance sheet we would add 100,000 shares at £1.00 into the issued share capital and 100,000 shares at £2.00 (the premium) into the share premium account.

Revaluation reserve

Please refer to our discussion on *pages 65 and 66*.

Retained earnings

When we refer to the retained earnings entry in the balance sheet we mean the accumulated profits of the business. Again, they do not represent cash; they only give an indication how some of the assets of the business are financed. It might be better to look at it the other way. Instead of retaining and accumulating profits over a period of time a business was to distribute all its profits. The following might be observed, see *Table 3.13*, if we consider two example companies; say Company A that retains and accumulates profits, and, Company B who distributes all its profits.

Table 3.13 Comparison of retaining or distributing profits

BALANCE SHEET (Company A – Retains all profits)

ASSETS	£	LIABILITIES	£
Non-current assets	300,000	Issued share capital	200,000
		Retained earnings	300,000
		Equity	500,000
Current assets	700,000	Current liabilities	500,000
	1,000,000		1,000,000

CLOSING BALANCE SHEET (Company B – Distributes all profits)

ASSETS	£	LIABILITIES	£
Non-current assets	200,000	Issued share capital	200,000
		Retained earnings	0
		Equity	200,000
Current assets	500,000	Current liabilities	500,000
	700,000		700,000

In *Table 3.13*, it can be seen that Company B has £300,000 less in retained earnings and, therefore, £300,000 less equity. This means that £300,000 less has been retained in the company. The balance sheet of Company A looks much healthier than Company B: it has spent an extra £100,000 on non-current assets while retaining an extra £200,000 in current assets.

Equity

Equity is simply the addition of issued share capital plus reserves. If the business were liquidated and received book values for all its assets, and it paid off all its debts, the remainder would equate to the shareholder's fund or equity.

3.5   Current liabilities adjustments

In this section we are only going to discuss the term accruals, which is often one of the components of current liabilities.

Accruals (due, not yet paid)

An amount relating to a period, which has not so far been taken into account because they have not yet been invoiced by the supplier, therefore, not included in the accounting system and not paid. Examples would be, wages (due not yet paid), interest (due not yet paid), electricity (due not yet paid). At the end of the accounting period accruals are in effect sundry creditors; the company owes the supplier for a product or service which no invoice has yet been recorded, and will not be paid until the next accounting period.

These amounts are added to the expense/cost in the income statement and added to the current liabilities section of the balance sheet at the end of the period in which they are incurred.

Example – Accrual of wages

Wages for October 200X have been paid for the weeks ending the 7th, 14th, 21st and 28th and amount to £36,000. At the end of the period, two days wages are due (30th and 31st October) amounting to £3,500.

In this example, wages paid during the month amount to £36,000. Using accruals and the matching principle, the wages for the period are £36,000 plus £3,500 accrued giving £39,500.

❑   The effect on the income statement would be to increase the expenses for the period, thereby reducing the retained profit for the period;

❑   Given the adjustment in the income statement, there would be an automatic reduction on the liabilities side of the balance sheet. To complete the accrual, a similar amount has to be added into the current liabilities section of the balance sheet. Therefore, at the end of the period, the employees would be a sundry creditor of the company relating to £3,500 of wages which was due (not yet paid).

Appendix A

1. Depreciation

Motor vehicle purchased on 1st January 2004 for £80,000, 4 year life, assume no residual value. Show transactions in the accounts to 1st January 2007.

Motor vehicles

Dr.					Cr.
Jan 1	Balance b/d	80,000			

Provision for depreciation – Motor vehicles

Dr.						Cr.
2004			2004			
Dec 31	Balance c/d	20,000	Dec 31	Income statement	20,000	
2005			2005			
Dec 31	Balance c/d	40,000	Jan 1	Balance b/d	20,000	
			Dec 31	Income statement	20,000	
		40,000			40,000	
2006			2006			
Dec 31	Balance c/d	60,000	Jan 1	Balance b/d	40,000	
			Dec 31	Income statement	20,000	
		60,000			60,000	
2007			2007			
			Jan 1	Balance b/d	60,000	

Income statement for the year ended 31st December

Dr.				Cr.
2004/2005/2006				
Depreciation motor vehicle	20,000			

Balance sheet as at 31 December 2006

ASSETS			*LIABILITIES*
Non-current assets:			
Motor vehicle at cost `	80,000		
less Depreciation	60,000		
Net book value	20,000		

2. Bad debts (written off)

Assume that the following debts were written off during the year:

3rd April   D. Danger Ltd   £400

16th July   U.N. Welcome Ltd   £1,200

9th Nov   U. Dunnit Ltd   £600

D. Danger Ltd

Dr.					Cr.
Apr 1	Balance b/d	400	Apr 3	Bad debts a/c	400

U.N. Welcome Ltd

Dr.					Cr.
Jul 1	Balance b/d	1,200	Jul 16	Bad debts a/c	1,200

U. Dunnit Ltd

Dr.					Cr.
Nov 1	Balance b/d	600	Nov 9	Bad debts a/c	600

Bad debts account

Dr.					Cr.
Apr 3	D. Danger Ltd	400	Dec 31	Income statement	2,200
Jul 16	U.N. Welcome Ltd	1,200			
Nov 9	U. Dunnit Ltd	600			
		2,200			2,200

Income statement for the year ended 31st December

Dr.			Cr.
Bad debts account	2,200		

3. Provision for doubtful debts

From the following notes the entries in the provision for doubtful debts account, the income statement and the balance sheet.

❑   Opening provision for doubtful debts at 1st January 2005 is, £500;

❑   Year ended 31st December 2005, debtor balances are £83,000; adjust provision for doubtful debts to, £800;

❑   Year ended 31st December 2006, debtor balances are £150,000; adjust provision for doubtful debts to, £1,000.

Provision for doubtful debts account

Dr.						Cr.
2005				2005		
Dec 31	Balance c/d	800		Jan 1	Balance b/d	500
				Dec 31	Income statement	300
		800				800
2006				2006		
Dec 31	Balance c/d	1,000		Jan 1	Balance b/d	800
				Dec 31	Income statement	200
		1,000				1,000
2007				2007		
				Jan 1	Balance b/d	1,000

Income statement for the year ended 31st December

Dr.				Cr.
2005				
Provision for doubtful debts	300			
2006				
Provision for doubtful debts	200			

Balance sheet as at 31 December 2006

ASSETS			LIABILITIES
Current assets:			
Trade and other receivables	150,000		
less Provision	1,000		
	149,000		

4. Accruals (due not yet paid)

From the following, show the entries in the wages account, the income statement and the balance sheet.

❐ Wages for October 200X have been paid for the weeks ending 7th, 14th, 21st and 28th and amount to £9,000 per week. At the end of the period, two days wages are due amounting to, £3,500;

❐ Wages for November 200X have been paid for the weeks ending 4th, 11th, 18th and 25th and amount to £9,000 per week. At the end of the period, four days wages are due amounting to, £6,500.

Wages account

Dr.					Cr.
Oct 7	Cash	9,000	Oct 31	Income statement	39,500
Oct 14	Cash	9,000			
Oct 21	Cash	9,000			
Oct 28	Cash	9,000			
Oct 31	Balance c/d	3,500			
		39,500			39,500
Nov 4	Cash	9,000	Nov 1	Balance b/d	3,500
Nov 11	Cash	9,000	Nov 30	Income statement	39,000
Nov 18	Cash	9,000			
Nov 25	Cash	9,000			
Nov 30	Balance c/d	6,500			
		42,500			42,500
			Dec 1	Balance b/d	6,500

Income statement for the period ended 31st October

Dr.		Cr.
Wages	39,500	

Balance sheet as at 31st October

ASSETS		LIABILITIES	
		Current liabilities:	
		Accruals (wages due)	3,500

5. Prepayments (paid in advance)

From the following, show the entries in the fire insurance account, the income statement and the balance sheet.

❏ The fire insurance account shows a debit balance of £210, representing an amount paid in advance and covering the period 1st Januanry to 31st March 200X. Further advance payments were made for fire insurance covering six monthly periods as follows; 1st April 200X, £480 and 1st October 200X, £500.

Fire insurance account

Dr.					Cr.
200X			200X		
Jan 1	Balance b/d	210	Dec 31	Income statement	940
Apr 1	Bank	480	Dec 31	Balance c/d	250
Oct 1	Bank	500			
		1,190			1,190
200X+1			200X+1		
Jan 1	Balance b/d	250			

Income statement for the period ended 31st December 200X

Dr.		Cr.
Fire insurance	940	

Balance sheet as at 31st December 200X

ASSETS		LIABILITIES
Current assets:		
Prepayments (fire insurance)	250	

Exercise 3.1

Equipment was purchased in January 2004 for £500,000 with an estimated economic life of 4 years and a residual value of £40,000. The company adopts a straight line method of depreciation.

Record the entries in the accounts for the years ended 31st December 2004 to 31st December 2006 and bring down the opening balance on the depreciation account for 1st January 2007.

Exercise 3.2

Equipment was purchased in January 2004 for £500,000 with an estimated economic life of 4 years and a residual value of £40,000. The company adopts a 40% reducing balance method of depreciation.

Record the entries in the accounts for the years ended 31st December 2004 to 31st December 2006 and bring down the opening balance on the depreciation account for 1st January 2007.

Exercise 3.3

Assume that the following debts were written off during the year:

4th March	Albert Doe & Sons	£900
18th Aug	Barney Brothers	£3,500
7th Oct	Jim Cunning	£1,700

Open accounts for each customer, show entries to record each bad debt then transfer the balance for the year to the income statement.

Exercise 3.4

Assume that the following debts were written off during the year:

19th Feb	Blight & Co	£3,300
6th May	B. Dreadenough	£800
15th Sept	Harry Hardup Ltd	£6,000

Open accounts for each customer, show entries to record each bad debt then transfer the balance for the year to the income statement.

Exercise 3.5

From the following notes record the entries in the provision for doubtful debts account, the income statement and the balance sheet.

Opening provision for doubtful debts at 1st January 2005 is £8,000;

Year ended 31st December 2005, debtor balances are £750,000; adjust provision for doubtful debts to £9,500;

Year ended 31st December 2006, debtor balances are £1,150,000; adjust provision for doubtful debts to £11,500.

Exercise 3.6

From the following notes record the entries in the provision for doubtful debts account, the income statement and the balance sheet.

Opening provision for doubtful debts at 1st January 2005 is £1,600.

Year ended 31st December 2005, debtor balances are £145,000; adjust provision for doubtful debts to £1,200.

Year ended 31st December 2006, debtor balances are £180,000; adjust provision for doubtful debts to £1,500.

Exercise 3.7

From the following, show the entries in the wages account, the income statement and the balance sheet.

Wages for October 200X have been paid for the weeks ending 7th, 14th, 21st and 28th and amount to £25,000 per week. At the end of the period, two days wages are due amounting to £9,500.

Wages for November 200X have been paid for the weeks ending 4th, 11th, 18th and 25th and amount to £26,000 per week. At the end of the period, four days wages are due amounting to £22,500.

Exercise 3.8

From the following, show the entries in the rent account, the income statement and the balance sheet.

The rent account shows a debit balance of £2,000, representing an amount paid in advance and covering the period 1st January to 31st March 200X. Further advance payments were made by cheque for rent covering six monthly periods as follows; 1st April 200X £4,200 and 1st October 200X £4,400.

CHAPTER FOUR

SOLE TRADER, PARTNERSHIP and CLUB ACCOUNTS

LEARNING OBJECTIVES

When you have finished studying this chapter and completed the exercises, you should be able to:

❏ Understand the differences between the main financial statements of sole traders, partnerships and clubs/societies;

❏ Prepare the main financial statements, with appropriate adjustments, for sole traders;

❏ Prepare the main financial statements for partnerships, including partnership appropriation and capital accounts;

❏ Prepare the main financial statements for clubs/societies including receipts and payments accounts, and income and expenditure accounts.

4.1 Introduction

In this chapter we will cover the preparation of final accounts for unincorporated bodies such as:

1.   Sole traders;

2.   Partnerships;

3.   Clubs/societies.

Each have similarities such as the balance sheet, but they all have unique differences. For example, sole traders and partnerships are conducting a business for the purpose of making profits. They differ in the way capital is provided, salaries determined and, profits and risks are shared. While a club or society is formed for the purpose of pursuing an activity, where members pay annual subscriptions and any other fees due; it is not formed for the purpose of making a profit.

The basic accounting transactions are the same for all types of businesses / organisations; it is only how ownership differs and, the effect on capital and profits/surpluses.

4.2 Rules (what is included in each of the accounts)

When a trial balance has been completed, the next stage is to check every item and identify which account it belongs to (i.e. trading account, income statement, or balance sheet). You will find it helpful, during your early attempts, to refer to the rules which follow, when preparing final accounts.

Trading account (TA)

Takes in the revenue for the accounting period, and deducts the purchases (adjusted for the difference between opening and closing stock). The output from the trading account is the gross profit/loss for the period.

Income statement (IS)

Takes the gross profit/loss and adds any other sources of income (e.g. interest received, rent received, income received), then deducts the expenses and provisions for the period. Expenses will include such things as, wages, rent, rates, lighting and heating, administration, distribution, marketing, computing, interest paid, audit fee, etc. Provisions are for those items where the exact amount and the date a liability will occur are uncertain; the two main provisions are for depreciation of assets, and for doubtful debts. The output from the income statement is the net profit/loss before taxation for the period.

Balance sheet (BS)

Is a statement (not an account) of the financial position of a company at a given period of time. It records all the non-current assets and current assets (i.e. balances the company **OWNS),** and all the current liabilities and long-term financing from shareholders and other sources (i.e. balances the company **OWES).** Examples of the main balance sheet items include:

Non-current assets	Long term financing
Land and buildings	Owners capital
Plant and machinery	Current account (partnerships)
Fixtures and fittings	
Vehicles and others	Long term loans
Current assets	**Current liabilities**
Inventories	Trade and other payables
Trade and other receivables	Bank overdraft
Short term investments	Current taxation
Cash and cash equivalent	

4.3 Sole trader

In this type of business/organisation, the ownership and control rest in one person. This person is entitled to any profits/losses arising but are also liable to the full extent of their personal resources for their business debts and liabilities. It is the least formal of all businesses since all decisions are made by the single owner. No need for formal agreements on how profits should be split or the amount of salaries/holidays to be given.

With a sole trader it is normal to operate on a single capital account. To this account is added any profits or losses, and drawings are deducted to give a closing balance on their capital account.

Apart from the above, the final accounts of the sole trader are similar in most respects to that of a limited company.

We will now produce two examples of the final accounts for sole traders. The first with adjustments covering closing stock and depreciation, while the second example will include other adjustments such as salaries due, insurance paid in advance and the provision for bad debts.

Example 4.1 – Sole trader

The following trial balance has been extracted from the books of Albert Smith as at 31st May 200X.

	Dr.	Cr.	Reference
	£	£	
Purchases	135,000		TA 2
Capital		93,750	BS 40
Drawings	15,000		BS 42
Premises	45,000		BS 31
Marketing and selling	9,000		IS 11
Trade and other receivables	30,000		BS 37
Opening inventories	18,000		TA 1
Depreciation of vehicles		7,500	BS 35
Bad debts	1,500		IS 12
Office equipment	7,500		BS 32
Revenues		225,000	TA 6
Wages and salaries	30,000		IS 13
Heating and lighting	4,500		IS 14
Depreciation of office equipment		2,250	BS 33
Trade and other payables		22,500	BS 44
Discount allowed	2,250		IS 15
Cash	2,250		BS 39
Bank	7,500		BS 38
Discount received		1,500	IS 21
Vehicles	45,000		BS 34
	352,500	352,500	

Notes:

Closing inventories	£27,900	TA 3 + BS 36
Depreciation of office equipment	£750	IS 16 + BS 33
Depreciation of vehicles	£5,400	IS 17 + BS 35

Required:

Prepare Trading account, and Income statement for the year ended 31st May 2000, and a Balance sheet as at that date.

You will notice that each line in the trial balance has a reference at the end. If we select opening stock as an example, you will see that it refers to TA 1, i.e. trading account, location (1). Notice that all the locations in the accounts are numbered and they correspond to a line in the trial balance.

We will use this system for the initial exercise in the preparation of final accounts, to show that each line in the trial balance has a single location, also to help with an 'audit' trail for the reader/student to follow. We will also use the double entry bookkeeping principles applied to the trading account and, the income statement. In *Chapter 5* we will use a vertical layout.

The content of the trading account is similar from one company/organisation to another, provided that they are involved in trading activities.

Albert Smith

Trading account

for the year ended 31st May 200X

Dr.					Cr
(1)	Opening inventories	18,000	(6)	**Revenues**	**225,000**
(2)	add Purchases	135,000			
(3)	less Closing inventories	27,900			
(4)	= Cost of sales	125,100			
(5)	Gross profit c/d	99,900			
		225,000			225,000

Note: Many accounts are 'built-up' during the year and their balances have to be transferred either to the trading account or the income statement. This completes the double entry exercise and clears the accounts ready for the start of a new period. Below, we can see the revenues account with a credit balance of £225,000; then the transfer, i.e. debit the sales account with £225,000 and credit the trading account with £225,000. All other entries for the trading account and, income statement would follow the same procedure; with only the balance sheet items remaining as balances in the accounts.

Revenues account

Dr.				Cr
(6)	**Trading account**	**225,000**	Balance c/d	225,000

The transaction on *page 87* is shown only for completeness, and would be carried out automatically given that a company/organisation was using accounting software. For the purpose of completing final accounts from a trial balance we will assume that all the accounts have been posted, i.e. balances cleared.

A tip. When entering a posting into the final accounts, place a tick against the item in the trial balance. That way, you will be able to see what has been posted and what remains to be actioned.

Albert Smith

Income statement

for the year ended 31st May 200X

Dr.   Cr

(11)	Marketing and selling	9,000	(20)	Gross profit b/d	99,900
(12)	Bad debts	1,500	(21)	Discount received	1,500
(13)	Wages and salaries	30,000			
(14)	Heating and lighting	4,500			
(15)	Discount allowed	2,250			
(16)	Depreciation of office equip.	750			
(17)	Depreciation of vehicles	5,400			
(18)		53,400			
(19)	Net profit c/d	48,000			
		101,400			101,400

When completing the income statement, start at the top of the trial balance and post each item in turn; then, action each of the relevant adjustments.

You will notice that any postings into the credit side will increase the overall profit, while any postings into the debit side will reduce the overall profit.

All the postings, line 11 through to line 15, just go 'straight in', i.e. no adjustments. In line 16, we action the adjustment relating to the depreciation of office equipment. Here we are entering an amount of £750 which is the annual depreciation charge. The posting is debit the income statement, and credit the depreciation of office equipment account. Unlike the items in the trial balance that close the accounts, adjustments to the trial balance result in an initial entry and automatically affect the balance sheet.

A similar posting is required at line 17, depreciation of vehicles.

Albert Smith

Balance Sheet

as at 31st May 200X

ASSETS			LIABILITIES		
Non-current assets			**Owners capital**		
(31) Premises		45,000	(40) Capital account – opening		93,750
(32) Office equipment	7,500		(41) add Profit for year		48,000
(33) less Depreciation	3,000	4,500	(42) less Drawings for year		15,000
(34) Vehicles	45,000		(43) Capital account – closing		126,750
(35) less Depreciation	12,900	32,100			
Current assets			**Current liabilities**		
(36) Inventories	27,900		(44) Trade payables		22,500
(37) Trade receivables	30,000				
(38) Bank	7,500				
(39) Cash	2,250				
		67,650			
		149,250			149,250

After carrying out postings to the trading account and, the income statement we should only be left with balance sheet items. In this balance sheet we are adopting the layout; assets on the left and liabilities on the right hand side. It can be seen that the total assets equals total liabilities, i.e. the balance sheet equation.

For the purpose of initial learning there is no right or wrong way of laying out a balance sheet, i.e. as above, *or* with assets on the right hand side and liabilities on the left hand side, *or* in some vertical layout.

There are two areas of the above balance sheet that need some explanation. The non-current assets section. We take office equipment (at cost) from the trial balance, i.e. £7,500. From this we deduct the accumulated depreciation to the start of this year, as shown in the trial balance, plus the annual depreciation charge entered into the income statement, i.e. £2,250 + £750 = £3,000. Finally, when deducted from the office equipment at cost, this gives a net value of £4,500. A similar process is followed for vehicles.

In the top right corner of the balance sheet we show the capital account (opening balance) taken from the trial balance. To this we add the profit for the period, then deduct the drawings for the period to arrive at the capital account (closing balance), i.e. £93,750 + £48,000 – £15,000 = £126,750.

Example 4.2 – Sole trader

The following trial balance has been extracted from the books of *Aymi's Fashions* as at 29th February 200X.

	Dr. £	Cr. £	Reference
Capital		57,500	BS 41
Drawings	9,000		BS 43
Premises	25,000		BS 31
Trade and other receivables	15,000		BS 37
Trade and other payables		9,500	BS 45
Revenues		150,000	TA 9
Opening inventories	12,000		TA 1
Advertising	800		IS 11
Bad debts	600		IS 12
Office equipment	5,000		BS 32
Purchases	115,000		TA 2
Rent received		1,500	IS 21
Salaries	15,000		IS 13
Insurance	1,500		IS 14
Returns inwards	1,500		TA 10
Returns outwards		800	TA 4
Cash	1,500		BS 40
Bank overdraft		5,000	BS 46
Depreciation of office equipment		1,500	BS 33
Depreciation of shop fixtures		5,000	BS 35
Carriage inwards	3,000		TA 3
Carriage outwards	1,500		IS 15
Provision for doubtful debts		600	Adj.
Shop fixtures	25,000		BS 34
	231,400	231,400	

Notes:

Closing inventories	£15,000	TA 6 + BS 36
Depreciation of office equipment	£500	IS 16 + BS 33
Depreciation of shop fixtures	£3,000	IS 17 + BS 35
Provision for doubtful debts, adjust to	£750	IS 18 + BS 38
Insurance paid in advance	£800	IS 14 + BS 39
Salaries due	£800	IS 13 + BS 47

Prepare a Trading account and Income statement for the year ended 29th February 200X and a Balance sheet as at that date.

In this example we follow the same procedures as the previous example, but also introduce a number of additional items that require some explanation.

Aymi's Fashions

Trading account

for the year ended 29th February 200X

Dr.   Cr

(1)	Opening inventories		12,000	(9)	Revenues	150,000
(2)	Purchases	115,000		(10)	less Returns inwards	1,500
(3)	add Carriage inwards	3,000				
(4)	less Returns outwards	800				
(5)			117,200			
(6)	− Closing inventories		15,000			
(7)	= Cost of sales		114,200			
(8)	Gross profit c/d		34,300			
			148,500			148,500

There are three additional items in the trial balance that affect the trading account.

Two of these relate to returns inwards and returns outwards. As their name suggests, returns inwards relates to goods returned to a company by its customers, while returns outwards relates to goods returned to a company's suppliers. The treatment in the trading account is to deduct returns outwards from purchases, and returns inwards from revenues.

The third item is carriage inwards. Normal practice requires that where carriage inwards is shown on an invoice it is posted separately. However, many invoices do not show carriage as a separate item. In final accounts, carriage inwards is assumed to be part of the cost of purchases and is added to purchases. On the other hand, carriage outwards, i.e. delivery costs to our customers is seen to be an expense of the business and, therefore, included in the income statement.

Aymi's Fashions

Income statement

for the year ended 29th February 200X

Dr.   Cr

(11)	Advertising	800	(20)	Gross profit b/d	34,300
(12)	Bad debts	600	(21)	Rent received	1,500
(13)	Salaries	15,800			
(14)	Insurance	700			
(15)	Carriage outwards	1,500			
(16)	Depreciation of office equip.	500			
(17)	Depreciation of shop fixtures	3,000			
(18)	Provision for doubtful debts	150			
		23,050			
(19)	Net profit for year	12,750			
		35,800			35,800

In the income statement above, there are four items that require some explanation.

The first is bad debts: In *Chapter 3* we saw that when a trade receivable is considered financially unable to pay the outstanding amount on their account, the balance is transferred to a bad debts account. This account builds up throughout the accounting period and is transferred to the income statement as an expense associated with the business.

The second is salaries: In the trial balance, salaries paid amount to £15,000. A note to the trial balance states that at the end of the accounting period there are salaries due of £800. This total figure is included in the income statement, i.e. £15,000 + £800 being the salaries for the period. The £800 salaries due will also be shown in the balance sheet as an accrual in the current liabilities section.

The third is insurance: The trial balance shows that £1,500 has been paid for insurance. While a note to the trial balance states that £800 of insurance has been paid in advance. This net figure is included in the income statement, i.e. £1,500 – £800 being the insurance for the period. The £800 of insurance paid in advance will also be shown in the balance sheet as a prepayment in the current assets section.

Finally, the provision for doubtful debts: (For a review of the provision for doubtful debts please refer to *Chapter 3*). In a note to the trial balance we are asked to make a provision for doubtful debts of £750. We must check the trial balance to see if there is an opening provision; in this case there is a balance of £600. This net figure is included in the income statement, i.e. £750 – £600. In the balance sheet we deduct the total provision, i.e. £750 from the trade and other receivables figure in the current assets section.

Aymi's Fashions
Balance sheet
as at 29th February 200X

	ASSETS				LIABILITIES	
	Non-current assets				**Owners capital account**	
(31)	Premises		25,000	(41)	Capital account – opening	57,500
(32)	Office equipment	5,000		(42)	add Profit for year	12,750
(33)	less Depreciation	2,000	3,000	(43)	less Drawings for year	9,000
(34)	Shop fixtures	25,000		(44)	Capital account – closing	61,250
(35)	less Depreciation	8,000	17,000			
	Current assets				**Current liabilities**	
(36)	Inventories		15,000	(45)	Trade payables	9,500
(37)	Trade receivables	15,000		(46)	Bank overdraft	5,000
(38)	less Provision	750	14,250	(47)	Salaries due	800
(39)	Insurance prepaid		800			15,300
(40)	Cash		1,500			
			31,550			
			76,550			76,550

In the previous example, we discussed the treatment of non-current assets and depreciation; also the opening capital account through profit for the year and drawings to arrive at the closing capital account balance.

In the above balance sheet our attention will focus on the adjustments required in the current assets and current liabilities sections. A tip to help understand the additional items that must be included, is to work through all the notes to the trial balance; each note *must* be included in the closing balance sheet.

At line 37 in the current assets section, we can see the figure for trade receivables, i.e. £15,000. At line 38 we show the provision for doubtful debts, i.e. £750 and to the right the net figure, i.e. £14,250. At line 39 we include the insurance paid in advance of £800.

Finally, at line 47 we include salaries (due, not yet paid). At the balance sheet date, the salaried employees are sundry creditors of the business.

4.4 Partnerships

In the sole trader we saw that he/she was the single owner of the business. In a partnership there are two or more owners.

A partnership is defined in *Partnership Act 1890* as *'the relationship which exists between persons carrying on a business in common with a view to profit'*.

❐ Therefore, a partnership is a relationship in business. It could be compared to the relationship in a marriage. The common aspect is that partners have to work to maintain the relationship. If/when the relationship ceases to work it is important to know how the partnership will be dissolved. This is one of the main benefits in preparing a partnership agreement at the outset. We will outline the main features of a partnership agreement below.

❐ It is also concerned with persons carrying on a business in common. This requires a clear definition of the boundaries of the business, the duties of the partners, and a common goal or purpose. Business in this context means 'every trade, occupation or profession'.

❐ Finally, with a view to profit. An important element in a partnership; for example, a social club is a number of people undertaking some activity in common but without the view to profit.

For those contemplating forming a partnership we would strongly advise that you seek legal advice. Unlike a marriage, which is supposed to be 'till death us do part', a partnership often has a limited life. For example, if two partners formed a business, where Partner A contributed most of the capital and Partner B contributed most of the skill. When successful, and Partner B had managed to build up sufficient funds, Partner B might question the need for Partner A. One of our advisers refers to partnerships as 'sinking ships'.

Partnership agreement

The partnership agreement, like insurance, does not mean much until something goes wrong. The agreement should be prepared by a solicitor and should set out the rules governing how the partnership operates. Among other things it should cover the following:

❐ Who the partners are and how much capital each should contribute;

❐ How the profits/losses should be shared between the partners;

❐ If interest is payable on capital accounts, current account balances and interest charged on drawings;

❐ Any partners who are entitled to salaries, including how the amounts should be determined;

❐ The formulae to determine the amount of drawings each partner is allowed.

Example 4.3 – Partnership accounts

In this example we will concentrate on the additional elements concerned with partnership accounts, i.e. the partnership appropriation account and the partners capital accounts.

The following trial balance has been extracted from the books of *ASF Catering* as at 31st January 200X.

	Dr. £	Cr. £
Trade and other payables		36,000
Revenues		270,000
Purchases	201,000	
Trade and other receivables	9,000	
Equipment	81,000	
Opening inventories	27,000	
Overheads	21,000	
Depreciation of equipment		21,000
Capital – Alastair		36,000
Capital – Susan		21,000
Capital – Fiona		12,000
Drawings – Alastair	15,000	
Drawings – Susan	21,000	
Drawings – Fiona	12,000	
Bank	9,000	
	396,000	396,000

Notes:

Closing inventories	£33,000
Depreciation of equipment	£12,000
Interest on capital at 15% per annum	
Salaries – Susan	£9,000
Salaries – Fiona	£6,000
Profits/losses share – Alastair	5
Profits/losses share – Susan	4
Profits/losses share – Fiona	3

ASF Catering
Trading account
for the year ended 31st January 200X

Dr.   Cr

Opening inventories	27,000	Revenues	270,000
Purchases	201,000		
	228,000		
– Closing inventories	33,000		
= Cost of sales	195,000		
Gross profit c/d	75,000		
	270,000		270,000

ASF Catering
Income statement
for the year ended 31st January 200X

Dr.   Cr

Overheads	21,000	Gross profit b/d	75,000
Depreciation of equipment	12,000		
Net profit	42,000		
	75,000		75,000

ASF Catering
Partnership appropriation accounts

	Alastair	Susan	Fiona	Total
Interest on capital (1)	5,400	3,150	1,800	10,350
Salaries (2)		9,000	6,000	15,000
Balance (3)	6,938	5,550	4,162	16,650
	12,338	17,700	11,962	42,000

Tutorial notes:

1. Interest on capital: A note to the accounts indicates that partners are allowed 15% on the balance of their capital accounts:

	Alastair	Susan	Fiona
Opening capital	*36,000*	*21,000*	*12,000*
Interest on capital at 15%	5,400	3,150	1,800

2. Salaries: A note to the accounts gives the salaries payable to Susan £9,000, and Fiona £6,000.

3. Share of profits/losses: The profit for the period is £42,000. From this, we deduct the interest on capital £10,350, and the total of the salaries £15,000 to give a net profit or balance of £16,650. A note to the accounts gives the proportion each partner is entitled to, i.e. 5 : 4 : 3.

	Alastair	Susan	Fiona	Total
Profit sharing proportions	5	4	3	12
Net profit or balance				16,650
Alastair £16,650 ÷ 12 x 5	6,938			
Susan £16,650 ÷ 12 x 4		5,550		
Fiona £16,650 ÷ 12 x 3			4,162	

ASF Catering
Partnership capital accounts

	Alastair	Susan	Fiona
Opening capital	36,000	21,000	12,000
add Profit appropriation	12,338	17,700	11,962
less Drawings	15,000	21,000	12,000
Closing capital	33,338	17,700	11,962

The partnership capital accounts are similar to the sole traders capital account. Simply, take the opening capital and add profit appropriation then deduct drawings to give the closing capital account balance.

ASF Catering
Balance sheet
as at 31st January 200X

ASSETS			LIABILITIES	
Non-current assets			**Capital accounts**	
Equipment	81,000		Alastair	33,338
less Depreciation	33,000	48,000	Susan	17,700
			Fiona	11,962
				63,000
Current assets			**Current liabilities**	
Inventories	33,000		Trade payables	36,000
Trade receivables	9,000			
Bank	9,000			
		51,000		
		99,000		99,000

In this example, we show the partners capital accounts as a single entry. An alternative method is to keep the capital accounts intact, and use partners current accounts to record profits/losses and drawings.

4.5 Club/Society accounts

We now turn our attention to club/society accounts. These are common in sports clubs, leisure clubs, social clubs, debating societies, etc. The main difference from the previous accounts are that they are run on behalf of the members for the members, not with the view to profit.

In many cases clubs/societies do not maintain full accounting records. Instead, they maintain a receipts and payments account which is similar to a bank/cash account. Other differences include:

❏ There might be a bar account which is similar to a combined trading and, income statement. Here the view is to make a surplus to help fund other activities enjoyed by the members. All clubs/societies are required to prepare an income and expenditure account and a balance sheet. The income and expenditure account is similar to the business income statement.

Example 4.4 – Club/Society accounts

In the example that follows we have an opening balance sheet and, a receipts and payments account, together with notes. These take the place of a trial balance.

We will produce a Bar trading account and, Income and expenditure account for the year ended 30th September 200X and a Balance sheet as at that date.

Fellow Accountants Golf Society
Opening balance sheet
as at 1st October 200X-1

ASSETS			LIABILITIES		
Non-current assets			**Accumulated fund**		
Premises		256,000	Opening capital fund		282,800
Equipment	37,050		add Surplus for period		25,200
less Depreciation	1,850	35,200	Closing capital fund		308,000
Current assets			**Current liabilities**		
Stock – bar	12,800		Creditors – bar purchases	8,000	
Subs. in arrears	7,200		Subs. paid in advance	4,000	
Insurance in advance	2,400		Sundry bar expenses due	800	12,800
Cash	7,200	29,600			
		320,800			320,800

Fellow Accountants Golf Society
Receipts and payments account
for the year ended 30th September 200X

Dr.			Cr.
Balance b/f	7,200	Wages	192,000
Subscriptions	184,000	Sundry bar expenses	4,800
Bar takings	220,800	Insurance	7,200
Locker rents	3,200	Rates	5,600
		Printing and stationery	3,200
		Bar purchases	163,200
		Balance c/f	39,200
	415,200		415,200

Notes:

Wages including bar attendant	£11,200
Insurance paid in advance	£3,040
Sundry bar expenses due	£480
Subscriptions due	£4,800
Subscriptions paid in advance	£2,400
Bar purchases due	£4,800
Bar stock	£8,800

Depreciation of furniture and equipment, 5% on a reducing balance

Fellow Accountants Golf Society
Bar trading account
for the year ended 30th September 200X

Dr.   Cr.

Opening inventories (1)	12,800	Bar takings	220,800
Purchases (2)	160,000		
	172,800		
− Closing inventories (3)	8,800		
= Cost of sales	164,000		
Wages – bar attendant (4)	11,200		
Sundry bar expenses (5)	4,480		
Profit from bar	41,120		
	220,800		220,800

Tutorial notes:

1. Opening inventories is taken from the opening balance sheet.

2. Purchases: £163,200 (receipts and payments account) + £4,800 (notes) – £8,000 (opening balance sheet) = £160,000.

3. Closing inventories is taken from the notes.

4. Wages – bar attendant is taken from the notes

5. Sundry bar expenses: £4,800 (receipts and payments account) + £480 (notes) – £800 (opening balance sheet) = £4,480.

Fellow Accountants Golf Society
Income and expenditure account
for the year ended 30th September 200X

Dr.			Cr.
Wages (1)	180,800	Subscriptions (6)	183,200
Insurance (2)	6,560	Locker rents (7)	3,200
Rates (3)	5,600	Profit from bar (8)	41,120
Printing and stationery (4)	3,200		
Depreciation of equipment (5)	1,760		
Surplus to capital a/c	29,600		
	227,520		227,520

Tutorial notes:

1. Wages: £192,000 (receipts and payments account) – £11,200 (notes) = £180,800.

2. Insurance: £7,200 (receipts and payments account) + £2,400 (opening balance sheet) – £3,040 (notes) = £6,560.

3. Rates: £5,600 (receipts and payments account).

4. Printing and stationery: £3,200 (receipts and payments account).

5. Depreciation: £35,200 (opening balance sheet) x 5% (notes) = £1,760.

6. Subscriptions: £184,000 (receipts and payments account) + £4,000 (opening balance sheet) – £7,200 (opening balance sheet) + £4,800 (notes) – £2,400 (notes) = £183,200.

    This is a particularly difficult adjustment. The diagram below shows subscriptions due at the beginning of the year. These would be collected and included in the £184,000, therefore have to be deducted; similarly, the £2,400 paid in advance is also included in the £184,000 and has to be deducted.

£7,200	**£4,000**	**£184,000**	**£4,800**	£2,400

7. Locker rents: £3,200 (receipts and payments account).

8. Profit from bar (taken from the bar trading account).

Fellow Accountants Golf Society
Balance sheet
as at 30th September 200X

ASSETS			LIABILITIES		
Non-current assets			**Accumulated fund**		
Premises		256,000	Opening capital fund		308,000
Equipment	35,200		add Surplus for period		29,600
less Depreciation	1,760	33,440	Closing capital fund		337,600
Current assets			**Current liabilities**		
Stock – bar	8,800		Creditors – bar purchases	4,800	
Subs. in arrears (1)	4,800		Subs. paid in advance (2)	2,400	
Insurance in advance	3,040		Sundry bar expenses due	480	7,680
Cash	39,200	55,840			
		345,280			345,280

Tutorial notes:

The preparation of the balance sheet is similar to sole trader and partnership accounts. A tip: when you are given an opening balance sheet, use it as a template to produce your closing balance sheet. Below we will restrict our explanation to subscriptions paid in arrears and in advance.

1. Subscriptions in arrears, i.e. due. This can be confusing, but subscriptions due is similar to a sundry debtor, therefore, it is included in the current assets section of the balance sheet.

2. Subscriptions paid in advance, i.e. prepaid. Again, these can be confusing. Subscriptions paid in advance is similar to a sundry creditor, therefore, it is included in the current liabilities section of the balance sheet.

Exercise 4.1

Hannah's Just Gardens, Trial balance as at 31st August 200X

	£	£
General expenses	4,200	
Rent	8,000	
Motor expenses	14,700	
Salaries	71,200	
Insurance	7,800	
Opening inventories	67,700	
Purchases	300,000	
Revenues		536,300
Motor vehicle	56,000	
Trade and other payables		103,200
Trade and other receivables	81,800	
Premises	400,000	
Bank	28,000	
Depreciation of motor vehicle		22,400
Capital		464,500
Drawings	87,000	
	1,126,400	1,126,400

Inventories at 31st August 200X was £99,200.

Depreciation of motor vehicle, over 5 years straight line.

General expense due £500.

Prepare a Trading account and Income statement for the year ending 31st August 200X and a Balance sheet as at that date.

Exercise 4.2

The Trial balance as at 31st December 200X was as follows:

	Dr.	Cr.
Trade and other payables		40,000
Revenues		300,000
Land and buildings	100,000	
Administrative overheads	60,000	
Purchases	200,000	
Trade and other receivables	30,000	
Vehicles	20,000	
Opening inventories	30,000	
Selling overheads	19,000	
Provision for doubtful debts		700
Trade investments (at cost)	20,000	
Audit fee	1,000	
Income from investments		2,000
Cash	5,000	
Drawings	15,000	
Owners capital		138,300
Interest paid	1,000	
Bank overdraft		20,000
	501,000	501,000

Closing inventories at 31st December 200X	£40,000
Adjust provision for doubtful debts to	£1,000
Administration costs due	£2,000

Prepare a Trading account and Income statement for the year ended 31st December 200X and a Balance Sheet as at that date.

Exercise 4.3

The Trial balance as at 30th September 200X

	£	£
Rent	31,200	
Insurance	6,100	
Bank overdraft		250,000
Lighting and heating	10,320	
Motor expenses	39,200	
Salaries and wages	97,000	
Revenues		712,000
Purchases	400,000	
Sundry expenses	16,120	
Motor vehicles	70,000	
Trade and other payables		165,000
Trade and other receivables	136,200	
Furniture and fittings	79,200	
Opening inventories	219,400	
Buildings	545,000	
Interest payable	15,000	
Cash at bank	22,680	
Drawings	125,560	
Capital		685,980
	1,812,980	1,812,980

Inventories at 30th September 200X was £199,200

Insurance paid in advance, £600

Bad debts to be written off, £6,000

Prepare a Trading account and Income statement for the year ending 30th September 200X and a Balance Sheet as at that date.

Exercise 4.4

The Trial balance as at 31st October 200X was as follows:

	Dr.	Cr.
Land and buildings	100,000	
Machinery	110,000	
Purchases	190,000	
Rates	4,000	
General expenses	30,000	
Loan at 10%		100,000
Wages and salaries	40,000	
Bad debts written off	1,000	
Distribution costs	25,000	
Trade and other receivables	25,000	
Depreciation of machinery		33,000
Opening inventories	40,000	
Bank	20,000	
Owners capital		86,000
Revenues		350,000
Loan interest	5,000	
Trade and other payables		38,000
Drawings	17,000	
	607,000	607,000

Notes:

Closing inventories at 31st October 200X, £20,000

Depreciation of plant and equipment, 10 years straight line.

Prepare a Trading account and Income statement for the year ended 31st October 200X and a Balance sheet as at that date.

Exercise 4.5

Smith and Jones are in partnership on the following terms:

1.   Interest at 5% per annum is to be allowed on opening capital account balances;

2.   Jones is entitled to draw a salary of £3,000;

3.   Profits/losses are shared two thirds Smith, one third Jones.

In addition, the following balances have been extracted from the accounts on 31st December 200X.

	Dr.	Cr.
Trade and other payables		34,800
Revenues		103,200
Discount allowed	1,800	
Cash	900	
Fixtures and fittings	5,400	
Purchases	86,400	
Trade and other receivables	37,200	
Freehold premises	30,000	
Opening inventories	27,600	
Bad debts	1,800	
General expenses	5,400	
Depreciation of equipment		900
Capital – Smith		12,000
Capital – Jones		5,400
Repairs to premises	1,800	
Drawings – Smith	1,800	
Drawings – Jones	4,800	
Bank overdraft		48,600
	204,900	204,900

Notes:
Closing inventories   £31,200
Depreciation of fixtures & fittings, 10 years straight line
Insurance prepaid (in general expenses)   £300

Prepare Trading account, Income statement, Parternship appropriation account, Partners capital accounts for the year ended 31st December 200X and a Balance sheet as at that date.

Exercise 4.6

Jim, Dougal and Rosie are in partnership on the following terms:

1. Interest at 12% per annum is to be allowed on opening capital account balances;

2. Salaries to be paid, Dougal £24,000, Rosie £20,000;

3. Profits/losses are shared between Jim, Dougal and Rosie in the ratio 3 : 2 : 1.

In addition, the following balances have been extracted from the accounts on 31st July 200X.

	Dr.	Cr.
Trade and other payables		64,000
Revenues		516,000
Purchases	268,000	
Trade and other receivables	48,000	
Equipment	220,000	
Opening inventories	56,000	
Overheads	60,000	
Depreciation of equipment		36,000
Capital – Jim		60,000
Capital – Dougal		40,000
Capital – Rosie		32,000
Drawings – Jim	36,000	
Drawings – Dougal	28,000	
Drawings – Rosie	20,000	
Bank	12,000	
	748,000	748,000

Notes:

Closing inventories	£44,000
Depreciation of equipment	£46,000

Prepare Trading account, Income statement, Parternship appropriation account, Partners capital accounts for the year ended 31st July 200X and a Balance sheet as at that date.

Exercise 4.7

The following particulars relate to the *B One Fitness Club*:

Opening balance sheet as at 31st March 200X-1

Non-current assets			Accumulated fund		125,000
Club house at cost		75,000			
Furniture and equipment		37,500			
		112,500			
Current assets			Current liabilities		
Subs in arrears	2,500		Trade payables	2,500	
Cash	13,750		Subs paid in advance	1,250	
		16,250			3,750
		128,750			128,750

Receipts and payments account for the year ended 31st March 2000

Balance b/f	13,750	Wages	63,750
Subscriptions	75,000	General expenses	3,750
Social takings	23,750	Insurance	2,500
		Rates	3,750
		Printing and stationery	2,500
		Balance c/f	36,250
	112,500		112,500

Notes:

Subscriptions due	£1,250
Subscriptions paid in advance	£750

Depreciation of furniture and equipment at 25% on reducing balance.

You are required to prepare the club's Income and expenditure account for the year ended 31st March 200X and a Balance sheet as at that date.

Exercise 4.8

From the following opening balance sheet and receipts and payments account you are required to prepare the club's income and expenditure account for the year ended 31st October 200X and a balance sheet as at that date.

Opening balance sheet 1st November 200X-1

Non-current assets			Opening capital fund		82,600
Club house		108,000	add Surplus for period		45,500
Equipment	22,750		Closing capital fund		128,100
less Depreciation	5,950	16,800			
Current assets			Current liabilities		
Stock – bar	5,400		Creditors – bar purchases	4,200	
Subs. in arrears	2,100		Subs. paid in advance	3,300	
Insurance prepaid	1,500		Sundry bar expenses due	1,500	9,000
Cash	3,300	12,300			
		137,100			137,100

Receipts and payments account for the year ended 31st October 200X

Dr.			Cr.
Balance b/f	3,300	Wages	72,000
Subscriptions	90,000	Sundry bar expenses	1,800
Bar takings	58,800	Insurance	2,700
Locker rents	3,600	Rates	2,100
		Printing and stationery	1,200
		Bar purchases	49,200
		Balance c/f	26,700
	155,700		155,700

Notes:
Wages include £3,000 for bar attendant

Insurance paid in advance	£1,320
Sundry bar expenses due	£420
Subscriptions due	£1,500
Subscriptions paid in advance	£2,100
Bar purchases due	£1,500
Closing bar stock	£3,600

Depreciation of equipment over 20 years straight line.

CHAPTER FIVE

F I N A L
A C C O U N T S
OF L I M I T E D
C O M P A N I E S

When you have finished studying this chapter and completed the exercises, you should be able to:

❏ Understand the requirements for the preparation of the main financial statements of limited companies;

❏ Prepare trading account, income statement, appropriation account and balance sheet in vertical formats;

❏ Describe the main components of published accounts;

❏ Have an appreciation of the formats for UK published accounts and the extent of UK accounting standards.

5.1 Introduction

The following example shows the preparation of the final accounts for limited companies. First we will provide a set of rules to determine which items go in which accounts, i.e. trading account, income statement, appropriation account, and balance sheet.

In the second part of the chapter we will describe the main components of published accounts, including the chairperson's statement, the directors' report, the auditors' report, accounting policies, notes to the accounts and historical summaries. This is a section that you will often refer to when using published accounts for assignment purposes.

Appendices to the chapter provide alternative layouts for published accounts together with a listing of UK Accounting Standards.

Final accounts of limited companies

These consist of:

Trading account;

Income statement;

Appropriation account;

Balance sheet.

5.2 Rules (what is included in each of the accounts)

When a trial balance has been completed, the next stage is to check every item and identify which account it belongs to (i.e. trading account, income statement, appropriation account or balance sheet). You will find it helpful during your early attempts to refer to the rules which follow, when preparing final accounts.

Trading account (TA)

Takes in the revenues for the accounting period, and deducts the purchases (adjusted for the difference between opening and closing inventories). The output from the trading account is the gross profit/loss for the period.

Income statement (IS)

Takes the gross profit/loss and adds any other sources of income (e.g. interest received, rent received, income received), then deducts the expenses and provisions for the period. Expenses will include such things as, wages, rent, rates, lighting and heating, administration, distribution, marketing, computing, interest paid, audit fee, etc. Provisions are for those items where the exact amount and the date at which a liability will occur are uncertain; the two main provisions are for depreciation of assets, and for doubtful debts. The output from the income statement is the net profit/loss before taxation for the period.

Appropriation account (AA)

Takes the net profit/loss before taxation and adds any accumulated profits from previous periods (shown in the trial balance as retained earnings. This gives the amount of profit which can then be appropriated between taxation, shareholders (by way of dividend), and the amount retained in the business which will be the retained earnings (closing) balance.

Balance sheet (BS)

Is a statement (not an account) of the financial position of a company at a given period of time. It records all the non-current assets and current assets (i.e. balances the company OWNS), and all the current liabilities and long term financing from shareholders and other sources (i.e. balances the company OWES).

Examples of the main Balance sheet items will include:

Non-current assets	Equity
Land and buildings	Issued share capital
Plant and machinery	Share premium
Fixtures and fittings	Revaluation
Vehicles and others	Retained earnings
	Long-term loans/debentures
Current assets	**Current liabilities**
Inventories	Trade and other payables
Trade and other receivables	Bank overdraft
Prepayments	Accruals
Short-term investments	Taxation due
Cash and cash equivalent	Dividends proposed

5.3 Example – Oak Limited

The Trial balance of *OAK Ltd* as at the 31st March 200X was as follows:–

		Dr.	Cr.
BS	Vehicles (at cost)	130,000	
TR	Purchases	720,000	
TR	Revenues		1,000,000
BS	Depreciation of vehicles		26,000
TR	Opening inventories	140,000	
BS	Trade and other receivables	85,000	
BS	Trade and other payables		44,000
BS	Long-term loans at 10%		60,000
BS	Share premium		25,000
AA	Retained earnings		25,000
IS	Wages	35,000	
IS	Rates	2,500	
IS	Heating and lighting	5,000	
IS	Salaries	20,000	
IS	Administration expenses	65,000	
BS	Furniture and fittings (at cost)	18,000	
BS	Depreciation of furniture and fittings		9,000
BS	Bank balance	50,000	
	Provision for doubtful debts		3,000
IS	Loan interest paid to 30th Sept 200X-1	3,000	
BS	Freehold property	200,000	
BS	Issued share capital		300,000
IS	Bad debts written off	3,500	
IS	Directors fees	15,000	
		1,492,000	1,492,000

Prepare a Trading account, Income statement and Appropriation account for the year ended 31st March 200X, and a Balance sheet as at that date.

The following notes are to be taken into account:
1. Inventories at 31st March 200X, £150,000;
2. Wages outstanding at 31st March 200X, £1,500;
3. Rates paid in advance amounting to £500;
4. Depreciation of vehicles over 5 years (straight line);
5. Depreciation of furniture and fittings, 5% on cost;
6. Provision for bad and doubtful debts, adjust to £3,500;
7. Dividend proposed, 50% of profit attributable to shareholders.

The notes to the trial balance are essentially adjustments which have not been recorded in the accounts. This means that each note affects the trading account, OR the income statement, OR the appropriation account but will always be shown in the balance sheet.

This example will be prepared using a vertical layout. It is also intended for internal use, therefore, has the Trading account, Income statement and the Appropriation account separated.

OAK Ltd

Trading account for the year ended 31st March 200X

	Dr.	Cr.
	£	£
Revenues		1,000,000
Opening inventories	140,000	
+ Purchases	720,000	
	860,000	
− Closing inventories	150,000	
= Cost of sales		710,000
Gross profit c/d		290,000

Check the extraction of each item from the trial balance and note where they are recorded in the trading account. You will notice that the receipts are listed on the right hand side (credit), while the costs are listed on the left hand side (debit). In this example, the receipts are greater than the costs, therefore, the resulting balance is a gross profit. The double entry is completed by recording the gross profit on the credit side of the income statement.

OAK Ltd

Income statement for the year ended 31st March 200X

	Note	£	£
Gross profit b/d			290,000
Wages	2	36,500	
Rates	3	2,000	
Heating and lighting		5,000	
Salaries		20,000	
Administrative expenses		65,000	
Loan interest	8	6,000	
Bad debts written off		3,500	
Directors fees		15,000	
Depreciation vehicles	4	26,000	
Depreciation furniture and fittings	5	900	
Provision for doubtful debts	6	500	
			180,400
Net profit before taxation c/d			109,600

The entries into the income statement follow a similar pattern to those in the trading account. Many of the costs / expenses can simply be recorded, however, those items which are included in the adjustments need special treatment. We will now explain how each adjustment is treated in the income statement.

Notes to explain items in the income statement

We have allocated an additional note for the interest due on the long-term loans. For an explanation see note 8 on the next page.

2. Wages outstanding, £1,500

To obtain the total wages for the period, we take the wages shown in the trial balance and add any wages outstanding (£35,000 + £1,500). This occurs when there are a number of working days at the end of the accounting period where wages have been earned but not yet paid.

3. Rates paid in advance, £500

To obtain the rates for the period, we take the rates shown in the trial balance and deduct any rates paid in advance (£2,500 – £500). This occurs when a company pays rates which includes a proportion that falls into the beginning of the next year.

4. Depreciation of vehicles

The provision for depreciation of vehicles is calculated, using the straight line method, over five years. The provision for the year is £130,000 divided by 5 which equals £26,000.

5. Depreciation of furniture and fittings

The provision for the depreciation of furniture and fittings is calculated using 5% on cost. The provision for the year is £18,000 times 5 divided by 100 which equals £900.

6. Provision for doubtful debts

The entry for the provision for doubtful debts is as follows:

	Closing provision required (note 6)	3,500
less	Opening provision (from the trial balance)	3,000
		500

The balance of £500 represents the additional provision required. The transaction would be; debit the income statement, and credit the provision for doubtful debts account. Should the closing provision be less than the opening provision the transaction would be reversed.

8. Long-term loan: interest at 10%

The entry in the trial balance for interest paid represents only six months interest. This means the calculation for loan stock interest for the income statement must include interest for the complete accounting period: £60,000 times 10 divided by 100 which equals £6,000.

OAK Ltd

Appropriation account for the year ended 31st March 200X

	Note	£
Profit before taxation b/d		109,600
– Taxation		0
Profit after taxation		109,600
– Dividend	7	54,800
Retained profit		54,800

7. Provide for dividend

Dividend is calculated at 50% of profit attributable to shareholders; £109,600 times 50 divided by 100 which equals £54,800.

In published accounts the trading, income statement and appropriation account would be shown in a single vertical layout with the previous year's figures also given. It is simply called an income statement and requires less detail than shown in this example. However, some of the detail can often be found in the notes to the accounts.

Earnings per share is another figure that is required to be shown in published accounts, together with an explanation of the calculation.

OAK Ltd

Balance Sheet as at 31st March 200X

NON-CURRENT ASSETS	Notes	COST	DEPN	N.B.V.
Freehold property		200,000		200,000
Vehicles	1	130,000	52,000	78,000
Furniture and fittings	2	18,000	9,900	8,100
		348,000	61,900	286,100

CURRENT ASSETS				
Inventories			150,000	
Trade and other receivables		85,000		
less Doubtful debts	3	3,500	81,500	
Prepaid	4		500	
Bank			50,000	
			282,000	

CURRENT LIABILITIES				
Trade and other payables		44,000		
Accruals	5	4,500		
Dividend proposed	6	54,800		
			103,300	
				178,700
Total assets less Current liabilities				464,800
NON-CURRENT LIABILITIES			60,000	
Net assets				404,800

EQUITY				
Issued share capital				300,000
Share premium				25,000
Retained earnings	7			79,800
				404,800

A balance sheet is not an account, it is simply a statement which records a true and fair view of the financial position of a company. We will now discuss some of the points which often need clarification.

1. Accumulated depreciation – Vehicles

Accumulated depreciation, shown in the closing balance sheet, is calculated by taking the depreciation provision, shown in the trial balance, and adding the depreciation provision for the current year (£26,000 + £26,000) which equals £52,000.

2. Accumulated depreciation – Furniture and fittings

Accumulated depreciation, shown in the closing balance sheet, is calculated by taking the depreciation provision, shown in the trial balance, and adding the depreciation provision for the current year (£9,000 + £900) which equals £9,900.

3. Trade and other receivables

Trade and other receivables are taken at the value shown in the trial balance less the provision for doubtful debts (£85,000 – £3,500) which equals £81,500. In published accounts, it is normal just to show the net balance for trade and other receivables.

4. Prepayments

Prepayments represent the amounts that have been paid in advance of an accounting period. The prepayment in this example is the deduction of £500 from the rates.

5. Accruals

Accruals represent the amounts due but not paid at the end of an accounting period. They could be listed under a heading 'sundry creditors'. The accruals in this example are the addition of loan interest due plus wages due (£3,000 + £1,500) which equals £4,500.

6. Dividend proposed

The dividend proposed was included in the appropriation account and will be recorded in the balance sheet as a current liability. The dividend covers the accounting period under review, but will not be paid until it is approved at the shareholder's meeting which could be a number of months into the next accounting period.

7. Retained earnings

This represents the retained profit for the year taken from the appropriation account, plus the retained profits from previous years taken from the trial balance (£54,800 + £25,000) which equals £79,800.

5.4   Main components of published accounts

Public limited companies (plcs), are required to publish reports and file them annually with the registrar of companies. Most annual reports contain more detail than is required, either by company law or by the stock exchange. The readers of published accounts range from shareholders who have a financial interest in the company; through suppliers and lenders; through to employees, whose interest is in the continuity of employment. Most annual reports will contain the following:

a.   The chairperson's statement;

b.   The directors' report;

c.   The auditors' report;

d.   Accounting policies;

e.   An Income statement;

f.   A Balance sheet;

g.   A Cash flow statement;

h.   Notes to the accounts;

i.   Historical summaries.

a.   The chairperson's (or opening) statement

According to the *Cadbury Report on 'The Financial Aspects of Corporate Governance' (1992)*, this statement is the most widely read part of company reports. It is generally a review of progress of the company and its business environment over the past year, together with some indications of the proposed direction for the company in the forthcoming year. Remarks by the chairperson will generally not be convertible into a forecast of the results for the company for the next year, although usually much of value can be gleaned from the statement in terms, not only of what is included (and excluded), but also from the tone in which information is conveyed.

b.   The directors' report

In contrast to the chairperson's statement, the content of the directors' report is laid down by statute and, to a lesser extent, by the requirements of the *Stock Exchange* for listed companies. Furthermore, the auditors are required to comment in their report if any information given in the directors' report is not, in their opinion, consistent with the company's accounts. The main requirements of the directors' report is provided in *Table 5.1*.

Table 5.1   Main requirements of the directors' report

❏   Principal activities and business review;

❏   Results and dividends;

❏   Changes in fixed assets;

❏   Changes in share capital;

❏   Names of directors, any movements, and details of their shareholdings;

❏   Research and development activities;

❏   A fair review of the year's business, and the end–of–year position;

❏   Likely future developments;

❏   Any important events since the year–end;

❏   Charitable and political contributions.

---

c. The auditors' report

By law, every limited liability company is required to appoint at each annual general meeting (AGM) an auditor (or auditors) to hold office from the conclusion of that meeting until the conclusion of the next AGM. The auditors are required to report to the shareholders on the accounts examined and laid before the company in a general meeting. It is important to understand that there is no responsibility as an auditor for the efficiency, or otherwise, of the business. Specifically, the auditors, appointed by the shareholders, have historically been required to report to them whether in their opinion:

❏   The balance sheet gives a true and fair view of the company's affairs;

❏   The income statement gives a true and fair view of the profit or loss for the year; and,

❏   The accounts give the information required by the *Companies Acts* in the manner required.

d. Accounting policies

Standard Statement of Accounting Practice (SSAP) 2, requires companies to include details of their chosen accounting policies in their statutory report. They will include details of their policies in relation to:

❑ Basis of accounting and consolidation;

❑ Non-current assets and depreciation;

❑ Inventories;

❑ Pension contributions;

❑ Deferred taxation;

❑ Foreign currencies;

❑ Goodwill;

❑ Leases.

e. Published income statement

The form frequently encountered is illustrated in the consolidated income statement in *Table 5.2.*

The income statement, in this case consolidated to show the effect on profit for the companies comprising the group, is characterised by 'layers' of profit, similar to those discussed in *Chapter 1.* The last item, the transfer to/(from) reserves, is found by using the following 9 steps:

1. Add together all of the income to obtain total revenue (turnover) for the group;

2. Add together the cost of sales;

3. Subtract cost of sales from total revenue to obtain gross profit;

4. Enter the distribution costs and administrative expenses;

5. Subtract the distribution costs and administrative expenses from the gross profit to obtain profit before financing costs;

6. Enter finance income and finance costs; then add the income and subtract the costs to obtain profit before taxation;

7. Enter taxation and subtract from the profit before taxation to obtain the profit for the year.

Table 5.2 *Consolidated income statement*

CONSOLIDATED INCOME STATEMENT
for the year ended 31st December 200X

	200X £'000	200X-1 £'000
Revenue	29,000	26,000
Cost of sales	−21,000	−20,000
GROSS PROFIT	8,000	6,000
Distribution and selling cost	−2,700	−2,000
Administration expenses	−3,000	−3,000
OPERATING PROFIT	2,300	1,000
Finance expense	−300	−600
PROFIT/(LOSS) BEFORE TAXATION	2,000	400
Taxation	−700	−140
PROFIT/(LOSS) FOR THE YEAR	1,300	260
EARNINGS PER SHARE:		
Undiluted	1.5p	−1.00p
Diluted	1.25p	

---

f. Balance sheet

Having considered the published income statement, let us now consider the published balance sheet.

The balance sheet, which is shown in *Table 5.3*, consists of the following:

1. The sum of all non-current assets (fixed assets) within the group;

2. The sum of all current assets within the group;

3. The sum of all group liabilities falling due within one year, called current liabilities;

4. Net current assets, which represent the current assets less current liabilities, often called working capital;

5. Total assets less current liabilities;

6. Net assets, which represent the difference between total assets and total liabilities;

7. Equity, which is the sum of the share capital and reserves of the group.

Table 5.3   *Published balance sheet*

CONSOLIDATED BALANCE SHEETS
as at 31st December 200X

	200X £'000	200X-1 £'000
NON-CURRENT ASSETS		
Tangible assets	7,000	5,000
	7,000	5,000
CURRENT ASSETS		
Inventories	8,000	6,000
Trade and other receivables	7,000	6,000
Cash or cash equivalent	7,000	3,000
	22,000	15,000
CURRENT LIABILITIES	10,000	6,000
NET CURRENT ASSETS (LIABILITIES)	12,000	9,000
TOTAL ASSETS LESS CURRENT LIABILITIES	19,000	14,000
NON-CURRENT LIABILITIES	7,000	3,000
NET ASSETS	£12,000	£11,000
EQUITY		
Called up share capital	6,000	5,900
Share premium account	4,500	3,900
Retained earnings	1,500	1,200
	£12,000	£11,000

Please note, that the contents illustrated in the consolidated balance sheets, *Table 5.3*, may differ from some you will encounter in practice. Apart from differences in the nature of the business, which will affect mix and even types of assets and/or liabilities, there are other reasons, for example, where subsidiaries are not wholly owned, thereby giving rise to what are known as 'minority interests' (external shareholdings outside the group).

As indicated in the illustration in *Table 5.3*, the total in the top part of the balance sheet is calculated as follows:

(NON-CURRENT ASSETS + CURRENT ASSETS) – TOTAL LIABILITIES = NET ASSETS

and that

NET ASSETS = EQUITY (SHAREHOLDERS' FUNDS)

The owners' equity/shareholders' funds comprises the sum of capital and reserves, and is sometimes also referred to as net worth. This section includes all of the called up share capital of a company. In some company accounts, and indeed in our example company, you will find an item in the reserves called the 'share premium account'. This arises where new shares are offered at an issue price which is more than their nominal or face value. The nominal value of the new shares will be included in issued share capital. The difference between the nominal value and the issue price is the share premium and will be credited to that account.

g. Cash flow statement

This statement is required to be produced by a UK accounting standard (FRS 1) and is also a US reporting requirement. The purpose of the statement is to provide an explanation of the sources where cash has been generated during the year, and how it has been used. The UK approach requires cash flows to be reported using the following standard headings:

❏   Operating activities;

❏   Returns on investment and servicing of finance;

❏   Taxation;

❏   Investing activities;

❏   Financing.

h. Notes to the accounts

In its published form, the income statement is in a summarised form which can only provide a limited indication of how well a business has performed. In working with such a statement you will often want more information to form a more complete view, some of which will be found in supporting notes to the accounts. You will rarely find all of the information you wish, because, for competitive reasons companies are often reluctant to provide more than the minimum required of them.

Greater detail on all items contained within an income statement are available from the notes to published accounts, the relevant note usually being cross referenced in a separate column in the income statement. What form do such notes take? The following is an illustration of a note that might be found for earnings per share:

> *The earnings per ordinary share are based on the profits after taxation and preference dividend of £1,800,000 (2005, loss £500,000) and 120,000,000 ordinary shares (2005, 100,000,000) being the weighted average number of shares in issue during the year.*

Other notes to accounts would typically include:

❏ Turnover and profit or loss for each different type of business;

❏ Turnover for different geographical markets;

❏ Details of net operating costs, including raw materials and consumables, depreciation, staff costs and auditors fees;

❏ Interest payable and receivable;

❏ Details of directors' remuneration, and employees with emoluments over £30,000;

❏ The average number of employees, total wages, social security and pension costs;

❏ Details of tax;

❏ Details of preference and ordinary dividends.

i.   Historical summaries

Historical summaries are not a legal requirement, but have been provided by the vast majority of large companies since asked for by the Chairman of the Stock Exchange some 25 years ago. The usual period covered is five years and the more usual items included are:

❏ Revenues;

❏ Profit;

❏ Dividends;

❏ Capital employed;

❏ Various ratios: such as earnings per share, return on capital, profit on turnover and assets per share. These have to be interpreted guardedly, because, with the exception of earnings per share, there is no commonly accepted standard for any ratio.

5.5 Interim reporting

Although the information provided in an annual report may be valuable, it becomes limited with the passage of time. More up-to-date information can be obtained from interim reports.

In addition to a requirement to produce annual reports, the *Stock Exchange's Yellow Book, Admission of Securities to Listing,* requires as a minimum the following to be provided on an interim basis:

❏ Net revenues;

❏ Profit before tax and extraordinary items;

❏ The taxation charge;

❏ Minority interests;

❏ Ordinary profit attributable to shareholders;

❏ Extraordinary items;

❏ Dividends;

❏ Earnings per share;

❏ Comparative figures;

❏ An explanatory statement to include information on any events and trends during the period as well as details about future prospects.

The whole interim report must be sent to all shareholders, or alternatively, it must appear in two national newspapers. Such reports are not usually audited and thus, lack the authority and accuracy which annual reports appear to possess. There are no guidelines on the preparation of interim reports in company law or accounting standards.

APPENDIX A – Formats for published accounts (IFRS)

INCOME STATEMENT

Revenue
Cost of sales
Gross profit
Distribution costs
Administration expenses
Profit from operations
Finance income
Finance expense
Profit before taxation
Taxation
Profit after taxation

Profit for the year
Earnings per share

CONSOLIDATED BALANCE SHEET

ASSETS

Non-current assets

Intangible assets

Tangible assets

Total non-current assets

Current assets

Inventories

Trade and other receivables

Cash and cash equivalent

Total current assets

Total assets

LIABILITIES

Current liabilities

Borrowings

Trade and other payables

Taxation

Total current liabilities

Non-current liabilities

Borrowings

Deferred taxation

Total non-current liabilities

Total liabilities

Net assets

EQUITY

Issued share capital

Share premium account

Retained earnings

Total equity

Appendix B – Accounting Standards

Standard Statement of Accounting Practice (SSAP)

SSAP 1   Accounting for associated companies

SSAP 2   Disclosure of accounting policies

SSAP 3   Earnings per share

SSAP 4   Accounting for government grants

SSAP 5   Accounting for value added tax

SSAP 8   The treatment of taxation under the imputation system in the accounts of companies

SSAP 9   Stocks and long-term contracts

SSAP 12   Accounting for depreciation

SSAP 13   Accounting for research and development

SSAP 15   Accounting for deferred tax

SSAP 17   Accounting for post balance sheet events

SSAP 18   Accounting for contingencies

SSAP 19   Accounting for investment properties

SSAP 20   Foreign currency translation

SSAP 21   Accounting for leases and hire purchase contracts

SSAP 22   Accounting for goodwill

SSAP 24   Accounting for pension costs

SSAP 25   Segmental reporting

Financial reporting statement (FRS)

FRS 1   Cash flow statements

FRS 2   Accounting for subsidiary undertakings

FRS 3   Reporting financial performance

FRS 4   Capital instruments

FRS 5   Reporting the substance of transactions

FRS 6   Acquisitions and mergers

FRS 7   Fair values in acquisition accounting

FRS 8   Related party disclosures

FRS 9   Associates and joint ventures

FRS 10   Goodwill and intangible assets

FRS 11   Impairment of fixed assets and goodwill

FRS 12   Provisions, contingent liabilities and contingent assets

FRS 13   Derivatives and other financial instruments: disclosures

FRS 14   Earnings per share

FRS 15   Tangible fixed assets (supersedes SSAP 12)

FRS 16   Current tax

FRS 17   Retirement benefits

FRS 18   Accounting policies

FRS 19   Deferred tax

FRS 20   (IFRS 2) Share based payment

FRS 21   (IAS 10) Events after balance sheet date

FRS 22   (IAS 33) Earnings per share

FRS 23   (IAS 21) The effect of changes in foreign exchange rates

FRS 24   (IAS 29) Financial reporting in hyperinflation economies

FRS 25   (IAS 32) Financial instruments: disclosure and presentation

FRS 26   (IAS 39) Financial instruments: measurement

FRS 27   Life assurance

FRS 28   Corresponding amounts

FRS 29   (IFRS 7) Financial instruments: disclosures

Exercise 5.1

The Trial balance of *Aero Engineers Ltd* as at 30th April 200X was as follows:

	Dr.	Cr.
Trade and other payables		72,000
Revenues		540,000
Land and buildings	234,000	
Administrative costs	108,000	
Purchases	360,000	
Trade and othe receivables	54,000	
Rent received		2,000
Vehicles	36,000	
Opening inventories	54,000	
Selling costs	34,200	
Trade investments	36,000	
Provision for doubtful debts		800
Audit fee	1,800	
Income from investments		3,600
Cash	9,000	
Retained earnings		94,400
Issued share capital		180,000
Interest paid	1,800	
Bank overdraft		36,000
	928,800	928,800

Notes:

1. Closing inventories at 30th April 200X, £72,000.

2. Depreciation of vehicles, straight line over six years, residual value £6,000.

3. Interest due at 30th April 200X, £360.

4. Adjust provision for doubtful debts to £500.

Required

Prepare a Trading account and Income statement for the year ended 30th April 200X and a Balance sheet as at that date.

Exercise 5.2

The Trial balance of *Tru Systems Ltd* as at 31st March 200X was as follows:

	Dr.	Cr.
Revenues		1,890,000
Land and buildings	819,000	
Interest paid	6,300	
Purchases	1,260,000	
Issued share capital		630,000
Trade and other payables		252,000
Discount allowed	12,200	
Vehicles	126,000	
Opening inventories	189,000	
Selling costs	119,700	
Audit fee	6,100	
Income from investments		12,600
Cash	31,500	
Bad debts written off	3,600	
Retained earnings		318,000
Administrative costs	378,000	
Trade investments	114,000	
Discount received		22,200
Trade and other receivables	185,400	
Bank overdraft		126,000
	3,250,800	3,250,800

Notes:

1. Closing inventories at 31st March 200X, £252,000.

2. Further bad debt write off, £800.

3. Administration costs due, £2,900.

Required

Prepare a Trading account and Income statement for the year ended 31st March 200X and a Balance sheet as at that date.

Exercise 5.3

The following Trial balance has been extracted from the books of *Icandoit Ltd* as at 30th June 200X.

	Dr.	Cr.
Trade and other payables		144,900
Long-term loans at 10%		147,000
Purchases	2,604,000	
Rent and rates	157,500	
Revenues		4,410,000
Trade and other receivables	630,000	
Directors' remuneration	115,500	
Income from investments		8,400
Equipment at cost	882,000	
Accumulated depreciation of equipment		319,200
Office expenses	102,900	
Issued share capital		420,000
Preference share capital at 8%		105,000
Dividend – preference shares	8,400	
Heating and lighting	58,800	
Sales expenses	114,800	
Bank	14,700	
Insurance	35,700	
Investments – quoted	58,800	
Retained earnings		277,200
Provision for doubtful debts		16,800
Opening inventories	281,400	
Vehicles at cost	168,000	
Accumulated depreciation of vehicles		84,000
Wages and salaries	675,000	
Auditor's remuneration	25,000	
	5,932,500	5,932,500

Notes:

1. Inventories at 30th June 200X amounted to £325,500.

2. Depreciation is to be provided on equipment and vehicles at a rate of 20% and 25% respectively on cost.

3. Provision is to be made for wages, due not yet paid, amounting to £25,200.

4. Rates paid in advance at 30th June 200X amounted to £6,300.

5. The provision for doubtful debts is to be made equal to 5% of outstanding trade receivables as at 30th June 200X.

6. Corporation tax based on the profit for the year of £126,000 is to be provided.

7. An ordinary dividend of £40,000 is proposed.

Prepare *Icandoit Limited's* Trading account, Income statement and Appropriation account for the year ended 30th June 200X, and a Balance Sheet as at that date.

Exercise 5.4

The following Trial balance has been extracted from the books of *Rusty and Dusty Musty Limited* as at 31st October 200X.

	Dr.	Cr.
Administrative expenses	441,000	
Bad debts written off	72,000	
Bank	63,000	
Trade and other payables		621,000
Trade and other receivables	2,700,000	
Depreciation of equipment		1,368,000
Depreciation of vehicles		360,000
Directors' remuneration	495,000	
Heating and lighting	252,000	
Income from investments		36,000
Insurance	153,000	
Interim dividend	36,000	
Investments – quoted	252,000	
Issued share capital (2,250,000 shares at £1.00)		2,250,000
Long-term loan at 12%		630,000
Equipment at cost	3,780,000	
Marketing and selling expenses	270,000	
Retained earnings		1,188,000
Provision for doubtful debts		72,000
Purchases	11,160,000	
Rent and rates	675,000	
Revenues		18,900,000
Opening inventories	1,206,000	
Vehicles at cost	720,000	
Wages and salaries	3,150,000	
	25,425,000	25,425,000

Notes:

1. Inventories at 31st October 200X amounted to £1,395,000.
2. A further bad debts write off amounting to £26,000.
3. Adjust provision for doubtful debts to 5% of outstanding trade receivables as at 31st October 200X.
4. Insurance paid in advance at 31st October 200X amounted to £27,000.
5. Depreciation is to be provided on equipment and vehicles at a rate of 20% and 25% respectively on cost.
6. Make provision for corporation tax of £540,000.
7. A final dividend of 6p per share is proposed.

Prepare Trading account, Income statement, and Appropriation account for the year ended 31st October 200X, and a Balance sheet as at that date.

Exercise 5.5

The following Trial Balance has been extracted from the books of *Uaddit Limited* as at 30th September 200X.

	Dr.	Cr.
Trade and other payables		360,000
Revenues		2,700,000
Land and buildings	1,080,000	
Marketing and selling costs	540,000	
Purchases	1,710,000	
Trade and other receivables	270,000	
Equipment	360,000	
Opening inventories	270,000	
Administration costs	171,000	
Depreciation of equipment		36,000
Vehicles	180,000	
Audit fee	9,000	
Rent received		18,000
Cash	45,000	
Retained earnings		387,000
Issued share capital		855,000
Depreciation of vehicles		90,000
Provision for bad debts		18,000
Rates	9,000	
Bank overdraft		180,000
	4,644,000	4,644,000

Notes:

1. Closing inventories at 30th September 200X   360,000
2. Depreciation of equipment   36,000
3. Depreciation of vehicles   18,000
4. Bad debts write off   9,000
5. Provision for bad debts   19,800
6. Administration costs due   32,400
7. Provision for corporation tax   58,500
8. Dividend 8% of net profit before tax

Prepare *Uaddit Limited's* Trading account, Income statement and Appropriation account for the year ended 30th September 200X, and a Balance sheet as at that date.

Exercise 5.6

The following Trial Balance has been extracted from the books of *Horace and Doris Morris Limited* as at 28th February 200X.

	Dr.	Cr.
Advertising	90,000	
Bank	21,000	
Trade and other payables		207,000
Long-term loan at 10%		210,000
Trade and other receivables	900,000	
Directors' remuneration	165,000	
Electricity	84,000	
Insurance	51,000	
Investments – quoted	84,000	
Income from investments		12,000
Equipment at cost	1,260,000	
Accumulated depreciation of equipment		456,000
Office expenses	147,000	
Issued share capital (750,000 shares at £1.00)		750,000
Interim dividend	12,000	
Retained earnings		396,000
Provision for doubtful debts		24,000
Purchases	3,720,000	
Rent and rates	225,000	
Revenues		6,300,000
Opening inventories	402,000	
Vehicles at cost	240,000	
Accumulated depreciation of vehicles		120,000
Wages and salaries	1,074,000	
	8,475,000	8,475,000

Notes:

1. Inventories at 28th February 200X amounted to £465,000.

2. Depreciation is to be provided on equipment and vehicles at a rate of 20% and 25% respectively on cost.

3. Provision is to be made for auditors' remuneration of £36,000.

4. Insurance paid in advance at 28th February 200X amounted to £9,000.

5. The provision for doubtful debts is to be made equal to 5% of outstanding trade receivables as at 28th February 200X.

6. Corporation tax based on the profit for the year of £180,000 is to be provided.

7. An final dividend of 10p per share is proposed.

Prepare *Horace and Doris Morris Limited*'s Trading account, Income statement and Appropriation account for the year ended 28th February 200X, and a Balance sheet as at that date.

CHAPTER SIX

FINANCIAL RATIO ANALYSIS

LEARNING OBJECTIVES

When you have finished studying this chapter and completed the exercises, you should be able to:

❑ Describe, calculate and interpret:

- Profitability ratios, including return on total assets (ROTA), profit margin% and revenue generation;

- Working capital or liquidity ratios, including current ratio and acid test;

- Gearing ratios, including borrowing ratio and income gearing ratio;

- Employee ratios, including revenues per employee and profit per employee;

❑ Describe certain weaknesses in traditional ratios including profitability and liquidity.

6.1   Introduction

Performance measurement is a key issue for all organisations. Management needs to measure the results of its actions, not only in comparison to competitor organisations, but in relation to its past performance too. This is a difficult area since the amount, complexity and interpretations placed on data, both published and unpublished, have an infinite variability.

This chapter attempts to show a simplified route through this maze. By explaining the development and use of the most important ratios, and the form which they are likely to be presented, you will be equipped with the skill necessary to take a critical view of an important area of company performance measurement.

One major challenge you will have to face as your career progresses, is to understand and make sense of internally generated and externally published financial information. In this chapter we will show how the sense of financial information can be achieved using ratio analysis, whereby one piece of financial data (e.g. profit) is expressed in terms of another (e.g. total assets), then the result is compared with the same ratio for another time period or another company.

It is possible to calculate any number of ratios and great care has to be exercised to ensure that an approach is adopted whereby only those which are relevant and essential are selected. This can be achieved in assessing profitability by adopting a hierarchical approach involving the calculation of a 'key' ratio and further related ratios. As we will show, the 'key' ratio relates to profit information from the income statement, and to the capital employed in the business in terms of assets found in the balance sheet. The rationale for its calculation is much the same as that for undertaking personal investment – you need to know how much return, or profit, will be generated in absolute terms, but also how it relates to the amount of money to be tied up.

It is important to apply agreed rules regarding the specification of the various components of any ratio in a consistent manner, and to interpret changes in the resulting ratios against previous levels, industry averages or simple benchmarks.

Our discussion of ratio analysis is not restricted to analysing profitability. We will consider other important areas of ratio analysis such as liquidity, financial structure (gearing) and employee based ratios.

We will reinforce the ratios to be discussed using examples based upon figures taken from the income statement and balance sheet, which are illustrated in *Table 6.1*, together with some additional information.

Table 6.1 Balance sheet, and income statement

Balance sheet as at 31st May 200X

	£m	£m	£m
NON-CURRENT ASSETS (Net book value)			400
CURRENT ASSETS			
Inventories		950	
Trade and other receivables		500	
Cash		50	
		1,500	
CURRENT LIABILITIES			
Trade and other payables	425		
Bank overdraft	675		
		1,100	
NET WORKING CAPITAL			400
TOTAL ASSETS less CURRENT LIABILITIES			800
LONG-TERM LOAN			120
NET ASSETS			£680
EQUITY			
Issued share capital (at £0.25 per share)			130
Retained earnings			550
			680

Income statement for the year ended 31st May 200X

	£m
Revenues	5,500
Cost of sales	–2,850
Distribution costs	–600
Administrative expenses	–1,800
Interest payable	–140
PROFIT BEFORE TAXATION	110
Taxation	–40
PROFIT AFTER TAXATION	70
Dividend	–20
PROFIT FOR YEAR	50

Notes: *Number of employees*   35,000

6.2   Profitability ratios

In this section we will illustrate how the key financial ratio, Return on Total Assets (ROTA)%, may be used as an analytical tool for gauging profitability performance at the business-level. Providing the necessary financial data is available it can be further sub-divided so that more detailed analysis of a number of interrelated ratios can be calculated.

The data required for its calculation is shown in *Table 6.2*, which has been extracted from *Table 6.1*.

Table 6.2   Basic data for calculation of profitability ratios

	Latest year £'m	Extracted from
Non-current assets	400	Balance sheet
Current assets	1,500	
Profit before taxation	110	Income statement
Interest payable	140	
Revenues	5,500	

1.   Return on total assets (ROTA)% – The key ratio

Return on total assets (ROTA)% seeks to provide the answer to a very simple question, 'What profit is generated as a percentage of total assets?' It is calculated by expressing profit before interest payable and taxation (PBIT) as a percentage of total assets. As a general rule, the higher the ratio the better.

For the example company, profit is taken before interest payable and taxation, i.e. £250 million (£110m + £140m). Total assets is the sum of non-current assets (excluding intangibles) plus current assets, i.e. £400m + £1,500m which gives £1,900 million.

Using this information, we can calculate (ROTA)% to give an indication of the return which a company achieves on its capital employed, sometimes referred to as return on capital employed, or ROCE.

$$\text{(ROTA)\%} = \frac{\text{Profit before interest payable and tax}}{\text{Total assets (excluding intangibles)}} \times 100$$

$$= \frac{\text{£250 m}}{\text{£1,900 m}} \times 100$$

$$= 13.2\%$$

(ROTA)% may fall because of a decrease in profits and/or an increase in total assets. (ROTA)% can be affected by the accounting principles or policies adopted which affect both the profit calculation and total assets. You may recall that we demonstrated the effect upon profit when using different methods for depreciating assets in *Chapter 3*. (ROTA)% can also be used to show whether or not a company is likely to produce a higher or lower level profit per £ of total assets than it has in the past, or relative to their competitors' or industry performance.

But what happens if the (ROTA)% calculated is lower than that generated in the previous year or by competitors? Is there any way of identifying possible reasons? The answer is yes. (ROTA)% is the 'key' ratio at the top of a business level ratio hierarchy which can be analysed in more detail by the introduction of revenues from the income statement. Introducing revenues for the period of £5,500 million enables another level of interrelated ratios within the hierarchy to be calculated which is shown in *Figure 6.1*.

Figure 6.1 Hierarchy of business level profitability ratios

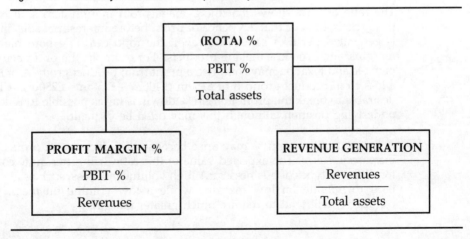

By expanding the key ratio we can see how the level of profitability is being achieved, which could be from a higher or lower PBIT as a percentage of sales, known as the 'profit margin' ratio, from a higher or lower level of sales to total assets, known as the revenue generation ratio, or from a combination of the two.

2.   Profit margin

The profit margin ratio gives an indication of the average profit margin achieved by a company. It is calculated by expressing profit before interest payable and taxation as a percentage of sales revenue.

Again, profit is taken before interest payable and taxation (PBIT) which for the example company we have already calculated as £250 million. Revenues is taken from the income statement, in common with PBIT, and is £5,500 million.

Using this information, we can calculate the ratio to find the profit margin percentage.

$$\text{Profit margin \%} \quad = \quad \frac{\text{Profit before interest payable and tax}}{\text{Revenues}} \quad \text{x} \quad 100$$

$$= \quad \frac{£250 \text{ m}}{£5,500 \text{ m}} \quad \text{x} \quad 100$$

$$= \quad 4.5\%$$

The ratio of 4.5% shows that the average profit margin across all the lines or products is 4.5% or that 4.5 pence of profit before interest payable and taxation is generated per £ of sales. However, the ratio can hide both high and low margins, and even loss making products. For example, the profit before interest payable and taxation may comprise a profit from product group A of £400m and a loss from product group B of £150m (£400m – £150m = £250m). Clearly, it is desirable to break the profit margin % down as far as possible to reflect the real underlying position, although this may often be difficult.

A lower profit margin % may arise because of a decrease in profits and/or an increase in sales. The expected value of this ratio will differ quite considerably for different types of businesses. A high volume business, such as a retailer, will tend to operate on low margins while a low volume business, such as a contractor, will tend to require much greater margins.

When comparing a profit margin ratio with previous years, or against competitors, any significant differences in the profit margin % can be further analysed with a view to identifying likely problem areas. The following headings represent a checklist of areas for further analysis:

o   Percentage growth in revenues;

o   Product mix from various activities;

o   Market mix for profit and revenues by division and geographical area;

o   Expansion of activities by merger or acquisition;

o   Changes in selling prices (usually only available from management accounts and not from published accounts);

o   Changes in costs (major cost items are shown in published accounts).

The UK accounting standard, *SSAP 25*, requires companies to provide an analysis of turnover and contribution to operating profit by principal activities. This information is found in the notes to the accounts as illustrated in *Table 6.3*.

Table 6.3   Analysis of turnover and operating profit

Division (or principal activity)	Revenues (Sales)		Profit before interest payable and tax	
	£'000	%	£'000	%
A	2,200	40	75	30
B	1,320	24	85	34
C	880	16	30	12
D	880	16	40	16
E	220	4	20	8
Total	£5,500	100	£250	100

This table provides useful information. The overall profit margin we calculated as being 4.5%, and with this information we can readily calculate the PBIT margin made by each division. For a complete interpretation you should obtain figures for previous years and industry averages. In this way you will be able to determine trends in turnover and/or PBIT by division (and/or geographic area).

Profit margin: Analysis by cost

The main categories of cost from the income statement can be expressed as a percentage of sales, with a view to identifying those costs which require further investigation. The logic behind such investigation is that any cost reduction should, all things being equal, feed through to the profit margin % and, therefore, improve (ROTA)%. Do bear in mind that the profit margin % and associated ratios will vary from industry to industry. Low volume businesses are often reliant upon higher margins than high volume businesses, such as retailing (e.g. a petrol station), which often operate on low margins meaning that cost control can be absolutely critical to their success.

In *Figure 6.2*, we show how the profit margin % ratio can be broken down into subsidiary ratios such as cost of sales, administration costs and other costs. In practice, these subsidiary ratios would be those appropriate to the analysis being performed.

Figure 6.2 Profit margin % – Analysis by cost

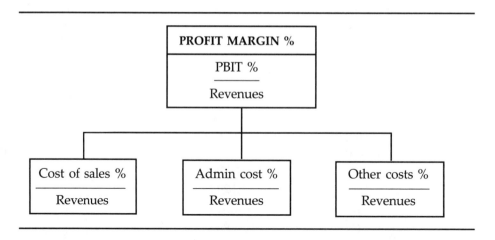

3. Revenue generation ratio

The revenue generation ratio shows the value of revenues generated from each £ of total assets. It is calculated by dividing revenues by total assets.

$$\text{Revenue generation ratio} \quad \frac{\text{Revenues}}{\text{Total assets}}$$

$$= \frac{£5,500 \text{ m}}{£1,900 \text{ m}}$$

$$= 2.89 \text{ to } 1$$

The revenue generation ratio indicates that the company has generated £2.89 of revenue for each £1.00 of total assets, and can also be calculated by division/principal activity if the information is available.

A low ratio could be due to a decrease in revenues and/or an increase in total assets. As a general rule, the higher the ratio the better.

The revenue generation ratio can be affected by increases or decreases in non-current assets, current assets and changes in the mix of assets. Increases in this ratio, can be achieved by an increase in revenues and/or a decrease in total assets.

Revenue generation: Analysis by asset

Figure 6.3   Revenue generation: Analysis by asset

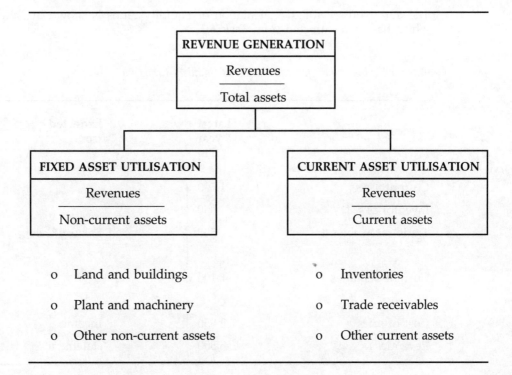

4.   Profitability ratios, summary

A summary of the three profitability ratios is given below:

1.	Return on total assets	13.2%
2.	Profit margin	4.5%
3.	Revenue generation ratio	2.89 to 1

Changes in the profit margin% and the sales generation ratio will have a direct impact upon (ROTA)%. Any improvement in either ratio should, all things being equal, should cause an improvement in the (ROTA)%

6.3   Liquidity (or working capital) ratios

An analysis of profitability ratios alone is totally inadequate for obtaining a well balanced view of the performance of a company. While profitability is undeniably important, the need to achieve a satisfactory liquidity position is vital for survival. It is a fact that many companies which have failed were profitable but unable to maintain a satisfactory level of liquidity.

The data required for the calculation of liquidity ratios is shown in *Table 6.4*, which has been extracted from *Table 6.1*.

Table 6.4   Basic data for calculation of liquidity ratios

	Latest year £'m	Extracted from
Current assets	1,500	
Inventories	950	
Trade receivables	500	Balance sheet
Current liabilities	1,100	
Cost of sales	2,850	Income
Revenues	5,500	statement

In this section, we will describe four ratios designed to measure different components of liquidity within the working capital cycle. These are:

1.   Current ratio;

2.   Liquid (or acid test) ratio;

3.   Inventory turn;

4.   Trade receivable weeks.

Figure 6.4   Working capital cycle

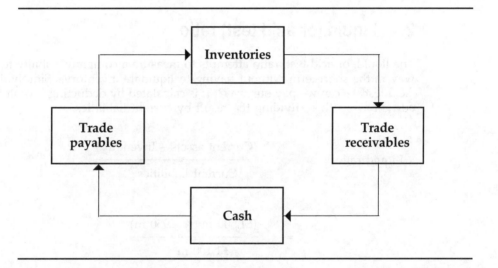

1.   Current ratio

The current ratio attempts to measure the ability of a company to meet its financial obligations falling due within one year. It is calculated by dividing current assets by current liabilities.

$$\text{Current ratio} \quad = \quad \frac{\text{Current assets}}{\text{Current liabilities}}$$

$$= \quad \frac{£1,500 \text{ m}}{£1,100 \text{ m}}$$

$$= \quad 1.36 \text{ to } 1$$

For decades, the interpretation of the current ratio has suffered against the unrealistic rule of thumb that current assets should be double that of current liabilities for all companies. This implies that the proportions of current assets and current liabilities should be the same for a fast food company with small inventory and virtually no trade receivables, through to the company undertaking a long-term contract with high inventory, high trade receivables and payables, and bank overdraft.

A very low current ratio indicates potential difficulties, the determination of low varying by the type of business. A high current ratio is not necessarily a good sign; it could mean that a company had idle resources. For example, the current ratio would increase if a company were to increase its inventory or increase its trade receivables. Similarly, the current ratio would decrease if a company took actions to decrease its inventory or decrease its trade receivables. We cannot say whether these actions are necessarily good or bad, and care should be taken when attempting to interpret both the size of the current ratio, and the movements year on year.

2. Liquid (or acid test) ratio

The liquid, or acid test, ratio attempts to measure a company's ability to pay its way in the short-term without having to liquidate inventory. Simply, it is the 'acid test' – can we pay our way? It is calculated by deducting inventory from current assets then dividing the result by current liabilities.

$$\text{Liquid ratio} = \frac{(\text{Current assets} - \text{Inventory})}{\text{Current liabilities}}$$

$$= \frac{(\text{£1,500 m} - \text{£950 m})}{\text{£1,100 m}}$$

$$= \quad 0.50 \text{ to } 1$$

What do we mean by paying our way in the short-term? For purposes of this ratio, the short-term is considered to be up to 13 weeks, and paying our way to mean that we can pay our debts as and when they fall due. It does not mean that every business needs to maintain the same level to cover all current liabilities.

In common with the current ratio, different liquid ratios apply to different industries. For example, in retailing it has become normal to find a level of around 0.25 to 1 cover for current liabilities. This is possible through cash trading, a high level of commitment from their suppliers and the fact that inventory could be liquidated in time to meet maturing debts. Similar to the current ratio, if these companies maintained a higher level of cover for current liabilities there would be idle resources.

3. Inventory turn

The inventory turn ratio is a measure showing the number of times inventory is 'turned over' on average in a given period (usually one year). It is calculated by dividing the cost of sales by inventory.

In published accounts it may be impossible to obtain a reliable figure for cost of sales. To maintain consistency, we suggest that you take revenues and deduct profit before tax, interest payable, selling and distribution costs, and administration costs. In this example (£5,500m – £110m – £140m – £600m – £1,800m), which gives £2,850 million. Inventory is taken from the current assets section of the balance sheet and will include raw materials, work in progress and finished goods. In this example, it is £950 million.

Using this information, we can calculate the inventory turn:

$$\text{Inventory turn} = \frac{\text{Cost of sales}}{\text{Inventory}}$$

$$= \frac{£2,850 \text{ m}}{£950 \text{ m}}$$

$$= 3.0 \text{ times}$$

A low inventory turn ratio indicates that a company may be holding too much stock. The actual size of the ratio will depend upon the mix of inventory held and the average holding in the industry. As a general rule, the higher the ratio the better.

If a company holds too much inventory then there are potential disadvantages arising from the cost of holding inventory, the possibility of obsolescence, and the cost associated with tying up additional working capital, to the detriment of other components within the working capital cycle.

4. Trade receivable weeks

The trade receivable weeks ratio shows the number of weeks on average that trade receivables take to pay their invoices. It is calculated by multiplying trade receivables by the number of weeks in the period, then dividing the result by sales revenue for the period.

If we consider calculation of the ratio for our example company, the trade and other receivables figure is taken from the current assets section of the balance sheet, i.e. £500 million. Sales revenue is taken from the income statement, i.e. £5,500 million. Using this information we can calculate the trade receivable weeks as follows:

$$\text{Trade receivables weeks} = \frac{\text{Trade receivables} \times \text{Number of weeks in the period}}{\text{Revenues}}$$

$$= \frac{£500 \text{ m} \times 52}{£5,500 \text{ m}}$$

$$= 4.7 \text{ weeks}$$

The lower the trade receivable weeks ratio, the more effective the system of credit control and as a general rule, the lower the ratio the better. The actual size of the ratio will depend upon the mix of trade receivables between large, medium and small customers and the average holding in the industry.

A high trade receivable weeks ratio means that a company is allowing customers too much time to pay their debts. Other customers might follow by extending the time taken to pay. Furthermore, the cost of financing additional trade receivables, the possibility of increased bad debts, and tying up additional working capital can often lead to detrimental effects on other components within the working capital cycle, e.g. a shortage of funds to finance stock requirements.

In addition to monitoring trade receivable weeks in aggregate, it is desirable, where possible, to undertake trade receivable age analysis to distinguish long outstanding debts from those that are more recent. For example, of the £500m trade receivables, the following breakdown by age may be the case:

Less than 4 weeks,	£200m	40%
More than 4 weeks and less than 8 weeks	£250m	50%
More than 8 weeks	£50m	10%

It is recognised that the longer a debt is outstanding the less likelihood there is that payment will be made at all. For this reason, most organisations will aim to decrease the proportion of long-term debts outstanding as far as possible.

5. Working capital ratios, summary

A summary of the four working capital ratios is given below:

1.	Current ratio	1.36 to 1
2.	Liquid (or acid test) ratio	0.50 to 1
3.	Inventory turn	3.0 times
4.	Trade receivable weeks	4.7 weeks

6.4 Gearing ratios

Businesses can secure finances from many sources, ranging from shareholders who are owners of the company to those who lend money to the business. One of the key distinctions between these two sources of financing is that, the interest payable on borrowed funds is deductible as an expense in calculating the tax payable. This is known as the 'tax shield'. Imagine a company with a £10m loan on which it is paying interest at 10%. The company's marginal rate of tax is 25%, and because of the deductability of the interest as an expense, the company will pay £750,000 that is 7.5% rather than 10%. The same does not apply, however, for funding from the issues of shares. In that case, dividends are paid from after tax income and there is no tax shield.

From this you might conclude that there is a distinct advantage for a company raising debt as opposed to equity. Depending upon relative rates of interest, this can be the case. By combining debt and equity, it can be shown that a company can lower the cost of its capital. However, there will come a point where increasing the proportion of debt to equity will be perceived as being a risk; first to new lenders who might doubt the company's potential to service the interest and, second to shareholders who might be concerned at the very high level of debt relative to equity. As a consequence, beyond a certain level, it is generally thought that a company's cost of capital from taking on more debt will actually increase.

Thus, while there is an advantage in holding both equity and debt, the relative proportions of each need to be carefully assessed for the risks involved. Hence, we calculate 'gearing' ratios to measure the proportion of debt to equity and other measures to assess the firm's ability to service its debts from current profits.

As with other ratios there are different definitions of gearing depending on the interests of the users. In the following section, we describe the two most popular measures of gearing: the borrowing ratio and the income gearing ratio.

1. Borrowing ratio

The borrowing ratio is a conservative measure showing the number of times total borrowings exceed equity. It is calculated by dividing total borrowings by equity (shareholders' funds).

Total borrowings is the sum of short-term loans (including bank overdraft) and long-term loans, in this example, £795m (£675m + £120m). Equity is the sum of issued share capital plus reserves, £680m (£130m + £550m). Reserves will include such items as share premium, revaluation reserve and, retained earnings.

Using this information, we can calculate the borrowings ratio:

$$\text{Borrowing ratio} = \frac{\text{Total borrowings}}{\text{Equity}}$$

$$= \frac{\text{£795 m}}{\text{£680 m}}$$

$$= 1.17 \text{ to } 1$$

A high borrowing ratio simply indicates that a company has placed a greater reliance upon borrowing than equity to finance its operations. The higher the ratio the more highly geared the company is said to be. Although it should provide a higher return to its shareholders when the economy is experiencing boom conditions, during periods of increased interest rates, economic recession or simply loss of customers, the opposite will apply. A company which has high gearing is particularly vulnerable and might find that it cannot continue to finance its borrowings.

2. Income gearing

The income gearing ratio measures the extent to which interest payable is covered from pre-tax profits plus interest payable. It is calculated by dividing interest payable by profit before interest payable and taxation, and expressing the result as a percentage.

Interest payable is taken from the income statement, which for the example company is £140m. Profit before interest payable and taxation (PBIT) is the sum of profit before taxation plus interest payable, £250m (£110m + £140m). Using this information we can calculate the income gearing ratio as follows:

$$\text{Income gearing} = \frac{\text{Interest payable}}{\text{Profit before interest payable and tax}} \times 100$$

$$= \frac{£140 \text{ m}}{£250 \text{ m}} \times 100$$

$$= 56 \%$$

The higher the income gearing ratio, the greater the amount of available profit a company is liable to pay as interest. The income gearing ratio shows the effect of a company's gearing policy. For example, if a company increased its borrowings this would tend to increase the income gearing ratio. The income gearing ratio also shows the effect on a company of changes in economic circumstances. If interest rates rise or consumer demand falls, the income gearing ratio will worsen.

The income gearing ratio provides an indication of the ability to service debt commitments from profit. In the case of the example company, it can 'cover' interest payable just over one and three quarter times, that is, the profit before interest payable and tax is 1.79 the size of the interest payable (£250m divided by £140m). When expressed in this form, the ratio is known as the 'interest cover' ratio and is calculated as follows:

$$\text{Interest cover} = \frac{\text{Profit before interest payable and tax}}{\text{Interest payable}}$$

3. Gearing ratios, summary

A summary of the two gearing ratios is given below:

1. Borrowing ratio   1.17 to 1

2. Income gearing   56%

6.5   Employee ratios

Organisations of all types try to ensure that they derive as much value as possible from the resources used. In many cases one of the most valuable, but also the most expensive resource, is associated with employees.

We illustrate four popular employee ratios used by a number of commercial organisations:

1.   Profit per employee;

2.   Revenues per employee;

3.   Non-current assets per employee;

4.   Borrowings per employee.

1.   Profit per employee

The profit per employee ratio shows the £ value of profit before taxation (PBT) generated by each employee. It is calculated by dividing profit before taxation by the average number of employees.

In the case of the example company, profit before taxation is £110 million. The average number of employees is usually found in the *Director's Report* or in the notes to the accounts. In this example the figure is given, i.e. 35,000. Using this information, we can calculate the profit per employee ratio.

$$\text{Profit per employee} \quad = \quad \frac{\text{Profit before taxation}}{\text{Number of employees}}$$

$$= \quad \frac{£110 \text{ m}}{35,000}$$

$$= \quad £3,143$$

It is important to ensure that the average number of employees used as the denominator are stated in full time equivalents. In some companies, the average number of employees will include part-time employees working between say 8 and 30 hours per week. If this is the case, then you should substitute aggregate remuneration for the denominator and express the result per £1,000 of employee remuneration. With employee remuneration given at £600 million, the calculation would be:

$$\text{Profit per £1,000} = \frac{\text{Profit before taxation}}{\text{Employee remuneration}} \times 1,000$$

$$= \frac{£110 \text{ m}}{£600 \text{ m}} \times 1,000$$

$$= £183$$

In the above example, the result is stated as £183 profit per £1,000 remuneration.

2. Revenues per employee

The revenues per employee ratio shows the £ value of revenue generated by each employee. It is calculated by dividing revenues, taken from the income statement, by the average number of employees.

$$\text{Revenues per employee} = \frac{\text{Revenues}}{\text{Number of employees}}$$

$$= \frac{£5,500 \text{ m}}{35,000}$$

$$= £157,143$$

3. Non-current assets per employee

The non-current assets per employee ratio shows the £ value of non-current assets per employee. It is calculated by dividing non-current assets, taken from the balance sheet, by the average number of employees.

$$\text{Non-current assets per employee} = \frac{\text{Non-current assets}}{\text{Number of employees}}$$

$$= \frac{£400 \text{ m}}{35,000}$$

$$= £11,429$$

4. Borrowings per employee

The borrowings per employee ratio shows the £ value of borrowings attributable to each employee. It is calculated by dividing total borrowings by the average number of employees. Borrowings is the sum of short-term loans, including bank overdraft and long-term loans of £795 million.

$$\text{Borrowings per employee} \quad = \quad \frac{\text{Total borrowings}}{\text{Number of employees}}$$

$$= \quad \frac{£795 \text{ m}}{35,000}$$

$$= \quad £22,714$$

Total borrowing per employee ratios should be compared against trends year-on-year or against competitors/industry figures. A low comparative ratio would indicate that a company was not utilising sufficient financing through debts and/or it was overstaffed.

5. Employee ratios, summary

The strength and popularity of employee ratios is in their simplicity, both in calculation and interpretation. A summary of all four ratios is given below.

1.	Profit per employee	£3,143
2.	Revenues per employee	£157,143
3.	Non-current assets per employee	£11,429
4.	Borrowings per employee	£22,714

6.6   Investor ratios

In this section, we will demonstrate three ratios which can be used by the investor to assist in investment decisions. The same ratios can also be used by the directors to measure the effect management decisions might have on the future share price and dividends. These ratios are:

1.   Earnings per share;

2.   Price earnings ratio;

3.   Net assets per share;

1.   Earnings per share (EPS)

Earnings per share is the only accounting ratio which is required by a financial reporting standard, i.e. FRS 14. The instructions for its calculation given in FRS 14 are an attempt to ensure that the ratio is calculated on a comparable basis, between one company and another.

Earnings per share is calculated by dividing profit attributable to equity holders by the average number of equity shares in issue, and ranking for dividend in respect of the period.

Profit attributable to equity holders (earnings) is based on the consolidated profit for the period after taxation and after deducting minority interests and preference dividends. In this example, £70 million. The number of equity shares is given, i.e. 520 million. Using this information, we can calculate earnings per share.

$$\text{Earnings per share (EPS)} \quad = \quad \frac{\text{Profit attributable to equity holders}}{\text{Number of shares}}$$

$$= \quad \frac{\text{£70 m}}{\text{520 m}}$$

$$= \quad \text{13.46 pence}$$

The earnings per share ratio is the basis for the calculation of a number of other investor ratios. It is also widely used at corporate level as a key measure of performance, i.e. companies are anxious to show that their earnings per share is increasing year-on-year. However, the ratio is not without its problems.

For example, an increase in earnings per share might be due to a decision to finance expansion though debt capital. In this case, we would expect the profit attributable to shareholders to increase, while the number of equity shares would remain constant. Is this a good sign, or a bad sign? What is the effect on the gearing?

2.   Price earnings (PE) ratio

The price earnings ratio, shows the relationship between the market price of shares and their earnings from the most recent published accounts. It is calculated by dividing the market price of an individual ordinary equity share by the earnings per share.

The market price of an individual equity share for a publicly quoted company is normally available in the financial press. In this example, it is given as 110 pence and earnings per share was calculated in the previous section, i.e. 13.46 pence.

Using this information, we can calculate the price earnings ratio.

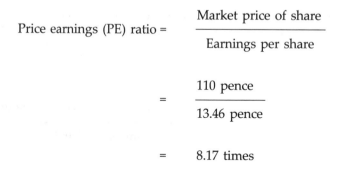

$$\text{Price earnings (PE) ratio} = \frac{\text{Market price of share}}{\text{Earnings per share}}$$

$$= \frac{110 \text{ pence}}{13.46 \text{ pence}}$$

$$= 8.17 \text{ times}$$

The price earnings ratio is expressed as a multiple, with the magnitude of the ratio providing some indication of how the market values the future earnings potential of a share. The emphasis here is upon the word future. The market will form a view about the future quality of earnings which will be expressed in the share price from which a PE ratio may be calculated. However, increases in earnings may not always bring about increases in the share price, and earnings may rise but not be associated with a share price increase.

There is no 'normal' level for price earnings ratios which differ over time, industry sector, and between countries. For example, price earnings ratios in July 1990 for companies classified in Textiles ranged from 3 to 57, but with most falling in the 6 to 13 range, while in the Banks, Hire purchase and Leasing classification, price earnings ratios ranged from 4 to 50, but with most falling in the 8 to 15 range.

3. Net assets per share

The net assets per share ratio shows the amount each equity share is covered by the net assets of a company. It is calculated by dividing the net assets by the average number of equity shares in issue and ranking for dividend in respect of the period.

Net assets here, is the sum of non-current assets (excluding intangibles) plus current assets minus current liabilities, taken from the balance sheet. In this example, £800 million. The number of equity shares is given, i.e. 520 million.

Using this information, we can calculate the net assets per share ratio.

$$\text{Net assets per share} = \frac{\text{Net assets}}{\text{Number of shares}}$$

$$= \frac{£800 \text{ m}}{520 \text{ m}}$$

$$= 153.85 \text{ pence}$$

The net assets per share ratio can produce misleading results because of the discretion that can be exercised in the valuation and depreciation policies to assets.

The net assets per share can be compared against the market price of a share. This usually takes the form of (market price per share ÷ net assets per share) which is known as the Market to Book, or MB ratio, a ratio we will review later within the context of business valuation.

There is benefit to be gained from knowing the amount net assets cover the market share price. At times, when a company is experiencing difficulties and the market share price falls, it is useful to identify the 'net asset backing'. As we have seen in the most recent recession, companies may be subject to serious speculation about their ability to generate both profit and cash flow. Such concern may well be expressed by a fall in the share price which can lead to vulnerability from predator companies. If the share price falls too far, then a company may appear to be an attractive bargain. One defence against such situations is to monitor and communicate the net assets per share figure to existing shareholders. In such a calculation, the directors will have to recognise realism by acknowledging that the values of assets in the balance sheet may differ substantially from their realisable value.

4.   Investor ratios, summary

1.   Earnings per share (EPS)   13.46 pence

2.   Price earnings (PE) ratio   8.17 times

3.   Net assets per share   153.85 pence

Appendix A: Total assets or Net assets

Bliss (1924), provides a useful definition of profitability when he writes 'The real measure of the earning power of a business is the operating profits earned on the total capacity used in such operations shown by the asset footing of the balance sheet'. Here it is not clear what he means by operating profits and these can be defined in a number of ways. What is clear, however, is the statement regarding the asset base – he means total assets.

Horngren (1970), confirms this when he states *"The measurement of operating performance (i.e. how profitably assets are employed) should not be influenced by the management's financial decisions (i.e. how assets are obtained). Operating performance is best measured by the rate of return on total assets."* Here again there is no precise definition given for profit, which it is assumed that he means 'rate of return'. While there is some debate regarding profit, the use of total assets seems to be widely supported, with *Dobson (1967)* being one of the earliest writers in the UK to agree with and suggest the use of total assets.

The UK position of using net assets can be traced back to a report in *Accountancy* in 1956, on the findings of a BIM study group that stated *"It should be understood that capital employed is here regarded in terms of a statement of net operating assets, (i.e. gross assets excluding intangible assets such as goodwill, less current liabilities), and this approach is necessary if further examination is to be made into the component parts of employed capital."* This statement has been the basis for the denominator of profitability ratios in the UK since that date.

Parker (1975), gives a fuller definition of the profitability ratio when he states the basis for profit and the basis for what he terms net tangible assets: *"Profit is taken before interest and tax in order to separate managerial performance from the effects of different financial structures and from changes in tax rates"* and Net tangible assets, defined in his glossary as *"Assets except for intangible assets, (i.e. goodwill, patents and trademarks), less current liabilities."*

Return on net assets (RONA) %

In this chapter we have outlined the calculation for the key profitability ratio using total assets as the denominator, i.e. (ROTA)%. We also showed the breakdown of (ROTA)% into the profit margin and the revenue generation ratio.

In the UK, the ratio most commonly used is return on net assets (RONA)%, i.e. profit before taxation and interest payable expressed as a percentage of net assets. Net assets is the sum of total assets minus current liabilities (or non-current assets plus net working capital).

It is important that we offer a word of caution about net assets. If you extract the figures from a published balance sheet you should be able to identify a description "total assets less current liabilities" which is the same as net assets for the purpose of financial ratio analysis. However, we often find the practitioner extracting 'net current assets' which is another name for net working capital and does not include non-current assets, and those described as net assets which, in published accounts, are after the deduction of long-term loans.

In what follows we will compare (RONA)% with (ROTA)% discussed earlier in this chapter.

Table 6.5 Basic data

		Col. 1	Col.2	Col.3
Non-current assets		5,000	15,000	15,000
+ Current assets		45,000	45,000	45,000
Total assets	(A)	50,000	60,000	60,000
Current liabilities		30,000	40,000	30,000
Net assets	(B)	20,000	20,000	30,000
PBIT	(C)	6,000	6,000	6,000

Table 6.5 Column 1, contains data extracted from a balance sheet. Column 2 and 3 both show the purchase of a non-current asset for £10,000, but in Column 2, the purchase is financed through short-term borrowings (included in the £40,000) whilst in Column 3 the purchase is financed using a long-term loan, therefore, not included in current liabilities.

From the basic data in *Table 6.5*, the (RONA)% and (ROTA)% are:

	Col. 1	Col.2	Col.3
(RONA)% (C) ÷ (B) x 100	30%	30%	20%
(ROTA)% (C) ÷ (A) x 100	12%	10%	10%

The most noticeable difference is in the absolute size of the ratios. Is it better to claim that the company is making a return on net assets of 30% or a return on total assets of only 12%?

On closer inspection we find with (RONA)% that the purchase of the non-current asset when financed through short-term borrowings has produced no increase in the profitability of the company, while with (ROTA)% there is a slight decrease. However, when long-term borrowings are used (i.e. Column 3) there is a significant reduction in (RONA)% (i.e. 30% to 20%) while (ROTA)% shows no movement.

This example serves to illustrate that (RONA)% can be affected significantly by the method of finance used. A company which uses short-term finance to purchase non-current assets and generate the same profits as in the preceeding period, (RONA)% will remain the same (the increase in non-current assets being off-set by the increase in short-term borrowings).

(ROTA)%, which is the method we recommend, is unaffected by the method of financing assets. This is evident from our example, where the same percentage results irrespective of the method of finance used, i.e. 10% in column 2 and in column 3.

Total assets or net assets

Consider the position of a company in poor financial health that uses short-term finance (just to keep things going). Its total assets are also increasing slightly. During the early stages, this company could produce an increase in profitability when using (RONA)%. Our example shows results for a three year period.

Our example company has the following data for the year to December 2004:

Non-current assets	£400,000
Current assets	£2,400,000
Current liabilities	£2,000,000
Profit before interest and tax	£200,000

Calculate:	**2004**
Return on net assets % (Profit ÷ (TA - CL) x 100)	25%
Return on total assets % (Profit ÷ TA x 100)	7.1%
Current ratio (CA ÷ CL)	1.20:1

A possible interpretation might indicate that the company was very profitable making a return on net assets of 25%. It was a good year for the company although the return when expressed as a percentage to total assets only shows 7.1%. It is clear that the deduction of current liabilities does have an effect on the overall size of the percentage.

During the year to December 2005 our example company had a number of problems and the following data was produced:

Non-current assets	£400,000
Current assets	£2,500,000
Current liabilities	£2,300,000
Profit before interest and tax	£200,000

Calculate: **2005**

Return on net assets % (Profit ÷ (TA - CL) x 100)   33.3%

Return on total assets % (Profit ÷ TA x 100)   6.9%

Current ratio (CA ÷ CL)   1.09:1

Return on net assets is looking good with an increase in profitability. However, the return on total assets is moving in the other direction. The current ratio has also reduced. Overall impression, if considering the net assets, is that we are doing fine.

In the year to December 2006 our example company still experienced problems and the following data was produced:

Non-current assets	£400,000
Current assets	£2,600,000
Current liabilities	£2,600,000
Profit before interest and tax	£200,000

Calculate: **2006**

Return on net assets % (Profit ÷ (TA - CL) x 100)   50%

Return on total assets % (Profit ÷ TA x 100)   6.7%

Current ratio (CA ÷ CL)   1.00:1

Here is a company that fits the classic view - it appears to be increasing its profitability but is experiencing liquidity problems. If we had continued for another year with our example company, would it have achieved a return on net assets of 100%!!

In the above example, the return on net assets is giving false information and often at a time when, possibly in trouble, the company needs reliable information. In our view that can only be given by expressing profit as a percentage of total assets.

Appendix B: What is Gearing?

There are a number of methods used to determine the gearing of a company. For the purpose of this example we are using the components of the borrowing ratio, i.e. total borrowings divided by equity.

Example

Two identical companies that are run by twins. One twin owns Company A, the other twin owns Company B. The have similar premises – in the same street, and they manufacture the same products, to the same specification, using the same machinery. All costs and volumes are the same. The employ similar staff, i.e. twins, each employing one twin. The only difference between the two companies is the way in which they are financed. Twin A financed Company A mainly from equity capital (shareholders), while Twin B financed Company B mainly from borrowings. The gearing for each company is shown as follows:

	A	B
Borrowings	20	80
Equity	80	20
GEARING	LOW	HIGH

It can be seen that the gearing for Company A is 20 ÷ 80 equals 0.25 to 1, while the gearing for Company B is 80 ÷ 20 equals 4.00 to 1. Why do we add back interest payable to the profit before taxation figure? The answer is to remove the effect of gearing when comparing the profitability of different companies.

In the *Table 6.6*, we show both companies have achieved an operating profit of £1,000. We have also assumed that interest payable is in proportion to the company's borrowing, therefore, Company A has £200 of interest payable while Company B has £800.

Table 6.6 Income statements for Company A and B

	A	B
Operating profit	1,000	1,000
less Interest payable	200	800
Profit before taxation	**800**	**200**
less Taxation (assume 25%)	200	50
Profit after taxation	600	150
less Dividend	300	75
Retained profit	300	75
No. of shares (assumed)	80	20
Retained profit per share	3.75	3.75

From *Table 6.6,* it can be seen that if we took profit before taxation as our figure for profit, it would be after the payment of interest on borrowings, but before the payment of dividends to shareholders for financing of the business. To overcome this, we take the profit figure before any financing of the business, i.e. operating profit.

Why do companies move towards higher gearing?

Quite simply, in good times it pays to finance a business by debt provided that the return is in excess of the cost of the debt.

	A	B
Borrowings	20	80
Equity	80	20
GEARING	LOW	HIGH
RETURN	LOW	HIGH

Companies that move towards higher gearing will provide a higher return to each individual share when the economic climate is good. If we take the previous example and add an extra £500 to the operating profit for both companies, the result is shown in *Table 6.7.*

Table 6.7 Income statements – Increase in operating profit

	A	B
	£	£
Operating profit	1,500	1,500
less Interest payable	200	800
Profit before taxation	1,300	700
less Taxation at 25%	325	50
Profit after taxation	975	650
less Dividend	300	75
Retained profit	675	575
No. of shares	80	20
Retained profit per share	8.44	28.75

We can see from the above table that an incremental operating profit of £500 means that the profit before taxation is increased by £500 since the interest payable is covered from the initial £1,000 profit. Given that both companies pay the same rate of tax and pay the same amount of dividend, means that the retained profit is £675 for Company A, and £575 for Company B. Extending the calculation we can produce a retained earnings per share of £8.44 for Company A, and £28.75 for Company B. We can now see that Company B achieves a higher return (per share) given an increase in the profits earned by the company. Higher gearing produces a higher potential return to shareholders.

What can happen to highly geared companies when there is an economic downturn?

Companies that move towards higher gearing should always keep a look out for the possibility of an economic downturn. Many companies fail to consider their financial structure and find that they are highly geared at the start of a recession. A substantial number of these companies will fail. The results of high gearing that produce a high return (per share) will place companies in a high risk category.

	A	B
Borrowings	20	80
Equity	80	20
GEARING	LOW	HIGH
RETURN	LOW	HIGH
RISK	LOW	HIGH

Companies that move towards higher gearing will provide a higher return to each individual share when the economic climate is good. If we take the previous example and deduct £500 from the operating profit for both companies, the result is shown in *Table 6.8*.

Table 6.8   Income statements – Decrease in operating profit

	A	B
Operating profit	500	500
less Interest payable	200	800
Profit/Loss before taxation	300	–300

Here we can see the risk involved. At times of recession, revenues often decline. This will inevitably cause a decline in profits, which in turn will cause a decline in the amount of funds coming into the business. The only thing which doesn't decline is the borrowings and the interest payments. In many cases interest rates will increase, therefore, causing an even larger outflow of funds and an eventual, long-lasting cash crisis.

Exercise 6.1

Given a gearing ratio (total borrowing/equity) of 0.72 to 1 and the following Balance sheet values:

Closing inventories	£210,000	Retained earnings	£140,000
Cash	£45,000	Bank overdraft	£70,000
Issued share capital	£110,000	Trade receivables	£105,000
Trade payables	£170,000		

a. What is the value of long term loans?

b. What is the value of non-current assets?

c. Calculate the current ratio.

d. Given a profit before tax and interest payable of £48,000 calculate the return on net assets (RONA)%

Exercise 6.2

The following figures have been extracted from the accounts of *BacDor Limited* for the year ended 31st July 200X:

	£'000		£'000
Revenues	25,500	Cost of sales	20,000
Profit before taxation	500	Interest payable	3,500
Issued share capital	1,000	Retained earnings	9,000
Long-term loan	9,000	Trade payables	16,000
Bank overdraft	6,000	Premises	9,000
Vehicles	6,000	Inventories	16,000
Trade receivables	9,000	Cash	1,000

a. Calculate ratios covering profitability, liquidity and gearing.

b. Interpret the ratios calculated (in a. above) with reference to industry average figures for the same period (shown below). Make suitable assumptions to assist with your interpretation.

1.	Profit ÷ Net assets	18%
2.	Profit ÷ Revenues	6%
3.	Revenues ÷ Net assets	3.00 to 1
4.	Current ratio	1.50 to 1
5.	Liquid ratio (or acid test)	0.70 to 1
6.	Inventory turn	4 times
7.	Trade receivables ratio	12 weeks
8.	Borrowings ÷ Equity	0.80 to 1
9.	Interest payable ÷ Profit before tax plus interest payable %	30%

Exercise 6.3

From the following data, calculate three profitability ratios, two liquidity ratios and two gearing ratios:

Profit before taxation	£22,000	Interest payable	£8,000
Inventories	£50,000	Issued share capital	£50,000
Long-term loans	£50,000	Non-current assets	£90,000
Trade receivables	£30,000	Bank overdraft	£20,000
Retained earnings	£20,000	Cash	£10,000
Trade payables	£40,000	Cost of sales	£480,000
Revenues	£700,000		

Exercise 6.4

The following figures have been extracted from the accounts of *I. Dilly & U. Dally Limited* for the year ended 31st January 200X:

	£'000		£'000
Revenues	8,000	Cost of sales	6,300
Profit before taxation	200	Interest payable	700
Issued share capital	200	Retained earnings	2,800
Long-term loan	1,800	Trade payables	5,000
Bank overdraft	2,000	Premises	3,000
Vehicles	1,500	Inventories	4,500
Trade receivables	2,500	Cash	300

a. Calculate ratios covering profitability, liquidity and gearing.

b. Interpret the ratios calculated (in a. above) with reference to the previous years figures shown below. Make suitable assumptions to assist with your interpretation.

1.	Profit ÷ Net assets	15%
2.	Profit ÷ Revenues	8.3%
3.	Revenues ÷ Net assets	1.81 to 1
4.	Current ratio	1.25 to 1
5.	Liquid ratio (or acid test)	0.60 to 1
6.	Inventory turn	2.1 times
7.	Trade receivables ratio	10 weeks
8.	Borrowings ÷ Equity	0.70 to 1
9.	Profit before tax ÷ Profit before tax plus interest payable %	45%

Exercise 6.5

Given the following Balance sheet values:

	£		£
Issued share capital	100,000	Wages accrued	20,000
Trade receivables	250,000	Retained earnings	50,000
Cash	20,000	Bank overdraft	80,000
Equipment	110,000	Closing inventories	150,000
Long-term loans	160,000	Trade payables	220,000

a. Calculate the (balancing) figure for land and buildings.

b. Calculate the gearing ratio (total borrowings to equity).

c. Calculate the current ratio.

d. Assume that the return on net assets is 15%, calculate the value of Profit (for the period).

Exercise 6.6

The following ratios have been calculated from the accounts of *N.O. Bother plc*

	2002	2003	2004	2005	2006
PROFITABILITY RATIOS:					
Profit before tax ÷ Net assets %	30.9	19.8	8.9	−1.5	−7.1
Profit before tax ÷ Revenues %	12.5	10	2.3	−0.6	−3.1
Revenues ÷ Net assets	2.47	1.98	3.80	2.43	2.32
WORKING CAPITAL RATIOS:					
Current assets ÷ Current liabilities	1.15	1.87	0.99	2.40	2.06
Liquid assets ÷ Current liabilities	0.28	0.46	0.21	1.02	0.90
Cost of sales ÷ Inventories	1.2	1.4	1.3	2.4	2.1
Trade receivables ÷ Average weekly revenue	3.9	4.4	4.7	5.3	4.2
GEARING RATIOS:					
Borrowing ÷ Equity	0.54	0.63	1.22	0.43	0.32
Interest payable ÷ P.B.I.T. %	8.0	20.0	128.6	−500	−25.0

The above profitability, working capital and gearing ratios have been calculated for the period 2002 to 2006. You are required to provide an interpretation of the movements in each ratio making any assumptions which you feel are necessary.

Exercise 6.7

The following figures have been extracted from the accounts of *RR Limited* for the year ended 31st March 200X:

	£000
Revenues	3,500
Premises	300
Interest payable	100
Share capital	400
Cost of sales	2,000
Trade payables	2,000
Cash	200
Bank overdraft	800
Vehicles	200
Inventories	2,100
Profit before taxation	200
Trade receivables	1,200
Retained earnings	800

1. You are required to calculate profitability, liquidity and working capital ratios for *RR Limited*.

2. Given the following ratios which reflect the averages for the same industrial sector, comment on the differences between the ratios calculated in above and the industry averages below.

Profit ÷ Net assets	32%
Profit ÷ Revenues	4%
Revenues ÷ Net assets	8.00 to 1
Current ratio	1.60 to 1
Liquid ratio (or acid test)	0.60 to 1
Inventory turn	3 times
Trade receivable weeks	12 weeks

Exercise 6.8

The following figures have been extracted from the accounts of *Percentage Limited* for the five years 2002 to 2006:

CONSOLIDATED BALANCE SHEET DATA FOR FIVE YEARS (£'000)

	2002	2003	2004	2005	2006
Non-current assets	26,000	70,000	80,000	96,000	135,000
Inventories	50,000	50,000	51,000	52,000	58,000
Trade receivables	24,000	25,000	26,000	28,000	24,000
Current assets	76,000	77,000	80,000	83,000	90,000
Trade payables	52,000	50,000	52,000	55,000	65,000
Bank overdraft	11,000	12,000	12,000	12,000	32,000
Current liabilities	65,000	64,000	67,000	70,000	100,000
Share capital	8,000	8,000	16,000	16,000	16,000
Retained earnings	10,000	49,000	51,000	64,000	376,000
Long-term loans	19,000	26,000	26,000	29,000	33,000

CONSOLIDATED INCOME STATEMENT DATA FOR FIVE YEARS (£'000)

	2002	2003	2004	2005	2006
Revenues	90,000	118,000	124,000	140,000	170,000
Cost of sales	78,000	103,000	104,500	111,400	135,000
Interest payable	3,000	3,000	3,500	3,600	10,000
Profit before tax	9,000	12,000	16,000	25,000	25,000

1. Calculate profitability ratios for the five years and provide a brief overview of what they reveal about the performance of the company.

2. Calculate liquidity ratios for the five years and provide a brief overview of what they reveal about the performance of the company.

3. Calculate gearing ratios for the five years and provide a brief overview of what they reveal about the performance of the company.

Exercise 6.9

The chairman of *H.O. Ratio Limited* has obtained figures from a comparison of a competitor.

Total assets	£258,750
Current liabilities	£125,000
Administrative expenses	£33,250
Current ratio	1.75 1
Liquid (or acid test) ratio	1.05 1
Average age of outstanding customer debts	
(based on a 52 week year)	12 weeks
Net profit ÷ Net current assets %	20%
Gross profit ÷ Revenues %	20%

1. From the information above, prepare in as much detail as possible, an Income statement for the year ended 31st October 200X and a Balance sheet as at that date.

2. Comment on the limitations in using ratio analysis as a means of measuring the financial performance of a company.

CHAPTER SEVEN

COMPANY FINANCIAL ANALYSIS

LEARNING OBJECTIVES

When you have finished studying this chapter and completed the exercises, you should be able to:

❑ Describe and set in context the non-financial approach for recognising corporate financial distress developed by Argenti;

❑ Describe and know when and how to apply Altman's 1968 ratio model;

❑ Describe the development and application of Robertson's 1983 ratio model;

❑ Carry out an analysis of a company using financial and non-financial techniques, including:

- Ratio analysis;
- Ratio models;
- Diary of events;
- Common-size statements;
- Cost analysis statements;
- Non-financial indicators.

❑ Identify published sources of company information.

7.1   Introduction

Research by academics over the last 25 years or so has revealed that statistical and non-statistical approaches can be used for analysing financial and non-financial data in order to form a view about corporate financial health. What these approaches are and how they differ are considered in this chapter.

We have shown that a great deal of judgement needs to be used when calculating and applying financial ratios. This is equally true when using 'ready-made' information from data services such as Datastream, despite their presentation of the ratios as a single score, which may be compared against the appropriate benchmarks also supplied.

The combination of ratios and statistical technique has now made it possible to forecast the likelihood of financial failure with some degree of success.

7.2   Argenti's non-financial indicators of corporate distress

When companies fail they tend to display non-financial signs of deterioration as well as financial ones. These non-financial indications include some elusive matters like 'bad management' and economic downturn, and others less elusive such as over-trading and excessive inventories.

Many individuals have considered the importance of non-financial factors but *Argenti (1976)* is noteworthy because of his attempt to rank the items in some order of importance.

To summarise the extent of corporate distress, *Argenti* has proposed an A-score. This is based on the assumption that, as a general rule, most companies fail for broadly similar reasons and in a broadly similar manner. The failure sequence is assumed to take many years, typically five or more, and to fall into three essential stages comprising:

1. Specific *defects* in a company's management and business practices in particular at the very top;

2. Subsequently, possibly years later, top management makes a major *mistake* because of the specific defects;

3. Ultimately, signs and *symptoms* of failure begin to appear and manifest as financial and non-financial matters.

Argenti has discussed these three stages in more detail which we shall now consider.

1. The inherent defects

The inherent defects identified by *Argenti* relate to:

a. Management;

b. Accountancy systems;

c. Change.

a. Management

He identifies a major defect as being an autocratic Chief Executive, particularly, where he or she is also the Chairperson. Such an individual will tend to be viewed as being 'the company' and will be surrounded by people whose advice he/she has no intention of taking.

The board may consist of passive, non-contributing directors, arguably a desirable situation for an autocratic leader, but not for the company. Secondly, the directors may lack all-round business skills. Thirdly, there may be a lack of strong financial direction. Poor working capital management is often good evidence of this. For example, there may be no substantial cash flow forecasting making it difficult to manage future borrowing. Finally, a lack of management expertise below board level can lead to failure.

b. Accountancy systems

Companies that fail are often found to have poor or non-existent accounting systems, a defect which can be related to poor financial direction. Other than working capital, budgetary control may be a particular problem. Either no budgets are prepared at all or the budgets are prepared but are not followed by adequate variance reports. The consequence is that employees do not know what is required of them or, if they do, they do not know whether they have achieved it.

Within such a defective accounting system costing may be a particular problem. Managers may not know what each product or service costs, and, if they do, they are not likely to be aware of the characteristics of reported costs, i.e. whether they are full costs or not.

c. Change

Many companies that fail are those which have either not noticed a change in their business environment or have not responded to it. *Argenti* cites signs of such defects as being old-fashioned product, old-fashioned factory, out-of-date marketing, strikes attributable to outmoded attitudes to employees, an ageing board of directors, and no development of information management competencies, such as those associated with computerisation.

2. The Mistakes

Three mistakes are identified by *Argenti* as being responsible for failure:

a. Over-gearing;

b. Over-trading;

c. The 'big' project or contract.

a. Over-gearing

Companies dominated by ambitious autocrats, and not constrained by a strong finance director, are particularly prone to taking on a higher level of gearing than its financial situation should allow.

b. Over-trading

Over-trading occurs when a company expands faster than its ability to generate funding. Expanding companies often over-trade and become prone to failure by relying upon loan finance often of a short-term nature.

c. The big project

Some companies are brought down by the failure of a large and over-ambitious project. A 'big project' can be physical, such as launching a major new product or service, but need not necessarily be tangible. The guaranteeing of a loan for a subsidiary company would fall within this category.

3. The symptoms

Argenti identifies a number of symptoms which can be observed as a company moves toward failure:

a. Financial signs;

b. Creative accounting;

c. Other signs.

a. Financial signs

Financial signs of failure such as deteriorating ratios were discussed in some detail in the previous chapter. Whilst of doubtless value their major shortcoming relates to their inability to indicate the likelihood of failure in a period of less than two or three years, unlike other non-financial symptoms.

b. Creative accounting

The prospect of failure has been known to encourage the accounting system to be used very imaginatively, particularly, where financial information is required to be reported to outside parties. Such imagination, when not obviously exercised for reasons other than to mislead, is known as creative accounting. Such creativity may manifest itself in a number of areas. The treatment of depreciation is one example, for which the exercise of creativity is likely to be severely constrained by the role of the auditor.

c. Other signs

A company heading for failure may exhibit numerous non-financial signs of distress as well as financial ones. Examples of which are; management salaries are frozen, capital expenditure decisions are delayed, product quality or service deteriorates, market share falls, the chief executive is ill, staff turnover rises, morale deteriorates, rumours abound, the dividend is not cut when there would seem to be sound reason for so doing.

At the very end of the process, when failure is imminent, all of the financial and non-financial signs become so severe that even the most casual observer can see them. These are referred to as 'terminal' signs.

The framework developed by *Argenti* provides a useful checklist for identifying financial distress and potential failure. *Argenti's* 'A Score' aggregates individual defects to assess a company's failure potential, and is shown in *Table 7.1.*

Table 7.1 Argenti's failure framework

Defects		Scores
Autocrat		8
Chairman and Chief Executive		4
Passive board		2
Unbalanced skills		2
Weak Finance Director		2
Poor management depth		1
No budgetary control		3
No cash flow plans		3
No costing system		3
Poor response to change		15
Total for defects	**(A)**	43
Mistakes		
High gearing		15
Over-trading		15
Big project		15
Total for mistakes	**(B)**	45
Symptoms		
Financial signs		4
Creative accounting		4
Non-financial signs		3
Terminal signs		1
Total for symptoms	**(C)**	12
Total overall possible score	**(A+B+C)**	**100**
Pass mark		**25**

Argenti recommends that the scores are given only if the observer is confident that an item is clearly visible in the company being studied. Only maximum or nil scores are allowed. This means that, for example, only if the observer is quite sure that the chief executive dominates the suspect company and has deliberately gathered a team of executives whose advice is ignored, a score of eight for 'autocrat' should be given, otherwise the score should be nil.

The overall pass mark according to the system is 25. Scores above that level are considered to show so many of the well-known signs which precede failure that the observer should be profoundly alarmed. Within the overall score, the sub-scores are also noteworthy. If a company scores more than the pass mark of 10 in the defects section, even if it scores less than 25 overall, it is viewed as being indicative of a company in danger of making one of the mistakes that lead to failure.

Argenti's approach to analysing indicators of corporate distress is valuable because it provides a useful checklist of issues and events that have been shown to be common to failing organisations. However, the scoring method he offers is highly subjective.

7.3   Altman's 1968 ratio model

In addition to the *Argenti* type approach, a number of researchers have developed financial/mathematical models. The most well known of these is the 'Z scoring' model developed originally by *Professor Altman (1968)*. Using a statistical technique, known as multiple discriminant analysis (MDA), long established for distinguishing between life forms in the natural sciences, *Altman* sought to determine whether any financial characteristics could be found to distinguish those firms that had failed from those which had not.

In developing his 1968 model, *Altman* selected 33 companies for the failed group. The criteria for selection required each company to be in manufacturing. The asset size ranged from $0.7 million to $25.9 million. The dates of the last set of accounts ranged from 1946 to 1965. The on-going group was selected using a paired sample, each failed company being paired with an on-going company both in terms of industry and size. The *Altman* approach can be summarised as follows:

1. Two matched groups of companies identified in the American manufacturing sector. One group comprising companies that have failed, the other a group of similar companies, known as on-going, that have not failed.

2. Financial ratios calculated for each group. Data for the failed group being taken from the last set of accounts, while data for the on-going group being taken from the same year.

3. The statistical procedure is then designed to produce a single score (Z score) which can be used to classify a company as belonging to the failed group or the on-going group.

4. The intended result is the identification of a set of ratios that can be weighted and summed to give a Score (Z) indicative of potential as distinct from past failure.

From an initial list of 22 financial ratios, the final model consisted of five ratios together with their respective weights and is shown as follows:

$$Z = 1.2 X_1 + 1.4 X_2 + 3.3 X_3 + 0.6 X_4 + 1.0 X_5$$

In this model, Z is the sum of the ratios times the weights, and the individual ratios are defined as:

X_1 = Working capital ÷ total assets

X_2 = Retained earnings ÷ total assets

X_3 = Profit before interest and tax ÷ total assets

X_4 = Market value of equity ÷ book value of total debt

X_5 = Revenues ÷ total assets

In determining the Z score, the failed group and the on-going group are combined and ordered according to their individual Z scores. It is then possible to specify two limits as follows:

o   An upper limit, where no failed companies are misclassified (none are included in the on-going), and;

o   A lower limit, where no on-going companies are misclassified (none are included in the failed).

Altman's attempt to discriminate between these two groups of companies was not perfect and misclassifications did occur between the upper and lower limit. The area between the upper and lower limit is what *Altman* describes as the 'zone of ignorance' or the 'grey area', where a number of failed companies and/ or on-going companies were misclassified. The limits and the zone of ignorance arising from *Altman's* 1968 model are shown in *Figure 7.1*.

Figure 7.1   Determining the cut-off for Altman's 1968 model

> 2.99	On-going companies		
Failed	2.99		
	2.78	On-going	*Zone of*
	2.68	On-going	*ignorance*
Failed	2.67		*or*
Failed	2.10		*Grey*
Failed	1.98		*area*
	1.81	On-going	
< 1.81	Failed companies		

In order to 'force' a classification, *Altman* identified a score where the misclassifications would be minimised. This 'cut-off' was between 2.67 and 2.68 which resulted in only one failed company and one on-going company being misclassified. To achieve a single cut-off point *Altman* selected 2.675 the mid-point.

Example

Ratio models have an appeal since they lend themselves to spreadsheet application to arrive at the total score (in the *Altman* model, the Z score). They are also much easier to interpret. In the *Altman* model, the Z score is used to classify the company into one of three groups, i.e. the on-going group, the 'grey area' or the failed group.

One of the problems with ratio models is trying to determine how each of the ratios are calculated. In the top section of *Table 7.2* we provide the basic data required to calculate Z scores for *Altman's* model together with capital letters against each item. Please note that you will need to obtain the share price for each year of calculation. To be consistent, we suggest that you take year-end prices.

In the bottom section of *Table 7.2* we show you how to combine certain of the figures, e.g. working capital equals current assets minus current liabilities (B – C).

Table 7.2   Basic data

Basic financial data		200X–1	200X
(A) Non-current assets		42,000	44,000
(B) Current assets		78,000	79,000
(C) Current liabilities		36,000	56,000
(D) Retained earnings		59,000	55,000
(E) Long-term loans		25,000	12,000
(F) Revenues		155,000	175,000
(G) Profit before tax		6,000	–3,600
(H) Interest payable		3,000	3,000
(I) Number of ordinary shares		48000	48000
(J) Share price (pence)		300	180
Combining the figures		200X–1	200X
(K) Working capital	(B – C)	42,000	23,000
(L) Total assets	(A + B)	120,000	123,000
(M) Profit before tax + interest payable	(G + H)	9,000	–600
(N) Market value of equity	(I x J ÷ 100)	144,000	86,400
(O) Total debt	(C + E)	61,000	68,000

In *Table 7.3* below, we show the final calculations to arrive at the Z scores. For ratio X_1 we take the working capital figure from row (K) and divide it by total assets from row (L); the result is then multiplied by the weight for X_1, i.e. 1.2 to arrive at a figure of 0.42 for 1998. Similar calculations are performed for the remaining ratios X_2 to X_5. The Z score is the sum of ratios X_1 to X_5 giving a total of 4.05 for 1998.

Table 7.3   Altman's 1968 ratio model

		Weight	200X–1	200X
X_1	Working capital ÷ total assets	1.2	0.42	0.22
X_2	Retained earnings ÷ total assets	1.4	0.69	0.63
X_3	PBIT ÷ total assets	3.0	0.23	–0.01
X_4	Market value of equity ÷ total debt	0.6	1.42	0.76
X_5	Revenues ÷ total assets	1.0	1.29	1.42
	Z score		4.05	3.02

Interpretation is against a cut-off, above 2.67, and the company is unlikely to fail in the coming year. In this example, the total Z score is above 2.67 for the years 200X-1 and 200X.

7.4   Application of corporate failure models

1.   Specific industry group

Financial ratio models like Z scoring should be developed for specific industry groups only. The model cannot be successfully used across industry boundaries.

In practice it can be difficult to know whether a particular company 'fits' the industry requirement of a model, e.g. a model developed for manufacturing companies can only be used for manufacturing companies. This can be found in *Altman (1982)*, where a list of 42 companies included those with names such as:

Allied Supermarkets;

City Stores;

Commonwealth Oil Refining;

General Recreation;

Mays Department Stores;

Murphy Pacific Marine Salvage Co.;

Sambo's Restaurants Inc.;

Shulman Transport Enterprises;

White Motors;

Wilson Freight.

While *Altman* did not indicate the industry type, it seems unlikely, given contemporary industry classifications, that any of the above companies fits the classification of an American manufacturing company.

Taffler (1980), demonstrated the need to recognise the industry type when he developed a separate distribution model. This means that each industry certainly needs its own model but whether different models should be used for each country is a moot point. Perhaps, in an ideal world, each company would have a model specifically designed for its own particular circumstances.

2. Using a model to observe trends.

Corporate prediction models are developed to operate on a single year's data. This means that the latest year's data is used to predict the possibility of failure. *Barnes (1984)* is particularly critical of the idea of observing Z score trends, when he states that "it involves using discriminant co-efficients for one period for financial ratios and Z scores for another."

3. Changing the specification of the ratios

The ratios contained in a model are determined at the time when the model is developed. Changing the specification of a ratio requires a complete re-evaluation of the model; perhaps even resulting in another ratio being chosen as doing the best job.

The main reason for wanting to change the specification of a ratio has centred on ratio X_4 in *Altman's* 1968 model. Ratio X_4 is a short-term gearing ratio, and is stated as market value of equity divided by the book value of debt. This ratio effectively restricts the use of the model to those companies that are quoted on a stock exchange. For example, a company not quoted will not have a market value of equity. As a consequence, one might be tempted to substitute the book value, that is shareholders' funds inclusive of reserves. The result is not the same, as *Altman (1983)* has illustrated.

Altman recalculated the Z score using the book value rather than the market value of equity for the same two groups of companies he used to develop the 1968 model. Changing ratio X_4 to the book value of equity divided by the book value of debt produced the following changes to the weights shown in *Table 7.4.*

Table 7.4   Change to weights – by adjusting Ratio X_4

		1968 Model	1983 Revised	% Change
X_1	Working capital	1.2	0.717	40.3
X_2	Retained earnings	1.4	0.847	39.5
X_3	Profitability	3.3	3.107	5.8
X_4	Gearing	0.6	0.420	30.0
X_5	Asset utilisation	1.0	0.998	0.0

From the above, it can be seen that a small change to the specification of an individual ratio produces substantial changes to the weights assigned to other ratios in the model. Furthermore, the 1.81 cut-off in the 1968 model is amended to 1.23 as a result of the revision to ratio X_4.

7.5   Robertson's 1983 ratio model

1.   Introduction

In addition to statistically oriented approaches other models have been developed. *Robertson (1983)* has developed a model which measures changes in financial health which:

❏ Suggests key elements (ratio categories) identifiable in failed companies and then constructs ratios to measure each element.

❏ Uses simple weights, to compensate for the natural differences in the individual ratio values, to arrive at a single score.

❏ Interprets the score by measuring changes in financial health from previous periods, i.e. measuring changes in the score year-on-year; traditional interpretation follows this procedure.

❏ Identifies changes in financial health and allows examination of the individual ratio movements in order that corrective action can be taken.

The final model comprised of the following ratios, each of which will be described in *Section 3.* The ratios are referred to by using R_1 to denote ratio 1 through to R_5 to denote ratio 5.

$$R_1 = \text{(Revenues - total assets)} \div \text{revenues}$$

$$R_2 = \text{Profit before taxation} \div \text{total assets}$$

$$R_3 = \text{(Current assets - total debt)} \div \text{current liabilities}$$

$$R_4 = \text{(Equity - total borrowings)} \div \text{total debt}$$

$$R_5 = \text{(Liquid assets - bank borrowings)} \div \text{trade payables}$$

The financial change model (FCM) takes a similar form to *Altman's* 1968 model where the total score is found:

$$FCM = 0.3R_1 + 3R_2 + 0.6R_3 + 0.3R_4 + 0.3R_5$$

The model was developed using a systems approach. This required a statement of 'key elements' identifiable in failed companies, followed by the development of ratios which have individual meaning and will help to measure each of the elements; finally the provision for feedback (by observing the movements in the scores obtained from the individual ratios) to allow corrective action to be taken if necessary.

2. Key elements

The identification of the key elements was produced using literature, especially *Argenti's* failure process (discussed earlier), also from a detailed examination of the data already collected for eight failed companies. The 'key elements' identifiable in failed companies were:

❑ **Trading instability**

Most failing companies experience a fall in sales generated from their asset base. This is true both of the declining product life cycle and the rapid expansion or over-trading company.

❑ **Declining profits**

The conditions encountered in trading instability can erode a company's profit margins and when combined with other uncontrolled costs can result in substantial losses.

❑ **Declining working capital**

If not checked, declining profits can lead to a decline in working capital, accelerating if the company turns into a loss situation. Further reductions in working capital can be caused by continued expansion of net-current assets, especially when financed from short–term borrowings.

❑ **Increase in borrowings**

Instead of tackling the problem of trading instability and profitability, the failing company increases borrowings to maintain its required level of working capital. This has a double effect in that:

a. It further reduces profits through additional interest payments;

b. It increases the gearing of a company at a time when it is most vulnerable.

The selection of ratios to be included was considered to be the most important factor in the development of the model. Each ratio was selected to reflect the elements that cause changes in a company's financial health. An explanation of each of the ratios is given below.

3. The Ratios finally selected

R_1 (Revenues – total assets) ÷ revenues

This is a measure of trading stability. It highlights the important relationship between assets and revenues. When a company increases its asset base, it is looking for a corresponding increase in revenues. Companies experiencing trading difficulties are unable to maintain a given level for this ratio. Deterioration indicates a fall in the revenue generated from the asset base. If the ratio is maintained it can produce a stabilising effect even for a company that has problems with costs and/or borrowings.

R_2 Profit before taxation ÷ total assets

Profit is taken after interest expense but before tax, because failing companies borrow more and suffer increases in interest payments in the years leading to failure. Total assets exclude intangibles and are used as the base because they are not influenced by financing policies and tend to remain constant or increase. Failing companies tend to show a decline in profits in the years leading to failure, often turning into a loss. The deterioration in profit is sufficient to cause this ratio to fall. However, many companies are involved in rapid expansion and this, if present, could cause a further decline in the ratio.

R_3 (Current assets – total debt) ÷ current liabilities

This is an extension of the net working capital ratio, and requires that long-term debt is also deducted from current assets. It measures a company's ability to repay its current debt without liquidating non-current assets. When compared over a number of years, failing companies show a marked deterioration in this ratio due to the current assets falling while total debt remains constant or even increases.

R₄ (Equity – total borrowings) ÷ total debt

This is a gearing ratio. A low ratio indicates a high proportion of debt which means high gearing with associated high risk. Failing companies experience a drop in equity through a combination of losses in operations and reorganisation/extraordinary costs, while at the same time borrowings tend to increase. This can turn a healthy balance in favour of equity into a negative balance where borrowings exceed equity. Should a company not borrow but instead obtain additional funds from shareholders, then this will have a stabilising effect and reduce the risk of moving toward high gearing and associated interest payments. It will also help to reduce borrowings and improve liquidity ratios.

R₅ (Liquid assets – bank borrowings) ÷ trade payables

This ratio tests changes in immediate liquidity. After deducting bank borrowings from liquid assets it is then possible to measure the immediate cover for trade payables. Increasing bank borrowings incurs additional financing costs for current and future periods and might require the company to agree to a fixed and/or floating charge over its assets.

4. Weights

The weights used were selected to adjust the natural values obtained from certain ratios. For example, the ratio of profit before tax divided by total assets could only, at best, produce a natural score of 0.20 (equivalent to a 20% return on total assets) while a liquidity ratio or a gearing ratio could easily produce a natural score of 1.00 or more. In this case the weights allow the profit ratio to be increased and/or the liquidity or gearing ratios to be reduced. Weights can also be used to increase the effect of one ratio and/or reduce the effect of another.

Each ratio should contribute equally to the overall score and by a series of simple arithmetic calculations a set of weights applicable to a group of companies (or even a single company) was arrived at. The resulting weights should be easy to use and experiments were carried out by changing the weights (for example doubling and halving a ratio weight). This showed, contrary to expectations, that changes in individual ratio weights did not significantly affect the total score when comparing a company year–on–year.

5. Interpretation of the score

In traditional ratio analysis, the same ratios are used across 'industries' with ratio values being interpreted by observing the movements from previous periods or from an industry average. Given that the model was developed for use across 'industries', it is appropriate to use similar interpretation, i.e. observing the movements in the total (and individual) scores.

In testing the model it was found that, when the total score fell by approximately 40 percent or more in any year, substantial changes had taken place in the financial health of a company. Immediate steps should be taken to identify the reasons for the change and take remedial action. If the score falls by approximately 40 percent or more for a second year running, the company is unlikely to survive, unless drastic action is taken to stop the decline and restore financial health.

In practice, the model should be used to identify all movements in the total score; further checks should then be carried out on the individual ratios contained in the model in order that action be taken to correct the situation.

6. Example

In this example we will use the same basic data from the *Altman* model, please note that there are some additional figures, while others are not required. In the top section of *Table 7.5*, we provide the basic data required to calculate the total score for *Robertson's* model together with capital letters against each item. In the bottom section of *Table 7.5*, we show you how to combine certain of the figures, e.g. total assets is the sum of non-current assets plus current assets (A + C).

Table 7.5   Basic data

Basic Financial data		200X–1	200X
(A)	Non-current assets	42,000	44,000
(B)	Inventories	40,000	45,000
(C)	Current assets	78,000	79,000
(D)	Bank overdraft	8,000	26,000
(E)	Trade payables	25,000	30,000
(F)	Current liabilities	36,000	56,000
(G)	Equity	59,000	55,000
(H)	Long-term loans	25,000	12,000
(I)	Revenues	155,000	175,000
(J)	Profit before tax	6,000	-3,600

Combining the figures			200X–1	200X
(K)	Total assets	(A + C)	120,000	123,000
(L)	Total debt	(F + H)	61,000	68,000
(M)	Current assets – total debt	(C – L)	17,000	11,000
(N)	Equity (shareholder's fund)	(G)	59,000	55,000
(O)	Total borrowings	(D + H)	33,000	38,000
(P)	Equity – total borrowings	(N – O)	26,000	17,000
(Q)	Liquid assets	(C – B)	38,000	34,000
(R)	Liquid assets – bank borrowings	(Q – D)	30,000	8,000

In *Table 7.6* below, we show the final calculations to arrive at the total scores. For ratio X_1 we take the revenues figure from row (I) and deduct total assets from row (K), the result is then divided by revenues from row (I) and multiplied by the weight for X_1 i.e. 0.3 to arrive at a figure of 0.07 for 200X-1. Similar calculations are performed for the remaining ratios X_2 to X_5. The total score is the sum of ratios X_1 to X_5, giving a value of 0.99 for 200X-1

Table 7.6   Robertson's 1983 ratio model

		Weight	200X–1	200X
R_1	(Revenues – T.Assets) ÷ Revenues	0.3	0.07	0.09
R_2	Profit before tax ÷ Total assets	3	0.15	-0.09
R_3	(C.Assets – T.Debt) ÷ C.Liabilities	0.6	0.28	0.12
R_4	(Equity – T.Borrowings) ÷ T.Debt	0.3	0.13	0.08
R_5	(L.Assets – B.Borrow.) ÷ Tr.Payables	0.3	0.36	0.08
	Total Score		0.99	0.28

Interpretation is on the movement in the total score year-on-year. The suggestion is that a fall of more than 40% indicates a significant decline in the financial health of a company. In this case we can see that there is a decline well above the 40%.

The model then allows examination of each of the individual ratio components to identify where the decline has taken place. The analyst should then revert to using traditional ratio analysis to drill down and find the cause(s). In this case we can see that the decline is spread over ratios R_2 to R_5 i.e. profitability, liquidity and gearing.

7.6   Working with published accounts

1. Introduction

We have considered the make-up of corporate reports and the general principles for their analysis using financial ratios in earlier chapters. However, financial ratio analysis is only one tool for interpreting published information much of which may be non-financial in nature.

In this chapter, we consider how the published information provided in corporate reports of both a financial and non-financial nature may be analysed in a structured manner to permit useful interpretation. We will use the *Polly Ester Holdings plc* case study which is included in *Appendix B, pages 417–425*. It might be useful to obtain a photocopy of the case study to allow easier access to the material. The following points should be noted:

1. The *Polly Ester* case study is used to demonstrate the strengths and weaknesses of financial ratio analysis. The case is chosen since it provides ideas and allows similar analysis to be undertaken on data for any company.

2. The case also shows the different levels of analysis which can be achieved with the use of the notes to the accounts.

3. Please be aware that the ratios for many companies are stable year-on-year, i.e. there is little movement in any of the ratios. This makes it extremely difficult to permit useful interpretation.

4. The sections which address each group of financial ratios include both a description and interpretation. It is not intended that this should be taken as a specimen or suggested answer to the financial analysis of the case.

5. In the early stages of your analysis it is extremely useful to 'build' spreadsheet models. This will allow you to experiment with the data.

6. Financial ratio analysis is simply one of a number of analysis techniques required for appropriate interpretation. The development of basic strategy models such as SWOT, can be used to identify changes year-on-year.

7. It is also important to collect published and commercial material on your chosen company, as well as those of competitors. This should make it easier to provide realistic explanations of any movements observed in the financial ratios.

2.   Diary of events

Corporate reports do in fact contain much useful information but it may not necessarily be (and is not usually) organised in the most appropriate way to permit analysis. All too often the inexperienced analyst will focus attention upon hard forms of analysis like the calculation of ratios without setting the scene appropriately.

In this section, we will consider how to organise the information provided in a useful way via the diary of events. You will find this invaluable for both interpreting corporate reports in practice and for their analysis in business strategy.

A diary of events is a log of significant changes which have taken place in a company during the year under consideration. It should be directed both at financial and non-financial information obtained primarily from published accounts, but which may be supplemented with that from other sources.

What form should the diary of events take? We have provided a basic checklist in *Figure 7.2.*

Figure 7.2   Diary of events

AUDIT REPORT

Have the accounts been qualified?

DIRECTORS

Have there been any significant movements in key personnel, e.g. resignations/appointments?

Who are the non-executive directors?

TRADING STABILITY

Is the company losing its way, e.g. unrelated diversification?

Are there any statements on deterioration in the marketplace?

Are there statements referring to "Worst year in company's history?"

Are there signs that the company is over-trading?

BORROWINGS

Is there evidence that the company has agreed to a fixed and/or floating charge on all assets?

How many banks does the company use?

FIXED ASSETS

Is the company selling off key assets?

Is there evidence of over-commitment to a big project which could cause the downfall of the company?

ACCOUNTS

Is there evidence of delay in paying bills, e.g. long creditor days?

Is there evidence of a delay in publishing the annual report?

SALES by activity and PROFIT by activity

Is there any significant movement in sales or profitability by activity?

CAPITAL EXPENDITURE

Is the company expanding from organic growth?

Is there evidence of expansion by acquisition?

ACCOUNTING POLICY and TREATMENT

Has the company made any significant changes to its accounting policy and the treatment of key items, e.g. goodwill and brands?

Table 7.7   *A simplified Diary of Events*

Movements in:		2003/04	2004/05	2005/06
Revenues	£'000	512,700 to 604,400	604,400 to 757,300	757,300 to 889,800
	%	17.9	25.3	17.5
Non-current assets	%	22.6	13.5	1.3
Borrowings	%	146.7	23.2	76.3
No. of shops		73	74	
Acquisitions		Green & Gillies Pencosmo		Nufurnish. Ind. Inc.
Disposals				Green & Gillies
Other		New textile plant		Franchise – Styleright
Directors				
Resignations		R.J. Somers	P. Peters	A. Moorhouse
Appointments				H. Waterman

Table 7.7 shows a simplified version of the Diary of Events. From the movement in sales it must be asked, how much longer could the company achieve increases in sales in excess of 17% per annum?

The comparison of the percentage increases in non-current assets when compared to the percentage increases in borrowings is stark. Further analysis shows a substantial increase in non-current assets 2003/04 due to an increase in new shops, acquisitions of *Green and Gillies* and *Pencosmo* and the addition of a new textile plant. 2005 was a year of consolidation, or was it? The diary of events does not provide any surprises, except for the resignation of P. Peters towards the end of the year. 2006 saw the purchase of *Nufurnishing Industries Inc*, a franchise deal with *Styleright* and the disposal of *Green and Gillies* having spent considerable cash over the previous two years since its purchase.

From the above it can be seen that the Diary of Events provides useful data and will assist the analyst when undertaking a full interpretation of a company.

3.   Common size statement base year = 100

The common size statement (in this case indexing all financial data to a base year 2003) will be used to highlight those figures that show extreme movements, or simply those that are out of line with, say, activity.

Table 7.8   Common size statement for Polly Ester Holdings plc

	2003	2004	2005	2006
Non-current assets	100	122.6	139.2	141.0
Investments	100	92.7	91.1	135.0
Inventories	100	146.8	166.5	230.3
Trade and other receivables	100	126.3	172.6	226.8
Current assets	100	137.1	160.0	212.6
Bank overdraft	100	435.4	103.7	1090.3
Trade and other payables	100	136.6	197.5	272.1
Current liabilities	100	184.5	133.6	333.7
Share capital	100	107.8	116.6	106.6
Long-term loans	100	75.6	485.7	33.3
Revenues	100	117.9	147.7	173.6
Cost of sales	100	119.2	164.6	210.4
Profit before tax	100	102.8	90.2	–7.1
Interest payable	100	185.9	381.4	657.8
Retail and distribution costs	100	120.9	152.0	184.0
Administration costs	100	114.0	128.0	177.2
Retail space (sq mtr)	100	122.2	139.6	153.4

The common size statement in *Table 7.8* shows an increase in retail space over the period of 53.4%, while retail and distribution costs have increased by 84% and bank overdraft by a staggering 1,090.3%.

Inventories, trade receivables and payables have risen faster than the retail space or revenue income. There is a substantial decline in profit before tax over the period 2005/06 together with an increase in interest payable.

4.   Cost analysis statement year-on-year

The common size statement shows that there are many significant changes throughout the period. It will now be useful to consider some of the changes in more detail. First we will prepare a cost analysis statement showing changes in income and costs year-on-year. This can be reconciled to the changes in the profit before tax figures year-on-year.

Table 7.9   Cost analysis statement year-on-year

	2003/04 £'000	2004/05 £'000	2005/06 £'000
Revenues	91,800	152,900	132,500
Cost of sales	37,800	89,500	90,000
Retail and distribution costs	35,200	52,300	53,900
Administration costs	11,700	11,700	40,900
Interest payable	3,400	7,700	10,900
Miscellaneous –(balancing figure)	1,800	200	2,300
Total costs	**89,900**	**161,400**	**198,000**
Profit / –Loss before tax	1,900	–8,500	–65,500
Included in the above:			
Operating lease/hire charges	9,500	5,500	15,100
Staff costs	33,100	29,100	35,300
Depreciation	12,900	6,800	8,000
Exchange differences –fav +adv	0	–3,200	–17,300
	55,500	**38,200**	**41,100**

In *Table 7.9* above, we can see that the incremental revenue for the period 2005/06 was £132.5 million, while the incremental increase in costs was £198 million, which produced a reduction in the profit before tax of £65.5 million.

When we examine the figures for 2005/06 it can be seen that the cost of sales and retail and distribution cost increases are in line with the previous year even though incremental revenues have fallen. Given a similar decrease in costs for both items, cost of sales should be nearer to £77.6 million and retail and distribution costs nearer to £45.3 million. An indication that an additional £21 million was 'consumed' given the pro–rata movement.

Still considering the figures for 2005/06, the most obvious movement is in administration costs, a £40.9 million increase over the 2004/05 figure. Over a three year period this figure increases to £64.3 million.

In the bottom section of the statement we show a breakdown of some of the cost increases included in the top section. An interesting movement is the £35.3 million increase in staff costs of 2005/06. Looking at the three year period we see substantial increases in staff costs, 2003/04 saw £33.1 million increase and 2004/05 saw £29.1 million increase, some £97.5 million in the three years.

5.   Robertson's 1983 ratio model

Earlier in this chapter it was seen that *Robertson's 1983 ratio model* measures changes in financial health year-on-year. The model can either be used as the beginning of any analysis to highlight where movements have taken place, then use basic ratio techniques to identify the source(s) of the problem. Similarly, it can be used at the end of a report to substantiate the earlier interpretation. We prefer to use it at the beginning. In this way it can be used as a course screen, say in credit control, to identify those companies that require further analysis.

Table 7.10   Robertson's 1983 ratio model

	2003	2004	2005	2006
(Revenues – T.Assets) ÷ revenues	0.09	0.07	0.08	0.08
Profit before tax ÷ total assets	0.56	0.44	0.34	–0.02
(C.Assets – T.Debt) ÷ C.Liabilities	0.20	0.04	0.05	–0.02
(Equity – T.Borrowings) ÷ T.Debt	0.31	0.12	0.09	–0.03
(L.Assets – B.Borrow) ÷ Tr.Payables	0.16	–0.17	0.14	–0.34
Total score	1.32	0.50	0.70	–0.33

Early development of the model suggested that a decline in the score in excess of 40% would indicate that substantial changes had taken place in the financial health of a company. This has been modified over the years to examine other movements, especially if they are the result of a change to one of the five component ratios.

In this case, we don't have to use a calculator. We can see that a decline in excess of 40% has occurred in the period 2003/04 and in the period 2005/06. The model punishes any increase in borrowings. Should the subsequent activity of a company benefit from these borrowings then the score will improve. However, many companies do not benefit from an increase in borrowings. We will check this out in a later section when we interpret changes in the gearing ratios. Similarly, in 2005/06 there is a substantial decline in profitability and this will be examined in the next section.

6. Profitability ratios

In this section we will use the analysis in *Table 7.11* to compare the results obtained by four different specifications for a profitability ratio. These are:

1. Profit before tax (PBT) expressed as a percentage of total assets.
    This is the preferred method when interpreting changes in profitability ratios year-on-year. It does not allow interest paid to be added back since this should only apply when comparing one company against another, i.e. to remove the effect of differences in gearing, one company to another. It also takes total assets as the denominator. In this case an increase in total assets will require, all things being equal, an increase in profit before tax and vice versa.

2   The second option takes profit before tax expressed as a percentage of total assets less current liabilities.

The same numerator as the first option but a different denominator. Total assets less current liabilities is the favoured option in the UK but suffers from its lack of robustness with respect to current liabilities. For example, an increase in short-term borrowings will not require a corresponding increase in profits for a company still to be as profitable. Also, a movement from short-term borrowings to long-term borrowings will reduce profitability. It can be seen that the practice of deducting short-term borrowings from total assets severely affects the profitability of a company.

3.   The third option takes profit before tax and before the payment of interest (PBIT) expressed as a percentage of total assets less current liabilities.

This is the favoured profitability ratio used in the UK. It can be seen that it suffers from:

i.   Adding back interest payable for the numerator and,

ii.   Deducting current liabilities from total assets for the denominator.

4.   The fourth option takes profit before tax and before the payment of interest (PBIT) expressed as a percentage of net assets (total assets less current liabilities less long-term loans).

This ratio has a number of disagreeable features and will tend to overstate profitability.

In *Table 7.11*, it can be seen that the first option shows a substantial decrease in profitability for the period 2006. It is caused mainly by a decrease in the profit margin (profit before tax expressed as a percentage of sales). What causes a decrease in the profit margin? Either a decrease in income (selling prices) and/or an increase in costs. From the cost analysis statement, *Table 7.9*, it was seen that there was a decrease in the incremental revenues (income) for the period, and a substantial increase in costs.

The cost analysis statement provides us with the explanations for the decline in profitability. This is backed up with the statement in the case study that the decline in profitability was: 'a loss of margin in overseas core business, substantial start–up losses in *Green and Gillies* and a sharp increase in interest charges'. Also:

'the reduction in margin can be attributed to the fact that, as sterling based manufacturer, the group has passed the point where they can raise prices to their customers to compensate for the effects on an overvalued pound, particularly in their most important market, North America'.

While this may be true, it does not explain the substantial increase in staff costs, £35.3 million in 2005/06, nor the increase in operating leases and hire charges of £15.1 million for the similar period.

It is interesting to note that the ratio of revenues divided by total assets is fairly constant over the period, unlike the second and third option where the corresponding ratio fluctuates from year to year with an overall increase.

Table 7.11   Profitability ratios

	2003	2004	2005	2006
First option (preferred):				
Profit before tax ÷ total assets %	18.6	14.7	11.2	–0.7
Profit before tax ÷ revenues %	13.1	11.5	8.0	–0.5
Sales ÷ total assets	1.41	1.28	1.39	1.37
Second option:				
Profit before tax ÷ (TA – CL) %	28.0	28.2	16.0	–2.0
Profit before tax ÷ revenues %	13.1	11.5	8.0	–0.5
Revenues ÷ (TA – CL)	2.13	2.46	1.99	3.74
Third option:				
PBIT ÷ (TA – CL) %	29.7	31.2	20.0	8.9
PBIT ÷ revenues %	13.9	12.7	10.0	2.4
Revenues ÷ (TA – CL)	2.13	2.46	1.99	3.74
Fourth option:				
PBIT ÷ net assets %	34.7	34.6	31.7	9.7
PBIT ÷ revenues %	13.9	12.7	10.0	2.4
Revenues ÷ net assets	2.50	2.73	3.16	4.07

In *Table 7.11*, it can be seen that the second, third and fourth options tend to overstate profitability, especially the fourth option. In the second and third option, the ratio of revenues divided by total assets less current liabilities increases from £1.99 to £3.74 for the period 2005/06. This means that either revenues has increased and/or total assets less current liabilities has decreased. Reviewing the basic data shows that revenues increased by 17.5%, while total assets less current liabilities decreased by 37.4%; the result being an increase from £1.99 to £3.74. This does not make sense. Further examination shows that current liabilities increased from £163.9 million to £409.5 million, mainly due to an increase in bank overdraft from £24.4 million to £257.2 million. Here we have a perfect example of changes in short-term financing affecting profitability.

The third option has all the problems just highlighted plus the extra 'benefit' from adding back any interest payments to the profit figure. In this option the company is still 'seen' to be making a profit. How can this be? The calculation requires that the loss before tax of £4.7 million is adjusted by adding back £26 million of interest payable; this produces a 'profit figure' for the numerator of £30.8 million!

The fourth option suffers from much of that contained in option two and three. However, because it also deducts long-term loans, it does not fall into the trap of movements between short and long-term borrowing. This meagre benefit does not overcome its major shortcoming of grossly overstating profitability. In this particular option it can be seen that profitability was relatively steady for the three years 2003 to 2005.

Here we must return to the real world and agree with *Horngren* that profitability should be measured on operating assets (i.e. total assets) irrespective of how they have been financed – the first option.

7. Working capital ratios / liquidity ratios

Working capital, or liquidity ratios, attempt to give an indication of a company's ability to pay its way in the short and medium-term. The medium-term is taken to mean up to one year, while short-term is taken to mean up to 13 weeks, i.e. 3 months. All working capital ratios should be compared against trends year-on-year and/or industry averages. Working capital ratios correspond to the working capital cycle of a company and represent the flow of goods/services through a business. The main items comprise inventory, trade receivables, cash and trade payables. Financial controls should certainly exist for the first three items.

The current ratio, (current assets divided by current liabilities) considers the whole of the working capital cycle and gives an indication of a company's ability to pay its way in the medium-term.

The liquid, or acid test, ratio takes current assets, deducts inventories then divides the result by current liabilities. It attempts to give an indication of a company's ability to pay its way in the short-term. Many academic writers suggest that this is a 'more stringent' ratio than the current ratio simply because it deducts stock. This is not the case in practice. The liquid ratio, in its present form, suffers from movements in bank overdraft. For example, if bank overdraft increases and it is used (correctly) to finance a proportion of current assets, then the ratio is unlikely to change. This begs the question "Has there been a change in short-term liquidity?"

The alternative ratio, know as cover for trade payables, takes current assets, deducts inventories and bank overdraft then divides the result by trade payables. Research shows this to be more responsive to changes in short-term liquidity than the liquid ratio.

The final two ratios examine separate components of the working capital cycle. Cost of sales divided by inventory, gives the average inventory turn. Here, the higher the better. Trade receivables divided by average weekly (or daily) revenues, give the average debtor collection period. It would appear that the lower the ratio, the better. However, the simple fact of reducing the amount of credit allowed to its customers might result in a company losing some or many of its customers.

Table 7.12 Working capital or 'liquidity' ratios

	2003	2004	2005	2006
Current ratio:				
Current assets ÷ current liabilities	1.54	1.15	1.85	0.98
Liquid ratio:				
Liquid assets ÷ current liabilities	0.43	0.26	0.46	0.22
Cover for trade payables:				
(LA – BO) ÷ trade payables	0.54	–0.58	0.47	–1.13
Cost of sales ÷ inventory	1.4	1.2	1.4	1.3
Trade receivables x 52 ÷ revenues	3.7	4.0	4.3	4.8

The working capital cycle ratios for *Polly Ester Holdings plc* are heavily influenced by substantial movements in short and long-term borrowings. In this case, the best way to interpret the current ratio is to ignore the movements in the intervening years, simply take the total movement from 2003 to 2006, i.e. 1.54 to 0.98. A substantial decline in the company's ability to pay its way in the medium term. The main cause of this being the increase in bank overdraft.

In this example, the liquid, or acid test, ratio seems to follow similar movements to the current ratio. Here the ratio is difficult to interpret.

The 'cover for trade payables' ratio gives a clear interpretation. It takes current assets, deducts inventories and bank overdraft to show the amount trade payables are covered. In this example, in 2003, trade payables are covered 54 pence in the pound, while in 2004 the cover for trade payables is negative 58 pence in the pound. In 2005 another cover for trade payables of 47 pence in the pound, then in 2006 a negative of £1.13 in the pound.

The first of the remaining two ratios is known as stock turn, i.e. cost of sales divided by stock. The ideal for the ratio – the higher the better. For *Polly Ester Holding plc* this ratio is fairly stable, between 1.4 and 1.2 times. If we take the 2006 value of 1.3, this means that the company turned its stock over 1.3 times on average per year. Or another way of looking at it is 52 divided by 1.3 gives 40 weeks stockholding (on average). This would be considered very high stockholding, typical stockholding for a retailer might be 10 to 12 weeks. With a inventory holding of £314.4 million in 2006 and a revised inventory turn of 2.6 times this would give 20 weeks inventory holding and release £157.2 million from inventory for alternative use, perhaps in reducing borrowings.

The final ratio, known as the debtor collection period, trade receivables multiplied by 52 then divided by revenues shows an increase. The size of this ratio is influenced by the trading environment the company finds itself in, i.e. it must provide similar levels of credit to its customers compared to its competitors. For *Polly Ester Holdings plc* the ratio increases from an average 3.7 weeks to 4.8 weeks over the period. This means that the company is allowing its debtors a further 1.1 weeks at average weekly revenues, i.e. £889.8 divided by 52 times 1.1 gives £18.8 million.

Taking the stock and debtor ratios together it should be possible to reduce the working capital by approximately £176 million and in turn reduce bank overdraft which in turn would reduce interest payable and increase profit before taxation.

8. Gearing ratios

There are good gearing ratios but there are also gearing ratios that are not sufficiently robust. Quite simply, gearing is the relationship between borrowings (interest bearing debt) and equity (the shareholders interest in the company). In *Table 7.13* we show the good ratios first. These are:

1. **The borrowing ratio**. This takes total borrowings and divides the result by equity to produce a ratio. Where the result is less than 0.5 a company would be considered to be low geared. Where the result is greater than 1.0 a company would be considered to be high geared. However, these figures are rather arbitrary. More importantly, the analyst should consider the movements in the ratio year-on-year.

2. **Income gearing**. The first gearing ratio gives an indication of the level of gearing. The income gearing ratio gives an indication on whether a company can afford that level of gearing. The ratio takes interest payable and expresses it as a percentage of profit before taxation plus interest payable. In effect it is the mirror of the traditional interest cover ratio. The rule-of-thumb for the interest cover ratio is that interest payments should be covered by profits before taxation and interest, at least four times. For our income gearing ratio this translates to 25% being the benchmark.

And the gearing ratios that are not sufficiently robust:

3. The third gearing ratio, debt expressed as a percentage of equity plus debt, is a particularly bad ratio. It ranks with bad computer viruses and should not be used in any commercial system. Debt is taken to mean the total of current liabilities plus long-term loans. Closer examination of the ratio will show that debt is included both in the numerator and the denominator. This means that debt could increase ten thousand fold and the figure would not exceed 100%. This ratio is commonly used in published accounts in their five year summaries (a document which is not subject to audit verification).

4. The fourth gearing ratio suffers again from its construction and is another bad ratio. It takes long-term borrowings and expresses these as a percentage of equity. This might work for many well managed companies, but for those companies in serious financial difficulties, the results are simply misleading. Companies in difficulty quickly find out that there is no distinction between short and long-term borrowings. When things get tough the majority of long-term borrowings suddenly become short-term bank overdrafts (with the banks taking security on the assets for continued support). With this ratio, which only recognises long-term borrowings for gearing, it could show that a company is low geared when in fact it is at its limits, or has exceeded its limits, at the bank(s).

Table 7.13   Gearing ratios

	2003	2004	2005	2006
Borrowing ratio:				
Borrowing ÷ equity	0.24	0.55	0.63	1.22
Income gearing:				
Interest payable ÷ P.B.I.T. %	5.5	9.6	19.9	122.4
Third gearing ratio:				
Debt ÷ (equity + debt) %	42	52.6	54.8	65.6
Fourth gearing ratio:				
LTL ÷ equity %	12.7	8.9	52.8	3.9

In *Table 7.13* the first two ratios, the borrowing ratio and income gearing ratio show:

1.   The borrowing ratio moves from low gearing in 2003, through medium gearing in 2004 and 2005, then into high gearing in 2006. The point here is that the fast movement from low to high gearing is often not accompanied by directors who can 'cope' with the increased demands and personal interest shown by their bank or bankers.

2.   The income gearing ratio shows that while gearing was increasing, for the period 2003 to 2005, the company could afford it. However, in 2006 'the roof fell in' when profits were reduced to losses and the income gearing moved to 122%. Here, the company could not afford this level of gearing. Two options, reduce the level of borrowings to an acceptable level and/or increase the level of profits. Both are extremely difficult to achieve when a company is in such a difficult position.

The *Polly Ester* case provides a good example of the deficiencies in the popular gearing ratios shown below.

3.   A brief examination of the third gearing ratio quickly shows its shortcomings. It does not differentiate to any significant degree, the level of gearing in 2003 compared to that in 2006. Movements from 42% to 65.6% simply fail to provide adequate information on the real movements, i.e. total borrowings increasing from £49.6 million in 2003 to £265.8 million in 2006.

4.   The fourth gearing ratio also fails to provide adequate information. If we were to believe the calculated ratios, it actually shows a decrease from 12.7% in 2003 to 3.9% in 2006.

These results obtained from ratios three and four above compare with other similar companies under research.

9. Employee ratios

Employee ratios must rank amongst the easiest of all ratios to calculate and interpret. Many apparently successful companies have used employee ratios to manage their business. This can lead to a number of unsatisfactory decisions, e.g. increasing the number of consultants since they do not appear on the denominator of the ratio, but they do cost more than a comparable full-time employee.

The only word of caution when using these types of ratios is to ensure that the number of employees shown in the denominator of the ratio is expressed in terms of full-time equivalents. Apart from that, you simply pick a figure, divide it by the number of employees and you have a ratio.

In *Table 7.14* we show examples of five employee based ratios. These ratios are selected in order to verify our analysis so far.

The first two ratios focus on the trading activity, i.e. revenues per employee and profit per employee. Ideally, we would want to see both ratios increasing at a steady rate. For example, as revenues increased we would expect an increase in the number of employees. Similarly, given an increase in revenues per employee year-on-year, we would expect to see a corresponding increase in profit per employee – or slightly better.

The next two ratios provide a view to the expansion of a business. Non-current assets per employee show whether or not a company is expanding through the purchase of non-current assets (e.g. purchase of new equipment), or whether it is expanding through the use of more labour (not the favoured approach these days). The second ratio shows the expansion of borrowings and can be viewed as a simple gearing ratio. It also shows whether an expansion in non-current assets is being financed through borrowing.

The last ratio, staff costs per employee highlights one of the major costs in most companies. For this ratio we would expect to see a gradual increase perhaps in line with inflation.

Finally, do be aware that the acquisition or disposal of parts of a business can have a substantial effect on employee ratios. For example, if a company made a major acquisition of a high tech business, we would expect staff costs per employee to increase in the year of acquisition and beyond.

Table 7.14 *Employee ratios*

	2003 £	2004 £	2005 £	2006 £
Revenues per employee	89,177	87,081	102,006	112,012
Profit per employee	11,715	9,975,	8,185	–598
Non-current assets per employee	29,897	30,359	32,220	30,508
Borrowings per employee	8,628	17,632,	20,313	33,459
Staff costs per employee	27,199	27,301	29,440	31,959

In *Table 7.14* we can see that the employee ratios are broadly in line with the analysis and interpretation performed so far.

Here we can see that the ratio of revenues per employee has increased, though profit per employee has reduced. Action to increase profit per employee would include, an increase in the selling price and/or a reduction in costs, e.g. a reduction in the cost of sales and/or distribution, selling and administration costs.

The ratio of non-current assets per employee shows an increase in the first three years followed by a decrease in the final year. The decrease in the final year might be caused by the disposal of *Green and Gillies*, with the non-current assets of that company now removed along with its employees, combined with an overall increase in employees. In this case, the ratio should have remained constant. It failed to do so because the number of employees actually increased. We find that there was a modest increase in non-current assets from £239.2 to £242.4 million, with a substantial increase in the number of employees 7,424 to 7,944.

The final ratio shows increases in staff costs per employee including inflation. Taken together with the increase in the number of employees for the period 2005/06 produces additional staff costs of £35.3 million.

10. Non–financial indicators

We have left the non-financial indicators until last. In practice, they would be firmly embodied during the data collection and analysis phases. Non-financial indicators might include:

1. Many of the strategy models, for example:

   a. Strengths, weaknesses, opportunities and threats (SWOT);

   b. Political, economic, social, technological (PEST);

   c. Environmental influences (see *Johnson and Scholes*);

    d.   *Porter's* five forces;

    e.   *Porter's* value chain and competitive advantage.

2.   A diary of events, see *Figure 7.2,* and our simplified version in *Table 7.7.*

3.   *Argenti's* failure framework which has its focus on defects, mistakes and symptoms. Still the best framework around.

4.   The careful use of external material both on the company and it competitors.

The final non-financial indicator is left to the end, simply to make a strong case for the inclusion of such data. In *Table 7.7,* we showed the movement of directors. In this case a number of directors resigned in 2004, 2005 and 2006. It is important to verify the positions of these directors including their replacements.

In the *Polly Ester* case we find that Mr. Philip Peters who was the finance director resigned on the 20th December 2005 (eleven days before the financial year end). During the whole of the period 2006, the company appeared to operate without a finance director. In fact, Mr H. Waterman, the new finance director was not appointed until the 15th April 2007, some 16 months later.

From the analysis and interpretation of the case we have seen that 2006 was a critical year in the life of this company. Substantial over-trading, combined with financing expansion mainly through borrowings, combined with escalation of basic costs, combined with an inability to pass on costs to customers resulted in a downturn of the companys' fortunes. Would things have been different had there been a finance director in post during this vital period? We think so, but the main point here is to provide a good example on the use and interpretation of non–financial indicators. They do have a bearing.

11. Summary

The analysis and interpretation of the *Polly Ester* case study is based solely on information contained in the published accounts. Depending on the requirements, we would tend to collect other material from a variety of sources on both the company and its competitors.

In the introduction to this chapter we set out to demonstrate the strengths and weaknesses of financial ratios. This has been achieved:

1.   With the preparation and interpretation of a simplified diary of events, showing movements in revenues, non-current assets and directors.

2.   With the analysis and interpretation provided by the common size statement and the cost analysis statement. The former providing an easy access to major movements, while the latter an explanation of changes in income and costs.

3. In *Robertson's* 1983 ratio model, we showed how it can be used to highlight where changes have taken place in the financial health of a company. Traditional ratio analysis techniques can then be used to find the root cause.

4. In the sections covering profitability, liquidity and gearing we have provided explanations of each ratio, the strengths and/or weaknesses and our suggestions on which ratios to use to build a robust analysis and interpretation.

5. The employee ratios, follow the practice of "keep it simple and straightforward" (KISS). Easy to prepare, easy to interpret.

6. Non-financial indicators provide additional content and depth to any analysis, especially the models used in strategy, *Argenti's* framework and the diary of events. We saw the value of this in the movement of directors, especially the resignation of the finance director in December 2005.

Appendix A – Sources of company information

The following are examples of sources of company information which can be found in most university/college libraries, local reference libraries, and in some company libraries. The list of necessity is selective. However, you should experiment by using any library, to which you have access, to find out details about a particular company or topic.

KOMPASS (is now online)

At http://www.kompass.co.uk you can search on the following criteria:
1. Products and services; 2. Company name; 3. Trade names; 4. Executives.

Kompass is also available for a number of other countries.

WHO OWN'S WHOM   (annual publication in two volumes)

Use this resource to find out: 1. Who is the immediate or ultimate parent; 2. How many enterprises belong to the same group; 3. Whether there are any sister companies; or, 4. Company associates and affiliates.

KEY BRITISH ENTERPRISES   (annual publication)

Key British Enterprises provides up-to-date information on the UK's top 54,000 companies. Companies are selected on the basis that they meet one of the following: 1. 80 or more employees; 2. Revenue in excess of £8 million; 3. Total assets in excess of £30 million.

DIRECTORY OF DIRECTORS   (annual publication in two volumes)

Volume I is an alphabetical list of the directors of the principal public and private companies in the UK, giving the names of the companies where they are directors.

Volume II is an alphabetical list of the principal public and private companies in the UK, giving the names of their directors, together with limited financial data for some companies.

COMPANY REGISTRATION OFFICE

The Company Registration Office, Crown Way, Maindy, Cardiff, CF14 3UZ, holds certain information on companies on microfiche. Public limited companies are required to lodge their annual return not later than 7 months after their year end, limited companies 10 months.

They also have online access at http://www.companieshouse.gov.uk

FAME (financial analysis made easy)

A database containing company information. It contains detailed information on 500,000 UK and Irish companies, and summarised information on an additional 1.2 million companies. (1.7 million companies in total).

For each company there is up to 10 years of historical information. A company record typically contains: income statement, balance sheet, cash flow statement, ratios and trends, SIC codes and activity information, credit score and rating, lists of directors, shareholders, subsidiaries and holding companies, registered and trading addresses, and details of miscellaneous information that has been filed at Companies House.

The software allows you to search for companies that fulfil your criteria (by over 100 criteria). You can also compare companies against each other and present your results in graphs and tables. The integral analysis software is very sophisticated. Information can be downloaded for further analysis or marketing. You can also use 'Addin' functionality to access FAME from within Excel or export data directly into tailor-made templates.

INTERNET

There are many good sites on the internet providing UK company information. By its very nature the internet is continually changing and evolving, therefore, many links no longer work. We now list a few useful sites, some included just for their links.

http://www.northcote.co.uk/   Access to a large selection of annual reports. Especially useful for copies of reports from previous years.

http://www.carol.co.uk   Similar to the above. Requires free registration before gaining access to reports.

http://ft.ar.wilink.com   Obtain copies of the most recent annual reports. Can either download a pdf or request mail delivery. Can select reports for a number of companies.

http://finance.uk.yahoo.com/   A good site, but most useful for collecting share price trends for the last five years.

http://www.bized.ac.uk/   This is a useful site that provides material for those studying undergraduate and masters level courses. Worth a regular visit.

http://www.icaew.co.uk/library/   The Institute of Chartered Accountants for England and Wales. For those seeking that little bit extra to support their studies.

Exercise 7.1

The following data has been collected for the TrustMe Company:

	2005	2006
Non-current assets	42,000	44,000
Inventories	40,000	45,000
Current assets	78,000	79,000
Bank overdraft	8,000	26,000
Trade payables	25,000	30,000
Current liabilities	36,000	56,000
Equity	59,000	55,000
Long-term loans	25,000	12,000
Revenues	155,000	175,000
Profit before tax	6,000	4,000

REQUIRED:

Calculate *Robertson's* 1983 ratio model;

Carry out further ratio analysis from the results.

Exercise 7.2

Collect the annual report and accounts for a defence, retail or manufacturing company for the last three years;

Carry out a suitable financial analysis using the techniques covered in *Chapters 6 and 7*. Non-financial analysis should also be covered but included in an Appendix to your report.

CHAPTER EIGHT

COST ACCOUNTING

LEARNING OBJECTIVES

When you have finished studying this chapter and completed the exercises, you should be able to:

❑ Describe the main elements of costs and the various classifications of costs;

❑ Calculate overhead recovery rates and prepare product costs using absorption costing techniques;

❑ Prepare product costs with materials and labour, and absorption of variable and fixed overheads;

❑ Describe and calculate costs using Activity Based Costing.

8.1   Introduction

Costs may often represent a significant proportion of an organisation's income and, therefore, are an important area to be able to manage. For example, from an examination of the 2005 report and accounts of the *European Aeronautic Defence and Space* it can be seen that 80.5% of the group's net revenue is accounted for by operating expenses (92.3% for *Tesco's* in 2006).

Cost management is a declared priority of the group, a point made in repeated Chairperson's statements. It is particularly important because profit depends upon knowing the cost of doing business. However, there is a major problem in knowing whether the costs incurred are really warranted. Are they really necessary? Could they be avoided? How can we tell?

Cost management is associated with cost accounting. The management of costs within an organisation may well be influenced by the way in which they have been accounted for. At its simplest, the concern with cost accounting is to determine what it costs to produce a good or provide a service. This can be very straightforward in a one product or one service organisation where all costs can be clearly identified with the product/service being provided. However, very few such organisations exist and in a multi-product or multi-service environment procedures have to be found and used if costs are to be identified with that which is produced or provided.

If you refer to most cost accounting texts you will discover that procedures have been developed primarily in manufacturing organisations to deal with the cost accounting problems of different types of operation. Thus, you will encounter descriptions and discussions about cost accounting techniques and approaches for organisations producing bespoke one-off products, and those dealing with batch operations, process operations and long-term contracts. These techniques will focus upon the various elements of cost like labour and materials and the problems of accounting for raw materials, work in progress and finished goods.

What is important for you to understand about cost accounting is that it is not a science, and that considerable judgement is typically employed. In accounting for costs, particularly indirect costs, considerable judgement is employed in the process of apportionment and absorption to products and/or services. How such judgement based apportionment and absorption is applied we review in section 8.4. Thereafter, we will consider one important development in cost accounting, and more importantly cost management known as Activity Based Costing, or ABC. This approach has a claimed advantage over traditional methods, because it attempts to relate the costs of an organisation to those activities responsible for generating them.

8.2   Elements of cost

Originally cost accounting methods were developed to provide ways of accumulating costs and charging these to units of product or service in order to establish stock valuations. These were principally related to historical calculations, but the advantages of using these methods for planning were soon realised and cost accounting was extended to the areas of budgeting and decision analysis.

Almost every decision made by management has an affect on cost, and a good understanding of the types of costs and how they are used for cost control and cost management is important for sound financial management.

Total costs of a product or service comprise three main elements:

1.   Materials – the cost of materials consumed in making the product or providing the service;

2.   Labour – the cost of wages and salaries of employees, who are involved in producing the product or providing the service;

3.   Expenses – the cost of other expenses; which will include occupancy costs, power, depreciation, interest charges, telecoms, etc.

As we shall see later in this chapter there are different possible treatments of these three basic elements, arising from differing views of how they should be analysed and reported, which allow for alternative views of the 'cost' of a product or service.

8.3   Classifications of cost

This expression covers the way in which costs can be grouped, or classified, for analysis and reporting. A very common usage is the grouping of costs by function, e.g. splitting the costs of the organisation into production, selling, distribution, administration, etc. These can be further subdivided into, say, departmental costs within each function, and is a system commonly used in the budgeting process.

Two other important classifications of cost are:

1.   Direct/indirect costs;

2.   Variable/fixed costs;

and an understanding of these is important as they are linked to two methods of costing, absorption costing and marginal costing, which you will meet later in this chapter.

1   Direct/Indirect costs

A direct cost, is a cost that can be traced in full to the product, service or function, etc., that is being costed; whereas an indirect cost is a cost that has been incurred in the making of a product, providing a service, etc., but that cannot be traced in full to the product, service or function.

As an example, if a management consultant is currently working for three clients, the actual time spent on each client can be identified and charged directly to the individual client's account, but the cost of the administrative facilities, such as, say, occupancy costs cannot be traced directly to each client, These are indirect costs, which have to be shared on some basis between the clients to arrive at a total client cost.

Materials costs, labour costs and expenses can be classified as a direct cost or an indirect cost. When the three basic elements of cost are classified in this way the total of the direct costs is known as prime cost and the total of the indirect costs is known as overhead. Total cost is the sum of prime cost and overhead.

2   Variable/Fixed costs

This classification is based on a basic principle of cost behaviour, which assumes that as activity increases so usually will cost. It will usually cost more to send 10 faxes than to send 5. It will usually cost more to produce 150 cars than to produce 120. However, not all costs will increase in the same way or by the same amount. A definition of cost behaviour is:

"The way in which costs of output are affected by fluctuations in the level of activity." (CIMA official terminology)

Costs which tend to vary directly with the volume of output are variable costs. The most obvious of these is direct materials, and the relationship between cost and volume can be shown graphically as follows:

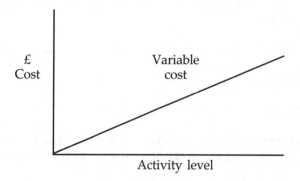

Costs which tend to be unaffected by increases or decreases in volume of output, and as such will be incurred regardless of output volume, are fixed costs. Examples of these would be rent and salaries. Of course in the long-term all costs are likely to change – the rent of the premises and employees' salaries would inevitably rise, but they do not alter as a direct result of making one more item. Graphically, a fixed cost would look like this:

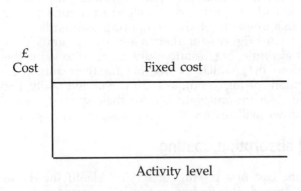

However, many items of a fixed cost nature are fixed within a particular activity level. For example, it could be that a number of administrators could handle a certain level of purchase orders, but beyond that certain level another administrator would have to be employed. This type of situation gives rise to what are called, stepped fixed costs, and also introduces the concept of the 'relevant range', that is the activity level over which the cost is fixed. A stepped fixed cost situation such as that described would appear graphically as follows:

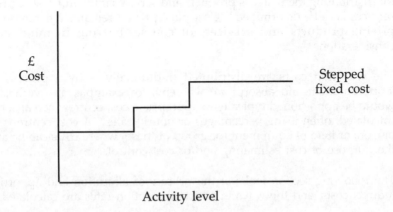

Some costs include parts that are variable and fixed. Such costs are usually called mixed, semi-variable or semi-fixed costs. Common examples are telephone and electricity charges, where there is a fixed rental element and a variable portion depending upon usage.

8.4 Techniques of costing

Costing is undertaken in organisations for the purpose of providing management with the information they need to be able to plan, control and make the necessary decisions. As such it has evolved, and continues to evolve, providing a 'toolkit' of methods and techniques that can be selected by management to suit their analytical and reporting purposes. There is no 'regulatory framework' requiring companies to produce costing statements etc., but some requirements of the accounting standards do demand that organisations prepare figures for their statutory accounts using particular techniques. For example, organisations are required to value their inventory at 'full production cost', which means that for their annual accounts they must use absorption costing techniques. However, internally, they are free to choose the most relevant and valuable for their type of operation. In the following section we will review the main costing techniques.

1. Overhead absorption costing

In determining the cost of a product or service, identifying the direct costs is normally straighforward. It is finding an equitable way of apportioning indirect costs (e.g. depreciation, heating and lighting) to products or services. Overhead absorption costing is the traditional method and is concerned with the process of charging an appropriate amount of indirect costs to products or services.

Indirect costs, allocation and apportionment

Organisations of all types incur indirect costs in the form of costs that cannot readily be identified with individual products or services. Given that such costs may well be a significant proportion of total costs, some means has to be found for distributing them across products and services if the full cost of products and services is to be determined. 'Cost plus' pricing remains a common method of pricing products and services, of course, bearing in mind key market considerations.

The way that costs are distributed traditionally is by a process known as 'apportionment and absorption' whereby, for example, an overhead like rent would be apportioned typically to appropriate cost centres then absorption rates calculated, often using percentages or hourly rates. A cost centre is a location, person, or item of equipment (or group of these) where costs can be attached for the purpose of cost estimating and/or cost control.

The following section looks at the process of allocation and apportionment of indirect costs, and the ways in which absorption rates are calculated and used.

1. Example

The *PVY Company* has two production departments, and, a raw material and finished goods store.

The budgeted costs for the last quarter of 200X are as follows:

	£
Rent	25,000
Maintenance to plant	18,000
Depreciation of plant	48,000
Lighting and heating	10,000
Supervision	13,000
Fire insurance	3,000
Power	15,000
Personnel services	12,000
General expenses	16,000

Additional information has been collected for use in allocating and/or apportioning the budgeted costs to departments.

	Dept. A	Dept. B	Store	Total
Number of employees	11	7	2	20
Area (square metres)	1,700	300	400	2,400
Machine hours (for quarter)	1,750	370	0	2,120
Direct labour hours (weekly)	460	308	87	855
Plant value	£560,000	£100,000	0	£660,000
Value of inventory used	£10,200	£1,800	0	£12,000
kW Hours, metered	125,000	25,000	0	150,000

The Factory Manager has given an estimate for supervision costs being the time spent in the two departments.

Department A   £10,000
Department B   £3,000

Complete an overhead analysis sheet showing clearly the basis used for apportionment. (Round all figures to the nearest hundred)

Table 8.1   Overhead analysis sheet

Budgeted costs	Basis of apportionment	Total £	Dept A £	Dept B £	Store £
Rent	Floor area	25,000	17,700	3,100	4,200
Maintenance to plant	Mach. hours	18,000	14,900	3,100	0
Depreciation of plant	Plant value	48,000	40,700	7,300	0
Lighting and heating	Floor area	10,000	7,100	1,200	1,700
Supervision	Tech.estimate	13,000	10,000	3,000	0
Fire insurance	Floor area	3,000	2,100	400	500
Power	kW Hours	15,000	12,500	2,500	0
Personnel services	No. employees	12,000	6,600	4,200	1,200
General expenses	Labour hours	16,000	8,600	5,800	1,600
		160,000	120,200	30,600	9,200
Service dept. (Store)	Inventory value	0	7,800	1,400	–9,200
		160,000	128,000	32,000	0

Example for the apportionment of rent to Department A:

$$\text{Department A} \quad = \quad \frac{£25,000}{2,400} \quad \times \quad 1,700$$

$$= \quad £17,700$$

The bases for apportionment, shown in *Table 8.1,* are used simply to illustrate the process. Apportionment is an art. It is possible to question the use of floor area as a means for apportioning the costs of items such as rent, lighting, heating and fire insurance, in fact it is possible to present a good case against any apportionment base.

Consider the case of using floor area for lighting and heating. Clearly, there is a requirement for different forms of lighting and heating in a variety of work situations few of which would correspond to floor area.

Similarly, consider the case of using machine hours to apportion the maintenance of plant. This suggests that the more a machine is used the more maintenance will be required and vice versa. Therefore, if we use a machine infrequently it will not require much maintenance! It also assumes that all machines cost the same and all are a similar age.

2. Overheads, absorption rates

Once the overhead allocation and apportionment process has been completed, the total overhead cost for a part of the business can be calculated by simple addition. For example, the total overhead for Department B we calculated as being £16,000. We can now use this figure to determine a future unit charge-out rate by absorbing it over a number of bases. One common base is labour hours, such that if labour hours were 2,000 we would have an overhead absorption rate of £8 per labour hour (£16,000 ÷ 2,000). In costing future products we would charge overheads to them according to the number of labour hours. Therefore, if a product required two hours of labour, a charge of £16 for overheads (£8 x 2) would be made.

How this approach can be applied using different bases and the effect of different methods of absorption we illustrate by continuing our example:

The *PVY Company* has prepared a Production cost budget for the last quarter of 200X as follows: (amounts have been rounded to the nearest 1,000)

	£	£
Direct materials		40,000
Direct labour – Department A	72,000	
– Department B	28,000	
		100,000
Prime cost		140,000
Overheads – Department A	128,000	
– Department B	32,000	
		160,000
Production cost		300,000

Department A is a machine based department with a total of 1,750 machine hours budgeted during the quarter. The labour rate in the department has been set at £12.00 per hour.

Department B is a labour based department with a total of 4,000 labour hours budgeted during the quarter. The labour rate in the department has been set at £7.00 per hour.

We will calculate an overhead absorption rate using each of the following bases:

a. Percentage on direct materials.

b. Percentage on direct labour   –   Whole company

c. Percentage on direct labour   –   Department A

d. Percentage on direct labour   –   Department B

e. Machine hour rate   –   Department A

f. Labour hour rate   –   Department B

The calculation of absorption rates (also known as overhead recovery rates) requires that an overhead cost is divided by an agreed absorption base. We will now show the calculations for the most popular methods, and comment on each one. (round up a percentage to a whole number)

a. Percentage on direct materials

$$\frac{\text{Overheads}}{\text{Material costs}} \times 100 = \frac{£160,000}{£40,000} \times 100 = 400\%$$

The percentage on direct materials is a simple method. However, it is difficult to find a situation in which to use the method. The problem is that it can only be used in a single (including single quality) material environment. If it were used in a mixed material environment, products would absorb overheads on the basis of their material cost.

b. Percentage on direct labour – Whole company

$$\frac{\text{Overheads}}{\text{Labour costs}} \times 100 = \frac{£160,000}{£100,000} \times 100 = 160\%$$

The percentage on direct labour is also a simple method but unlike materials is widely used. In this example, overheads would be absorbed at 160% of the total labour cost for each product or service. The major problem with this method arises when there are different levels of labour costs in different departments or cost centres. In order to address this problem most companies calculate separate absorption rates for each department or cost centre.

An example is shown in c and d. It can be seen that instead of using 160% for the whole company, we would now use 178% absorption rate to recover overheads in Department A, and 115% absorption rate to recover overheads in Department B.

c. Percentage on direct labour – Department A

$$\frac{\text{Overheads}}{\text{Labour costs}} \times 100 = \frac{£128,000}{£72,000} \times 100 = 178\%$$

d. Percentage on direct labour – Department B

$$\frac{\text{Overheads}}{\text{Labour costs}} \times 100 = \frac{£32,000}{£28,000} \times 100 = 115\%$$

One of the most popular methods to absorb overheads is using the hourly rate. This method also requires that separate absorption rates are calculated for each department or cost centre. In this example, we would absorb overheads for Department A based on the number of machine hours required times the rate of £32 per machine hour. Similarly, if the product used labour hours in Department B, there would be an absorption of overheads based on the number of labour hours required times the rate of £4 per labour hour. See calculations below.

e. Machine hour rate – Department A

$$\frac{\text{Overheads}}{\text{Machine hours}} = \frac{£128,000}{1,750} = £73.14 \text{ per machine hour}$$

f. Labour hour rate – Department B

$$\frac{\text{Overheads}}{\text{Labour hours}} = \frac{£32,000}{4,000} = £8.00 \text{ per labour hour}$$

3. Overheads, comparison of absorption methods

We have described the calculation of absorption rates and commented on each. However, there still remains the question, 'What absorption method should we use?' We will complete this example by showing the effect of using each of the absorption methods on the production costs of two products. Each product comprises different proportions of materials and labour. The example will use the following data:

❑   The executives of the *PVY Company* are trying to agree the method to be used for absorbing overheads to products.

❑   The following information is available to calculate the prime costs for Products 101 and 102.

		Product 101 per unit	Product 102 per unit
Direct material cost		£11	£28
Direct labour hours	– Department A	4 hours	2 hours
	– Department B	3 hours	4 hours

For convenience, we now restate the direct labour rate which was used in the previous section.

Direct labour rate	– Department A	£12.00 per hour
	– Department B	£7.00 per hour

An estimate of machine hours for both products is as follows:

Machine hours (per 100 units)	Product 101	47 hours
	Product 102	15 hours

Using the information for Products 101 and 102, we will prepare a table to show the effect of using absorption methods based on materials, direct labour and hourly rates.   Costs will be calculated per 100 units.   (when calculating the overhead, round to the nearest £100)

In *Table 8.2*, we have taken the direct material cost for Product 101 and multiplied it by 100 (£11 x 100) to give £1,100. The direct labour cost is found by multiplying the direct labour hours per unit for Product 101 spent in Department A by 100 (4 hours x 100) to give 400 hours, then multiplying the hours by the direct labour hourly rate (400 hours x £12) to give £4,800. A similar calculation is performed for Department B. Finally, the direct material costs and the direct labour costs are added (£1,100 + £6,900) to give the prime cost of £8,000 for Product 101. Now check the calculations for Product 102.

Table 8.2   *Comparison of absorption methods*

		Cost per 100 units			
		Product 101		**Product 102**	
		£	£	£	£
Direct material			1,100		2,800
Direct labour:					
Dept. A (£12 p.h.)	400 hrs	4,800		200 hrs 2,400	
Dept. B (£7 p.h.)	300 hrs	2,100		400 hrs 2,800	
			6,900		5,200
Prime Cost			8,000		8,000
1. 400 % on Direct materials			4,400		11,200
			12,400		19,200

In this first example, we have multiplied the direct materials for each product by 400%. For Product 101 (£1,100 x 400%) to give the overheads of £4,400. Finally, we added the overhead to the prime cost (£4,400 + £8,000) to give the total production cost of £12,400. Similar calculations for Product 102 gives a total production cost of £19,200. Both costs are arithmetically accurate, but they are heavily influenced by the material cost and subsequent overhead absorption using materials.

2. 160% on Total labour	11,000		8,300
	19,000		16,300

When using a percentage on total labour the calculations are similar. In this case we use the total labour cost for Product 101, (£6,900 x 160%) to give the overheads of £11,000 and £8,300 for Product 102. You will notice the difference between the two methods, with Product 102 now lower, due to the direct labour costs.

3. 178% on Labour Dept. A	8,500		4,300
4. 115% on Labour Dept. B	2,400		3,200
	10,900		7,500
	18,900		15,500

When using individual absorption rates, we take the rate and multiply it by the direct labour cost for a department. For example, for Product 101 we take the direct labour cost of (£4,800 x 178%) to give £8,500 of overheads for Department A, then add the direct labour cost of (£2,100 x 115%) to give £2,400 of overheads for Department B. Total absorbed overheads for both departments amounting to £10,900. Similar calculations for Product 102 produce total absorbed overheads of £7,500. We discussed the problem of using a percentage on total labour in the previous section. We can now see the effect of using individual absorption rates for each department or cost centre.

5.	£73.14 M.hour Dept.A	47 hrs	3,400	15 hrs	1,100
6.	£8.00 L.hour Dept.B	300 hrs	2,400	400 hrs	3,200
			5,800		4,300
			13,800		12,300

In the final section, we have used the hourly rate method. If Product 101 requires 47 machine hours in Department A, the absorbed overhead is (47 hours x £73.14) which gives £3,400. Overheads are absorbed in Department B using direct labour hours, the overhead is (300 hours x £8.00) which gives £2,400. To complete the calculations we add the two overhead figures to give £5,800, then add in the prime cost of £8,000 to give £13,800.

The purpose of the above example is to demonstrate the differing ways in which the overhead <u>could</u> be attributed to products. The method applied should be that which most closely aligns overhead and product. Most commonly used are time-based methods, (i.e. labour hour, machine hour) although there is growing interest in using 'an activity base'. This is discussed in more detail in *Section 8.5*.

Before moving on to consider other techniques of costing, we will now look at the construction of a quotation for an order, which is based on absorption costing principles.

8.5   Example – Quotation for an order

Mouldit Ltd makes a range of products in expanded polystyrene (cups, trays, DIY materials etc.). The budget for the six months to 31st October 200X is as follows:

	£	£	£
Revenues			780,000
Polystyrene (20,000 kg)	200,000		
Direct labour (4,000 hours)	50,000		
Variable overhead	150,000		
Total variable costs		400,000	
Fixed overhead		250,000	
Total cost			650,000
Budgeted profit			130,000

You have been asked to quote for an order which is estimated to require 380 kg of polystyrene and 100 hours of direct labour.

The order is from a regular customer. The company applies normal absorption costing principles. Variable overhead is assumed to be related to direct labour hours, and fixed overhead and profit are based on a percentage of total variable cost and total cost respectively.

Table 8.3   Calculation of quote price

		£
Materials	380kg at £10.00 per kg	3,800
Labour	100 hours at £12,50 per hour	1,250
Variable overhead	100 hours at £37,50 per hour	3,750
Total variable costs		8,800
Fixed overhead	£8,800 x 62.5 ÷ 100	5,500
Total cost		14,300
Budgeted profit	£14,300 x 20 ÷ 100	2,860
Quote price		17,160

The steps to be taken in the calculation of the product cost/quote price are shown below:

1. Materials: Calculate the price per kilogram, i.e. £200,000 ÷ 20,000 kg = £10.00 per kg.

2. Labour: Calculate the labour hour rate, i.e. £50,000 ÷ 4,000 hours = £12,50 per labour hour.

3. Variable overhead: Calculate the variable overheads on a labour hour basis, i.e. variable overheads divided by labour hours = £150,000 ÷ 4,000 hours = £37.50 per labour hour.

    Please note, in 2. above, we have found that the labour hour rate is £12.50 per labour hour, while in 3. above, we have found that the variable overhead rate is £37.50 per labour hour. Therefore, for each hour worked we have to recover £12.50 to pay the wages plus £37.50 to cover our variable overheads.

4. Total variable cost is the sum of materials + labour + variable overheads, i.e. £3,800 + £1,250 + £3,750 = £8,800.

5. Fixed overhead: We are told that this will be recovered as a percentage of total variable cost. Therefore, we have to calculate this percentage, i.e. £250,000 ÷ £400,000 x 100 = 62.5%.

6. Total cost is the sum of total variable cost plus fixed overhead, i.e. £8,800 + £5,500 = £14,300.

7. Budgeted profit: We are told that budgeted profit will be added as a percentage of total cost, therefore, we have to calculate this percentage. Budgeted profit is £130,000 and total cost is (£250,000 + £400,000) = £650,000. Therefore, the percentage is £130,000 ÷ £650,000 x 100 = 20%.

8. The price to quote is the total cost plus the budgeted profit, i.e. £14,300 + £2,860 = £17.160.

In summary, in determining the cost of a product or service the direct costs are normally straightforward. It is the apportionment of overheads that provides the challenge. Overhead absorption costing is a mechanism to enable the total production cost, including overheads, to be identified with a product or service to enable management to more fully understand and appreciate the determinants of product/service cost and profitability. However, it does have its opponents. Concern about the 'traditional' methods of apportioning and absorbing overhead accurately, led to the original development of activity based costing (ABC) which is covered in the next section. Concern about the validity of apportioning fixed costs over products/services and including fixed costs in stock valuations led to the development of an alternative method of costing. This is marginal costing and will be reviewed in *Chapters 8 and 9*.

8.6 Activity based (costing) analysis

1. Introduction

Traditionally, the costing of products was associated with manufacturing organisations. Costing systems, decades ago, were required by companies that manufactured a narrow range of products where direct labour and materials were the dominant factory costs. For such organisations, overhead costs were relatively small and the distortions arising from overhead allocations were not significant.

We have illustrated how costs are apportioned to cost centres by applying judgement, for example rent and rates, on the basis of floor space occupied. Once all such overheads have been allocated, they could then be absorbed to products or services on the basis of labour hours.

Although such cost apportionment and absorption methods have been developed in manufacturing organisations they are not readily transferrable to the growing service sector. In services the relationship between costs and the activities from which costs arise is more problematic. It is this background which has led to the development of Activity Based Costing (ABC).

For financial service providers, like banks, activity-based costing has particular attractions because such organisations operate in a highly competitive environment and they incur a large amount of support overhead costs that cannot be directly assigned to specific cost objects. Furthermore, their products and customers differ significantly in terms of consuming overhead resources.

ABC systems assume that activities cause costs to be incurred and that products (or other selected cost objects, such as customers and branches in the case of a bank) consume activities in varying amounts. A link is made between activities and products by assigning the cost of activities to products based on an individual product's demand for each activity.

The development of an ABC system will involve the following:

1.   The identification of the key activities that take place in the organisation;

2.   The creation of a cost pool for each major activity;

3.   The assignment of costs to activity cost pools;

4.   The determination of the cost driver for each activity cost pool;

5.   The determination of the unit cost for each activity;

6.   The assignment of the costs of activities to selected cost objects (for example, products) according to the cost object's demand for each activity.

Stage 1 identifies the major activities performed in the enterprise. Activities are simply the tasks that people or machines perform in order to provide a product or service. For example, in retail banking this would correspond with processing a deposit, issuing a credit card, processing a cheque, setting up a loan, opening an account or processing monthly statements, and so on. In a support activity like a personnel department, activities would be recruitment, remuneration, training, union negotiations, personnel administration and staff welfare.

Stage 2 creates a cost pool for each activity.

Stage 3 costs are analysed and assigned to the appropriate activity pool. For example, the total cost of processing a deposit might constitute one activity cost pool in a retail bank for all deposit processing related costs, with separate cost pools being created for each type of deposit account, if different types of deposits consume resources differently. In a personnel department, recruitment may constitute an activity pool for recruitment related costs like advertising, interviewing, contracts, and induction.

Stage 4 then identifies the factors that influence the cost of a particular activity. The term 'cost driver' is used to describe the events or forces that are the significant determinants of the cost of the activities. For example, if the cost of processing deposits is generated by the number of deposits processed, then the number of deposits processed would represent the cost driver for deposit processing activities. In the case of a personnel department, the cost drivers would be staff recruited, staff retired, staff on payroll.

The cost driver selected for each cost pool should be the one that, as closely as possible, mirrors the consumption of the activities represented by the cost centre. Examples of cost drivers that might be appropriate for other retail banking activities include:

❑ Number of applications processed for setting up a loan;

❑ Number of statements mailed for processing monthly statements;

❑ Number of mortgage payments past due date for processing activities relating to mortgage arrears.

Stage 5 divides the cost traced to each activity cost pool by the total number of driver units, in order to calculate a cost per unit of activity.

Stage 6 finally, the cost of specific activities is traced to products (or services) according to their demand for the activities by multiplying unit activity costs by the quantity of each activity that a product consumes.

The total cost of a product or service is then found by adding the individual costs of the activities that are required to deliver the product or service. In other words, a product or service can be viewed as a bundle of activities. ABC focuses on the costing of these activities and the bundling of them into products, customers or any other cost objects.

ABC seeks to measure, as accurately as possible, those resources consumed by products or services, whereas traditional costing systems just allocate and apportion costs to products or services. The ABC approach seems to offer considerable advantages as can be seen if we reconsider our retail banking example. The traditional approach might allocate deposit transaction processing costs to customers, or different types of deposit accounts, on the basis of the number of customer accounts. This would distort product costs if deposit processing costs are driven by the number of transactions processed. Allocating cost according to the number of customers will lead to low value deposit accounts that involve numerous 'over-the-counter' transactions being under-costed, whereas high value long term savings accounts requiring very few transactions will be over-costed. In contrast, an ABC system would establish a separate cost centre for deposit processing activities, ascertain what causes the costs (that is, determine the appropriate cost driver, such as the number of transactions processed) and assign costs to products on the basis of a product's demand for the activity.

2. How is ABC applied?

Activity-based profitability analysis is best thought of in hierarchical terms. First, the costs of undertaking the various activities should be listed, and those that can be analysed by products should be deducted from revenues, so that a contribution to profits can be derived for each product. Products in our retail banking example are deposit accounts and loans, and an example of a specific cost would be an advertising campaign aimed at one specific type of loan.

The next level is the product line or product group. For example, deposit accounts and loans may represent some of the individual products within the product line. Although some expenses can be traced to them individually, some of those incurred are common to all products within the product line and are not identifiable with individual products. These expenses are function, or product-line-sustaining expenses and are traced to product lines but not to individual products within the line.

Not all costs can be readily assigned to products. Some costs are common and joint to all products. These costs are called business or 'facility-sustaining expenses' and include such items as top management salaries. When deducted as a lump sum from the total of all the profit margins from all the individual product lines yield the overall profit of the enterprise or a particular strategic business unit.

3. Example

The following example is set in a manufacturing environment and will trace the factory overhead costs through two components. First, we will calculate the factory overhead costs allocated using traditional costing techniques, then using ABC cost drivers. Typically, these examples are 'prepared' in order to show that the ABC technique is 'more comprehensive in that it apportions each element of overhead relative to its consumption for each activity and will provide a more realistic basis for determining the overhead for each line of business'. To conclude this example, we will question the overheads used in the example and rework using a more balanced set of overheads while still retaining machine hours as the absorption rate.

In this example, we have two components RUF and TUF that are similar in appearance and use the same processes and machinery. The following data has been gathered:

	RUF	TUF
Budget volume (components)	3,000	24,000
Machine hours per component	3	3
Number of purchase orders	100	300
Number of setups	50	80
Total machine hours	9,000	72,000

Fixed factory overheads:

Volume related	£160,000
Purchasing related	£130,000
Setup related	£250,000
	£540,000

First, we will recover factory fixed overheads using traditional overhead absorption techniques.

Table 8.4   Traditional overhead apportionment

Fixed factory overheads   ÷   Total machine hours
£540,000 ÷ 81,000 hours = £6.667 per machine hour

		RUF			TUF
Cost per component:					
	(£6,667 x 3hrs)	£20.00	(£6.667 x 3hrs)		£20.00
Overhead costs absorbed:					
	(3,000 x £20)	**£60,000**	(24,000 x £20)		**£480,000**

In *Table 8.4*, we calculated a machine hour rate of £6.667. We then calculated the cost per unit for each component; since the machine hours are the same for both components it follows that the cost per unit will also be the same, i.e. £20.00 per unit. The last section shows the total overheads absorbed by RUF and TUF, i.e. £60,000 and £480,000.

We will now show the ABC method of apportionment that calculates absorption rates based on costs traced to activities divided by the consumption of these activities. In this example we have to calculate three rates as follows:

Volume related rate:

£160,000 ÷ 81,000 machine hours = £1.9753 per machine hour

Purchasing related rate:

£130,000 ÷ 400 purchase orders = £325 per purchase order

Setup related rate:

£250,000 ÷ 130 setups = £1,923.08 per setup

Table 8.5   ABC method of apportionment

		RUF		TUF
Volume costs	(9,000 x £1.9753)	17,778	(72,000 x £1.9753)	142,222
Purchasing costs	(100 x £325)	32,500	(300 x £325)	97,500
Setup costs	(50 x £1923.08)	96,154	(80 x £1923.08)	153,846
		146,432		393,568

It is clear that the two methods give widely different results. The traditional method apportions only £60,000 to RUF, while the ABC method apportions £146,432. The assumption here is that the traditional method favours the lower volume component because it does not take into account the high costs on the non-volume related activities, i.e. purchasing and setups. This indeed would be worrying, if it were the case. However, there does seem to be an imbalance between the breakdown of the fixed factory overheads. Let us consider the components that might be found in fixed factory overheads and recalculate.

Fixed factory overheads	£
Rent	75,000
Heating and lighting	35,000
Maintenance	50,000
Depreciation of machinery	170,000
Insurance	10,000
Supervision	35,000
Purchasing/receiving	75,000
Setup costs	90,000
	540,000

From the above figures it can be seen that depreciation of machinery is the largest item. Purchasing and setup costs have been reduced. In this case purchase orders per unit would be £75,000 ÷ 400 = £187.50. It is considered unlikely that setup costs would exceed depreciation, else there should be a case for a capital project to reduce setup costs.

Table 8.6   Traditional method of apportionment – Alternative

	Total	RUF	TUF
Rent	75,000	10,000	65,000
Heating and light	35,000	5,000	30,000
Maintenance	50,000	10,000	40,000
Depn of machinery	170,000	20,000	150,000
Insurance	10,000	3,000	7,000
Supervision	35,000	5,000	30,000
Purchase orders	75,000	20,000	55,000
Setup costs	90,000	35,000	55,000
	540,000	**108,000**	**432,000**

In the above example, we have left out the bases of apportionment, these might be floor area, machine hours, labour hours, plant value, number of employees, technical estimate. Using the traditional method of apportionment and spreadsheets it is possible to construct complex bases that will compare favourably against other methods, e.g. ABC.

However, in order to compare like with like we have recalculated the apportionment using an ABC technique and the fixed factory overheads in *Table 8.6*.

Table 8.7   ABC method of apportionment – Alternative

	RUF		TUF	
Volume costs	(9,000 x £4.62963)	41,667	(72,000 x £4.62963)	333,333
Purchasing costs	(100 x £187.5)	18,750	(300 x £187.5)	56,250
Setup costs	(50 x £692.31)	34,616	(80 x £692.31)	55,384
		95,033		**444,967**

From this brief review of the traditional compared to the ABC techniques it is clear that the whole activity of attempting to apportion overhead costs is open to question.

Exercise 8.1

a. From the following information, calculate the production cost for job numbers A1127 and A1131.

b. Discuss the problems associated with the use of floor area and plant value as a basis for apportionment.

JOBS

Direct costs:			A1127	A1131
Direct materials			£184.00	£262.00
Direct labour Shop 1	@	£10.00 per hour	9 hrs	11hrs
Direct labour Shop 2	@	£14.00 per hour	nil	7 hrs
Outwork			£99.00	£55.00

The following information is contained in the annual budget for 200X:

Direct labour	Shop 1	6,000 hours
Direct labour	Shop 2	9,000 hours

Works overhead:	£
Indirect labour	8,400
Salaries	42,000
Depreciation	18,900
Maintenance	19,600
Rent and rates	~~32,200~~
	121,100

Additional Information:	Shop 1	Shop 2
Plant value	£75,600	£113,400
Floor area (square metres)	3,000	3,000
Maintenance (estimate)	£12,000	£7,600

The direct labour hour is to be used for the calculation of overhead absorption rates.

Exercise 8.2

a. From the following information, calculate the production cost for job numbers E102 and E110.

b. Discuss the problems associated with the use of floor area and plant value as a basis for apportionment.

JOBS

Direct costs:			E102	E110
Direct materials			£71.80	£228.04
Direct labour Shop 1	@	£7.50 per hour	16 hrs	12hrs
Direct labour Shop 2	@	£10.50 per hour	nil	8 hrs
Outwork			£65.00	£40.00

The following information is contained in the annual budget for 200X:

Direct labour	Shop 1	5,000 hours
Direct labour	Shop 2	15,000 hours

Works overhead:	£
Indirect labour	12,000
Salaries	30,000
Depreciation	16,600
Maintenance	14,000
Rent and rates	20,000
	92,600

Additional information:	Shop 1	Shop 2
Plant value	£62,000	£104,000
Floor area (square metres)	2,000	4,000
Maintenance (estimate)	£4,400	£9,600

The direct labour hour is to be used for the calculation of overhead absorption rates.

Exercise 8.3

You are asked to prepare a quote for an order which is estimated to require 544 kg of materials, and 220 hours of direct labour. The order is from a regular customer. The company applies normal absorption costing principles. Variable overhead is assumed to be related to direct labour hours, and fixed overhead and profit are based on a percentage of total variable cost and total cost respectively.

The budget for the six months to 31st December 200X is as follows:

Revenues		£468,000
Direct materials 24,000 kg	£120,000	
Direct labour 5,000 hours	£75,000	
Variable overhead	£45,000	
Total variable cost		£240,000
Fixed overhead		£120,000
Total cost		£360,000
Budgeted profit		£108,000

The price you would quote is

Exercise 8.4

The overhead recovery rate for Shop 1 is £42.00 per machine hour, and the overhead recovery rate for Shop 2 is £20.00 per labour hour. The labour rates for Shop 1 and Shop 2 are £14.00 per hour and £10.00 per hour respectively. Administrative costs are charged at 30% of manufacturing costs and profit is added at 20% of total costs.

You are asked to prepare a quote given the following:

Direct materials	£200.00
Direct labour – Shop 1	5 hours
Direct labour – Shop 2	3 hours
Machine hours – Shop 1	10 hours

The price to quote is

Exercise 8.5

The apportionment and absorption of overheads can often cause concern. List four basis of apportionment and four methods of absorption.

Exercise 8.6

You are asked to prepare a quote for an order which is estimated to require 550 kg of materials and 220 hours of direct labour. The company has a shortage of direct labour with 5,000 hours being the maximum available for the period.

The budget for the six months to 31 December 200X is as follows:

Revenues			£650,000
Direct materials 25,000 kg	£100,000		
Direct labour 8,000 hours	£112,000		
Variable cost	£88,000		
Total variable cost		£300,000	
Fixed costs		£200,000	
Total cost			£500,000
Budgeted profit			£150,000

The price you would quote is

Exercise 8.7

The budget for *L. Driver Ltd* provide the following estimates for the current year ending 31st October 200X.

	Machine	Assembly
Machine hours	3,500	6,000
Direct labour hours	10,500	12,000
Hourly wage rate	£12.00	£7.50
Production overhead	£126,000	£90,000

In response to a request for a quotation from Fairway Ltd, the estimating department have provided the following costs and timings:

Direct materials	£144.00
Direct labour – Machine shop	3 hours
Direct labour – Assembly	5 hours
Machine hours – Machine shop	4 hours
Delivery charge – External carrier	£30.00

1. Calculate the predetermined overhead absorption rates that need to be applied to jobs passing through the factory for the current year.

2. Calculate the price to quote to Fairway Ltd, given that administrative costs are charged at 25% of manufacturing costs, and profit is added at 15% of total costs.

Exercise 8.8

A company produces two components, A1123 and A1139, that are similar in appearance and use the same processes and machinery. The following data has been gathered:

	A1123	A1139
Budget volume (components)	5,000	25,000
Machine hours per component	4	4
Number of purchase orders	150	350
Number of setups	70	120
Total machine hours	20,000	100,000

Fixed factory overheads:

Volume related	£250,000
Purchasing related	£125,000
Setup related	£150,000
	£525,000

a. Prepare statements showing the apportionment of fixed factory overheads using:

i   Traditional apportionment techniques.

ii   Activity based costing techniques.

b. Comment on the results.

COST-VOLUME -PROFIT ANALYSIS

LEARNING OBJECTIVES

When you have finished studying this chapter and completed the exercises, you should be able to:

❑ Describe the main differences between fixed and variable costs, relevant and irrelevant costs;

❑ Calculate and interpret break-even in units, minimum selling price and volume required to meet a target profit;

❑ Prepare and interpret break-even charts;

❑ Understand the limitations of cost, volume and profit (CVP) analysis;

❑ Prepare and interpret statements using relevant costs.

9.1   Introduction

Not all managerial action can be preplanned and handled within a budgetary context. The reality of management is that periodically events will arise on a non-routine or adhoc basis which require a decision to be taken. What tends to make such events difficult to deal with is that they are rarely the same. However, there are some guidelines that are generally applicable which can be summarised as:

p   Establish the exact nature of the issues requiring a decision to be taken;

p   Identify alternative courses of action;

p   Identify the most appropriate data, irrespective of its source;

p   Measure data correctly and logically analyse it;

p   Ensure that financial and non-financial data is well presented to facilitate information sharing and its correct interpretation.

In this chapter we are primarily concerned with decisions directed towards the short-term, which is frequently defined as one year or less, and the accounting information required to make these decisions. Decisions with implications greater than one year are discussed in the next chapter, however, it must be emphasised that much of the discussion about organising and analysing short-term decisions is relevant to dealing with long-term decisions.

As we will illustrate, dealing with short-term decisions requires a sound understanding of the economic issues of each situation to ensure an appropriate action is taken. In particular, use of the right data in the right way for each decision is critical for making good decisions. Unfortunately, there can often be confusion concerning the correct data to use because of a temptation to rely upon systems developed and currently operating to provide data for routine accounting purposes, such as budgetary control. Such systems will often have been developed for specific purposes relating to the control of activities and the information provided by it which is often inadequate for answering the key question for managing decisions which is:

'How do costs and revenues differ if one

course of action is adopted rather than another?'

Answering this key question requires the ability to identify costs and revenues which are likely to change as a consequence of the decision, irrespective of their source. For example, in a decision whether to discontinue an operation or not, the historical cost of the stock from the accounting system may often be irrelevant. The crucial question is, what alternative uses there are for the stock. If the only alternative is to sell the stock, the relevant information is its resale value which may be totally different from its historical cost. It also should not be ignored that there will often be non-financial information to be taken into consideration which may have a significant impact upon a particular situation, such as the effect on labour relations in the case of discontinuing an operation. Once all relevant points have been considered, it is critical that the resulting information is presented in the most appropriate form to ensure it is interpreted and correctly acted upon by the parties involved.

In this chapter we will consider the evaluation of non-routine decisions with the aid of a number of illustrations which represent the subtle differences in emphasis as to the type of data required. We first focus upon those decisions which require the analysis of cost behaviour and its application in what is now popularly called cost-volume-profit analysis. This type of approach can be useful for studying such issues as, what is the effect on profit when a new product range is introduced? It is also relevant to managers in not-for-profit organisations, mainly because knowledge of how costs fluctuate in response to changes in volume is valuable regardless of whether profit is an objective. No organisation has unlimited resources!

9.2   Cost-Volume-Profit relationships

A good understanding of how cost, volume and profit relate to one another can be invaluable in dealing with certain types of short-term decisions. Consider for example a request by a customer to provide a large consignment of standard product at a substantial discount. In order to establish the viability of such a request, one issue likely to be of importance, is the profitability that will result. We will illustrate how using Cost-Volume-Profit (CVP) analysis such a request can be readily evaluated, but before then, it is important to be aware of some basic terminology associated with its use.

1.   Fixed and variable costs

At its simplest, cost-volume-profit analysis is reliant upon a classification of costs in which fixed and variable costs are separated from one another. Fixed costs are those which are generally time related and are not influenced by the level of activity. For example, the rent payable by a manufacturer for factory space will not be related to the number of items produced. Whether times are good or bad the cost will have to be incurred and the same will apply to any other costs which are contractually incurred. If activity is to be increased beyond the capacity of the current premises additional rent would have to be incurred, but within what is known as the 'relevant range' of activity the cost is fixed. Variable costs on the other hand are directly related to the level of activity; if activity increases, variable costs will increase and vice versa if activity decreases.

Fixed and variable costs can be readily understood when portrayed graphically as illustrated in *Figure 9.1.*

Figure 9.1 Illustration of fixed and variable costs

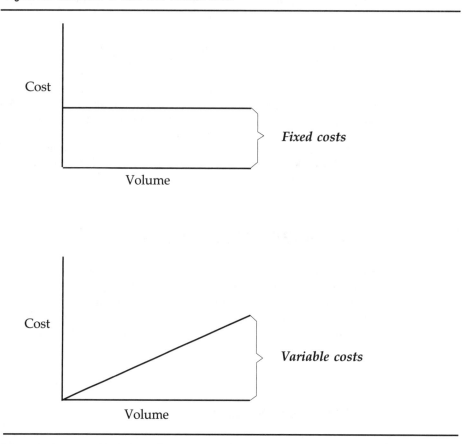

Fixed costs are shown to be constant for all levels of activity within the relevant range, whilst variable costs can be seen to increase in proportion to the level of activity. The sum of the fixed and the variable costs equals the total costs to be incurred over the level of activity within the relevant range.

In considering cost-volume-profit relationships it is usual to consider cost behaviour within the context of a model comprising only straight lines. This assumption can, of course, be relaxed to accommodate non-linear relationships, but it does make the analysis more difficult, and in considering whether to do so, it is important to determine whether the benefit derived from greater accuracy of the input data will warrant the effort required to be expended.

Finally, you should not ignore the fact that costs may be simultaneously affected by more than one activity base. For example, labour costs associated with road haulage may be affected by both the weight and the number of units handled.

2.   Uses of cost-volume-profit analysis

The ability to analyse and use cost-volume-profit relationships is an important management tool. The knowledge of patterns of cost behaviour offers insights valuable in planning and controlling short and long run operations. The example of increasing capacity is a good illustration of the power of the technique in planning. The implications of making changes upon profit can be determined as well as the requirements to achieve a given level of profit. The technique can be used to work forwards or backwards and, as should be only too obvious, it is ideal for spreadsheet analysis, whereby the effects of all sorts of modifications and assumptions can be evaluated.

The technique is also useful within the context of control. The implications of changes in the level of activity can be measured by flexing a budget using knowledge of cost behaviour, thereby permitting comparison to be made of actual and budgeted performance for any level of activity.

9.3   An example of cost-volume-profit analysis

The following data relates to a new product due to be launched on the 1st May:

Selling price	£20.00 per unit
Forecast volume	120,000 units
Variable costs	£16.00 per unit
Fixed costs	£300,000

We will apply the principles of CVP analysis to the following five situations, each has been treated as being independent of the other

1 Break-even point in units;

2 Break-even point in units, if variable costs per unit increase to £17.00;

3 Break-even point in £ sterling, if the fixed costs increase to £336,000;

4 Minimum selling price to meet a profit target of £120,000;

5 Volume of revenues required at a selling price of £19.00 per unit.

Finally, we will prepare a break-even chart using the original data.

The first step in tackling such a problem, is to calculate the total contribution and the contribution per unit.

	£	£ per unit
Revenues	2,400,000	20.00
less Variable costs	1,920,000	16.00
CONTRIBUTION	480,000	4.00
less Fixed costs	300,000	
Profit	180,000	

1. We calculate the break-even point by dividing the costs to be incurred, irrespective of the level of activity (i.e. fixed costs), by the contribution each unit will generate:

$$\text{Break-even point (units)} = \frac{\text{Fixed costs}}{\text{Contribution per unit}}$$

$$= \frac{£300,000}{£4.00}$$

$$= 75,000 \text{ units}$$

2. Where the variable costs per unit change, so too will the contribution per unit:

	£ per unit
Revenues	20.00
Variable costs	17.00
Contribution	3.00

With an unchanged £20.00 selling price and a revised variable cost of £17.00 a contribution per unit of £3.00 will result. Assuming that the fixed costs remain unchanged at £300,000, the break-even point in units is 100,000 (£300,000 ÷ £3.00).

3. Break-even always arises where total cost equals total revenue. To find the break-even point in value, rather than volume, we first calculate the break-even point in units, then multiply it by the selling price.

   In this case, where fixed costs are £336,000 (with no other changes), the break-even point in units will be £336,000 divided by £4.00, which equals 84,000 units. Break-even in value can be found by multiplying 84,000 by £20.00, which equals £1,680,000.

4. The minimum selling price to meet a target profit is found from the sum of the contribution per unit plus the variable cost per unit. The contribution per unit can be found by dividing the required units into the sum of the fixed costs and the profit target. For example, we are told that the profit target is £120,000, added to fixed costs of £300,000 gives £420,000 (i.e. the contribution in value). The contribution per unit can now be found by dividing £420,000 by 120,000 units to give £3.50. Therefore, the minimum selling price is £3.50 plus the unit variable cost of £16.00 which equals £19.50.

5. The calculation of total volume to cover fixed costs and meet the target profit is similar to the approach used to determine the break-even volume. The only difference is that the profit target is added to the fixed costs in order to calculate the number of units (volume) required to cover fixed costs and to cover the profit target from a given contribution per unit.

   In this case, the requirement is to identify the volume to cover fixed costs and profit assuming that the selling price per unit is decreased to £19.00. Where the selling price is £19.00, the unit contribution falls to £3.00:

	£ per unit
Revenues	19.00
less Variable costs	16.00
Contribution	3.00

   The volume of sales under these circumstances, is found by adding the fixed costs of £300,000 to the profit target of £180,000 and then dividing the result by £3.00, to give 160,000 units.

Break-even analysis can also be plotted on a graph. The basic data required is total forecast volume, total revenues, total fixed costs and total variable costs. A break-even graph, using the original data from the previous example, is shown in *Figure 9.2.*

Figure 9.2   Break-even graph

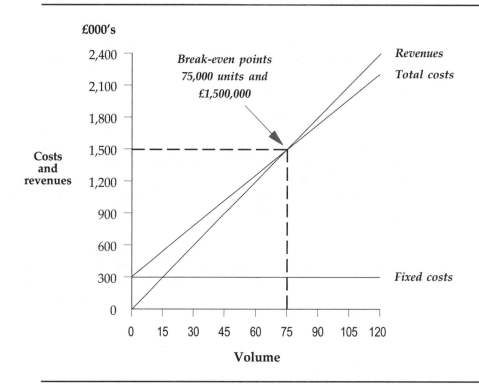

One of the most difficult tasks when preparing a break-even chart is determining the intervals between the values (e.g. units of 15 for the volume). You must also consider the overall size of the graph, its position on the page and give it a suitable heading.

In the above graph, the following steps need to be taken:

1.   First, plot the total fixed costs, i.e. £300,000, a straight line across the page;

2.   Next, plot the total variable costs, i.e. £1,920,000, from £300,000 at zero units to £2,220,000 (£1,920,000 + £300,000) at 120,000 units;

3.   Finally, plot the total revenues, i.e. £2,400,000, from £0 at zero units to £2,400,000 at 120,000 units.

Break-even is the point where total costs equal total revenues. Also at this point, the total cost per unit equals the selling price per unit. To the left of the break-even point, the total costs exceed the total revenues and represents the loss segment, while to the right of the break-even point the total revenues exceed the total costs and represents the profit segment.

Break-even is shown to be 75,000 units in terms of volume and, £1,500,000 costs and revenues. It can be seen that the only values to affect break-even are any change in:

1. Total fixed cost. For example, should total fixed costs increase then break-even will also increase;

2. Variable costs which in turn will affect total costs. For example, an increase in variable costs will increase the break-even volume;

3. Selling prices which in turn will affect the total revenues line. For example, a decrease in selling prices will increase the break-even volume.

9.4   Contribution margin and gross margin

We have shown the contribution margin to be the excess of revenues over all variable costs. It can be expressed as a total amount, a unit amount, and a percentage.

You should be aware of the potential for confusion about the difference between contribution and gross profit. Gross profit is a widely used concept, particularly in the retailing industry and is the excess of revenues over the cost of goods sold. However, the cost of goods sold will usually be very different in nature and amount from the contribution. The cost of goods sold relates solely to the direct costs associated with those items sold and any attributed overhead. It, therefore, usually contains elements of both fixed and variable costs unlike the contribution margin which is calculated with sole reference to variable costs.

Wagner plc manufactures an instrument which has a variable cost structure as follows:

	£
Materials	54.00
Labour	13.50
Variable costs	5.40
	72.90

The instrument sells at £121.50 each. The company expects revenues from this product in the current year of £1,822,500 and fixed overhead expense attributable to this product is budgeted at £189,000. A wage agreement with the employees states that a 10% increase will be paid to labour in the forthcoming year, whilst the managing director believes that from the beginning of the new financial year material prices will rise by 7.5%, variable overhead by 5%, and fixed overheads by 3%.

1. Calculate the new selling price if the contribution/revenues ratio is to be maintained.

2. Calculate the revenue volume required in the forthcoming year, if the price remains the same and the profit target is to be maintained. (The selling price is to remain at £121.50 in spite of the increase in costs).

	Existing variable cost		Revised variable cost
	£	%	£
Materials	54.00	7.5	58.05
Labour	13.50	10.0	14.85
Variable costs	5.40	5.0	5.67
	72.90		78.57

1. Revised selling price

Contribution to revenues ratio $\quad = \quad \dfrac{(121.50 - 72.90) \times 100}{121.50}$

$$= \quad 40\%$$

Thus, to maintain the current contribution to revenues ratio, the revised variable cost must equal 60% of the selling price.

Revised selling price $\quad = \quad \dfrac{£78.57 \times 100}{60}$

$$= \quad £130.95$$

2. Alternative sales volume required:

Existing sales volume $\quad = \quad \dfrac{£1,822,500}{£121.50}$

$$= \quad 15,000$$

Existing profit level:

Contribution (15,000 x £48.60)	729,000
less Fixed costs	189,000
	540,000

$$\text{Revised fixed costs} \quad = \quad \frac{£189,000 \times 103}{100}$$

$$= \quad £194,670$$

Existing profit level	540,000
Revised fixed costs	194,670
Contribution required	734,670

$$\text{Sales volume required} \quad = \quad \frac{£734,670}{(£121.50 - £78.57)}$$

$$= \quad 17,113$$

9.5.   Limitations of cost-volume-profit analysis

A major limitation of conventional CVP analysis that we have already identified is the assumption and use of linear relationships. Yet another limitation relates to the difficulty of dividing fixed costs among many products and/or services. Whilst variable costs can usually be identified with production services, most fixed costs usually can only be divided by allocation and apportionment methods reliant upon a good deal of judgement (covered in *Chapter 8*). However, perhaps the major limitation of the technique relates to the initial separation of fixed and variable costs. This can often be difficult to achieve with any sort of precision because many costs do not fall neatly into one or other of the two categories, and methods for separating fixed and variable costs may be required to use the technique. If this is the case, then you should be particularly mindful about applying a great deal of sophistication to any analysis because this may serve to cloud the key topic which is the quality of the data input.

The quality of input data is an important point and one you will find we often emphasise. In our opinion, too much emphasis has been placed upon how to make techniques more sophisticated without sufficient consideration of the quality of the data they are applied to. With this in mind, let us consider briefly how fixed and variable costs can be separated.

Judgement must be applied to the data in an attempt to separate those costs which can be considered wholly fixed or wholly variable. Bearing in mind that we are considering a defined range of activity; examples of fixed costs would be salaried staff and occupancy costs, such as rents and rates, whilst materials costs and sales commissions are illustrations of typical variable costs to a commercial oriented manufacturing operation.

Of course, the likelihood of separating a substantial proportion of total costs in this way is often very low and the remainder will fall somewhere between the two extremes of wholly fixed and wholly variable costs. This remainder, known as semi-fixed, or semi-variable costs, need to be separated in order to make cost-volume-profit analysis operable.

A number of methods are available to make such a separation possible ranging from comparing costs at high and low levels of activity, to regression analysis, whereby using statistical analysis a line of best fit is found from available cost data. Irrespective of the method applied, the result will only be an approximation! Yes, it is possible to minimise the approximation but you should weigh the cost of so doing against the relative likely benefit which will be achieved.

9.6   Relevant costs

The application of the principles of CVP analysis does suffer one major limitation for many decisions, other than those discussed earlier. In situations where there are different potential courses of action, relevant data for evaluating the alternatives is required and the cost behaviour information used in CVP analysis is unlikely to meet all of its requirements. What must be identified in such circumstances is the amount by which costs will change if one course of action is taken rather than another.

Surely, you must be thinking, this is simply an extension of cost-volume-profit analysis, but this need not be so. In discussing and applying cost-volume-profit analysis we did not question the relevance of the input data used to the decision in question. Questioning cost relevance is an important part of choosing between alternative courses of action.

As a manager, you must avoid using irrelevant information for evaluating alternatives no matter how impressive it may appear to be. The problem is, how do you avoid the use of irrelevant information and identify that which is relevant?

First, the accounting information used in any decision must relate to the future, not the past. It is essential that only costs and revenues yet to be incurred are used for purposes of decision making. This is because they alone will be incurred as a result of taking the decision in question. Past costs and revenues, which are often referred to as 'sunk' costs and revenues, are irrelevant to decision making, apart from their use in helping to forecast the future.

Second, where you are faced with a decision, the only relevant costs or revenues are those which are different under the alternative courses of action. Such costs are often referred to as *differential or incremental* costs. An understanding of how to use differential costs is important because most decisions will require at least two courses of action to be considered, given that one is merely to confirm current practice!

1.   Cost relevance in action

E. Tee, an aspiring manager, recently hit by the increase in interest rates upon his newly acquired mortgage, has a problem with the financial arrangements for his golf. He can either pay £9.00 every time he plays or £140.00 for a non-refundable season ticket plus £2.00 for every round played. Which should he choose? This you should immediately recognise as being similar in principle to the earlier discussion of cost-volume-profit analysis. In order to make a decision between these two alternatives we can work out how many times E. Tee would have to play so that he is indifferent between either of the two. This point of indifference, where he is no better or worse off, is like the break-even point discussed earlier. It is found by taking the cost of the annual season ticket and dividing it by the savings (the differential cost/benefit) achieved each time E. Tee would play.

$$= \frac{\text{Annual season ticket}}{\text{Saving on each round}}$$

$$= \frac{£140.00}{£7.00}$$

$$= \quad 20 \text{ times}$$

E. Tee would have to play more than 20 times in the year before a season ticket and £2.00 payment for each round would be a worthwhile decision. Since E. Tee likes golf and intends to play twice a week for the whole year he purchases an annual season ticket for £140.00.

Simple so far, but true to life complications arise. One month later, he identifies another problem which he cannot solve. He has visited another golf club which is nearer to his home. There is a single payment of £360.00 for membership with no additional green fees. The course is not heavily used, and it takes approximately three hours to complete a round compared to the four hours at the present club. What should he do? What about the £140.00 he has recently paid for his annual season ticket? The £140.00 is not relevant to this decision. It has already been paid, is not refundable and it will be the same irrespective of the decision he takes. Only the additional costs (incremental costs) and the additional savings (incremental receipts) are relevant to this new decision, i.e. those costs which will change as a result of making the decision.

The incremental costs in this case would be the £360.00 membership fee, and the incremental savings would be the £2.00 per round he has to pay at the present club.

$$= \frac{\text{Incremental costs}}{\text{Incremental savings}}$$

$$= \frac{£360.00}{£2.00}$$

$$= \quad 180 \text{ times}$$

Therefore, E. Tee would have to play approximately three and half times a week for it to be financially worthwhile joining the other golf club. If, on the other hand, E. Tee could save £1.00 on travel by joining the other golf club (which is nearer to his home), break-even would be achieved after 120 rounds (£360 divided by [£2.00 + £1.00]). However, there are a number of other aspects not necessarily of a financial nature which should be considered before changing to another club. Examples are:

❑ The time taken to play and travel;

❑ The possibility of sharing travelling;

❑ Who else plays;

❑ The amenities and social aspects;

❑ The quality of the facilities.

2.   Cost relevance – an example

A firm of boat builders has just had an order for a luxury yacht cancelled after it has been finished. The only potential buyer is Mr Apostolides; who said that he might buy the yacht on the following conditions that:

1. The price to him was no more than £37,500;

2. Certain specified conversion work was undertaken;

3. He could take delivery within one month.

The firm's accountant submits the following price estimate to help management decide whether a sale to Mr Apostolides would be worthwhile and to decide the minimum price that could be charged.

Table 9.1   Cost of building the yacht: – price estimate

		£
Materials at cost		21,000
Labour		18,000
		39,000
Variable costs (100% on direct cost)		39,000
		78,000
less Deposit, retained when order cancelled		22,500
		55,500
Add, Conversion work:		
Materials at cost	4,500	
Labour	1,500	
	6,000	
Fixed costs (100% on direct cost)	6,000	
Administration (25% on production cost)	1,500	
		13,500
Total cost		69,000
Add, profit mark-up (5%)		3,450
Suggested price to Mr. Apostolides		72,450

The following information is available:

1. Three types of materials were used in the original building of the yacht:

    a. **Type one** cost £10,500; at present it could only be sold to a scrap merchant for £3,000, but to put it in a suitable form for sale it would take 20 hours of labour at £5 per hour. This work would be undertaken by the firm's maintenance department which is very quiet at this time.

    b. **Type two** cost £7,500; at present it could only be sold as scrap for £3,000, again, after 20 hours of labour had been spent on it by the maintenance department. Alternatively, it could be kept for use next year as a substitute for a material which is expected to cost £4,500, but an additional 40 hours of highly skilled labour, over and above that spent to make the material suitable for resale, would then have to be hired at £7.50 per hour.

    c. **Type three** cost £3,000; it could now be sold for £2,250. Alternatively, it could be kept until next year as a substitute for a material which is expected to cost £3,000, but because of its special nature would have to be stored at an additional cost of £300.

2. There are two further types of materials to be used for the conversion:

    a. **Type four** was ordered last year at a price of £3,000, delivery was delayed and its realisable value has fallen to £1,500. In recognition of this, the suppliers have given the firm a discount of £900. The material could be used only for this one job.

    b. **Type five** has been in stock some time and originally cost £1,500. Its high content of precious metal means that it could now be sold for £3,750, but metal brokers would charge 10% commission for selling it.

3. Of the £1,500 conversion labour charge, £1,350 represents the skilled men that would have to be specially hired, the other £150 represents the time spent by the foreman who is a permanent employee.

4. The plans and specifications for the yacht could be sold for £3,750 if it is scrapped.

The accountant's cost statement indicates that Apostolides's offer of £37,500 would be significantly below the cost of £72,450. Is that the right conclusion? If you think it necessary, redraft the original schedule in the way you think might be more helpful to management. Your answer should include any assumptions you have made.

Table 9.2   Value of yacht, as is

			£
Material type 1	Note 1		3,000
Material type 2	Note 2		4,200
Material type 3	Note 3		2,700
Value in current state			9,900
Plans			3,750
		(A)	13,650
Conversion cost:			
Material type 4	Note 4		1,500
Material type 5	Note 5		3,375
Labour			1,350
		(B)	6,225
Apostolides's offer			37,500
less Minimum price if converted		(A – B)	19,875
Additional contribution if converted and sold to Mr. Apostolides			17,625

Notes:

1. Realisable scrap value, no labour charge as maintenance department over (under) capacity;

2. Replacement list value of £4,500 less skilled labour charge £300 (40 hours x 7.50 per hour). No maintenance labour as in Note 1;

3. Replacement cost less storage cost (£3,000 – £300);

4. Realisable value;

5. Realisable value;

6. Foreman, fixed cost.

Exercise 9.1

The following data has been extracted from the budget of *Hogan Ltd.*, for the six months ending 30th June 200X.

Sales (at £30 each)		£210,000
Variable costs	£140,000	
Fixed costs	£40,000	
Total cost		£180,000
Profit		£30,000

1. Calculate the break-even point in units.

2. Assuming that each of the following are independent of one another, calculate the break-even point assuming an increase in:

   a   Fixed costs by 10%;

   b   Variable costs by 5%;

   c   Selling price by 4%;

   d   Revenue volume by 8%.

Exercise 9.2

The following data relates to a new product due to be launched on the 1st March 200X.

Selling price	£25.00	per unit
Forecast volume	30,000	units
Variable costs	£15.00	per unit
Fixed costs	£200,000	

Assuming that each of the following are independent of one another, calculate the:

1. Break-even point in units, and £ sterling;

2. Break-even point in units, if variable costs per unit increase to £16.00;

3. Break-even point in £ sterling, if the fixed costs increase to £235,000;

4. Minimum selling price to meet a profit target of £70,000;

5. Volume of revenue required at a selling price of £23.00 per unit;

6. Additional units required to cover an advertising campaign of £40,000.

Exercise 9.3

A business makes and sells a single product from a plant with a capacity of 60,000 units per year. The results for the six months ended 31st December 200X are shown below:

	£'000	£'000
Sales (20,000 units at £300 per unit)		6,000
Direct materials	2,200	
Direct labour	640	
Production overheads (90% fixed)	1,600	
Selling and administration overheads (all fixed)	1,960	6,400
		– 400

The directors agree that this result is unsatisfactory. They propose cutting the price by £20, which they believe will stimulate sufficient revenues to utilise all of the capacity during the six months to 30th June 200x+1.

1. Calculate the break-even point in units for the six months to 31st December 200X;

2. Calculate the break-even point in units for the six months to 30th June 200X+1;

3. Calculate the profit for the six months to 30th June 200X+1, assuming that the increase in revenues can be achieved;

4. Calculate the profit and break-even point for the next financial year if market conditions do not allow the price to be increased from the new level set by the directors, but fixed costs do increase by 10% and variable costs by 4%;

Exercise 9.4

The following data has been collected: Selling price £84 per unit, Total variable costs £220,000, Forecast volume 5,500 units and Fixed costs £195,000.

1. Profit for the period is:

2. Break-even point in units and sterling is:

3. Break-even point in units, if variable costs increase by 10% is:

Exercise 9.5

E. Tee Ltd., manufactures three models of electric powered golf trolleys: Standard, Super, and Deluxe.

Budgeted fixed costs for the year ending 30th November 200X are £1,000,000.

The following data shows the selling prices and volumes, together with the costs per unit for each of the models.

Models	Standard	Super	Deluxe
Revenue volume	4,000	3,000	1,000
Selling price	£300	£375	£550
Direct materials	£90	£120	£160
Direct labour	£45	£45	£90
Variable overheads	£20	£30	£50

The Deluxe model has not been selling due to a cheaper import which has obtained an increased share in that market. E. Tee Ltd., has a choice, to either drop the selling price of the Deluxe model by £75 which they feel will increase sales volume by 50%, or to drop the Deluxe model from their range.

The extra labour, which is currently employed on the Deluxe model could be transferred to increase the production of the Standard or the Super model, or of both models equally.

1. State what the profit would be if E. Tee Ltd., continued with their budget plan;

2. Evaluate the choices available to E. Tee Ltd., and state which choice you would recommend.

Exercise 9.6

The following data has been collected: Selling price £25.00 per unit, Variable cost £15.00 per unit, Forecast volume 25,000 units and Fixed costs are expected to be £200,000 for the period.

1. The profit for the period is:

2. The break-even in £ sterling is:

3. The minimum selling price, if fixed costs increase to £260,000, is:

    (assume other relevant figures remain the same)

Exercise 9.7

The following data relates to a new product due to be launched on the 1st July 200X:

Selling price	£35.00	per unit
Forecast volume	50,000	units
Variable costs	£26.00	per unit
Fixed costs	£350,000	

Assuming that each of the following are independent of one another, calculate the:

1. Break-even point in units and £ sterling;

2. Break-even point in units, if variable costs decrease to £23.00 per unit;

3. Break-even point in units and £ sterling, if fixed costs increase to £370,000;

4. Minimum selling price to meet a target profit of £120,000;

5. Volume of revenue required at a selling price of £38.00 per unit;

6. Additional units required to cover an advertising campaign of £60,000.

Exercise 9.8

The following data has been collected: Selling price £24.00 per unit, Variable cost £16.00 per unit, Forecast volume 35,000 units and Fixed costs are expected to be £200,000 for the period.

1. The profit for the period is:

2. The break-even in £ sterling is:

3. The minimum selling price, if fixed costs increase to £260,000, is:

(assume other relevant figures remain the same)

Exercise 9.9

The following data relates to a new product due to be launched on 1st August 200X:

Selling price	£42.00	per unit
Forecast volume	70,000	units
Variable costs	£33.00	per unit
Fixed costs	£490,000	

Assuming that each of the following is independent of one another, calculate the:

1. Break-even point in units and £ sterling;

2. Break-even point in units, if variable costs decrease to £30.00 per unit;

3. Break-even point in units and £ sterling, if fixed costs increase to £550,000;

4. Minimum selling price to meet a target profit of £180,000;

5. Volume of revenue required at a selling price of £45.00 per unit;

6. Additional units required to cover an advertising campaign of £72,000.

CONTRIBUTION ANALYSIS

CHAPTER TEN

When you have finished studying this chapter and completed the exercises, you should be able to:

❑ Prepare statements to show whether a company should continue with apparently unprofitable products, divisions, branches.

❑ Apply the concept of relevant costs to:

- identify the best use of scarce resources;
- the make or buy decision;
- competitive tendering;
- the decision to accept or reject a special order.

❑ Describe and understand the differences between Absorption costing and Marginal costing.

❑ Use a framework to aid the structuring of decisions.

10.1   Introduction

In the previous chapter, we introduced the characteristics of financial information required for short-term decision making which must be differential between alternative choices and relate to the future. We will reinforce these two requirements and, where appropriate, apply the principles of CVP analysis with reference to five common applications of short-term decision techniques.

❏ Whether to continue with apparently unprofitable products, divisions, branches;

❏ How to make the best use of available scarce resources;

❏ Whether to make/use internal resources or buy from outside;

❏ Whether or not to use competitive tendering;

❏ Whether or not to accept a special order.

To answer the above, we need to use contribution analysis. What is contribution? In the previous chapter, we saw that revenues minus variable costs gave a contribution to fixed cost plus profit. We also saw that fixed cost plus profit equals contribution. Contribution analysis puts the emphasis on maximising contribution, which in turn will maximise profit. The focus on contribution also helps to highlight those variables that have an immediate impact on profit, i.e. those items that will change OR can be changed.

10.2   Whether to continue with apparently unprofitable products, divisions, branches

This application of short-term decision making techniques will consider using the following example:

> *T.O. Wood Ltd* manufactures and sells three products, X, Y and Z. The internally prepared product profitability statement for the company is shown in *Table 10.1*. Fixed overhead costs are absorbed as a percentage of labour costs and have been rounded to the nearest £100,000. Products X and Z are machine intensive while Product Y is labour intensive. Management is considering whether to drop Product Y because it is making a loss, the assumption being that they could increase the total profit of the company by £100,000 by dropping Product Y. Do you agree?

Table 10.1   T.O. Wood Ltd – Product profitability statement

		X £'000	Y £'000	Z £'000	Total £'000
(a)	Revenues	1,500	1,600	800	3,900
(b)	Material costs	500	400	100	1,000
(c)	Labour costs	400	800	300	1,500
(d)	Fixed costs	300	500	200	1,000
(e)	Total costs	1,200	1,700	600	3,500
(f)	**Profit/(Loss)**	**300**	**–100**	**200**	**400**

With reference to line (d), Product Y is absorbing 50% of the total fixed costs many of which may not be avoided even if the company were to drop Product Y. In such a situation where there is a limited differential effect upon fixed costs in continuing or dropping Product Y, they are not relevant in making the decision.

On the assumption that fixed costs are not avoidable in the short-term we have rearranged the contents of Table 10.1 to show a distinction between those costs likely to be avoidable and those that are not:

Table 10.2 T.O. Wood Ltd – Product contribution and profitability statement

	X £'000	Y £'000	Z £'000	Total £'000
Revenues	1,500	1,600	800	3,900
Material costs	500	400	100	1,000
Labour costs [1]	400	800	300	1,500
Total variable costs	900	1,200	400	2,500
Contribution	600	400	400	1,400
Fixed costs				1,000
Profit				400
Contribution ÷ Revenues %	40	25	50	

[1]   Labour costs are usually considered to be variable costs because they do respond to changes in the level of activity, albeit that this response may not be immediate.

In the rearranged *Table 10.2*, the value of retaining Product Y is shown assuming that no fixed costs are avoidable. Product Y can be seen to contribute £400,000 towards the fixed costs. If dropped, *T.O. Wood Ltd* would lose this contribution, with the result being a reduction in the total contribution by £400,000. Furthermore, this £400,000 reduction in contribution would completely wipe out the £400,000 profit currently obtained from making all three products.

This example illustrates one issue which must be considered in short-term decision analysis that arises from the allocation of fixed costs. Where fixed costs have been identified with products, as in this example, it is tempting, but usually wrong, to assume that they will necessarily disappear when a product is dropped. In fact, in many organisations all that is known with any certainty is the total fixed costs likely to be incurred. Their allocation across products or services is frequently heavily dependent upon judgement.

T.O. Wood Ltd is a useful illustration of CVP analysis. This technique can frequently be usefully extended by relating the contribution per product to the revenues to produce what is known as the contribution to revenues (C/R) ratio. The contribution to revenues ratio is potentially useful when costs have been separated into fixed and variable categories. This is because the effect on total profit of a given volume change for any product(s) can be assessed using knowledge of the contribution to revenues ratio. Let us consider the calculation and application of the C/R ratio.

The contribution to revenues ratios for X, Y and Z, are found by expressing the contributions of £600,000, £400,000 and £400,000 as a percentage of the revenues of £1,500,000, £1,600,000 and £800,000, respectively. The resulting contribution to revenues ratios are 40%, 25% and 50%. The effect on profit of an extra £1,000,000 of revenues being generated by each of the products, assuming that fixed costs would remain the same, would be £400,000, £250,000 and £500,000, for X, Y and Z, respectively. Therefore, given the potential to increase revenues by £1,000,000 the first product to be selected would be Product Z which has the highest contribution to revenues ratio. Thus the assumption that fixed costs are time related and remain unchanged for such an increase in activity, and, that there is no differential effect between products, then the highest profit will be generated from increasing revenues of Product Z.

You will note that we have been able to consider the potential financial benefits of an increase in revenues by considering the C/R ratio alone. Given that the relationships in the model are understood it is not necessary to undertake lengthy calculations to gauge the benefit.

Of course we have assumed no resource constraints. Where these exist the contribution to revenues ratio is not a useful distinguishing mechanism between alternative products, as we will see in the next section.

10.3 How to best use available scarce resources

In some production and distribution decisions, management may be confronted with the question of how best to allocate the firm's limited resources. Where demand for the product is greater than the production or distribution capabilities available, a company should seek to maximise its total contribution margin from these limited resources.

Limited resources can arise from one, or a combination, of the following:

o Shortages of raw materials or purchased goods;

o Shortage of certain labour skills;

o Restricted space for production, in the warehouse or in a retailing outlet;

o Maximum machine capacities.

It may not only be on the supply side that limitations prevail. It is also quite possible that a firm will face limitations upon the amount it can produce and/ or sell because of:

o Customer demand for one or more products and/or services;

o Government restrictions.

In such circumstances, the challenge is to obtain the maximum possible benefit from the market opportunities and the resources available.

Where there is one single constraint, it is possible to carry out an analysis to determine the best mix of products to maximise total contribution margin. At its simplest, the analysis requires the contribution margin for a product to be divided by the unit of scarce resource, i.e. limiting factor. That product or service with the highest contribution per unit of the scarce resource is the most desirable whilst the resource constraint operates. The application of the contribution per unit of scarce resource will be demonstrated with reference to *T.O. Wood Ltd,* where management is considering the most desirable mix of products to incorporate into their annual budget.

Market research information has produced the estimated revenues of *T.O. Wood's* present products together with further estimates of two new products, P and Q. There is no revenue constraint, but there is a constraint on machine capacity of 4,800 hours and, given this constraint, management needs to know the mix of products which should be produced so they are able to maximise the total profit margin. The product data is summarised in *Table 10.3*.

Table 10.3   T.O. Wood Ltd – Possible alternative products

	Existing Products			New Products	
	X	Y	Z	P	Q
Machine hours	2,000	800	2,000	800	1,000
	£'000	£'000	£'000	£'000	£'000
Revenues	1,500	1,600	800	700	1,000
Material costs	500	400	100	200	400
Labour costs	400	800	300	200	200
Total variable costs	900	1,200	400	400	600
Contribution	600	400	400	300	400
Cont'bn to revenues ratio	40%	25%	50%	43%	40%

Unfortunately, as we will illustrate, the current product analysis is inadequate for selecting the appropriate product mix to maximise profit. What is required, is an analysis of the contribution yielded per machine hour for each product. This is provided in *Table 10.4*, which has been used to rank the products from those which show the highest contribution per machine hour through to the lowest.

Table 10.4   Best use of scarce resources – Ranking

	Existing products			New products	
	X	Y	Z	P	Q
(a) Machine hours	2,000	800	2,000	800	1,000
	£,000	£,000	£,000	£,000	£'000
(b) Contribution	600	400	400	300	400
Contribution per machine hour [(b) ÷ (a)]	£ 300	£ 500	£ 200	£ 375	£ 400
Ranking	4	1	5	3	2

The analysis shows that Product Y, ranked first, provides the highest contribution per machine hour. Each unit requires less of the scarce resource than the other products, and it contributes £500 per machine hour.

The ranking, illustrated in *Table 10.4*, provides the order which will result in the best use of scarce machine hours. Given the total constraint of 4,800 hours and the selection of Product Y, which requires 800 hours, the remaining 4,000 hours would be allocated to products Q, P and X. This allocation to the four products does not exhaust the 4,800 hours available, and 200 hours still remain available. This 200 hours spare capacity could be used to ease production scheduling, or it might be used to produce a proportion of Product Z.

You will have doubtless noted by selecting the product mix using contribution per machine hour, Product Z with the highest contribution revenues ratio is the least desirable. Whilst it may produce the largest effect on contribution for a given increase in revenues, it suffers from being inefficient in terms of machine hour use. Hopefully, you will be thinking why not buy or lease a new machine or investigate subcontracting production. This line of thinking is entirely appropriate, as is questioning whether *T.O.Wood* should focus more heavily on Product Y. However, your attention would not have been so readily directed at these questions without the analysis we have outlined.

Assuming that the 200 hours are retained to ease production scheduling, the following revised product income statement shows the results of maximising total contribution per machine hour available.

Table 10.5 Product contribution and total profit statement

	Y	Q	P	X	Total
Machine hours	800	1,000	800	2,000	4,600
	£'000	£'000	£'000	£'000	£'000
Revenues	1,600	1,000	700	1,500	4,800
Material costs	400	400	200	500	1,500
Labour costs	800	200	200	400	1,600
Total variable costs	1,200	600	400	900	3,100
Contribution	400	400	300	600	1,700
Fixed costs					1,000
Profit					700

Where more than one constraint exists, the problem will be reliant upon operations research methods, like linear programming, for its solution. Such techniques are beyond the scope of this book.

10.4 The decision to make or buy

If you are not involved in a manufacturing environment, you may be tempted to skip this section on the grounds that make or buy decisions will be irrelevant to you. Nothing could be further from the truth! This we will demonstrate in the next section, which is concerned with the evaluation of providing internal services against the use of outside contractors, and represents a good illustration of an application of make or buy principles.

Stated very simply, in a make or buy decision, buying is preferable on economic grounds when the relevant costs for making are greater than the price quoted by the supplier. As with many decisions, what often confuses the analysis is the distinction between those costs that are relevant to making the decision and those that are not. The distinction between relevant and non–relevant costs for make or buy decisions is exactly the same as described earlier insofar as relevant costs are future orientated and differential. However, to aid your understanding of their applications to make or buy decisions we will relate it to the following example.

The purchasing manager of *T.O. Wood Ltd* has been investigating the possibility of buying a certain component from an outside supplier. *L. Driver Ltd* is prepared to sign a one year contract to deliver 10,000 top quality units as needed during the year at a price of £5.00 per unit. This price of £5.00 is lower than the estimated manufacturing cost per component of £6.00, which is made up as follows:

Table 10.6   Product cost statement

	Unit cost £.00
Direct material costs	1.20
Direct labour costs	1.80
Factory variable cost	0.60
Annual machine rental	0.40
Factory fixed cost – Allocated	0.50
– Apportioned	1.50
	£6.00

It appears at first sight that it will make better economic sense to buy rather than to make, however, let us consider whether all of the items within the product cost breakdown are relevant, i.e. 'If the decision is made to buy, which of the costs will be avoided?' An investigation of the components reveals that direct materials, direct labour, factory variable costs, annual machine rental and factory fixed costs – allocated would all be avoided. As the total of these relevant costs amounts to £4.50, which is less than the price of £5.00 quoted by the supplier, the decision should be to continue making the component. The remaining £1.50 of costs relating to apportioned fixed costs would presumably have to be borne elsewhere in the company and because they do not differ, irrespective of the course of action, are irrelevant.

Even if the analysis had indicated it to be more desirable to buy on economic grounds, there would still be factors to be considered other than the purely financial ones. For example, loss of know-how in producing this component, the loss of certain skilled labour, not being able to control future cost increases and, therefore, final product prices, the ability to fill up capacity in slack times, and the possibility of finding it difficult to obtain supplies at a reasonable price during boom times, which must all be taken into consideration.

10.5 Competitive tendering

As indicated, the principles used in the make or buy decision can also be applied to an evaluation of services, to answer the question, 'Do we provide service using our own resources or do we invite outside suppliers to compete to provide the service?'

There are many examples of organisations using competitive tendering in an attempt to obtain savings in the services they provide. These include, local authorities with refuse collection; health authorities with domestic, catering and building maintenance services; and the Royal Navy with ship repair.

What is the basis used to determine whether an organisation should provide a service in-house or accept an offer from an outside supplier? The financial criteria are exactly the same as the make or buy decision, such that an organisation should provide an in-house service when the relevant costs associated with its provision are less than the price quoted by outside suppliers. These relevant costs are once again those costs which would be avoided if the provision of the service were to cease, and would tend to include materials consumed and wages. However, you must be constantly aware of irrelevant costs like historical as opposed to future values of stocks and other assets, and allocated costs which can often cloud a decision. A thorough review of all costs associated with such a service must be undertaken.

Once again please note that our discussion has been concerned with financial criteria only. As we have emphasised on a number of occasions, there will always be non-financial issues, often of equal importance, to take into consideration before a decision can realistically be taken.

10.6   The decision to accept/reject a special order

One issue likely to be appropriate to all managers at some time in their careers is whether to accept what we will refer to as a special order. By this we mean, 'Are there circumstances in which it might make sense in financial terms to sell products or services at a lower price than normal, or alternatively, to provide a service internally at less than its full cost?'

In considering such decisions, it is most important to be quite clear about the meaning of the term *full cost*. In many organisations external and internal prices for products and services are generated with reference to the full or total cost of its provision plus a percentage margin, a practice known as *cost-plus pricing*. Within the full cost, there will usually be allocated and apportioned fixed overheads required to be covered, irrespective of whether a special order is accepted. Such non-relevant costs must be ignored since the criteria for accepting a special order must only consider whether the direct benefits which result, exceed those costs that could be avoided by not taking it.

Such evidence, as exists from surveys of pricing, reveals that some organisations do accept special orders using some form of the contribution analysis, although the bias towards its use is not as significant as many textbooks would imply.

You should be aware that the acceptance of a special order with reference to direct costs and benefits can be problematic if it generates a special order 'culture'. If all orders are priced as special, how will fixed overheads ever be recovered!

There are also other considerations to be taken into account that may have financial consequences. For example, if it became widely known that special orders were negotiable then the subsequent marketing and selling of products, or services, may be far more difficult, and require a good deal more effort to be expended than currently.

As a general guideline then, in these types of decisions, a company must consider:

1   Whether the acceptance of a special order will tie up capacity which could be used for profitable orders at some time in the future. If it does so then it should avoid the special contract.

2   Whether the acceptance of a contract will affect the regular revenue of the product, and ultimately the future pricing structure of that product. Generally speaking, a special contract should not be accepted if it will affect consumer behaviour adversely within the same marketplace. General knowledge of the availability of special orders may well lead to "consumer games" with the supplier. Special orders might relate to Government contracts or customers in a separate market segment; possibly in an overseas market.

In the example that follows, we will produce:

1. Budgeted income statement (without the special order);

2. Total income statement (including the special order);

3. Income statement (showing incremental income and costs for a special order).

Example

The *Jolly Inc.* company is considering whether it should accept a special order for 15,000 units from a customer in Malaysia who has offered an ex-factory cost of £48.00 per unit. The overseas customer will pay all delivery and insurance costs, and revenues will be restricted to its own country. In this example, we will assume that the company does not sell any units in Malaysia. The following data relates to the volumes, prices and costs for the year.

Production capacity	80,000 units
Forecast revenues volume	60,000 units
Selling price	£72.00
Materials	5kg at £3.00 per kg
Labour	2 hours at £9.00 per hour
Variable overheads	£1.50 per labour hour
Fixed production overheads	£420,000
Selling costs	£360,000
Administration overheads	£500,000

Table 10.7   Budgeted income statement

Forecast revenues volume: 60,000 units

		£	£
Revenues	(60,000 x £72.00)		4,320,000
Direct materials	(60,000 x 5kg x £3.00)	900,000	
Direct labour	(60,000 x 2hrs x £9.00)	1,080,000	
Variable overhead	(60,000 x 2 hrs x £1.50)	180,000	
Fixed overhead		420,000	
Total production cost			2,580,000
= Gross margin			1,740,000
Selling costs			360,000
			1,380,000
Administration costs			500,000
= Net profit			880,000

From the above statement it can be seen that the *Jolly Inc.* company is budgeted to make a profit of £880,000 for the year. It has used 60,000 units and has spare capacity of 20,000 units this year. Calculations are show where required. Fixed overheads, selling costs and administration costs are all considered fixed costs.

Table 10.8   Total income statement including special order

Expected revenues volume: 75,000 units

		£	£
Budgeted revenues	(60,000 x £72.00)		4,320,000
Revenues from special order	(15,000 x £48.00)		720,000
Total revenues			5,040,000
Direct materials	(75,000 x 5kg x £3.00)	1,125,000	
Direct labour	(75,000 x 2hrs x £9.00)	1,350,000	
Variable overhead	(75,000 x 2 hrs x £1.50)	225,000	
Fixed overhead		420,000	
Total production cost			3,120,000
= Gross margin			1,920,000
Selling costs			360,000
			1,560,000
Administration costs			500,000
= Net profit			1,060,000

In *Table 10.8*, the effect of the additional volume can be seen. We have added in the incremental revenues of 15,000 units that increases total revenues to £5,040,000. We have also increased the total volume for materials, labour and variable overheads to 75,000 units and kept fixed production overheads, selling costs and administration costs at their budgeted level. Should there be additional costs associated with the special order, these would have to be included.

A comparison of *Table 10.7 and 10.8* shows that the net profit figure would increase from £880,000 to £1,060,000 if the special order was accepted. From a financial point of view the special order should be accepted. However, this might only be beneficial in the short-term; if volume was expected to expand within the existing customer base the company would not be able to obtain its expected market share. In general, special orders should be short-term, accepted to fill a capacity gap and contribute additional profit to the company, i.e. incremental revenue exceeds incremental costs.

We now show an Income statement that highlights incremental revenue and costs. This statement, shown in *Table 10.9*, has been prepared to show an alternative method of analysis. By taking the Budgeted income statement in *Table 10.7*, plus the Income statement shown below, we obtain the same final result as *Table 10.8*.

Table 10.9 Income statement showing incremental income and costs for special order

Special order for 15,000 units

		£	£
Revenues	(15,000 x £48.00)		720,000
Direct materials	(15,000 x 5kg x £3.00)	225,000	
Direct labour	(15,000 x 2hrs x £9.00)	270,000	
Variable overhead	(15,000 x 2hrs x £1.50)	45,000	
Total production costs			540,000
= Gross margin			180,000

In the differential, or incremental statement shown above, the total production costs of £540,000 is deducted from the revenue of £720,000 to give a gross margin of £180,000. Here we can see that fixed production overheads are not included, since they have been 'recovered' from our existing budgeted activity. Similarly, selling costs are not included since it is unlikely that additional selling costs could be attributed to the special order. The same applies to the administration costs, the assumption being that there is sufficient capacity to deal with the special order, i.e. no direct costs should be incurred.

10.7   Marginal costing v absorption costing

We will complete this section of the book, which has covered costing, cost-volume-profit analysis and contribution analysis, with a look at the technique of marginal costing versus absorption costing.

Many of the examples in this chapter assumed a marginal costing approach, i.e. contribution analysis. You will have noticed the problem associated with using full cost to base decisions to:

❏   Drop a loss making product, division or business; or

❏   Allocate the best use of scarce resources; or

❏   Stop using facilities within the organisation and buy from outside; or

❏   Accept or reject a special order.

In each case, the use of full costing, i.e. absorption costing gives an incorrect message to the decision maker.

Absorption costing

❏   Those in favour of absorption costing will be satisfied that all known costs are covered, e.g. variable costs, fixed production costs, selling, distribution and administration costs.

❏   By valuing closing inventories at full production cost it matches costs with revenues for the period, i.e. a proportion of the costs are carried forward to the next period.

❏   Absorption costing removes the need to separate variable and fixed costs which is one of the main problems associated with marginal costing.

❏   With the final output being total costs, i.e. all variable and fixed costs, it can provide a basis for pricing for those businesses that operate on a cost plus method of pricing.

❏   Absorption costing would tend to be suited to low volume and/or large one-off items.

❏   Finally, absorption costing is the recommended method for external reporting; specifically, the valuation of stock.

Marginal costing

❏ Two of the main benefits of marginal costing are:

    1. That it removes the need to decide on bases of apportionment for each element of fixed cost and, the calculation of overhead recovery rates such as machine hour rate and labour hour rate;

    2. It removes the under/over absorption of fixed overheads due to changes in production volumes.

❏ The application of marginal costing simply requires that fixed costs are deducted as a 'lump' from contribution to give a profit figure.

❏ Marginal costing uses variable/direct costs that can be determined and located to a product.

❏ Marginal costing tends to suit high volume mass production products but is equally applicable to retail and similar environments.

❏ Provides data for short-term decision making, e.g. most profitable products, make or buy, best use of scarce resources.

Example

In the example that follows, we will show the difference in reported factory contribution/profit using marginal costing and absorption costing. We will then reconcile the difference between the two methods.

The following data has been collected prior to the preparation of absorption and marginal production cost statements for January and February.

Standard costs per unit:

	£
Direct materials	4.00
Direct labour	7.00
Variable manufacturing overhead	3.00
Standard variable cost	14.00

Other data:

Fixed manufacturing overhead	£375,000 per month
Expected production	75,000 units
Selling price	£26.00

Actual production data:

	Jan	Feb
Opening inventories	0	11,000
Production	73,000	68,000
Revenues	62,000	74,000
Closing inventories	11,000	5,000

Marginal costing

Table 10.10 shows the calculation of contribution after factory fixed overheads. At the beginning of the table we repeat some of the basic data from the example. Tutorial notes are appended to support certain calculations. It is assumed that the reader is familiar with contribution layouts.

Table 10.10   Marginal cost of production

	Jan	Feb
Revenues volume	62,000	74,000
Production volume	73,000	68,000
Closing inventories volume	11,000	5,000
Selling price per unit	£26.00	£26.00
Standard variable cost	£14.00	£14.00

	£	£	£	£
Revenues (1)		1,612,000		1,924,000
Opening inventories (2)	0		154,000	
Factory costs (3)	1,022,000		952,000	
	1,022,000		1,106,000	
less Closing inventories (4)	154,000		70,000	
		868,000		1,036,000
Contribution		744,000		888,000
less Factory overheads		375,000		375,000
Contribution after factory overheads		369,000		513,000

Tutorial notes:

1. The revenues figure is calculated, e.g. for February 74,000 units x £26.00 per unit = £1,924,000.

2. The opening inventories figure is calculated; opening inventories units times standard variable cost per unit, e.g. for February (please note that the closing inventories for January is the opening inventories for February) 11,000 units x £14.00 per unit = £154,000.

3. Factory cost is calculated; production volume x standard variable cost per unit, e.g. for February 68,000 units x £14.00 per unit = £952,000.

4. Closing inventories is calculated; closing stock units times the standard variable cost per unit, e.g. 5,000 units x £14.00 per unit = £70,000.

Absorption costing

Table 10.11 shows the calculation of gross profit. At the beginning of the table we repeat some of the basic data from the example. Tutorial notes are appended to support certain calculations. The main difference here is that an absorption rate must be calculated for factory fixed overheads and added to the standard variable cost. We will show this calculation after *Table 10.11*.

Table 10.11   Absorption cost of production

		Jan		Feb
Revenues volume		62,000		74,000
Production volume		73,000		68,000
Closing inventories volume		11,000		5,000
	£	£	£	£
Revenues (1)		1,612,000		1,924,000
Opening inventories (2)	0		209,000	
Total production cost (3)	1,387,000		1,292,000	
	1,387,000		1,501,000	
less Closing inventories (4)	209,000		95,000	
		1,178,000		1,406,000
Gross profit		434,000		518,000

The calculation of the absorption cost of production is as follows:

(Fixed factory costs ÷ budgeted production volume) + standard variable = cost per unit

(£375,000 ÷ 75,000) + £14.00 = £19.00 per unit

Tutorial notes:

1. The revenues figure is calculated; e.g. for February 74,000 units x £26.00 per unit = £1,924,000. This is the same as the marginal cost method.

2. The opening inventories figure is calculated; opening inventories units times the absorption cost of production per unit, e.g. for February (please note that the closing inventories for January is the opening inventories for February) 11,000 units x £19.00 per unit = £209,000.

3. Factory cost is calculated; production volume x the absorption cost of production per unit, e.g. for February 68,000 units x £19.00 per unit = £1,292,000.

4. Closing inventories is calculated; closing inventory units times the absorption cost of production per unit, e.g. 5,000 units x £19.00 per unit = £95,000.

Reconciling the difference

The main differences between marginal costing and absorption costing are that in absorption costing:

o Fixed factory costs are absorbed based on budgeted production levels, with adjustments carried out for under or over absorption;

o Fixed factory costs are absorbed into closing inventories and, ultimately, opening inventories.

We will now reconcile the differences between the two methods.

Table 10.12   Reconciling the differences between marginal and absorption costing

	Jan	Feb
Absorption costing method (1)	434,000	518,000
Marginal costing method (2)	369,000	513,000
	65,000	5,000
add Production volume variance (3)	– 10,000	– 35,000
Difference	**55,000**	**– 30,000**
Opening inventories (4)	0	55,000
Closing inventories (5)	55,000	25,000
Difference (6)	**55,000**	**– 30,000**

Tutorial notes:

1. These figures are taken from *Table 10.10*.

2. These figures are taken from *Table 10.11*.

3. Production volume variance is calculated as follows:

   (Actual – budget production) x fixed cost recovery rate

   Therefore, for:

   January = (73,000 – 75,000) x £5.00 = – £10,000

   February = (68,000 – 75,000) x £5.00 = – £35,000

4. There was no opening inventories in January. In February the opening inventories is the January closing inventories of £55,000.

5. The closing inventories for January is the difference between the closing inventories in *Table 10.10* and the closing inventories in *Table 10.11*, i.e. £209,000 – £154,000 = £55,000.

   The closing inventories for February is the difference between the closing inventories in *Table 10.10* and the closing inventories in *Table 10.11*, i.e. £95,000 – £70,000 = £25,000.

6. Check the January difference is as follows; (11,000 units – 0 units) = 11,000 x £5.00 = £55,000.

   Check the February difference is as follows; (5,000 units – 11,000 units) = 6,000 x £5.00 = £30,000.

10.8　Structured decision analysis

Clear thought and the application of certain key principles is critical for making sound decisions. We have offered these key principles using a number of applications which you may be able to apply to your own circumstances. All too often a major barrier to decision making is a lack of structure and we offer the following as a guideline:

o　Clearly define the problem and the scope;

o　Consider all possible alternative courses of action which could lead to a solution;

o　Discard those alternatives which, on a common sense appraisal, are 'nonstarters' for one reason or another;

o　Evaluate the cost and benefit differences between each of the remaining courses of action;

o　Weigh up the non-financial factors related to each course of action;

o　Take into account both financial and non-financial factors important to the decision; make the necessary trade-offs and decide.

All common sense you might be thinking? We would agree, but in our experience it is all too easy to overlook, underestimate, or evaluate incorrectly one or more of the steps.

Exercise 10.1

A company making a single product has a factory in Swindon and distribute its production through three depots situated in Swindon, Bristol and Reading.

It is estimated that during the coming year 99,000 units will be manufactured and sold at a price of £22 per unit, the volume being spread as follows:

Swindon	67,000 units
Bristol	22,000 units
Reading	10,000 units

Standard costs of production are:

Direct materials	£6.50 per unit
Direct labour	£3.40 per unit
Variable production overheads	150% on direct labour
Fixed production overheads	£250,000 per year

The cost of selling and distribution incurred by the depots are estimated as follows:

Fixed costs

Swindon	£70,000 per year
Bristol	£60,000 per year
Reading	£60,000 per year

Variable costs

Swindon	8% of revenues
Bristol	10% of revenues
Reading	12% of revenues

Management is considering closing the Bristol and/or Reading depots. If this is done it is expected that all revenues in these areas will be lost, but the revenues in Swindon will not be affected.

1. From the figures provided, prepare a statement indicating why management is thinking of closing the depots in Bristol and/or Reading.

2. Present additional information to help management make a decision in regard to this problem, and make recommendations from your figures.

Exercise 10.2

A meeting has been arranged of the executives of *W.E. Look Ltd.*, to consider the budget for the coming year. They are not convinced that the products they produce and sell are giving the optimum profit. Until they move into the new factory in two years time there will be severe restrictions on capacity.

The current machine capacity is 160 hours per week with no other major restrictions (i.e. materials, labour etc.)

The following information has been collected for the products the company is able to sell per week with no seasonal trends.

Products	A	B	C	D	E	F	G
				£000			
Revenues	7.0	2.0	2.0	4.0	6.0	2.0	4.0
Materials	4.0	0.8	0.7	2.5	3.0	0.6	0.6
Labour	2.0	0.6	1.0	1.0	1.0	0.6	2.0
Machine hours	40	20	20	60	80	20	120

Fixed costs will remain constant at £115,440 per year, regardless of product mix.

1. Prepare a statement showing which products should be produced to give the optimum profit from available capacity.

2. Prepare an income statement – for a single week.

Exercise 10.3

Mouldit Ltd makes a range of products in expanded polystyrene (cups, trays, DIY materials etc.). The budget for the six months to 31st October 200X is as follows:

	£	£	£
Revenues			780,000
Polystyrene (5,000 kg)	200,000		
Direct labour (10,000 hours)	50,000		
Variable overhead	150,000		
Total variable costs		400,000	
Fixed overhead		250,000	
Total cost			650,000
Budgeted profit			130,000

You have been asked to quote for an order which is estimated to require 100 kg of polystyrene and 240 hours of direct labour. Prepare separate quotes for each of the circumstances shown below.

1. The order is from a regular customer. The company applies normal absorption costing principles. Variable overhead is assumed to be related to direct labour hours, and fixed overhead and profit are based on a loading of total variable cost and total cost respectively.

2. Labour is in short supply and the budget includes the maximum hours available. During the half year you expect to receive more orders than you will be able to fulfil.

3. There is a potential new customer who is looking for a regular supplier. This is, in effect, a trial order and you would like to do business with them in the future. A competitor is believed to be quoting about £16,300.

Exercise 10.4

Simply Packers Ltd has its own internal department which produces a standard size carton for packaging the company's products. 360,000 of these cartons are used annually and the detailed budgeted costs of production are as follows:

Direct materials	£84,000	Direct labour	£18,000
Electricity (power costs)	£4,500	Depreciation of plant	£13,500
Repairs to plant	£3,000	Fixed production overheads	£15,000

An outside supplier has quoted to supply all the cartons on a regular basis throughout the year at a price of £325 per 1,000. In the event of accepting this offer the section will be closed and the specialist plant sold for £28,000. The company will also incur additional fixed costs of £9,000 per year for inspection and storage of the cartons.

1. Prepare a financial statement to help management decide whether they should buy in the cartons.

2. Identify any other factors which should be taken into consideration.

Exercise 10.5

The current availability of labour is 200 hours per week, with no other major restrictions. The following information has been collected for the products the company is able to sell per week with no major restrictions:

Products	A	B	C	D
Revenues	14,000	4,000	4,000	8,000
Materials	8,000	1,600	1,400	4,800
Labour	4,000	1,200	2,000	1,600
Labour hours	80	40	40	80

Prepare a table to show the ranking of products that would produce the greatest profit.

Exercise 10.6

Whines Ltd., manufactures and assembles small electric motors. 32,000 units of part 1790 are manufactured each year to which the following production costs apply:

Direct materials	£16,000
Direct labour	£24,000
Variable production overheads	£16,000
Fixed production overheads	£32,000

Wedge Ltd., has offered to sell *Whines Ltd.*, 32,000 units of part 1790 at £2.50 per unit. If the company accepts the offer, £12,000 of fixed overheads, applied to part 1790, could be eliminated. Additionally, some premises used during the manufacture of part 1790 could be rented to a third party at an annual rental of £8,000.

1. Explain whether *Whines Ltd.* should accept the offer from *Wedge Ltd.* or not

2. What other factors might the management of *Whines Ltd.* wish to consider before arriving at a decision.

Exercise 10.7

Dymond Ltd. manufactures specialist jewellery for fashion shops. For the last year, the company has been operating at 60 per cent of its capacity and its results were as follows:

Revenues	(240,000 units at £12 each)	£2,880,000
Variable costs	(at £7.80 per unit)	£1,872,000
Fixed costs		£700,000
Profit		£308,000

A major retailer has offered to purchase the output from the excess capacity for the next three years at a price of £9.60 per unit. If the offer was accepted, fixed costs would increase by £150,000 per year.

Evaluate the offer from the major retailer.

Exercise 10.8

The company accountant of *L. Driver Ltd* has drawn up the following statement to assist production management in their decision on product production for the coming year.

Product	A	B	C	D	E	F
Selling price (£)	420	570	510	480	540	570
Materials	190	160	130	205	240	150
Labour	40	90	90	50	70	90
Variable overheads	50	25	25	40	35	55
Fixed overheads	60	135	135	75	105	135
	340	410	380	370	450	430
Profit per unit	80	160	130	110	90	140
Ranking for production	6	1	3	4	5	2
Estimated maximum volume per annum (units)	400	1000	300	800	500	300

Specialist labour is required to produce the products and earns £8.00 per hour; the company can hire only 25,000 labour hours during the coming year. All other resources can be obtained in the desired quantities. Fixed overheads are charged at 150% of labour cost under the company's current costing system.

1. Produce an alternative method of ranking the company's products to make the best use of the shortage of specialist labour.

2. What other factors should be taken into consideration?

Exercise 10.9

The decision to "make or buy" is often misunderstood. Discuss, with reference to examples.

(refer to the text, *pages 272-273*, for an answer)

Exercise 10.10

The current availability of labour is 160 hours per week, with no other major restrictions. The following information has been collected for the products the company is able to sell per week with no major restrictions:

Products	A	B	C	D
Revenues	16,000	6,000	6,000	10,000
Materials	9,000	2,600	2,400	5,800
Labour	4,000	1,200	2,000	1,600
Labour hours	80	40	40	80

The Ranking is:

Exercise 10.11

AMILL is a chemical used in the production of *XZX Ltd's* range of fertilisers. Following a fire at the chemical works, supply is restricted to 12,000 kg per month, at a cost of £6.00 per kg.

Before supplies were restricted *XZX Ltd's* budget was:

	A	B	C	D
Revenues (in kgs)	18,000	21,600	18,000	28,800
Selling price (per kg)	£3.24	£4.92	£4.62	£6.00
Variable costs per kg of output:				
AMILL	£0.90	£1.44	£1.08	£2.40
Other direct materials	£0.30	£0.48	£0.48	£0.72
Direct labour	£0.48	£0.66	£0.60	£0.84
Production overhead	£0.12	£0.18	£0.12	£0.24

Fixed costs (£30,000 per month)

Calculate the maximum profit possible, per month, while AMILL is in short supply.

Exercise 10.12

Sam and Ella Chick Company are considering whether they should accept a special order for 35,000 units from a potential overseas customer who has offered an ex-factory cost of £18.00 per unit. The following data relates to the volumes, prices and costs for the year.

Production capacity;	200,000 units
Forecast revenues volume;	125,000 units
Selling price;	£25.00
Materials;	2kg at £2.00 per kg
Labour;	1 hour at £7.00 per hour
Variable overheads;	£2.00 per labour hour
Fixed production overheads;	£420,000
Selling costs;	£200,000

Prepare two income statements. The first to include budget forecast and special order; the second to show only the differential effect of the special order.

Exercise 10.13

The following data has been collected prior to the preparation of absorption and marginal production cost statements for January and February.

Standard costs per unit:

Direct materials	£10.40
Direct labour	£18.20
Variable production overhead	£7.80
Standard variable cost	£36.40

Other data:

Fixed production overhead	£975,000	per month
Expected production	195,000	units
Selling price	£67.60	per unit

Actual production data:	Jan	Feb
Opening inventories	0	30,000
Production	190,000	175,000
Revenues	160,000	195,000
Closing inventories	30,000	10,000

Prepare absorption and marginal cost statements for January and February.

CHAPTER ELEVEN

BUDGETING
and
BUDGETARY CONTROL

LEARNING OBJECTIVES

When you have finished studying this chapter and completed the exercises, you should be able to:

❏ Identify the diverse range of organisations where budgeting is appropriate;

❏ Outline the activities which can be identified as an integral part of the budgeting process;

❏ Describe the main budgeting techniques including flexible budgets, zero based budgeting and rolling budgets;

❏ Explain the key elements in administrating a budget;

❏ Prepare and interpret cash budgets.

11.1   Introduction

In *Chapter 1,* we reviewed the main financial statements together with the accounting principles and policies important in drafting them. Here we place these financial statements into context by reviewing business planning, its links with budgeting, and how the main financial statements can be used effectively in business planning.

In common with earlier chapters, it is important to stress that the purpose of this chapter is *not* to make you into a financial specialist. Although the output from the budgeting process may be expressed in financial terms, the purpose underlying budgeting is to ensure that scarce resources are allocated as efficiently and effectively as possible. In other words, budgeting is a *managerial process.*

The result of budgeting, we will illustrate as being a set of financial statements in the form of an income statement, balance sheet and cash flow forecast. These statements are prepared, and approved prior to a defined future period, for the purpose of attaining specific objectives.

Budgeting is used in organisations of all types to help in the development and co-ordination of plans, to communicate those plans to the people who are responsible for carrying them out, to secure co-operation of managers at all levels and as a standard against which actual results can be compared. You will find budgeting used in a diverse range of organisations and activities including:

❑   Central and local government;

❑   The health service;

❑   Education;

❑   Large companies;

❑   Small businesses (such as the local garage);

❑   Churches;

❑   Charities;

❑   Television and radio networks;

❑   Local clubs;

❑   The family.

The analogy of our discussions with the family budget may be helpful. For example, a budget could be compared with the preparation of a shopping list. In its preparation we would be able to make changes to the list to ensure that personal objectives were met both for the goods obtained and money spent.

During the actual shopping activity, regular comparisons of actual spend against budget could be undertaken and, if necessary, changes could be made to attain our objectives.

Why budget? Consider the alternative to shopping without making a mental or written list. The outcome might be that many of the important items would not be bought and/or a situation of overspend reached, a feature of many bankrupt companies!

11.2   Planning the business through budgets

Organisations plan for the future in a number of ways. One useful way of looking at the process is to consider it in relation to the planning horizon – that is, the time span to be covered. One straightforward framework considers planning in the following three phases:

1.   Long-term;

2.   Medium-term;

3.   Short-term.

There is no universally accepted definition of the period of time for which each plan should apply; it very much depends on the type of business – its markets, product life cycles, etc. However, the purpose of each phase in the planning process is quite clear.

Long-term planning; is essentially a strategic exercise aimed at assessing trends and, identifying and choosing between alternative courses of action over a period of many years.

Medium-term planning; is a more practical exercise aimed at optimising the use of resources over a manageable future period, bearing in mind the strategies identified in the long-term planning process.

Short-term planning or budgeting; is a more detailed process in which the medium-term objectives can be modified and adapted in response to immediate pressures and constraints. The short-term plan or budget normally covers periods of up to one year. It is this document (or set of documents) with which we will be most concerned in this chapter.

11.3 Budget environment

Successful budgeting is difficult, particularly in large complex organisations. To achieve success attention has to be paid to a number of activities which can be identified as being an integral part of the budgeting process. These are:

1. Defining objectives;

2. Planning;

3. Organising;

4. Controlling;

5. Co-ordinating;

6. Communicating;

7. Motivating.

1. Defining objectives

A budget must relate to and support the achievement of an organisation's financial objectives. Rational financial objectives should be set, bearing in mind the risk associated with them and the uncertainty of the future in relation to the return which shareholders expect from their investment.

Budget objectives or targets have two further characteristics. They should be capable of:

❑ Attainment by the managers concerned; and,

❑ Objective measurement.

The budgeting process cannot be seriously undertaken until top management has defined in measurable terms the objectives of the business to be achieved during the period of the budget. Objectives might include:

❑ The achievement of a specified percentage return on capital employed;

❑ The reduction of borrowing by a specified amount;

❑ An increase in market share by a specified percentage;

❑ The introduction of a specified number of new products;

❑ The reduction of labour turnover by a specified figure.

A good framework is captured in the acronym S.M.A.R.T. which stands for; Specific, Measurable, Achieveable, Realistic and Time banded.

Whether the objectives set are acceptable will depend on:

❑ What has been achieved in the current and previous years;

❑ Comparison with the performance of other business units working in similar business environments;

❑ Management's opinion of what can be achieved in the business environment of the near future.

The above are only a few examples of possible business objectives. They will usually relate to a range of activities within a company and not necessarily be restricted to purely financial or profit orientated objectives.

One key issue in defining objectives, concerns those factors which limit the ability of an organisation to do exactly as it would wish. These are known as *limiting factors,* and can be broken down into two types:

a. External factors over which an organisation has no direct control. The external factors might be the availability of:

❑ Sales demand in the marketplace;

❑ Raw materials;

❑ Scarce and specialised equipment;

❑ Skilled employees.

In many cases external limiting factors can be related to the economic climate.

b. Internal factors over which it has a considerable amount of control. The factors which may limit the firm internally could include:

❑ Productive capacity of the company;

❑ Capacity and skill of the workforce;

❑ Availability of cash.

All organisations will encounter constraints which limit their ability to do exactly as they wish. Some of these will be obvious, others not so obvious. The attainment of budgetary goals is limited by the capacity and commitments of the organisation as it currently exists. It is vital to identify and monitor closely the more important limiting factors in an organisation in order to set realistically attainable targets and budgets.

Limiting factors are identified in the external environment by the use of subjective judgement. Consideration of the social, technological, economic and political domains together with the competitive environment are a key part of strategic analysis and decision making which can be used to inform the budgeting process.

The limiting factors internal to the organisation are much less problematic. Objective measurements can be made of skills, capacities and other resources available, which may limit the provision of goods or services to the market.

Careful and systematic consideration of both external and internal constraints may lead to the identification of previously unknown limiting factors, thus alerting management to problems likely to occur during implementation of a particular strategy.

Once top management has agreed overall company objectives, then particular areas of responsibility can be assigned to lower levels of management and the budgetary process can commence.

2. Planning

Planning within the budgeting process takes place by the expression of departmental, functional or cost centre activities for the forthcoming year within individual budgets. These budgets will relate to the business objectives set by, or agreed with, top management for the year and will usually be part of the overall budget, commonly called the *master budget*.

Good planning provides the opportunity to evaluate alternative courses of action, so that resources may be used effectively under conditions of minimum risk.

There are many different types of plans which will need to be developed into budgets, examples of which are:

❏ Revenue plans;

❏ Purchasing plans;

❏ Manpower plans;

❏ Research and development plans;

❏ Capital expenditure plans;

❏ Marketing plans and business plans.

How are these plans linked and drawn together as budgets? As indicated in the last section, most organisations should have some idea of which aspects of the business limit their ability to generate profits; that is, where their major limiting factors are to be found. This should be the point at which they enter the budgeting process.

Very often, demand and the availability of the resources to meet it will be major constraints. For example, in times of buoyant sales prospects, actual revenues may be limited by the maximum physical productive capacity of the organisation. On the other hand, where forecast volume is below the productive capacity of the business, the projected budget for the use of resources will be based on those revenue forecasts.

Figure 11.1 Master budget and financial objectives

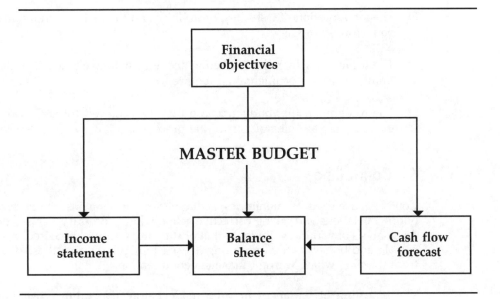

Theoretically, once the limiting factors have been identified the budgeting process should be simple to complete. In practice, however, the process is rather more complex, since the tendency is for the various budgets to be prepared in a predetermined sequence, each budget feeding information to the next. As problems of incompatibility between budgets occur, theY are solved by going back through the process and re-budgeting as necessary. The entire exercise becomes one of negotiation and agreement between the various parties to the process.

Alternative scenarios can be analysed through a master budget which is illustrated in *Figure 11.1*. This consists of an income statement, balance sheet and cash flow forecast. Once approved, the master budget allows management to plan and co-ordinate the future direction of the business.

3. Organising

A budget will not happen on its own. The more physical and human resources that are involved, the less likely is it to be conceived or achieved without good organisation.

Organising necessitates an understanding of the organisation structure, tasks, processes and systems, and people involved if any agreed budget is to have any chance of success. In particular, its success requires the following characteristics:

❏ The definition of the organisation structure so that possible areas of overlap can be identified and removed, or at least reduced;

❏ The identification of tasks, responsibilities and the methods individuals will be measured by;

❏ The means by which the budgeting activities will take place, including any training and/or documentation required;

❏ The recognition that budgeting can only be achieved through people and that they are an integral part of the process and any systems developed.

4. Controlling

Control is achieved by monitoring actual performance against the budget plan, noting deviations and taking corrective action where necessary. This is done by the analysis of variances similar to that of standard costing (discussed in *Chapter 12*). In addition, exception reporting is used to highlight only those deviations from the plan which warrant management attention.

The reporting of variances may be made before expenditure occurs where proposed spending is set against the budget or after the event when actual spending is compared to the plan. The former allows management to modify spending (for example, by seeking a cheaper source of supply) while the latter enables management to adjust future spending or ask for extra resources to conform to the plan.

5. Co-ordinating

Co-ordinating is an integral part of the budgeting process. Having organised, as discussed earlier, there is the need to look at the sequencing and interrelationships of the individual budget components.

As with limiting factors, it is difficult to view any process without considering its effect on other processes. Co-ordinating can be seen as a balancing activity which seeks to allocate priorities by predetermined agreement and also to unite a number of individual activities into a whole.

The different viewpoints of the co-ordinating process are usually apparent when agreeing company objectives. The activities will take into account the overall balance within the company, also such things as competitors and customers, economic political and social change, and if there is a need to change the future direction of the company.

6. Communicating

Within any budgeting system communication is important. Everyone concerned needs to know about:

❏   Objectives;

❏   Guidelines;

❏   Completed budgets and revisions;

❏   Actual results;

❏   Deviations from budget;

❏   Corrective action to be taken; and,

❏   Revisions to be included into forecasts which are produced for relevant management in an agreed format.

7. Motivating

The budgeting process is often considered as a purely mechanical exercise. It is argued, however, that the process is just as much a political as a mechanical process. Any system which seeks to allocate scarce resources through a decision making hierarchy which is characterised by its unequal distribution of power, is bound to be influenced by internal politics. This may tend to upset the objective calculations of the designers.

Problems caused by political influences include the pursuit of personal or group objectives at the expense of the whole organisation (lack of goal congruence), built-in slack in budget estimates, where targets tend to be imposed from above and the adoption of short-term perspectives at the expense of long-term profit optimisation.

The problem is, how can we know that if we take certain actions, then individuals will respond in a particular manner? For example, why do some managers like the budgeting process? Is it the challenge? Is it the power that information gives? Is it the 'games' they can play? Is it because they understand the system? Is it because they can see the purpose of the budgeting system? Is it because they are winning?

11.4 Budgetary control

Of equal importance to planning in the budgeting process is the need to establish a monitoring system to ensure that budget targets are met. Such a system is concerned with the:

❑ Comparison of actual results against budget;

❑ Identification, recording and communication of controllable differences; and,

❑ Taking corrective action either to maintain budget levels or, replan to meet recent developments.

The comparison of actual against budgeted performance requires that the budget is divided into monthly/four weekly periods against which actual results for each period may be compared.

Figure 11.2 Buget split into 12 monthly periods

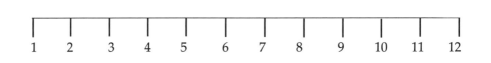

Comparison against the annual budget might be acceptable at the start of the year but it will quickly become out of date as key factors in the environment change. This will normally affect both revenue streams and cost structures. Reasons can include both opportunities and threats that the organisation should acknowledge at the earliest opportunity. For example, there is little point "sticking to the budget" when a substantial contract is awarded or that unforseen increases in energy costs must now be absorbed.

To facilitate the control process, organisations may adopt a reforecasting process that is either called the *Year's forecast or Outturn*. We will now expand this important technique with a description and example.

Year's forecast or outturn

Years forecast and outturn, are names given to the same technique and will deliver the same result. For the purpose of this section we will use year's forecast.

Many large organisations will prepare a year's forecast on a four weekly cycle while others might prepare their forecasts three times per year, e.g. at period 1-3, period 1-6 and period 1-9.

Why prepare these year's forecasts? Essentially, the year's forecast does what it says; it puts the focus on the year end position, i.e. the out turn.

Figure 11.3 Year's forecast

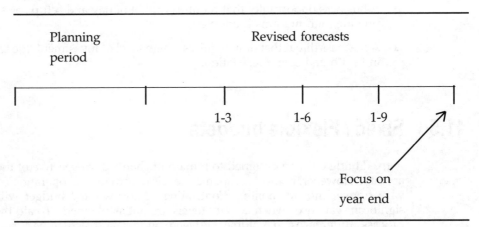

It also allows for periodic reviews to be held where budget holders are required to provide their latest forecasts. This can result in a budget holder declaring a surplus, which, together with other surpluses allows management to redirect funds throughout the year. However, it can also result in other budget holders declaring a deficit where they will be required to explain the reasons for their deficits.

A years forecast should remove the idea of :

"this is the budget, good or bad we are sticking to it".

if the budget is in surplus – then spend it.

An interesting comparison can be made when considering what a budget holder would do with a surplus if it were their own business. Would they spend the surplus simply because it was in the budget? We think not. However, what a system employing a years forecast does require is trust. Budget holders who declare a surplus one year shouldn't be constrained to that reduced level when setting their budgets for the next year. The implication in such a case gives a clear indication that budgets are set on the previous year levels plus or minus certain economic percentages. One would hope that budgets and three year plans were prepared to achieve specific objectives.

Reasons for difference

When a revised year's forecast is presented for approval it needs to be accompanied by a statement that explains the reasons of difference from the current forecast. Examples of reasons for difference might be:

❑ Increased competition in the market, leading to a reduction in revenue and/ or an increase in marketing costs;

❑ A crop failure leading to increased raw material costs;

❑ A business opportunity that requires capital outlay and setup costs, but will provide high margins if adopted;

❑ A business threat that now requires a high level of investment due to changes in health and safety legislation.

11.5　Fixed / Flexible budgets

A fixed budget is one designed to remain unchanged irrespective of the level of activity. However, in most companies, levels of activity and operating conditions vary from month to month. Controlling against a fixed budget will lead to significant variances when activity levels are not as planned. To aid the control process, differences in volume between budget and actual performance are incorporated in a revised, or flexible, budget.

It is important to ensure that the comparison of budgeted and actual performances matches like with like. For example, if actual revenue volumes are higher than budgeted, then certain items in the budget which are volume related should be increased. If this process was omitted a simple comparison would show an overspending on variable cost items, the result of which would be to record an unrealistic difference from budget. This is illustrated in *Table 11.1* on page 305, where the planned level of activity was the production and sale of 48,000 meals, whereas the reality was that 60,000 meals were produced and sold.

Table 11.1 Comparison of budget and actual

Budget activity level:48,000 meals
Actual activity level: 60,000 meals

	Unit cost per meal £	Variable cost 48,000 meals £	Fixed cost 48,000 meals £	Total budget 48,000 meals £	Total actual 60,000 meals £	Variance £
Revenues	1.75			84,000	103,200	19,200
Ingredients	0.35	16,800		16,800	20,280	–3,480
Wages	0.55	26,400		26,400	33,000	–6,600
Electricity	0.10	4,800	1,000	5,800	6,750	–950
Administration			12,000	12,000	11,500	500
Depreciation			9,000	9,000	9,000	0
Total costs		48,000	22,000	**70,000**	**80,530**	**–10,530**
Profit				14,000	22,670	8,670

It can be seen that there are significant negative cost variances, which result in the actual total cost being £10,530 higher than budget. However, this is offset by higher actual revenues – £19,200 higher than budget – resulting in £8,670 profit greater than budget. On a line by line basis this is not very helpful for control purposes. For example, wage costs are significantly higher than planned, but they were for a different level of operation. For in-year-management, the budget levels must be adjusted, in order to make a valid comparison with the actual level of activity. A flexible budget can be used to show this. Cost and revenues at the actual level of activity are recorded and matched against actual costs and revenues to identify the variances that are not related to differences in volume.

Obviously any variation in profit as a result of volume change is also important to know, but for control purposes, knowledge of variances due to efficiency and expenditure differences are vital. To produce the flexible budget a knowledge of those costs that change as activity levels change, as opposed to those that are fixed in the period is essential. *Table 11.2* illustrates the variances when actual performance (costs and revenues) is matched against the budget for the actual level of activity, i.e. actual costs and revenues for 60,000 meals and the budget for the 60,000 meals. It can be seen that the high unfavourable total cost variance of £10,500, when actual is compared to original budget, is more realistically reported as £1,470 favourable when the budget is flexed to represent the actual level of activity. However, because of the unfavourable revenue variance, when the volume increase is taken into account, the profit variance reported of £8,670 against the original budget becomes £330 unfavourable.

Table 11.2   Flexed budget v actual

Flexed budget activity level: 60,000 meals
Actual activity level: 60,000 meals

	Unit cost per meal	Variable cost 60,000 meals	Fixed cost 60,000 meals	Total flexed budget 60,000 meals	Total actual 60,000 meals	Variance
	£	£	£	£	£	£
Revenues	**1.75**			**105,000**	**103,200**	**−1,800**
Ingredients	0.35	21,000		21,000	20,280	720
Wages	0.55	33,000		33,000	33,000	0
Electricity	0.10	6,000	1,000	7,000	6,750	250
Administration			12,000	12,000	11,500	500
Depreciation			9,000	9,000	9,000	0
Total costs		60,000	22,000	**82,000**	**80,530**	**1,470**
Profit				23,000	22,670	−330

In summary, using flexible budgeting allows separation of the causes of variance between those that are volume related, and those that are related to efficiency or expenditure.

11.6   Budget administration

What are the key elements in administering a budget? We recommend that you review those we provide and compare them with practices in your own organisation. See if you can identify possible areas for improvement.

1. Budget guidelines

Budget guidelines are a means of conveying important budget assumptions to budget holders. They should be prepared at least annually and should include various percentages for budget holders to apply to expense items. They might also include information relating to overall movements in revenue volumes, the increase/reduction in certain sectors of the business, or the requirement to implement a particular aspect of health and safety.

2. Budget manual

A budget manual should contain sufficient information to enable managers to operate the budgeting system within a particular business, division or department. It should explain all the terms which are used in the budgeting system and provide worked examples of the main documents. A budget manual should not only deal effectively with the detail that a budget holder requires but also provide an overview of the total system.

3. Budget period

The main budget period within business is usually one year. However, many companies consider their three year plan to operate within the budgeting system. The usual method of operating such a three year plan is that the annual budget forms the first year of a three year plan. The second year is usually shown in less detail, with the third year simply taking a broad overview.

4. Budget factor

In any business there can be a number of factors which restrict its potential growth, a common one being revenue volume. Whatever the factor that restricts potential growth it should be identified and made explicit. For example, if revenues are considered to be such a factor then all other budgets should be prepared in an attempt to maximise revenues. Other budget factors could include; shortage of skilled labour, shortage of materials, storage of material, storage space or a specific item of plant within the manufacturing process.

5. Budget timetable

In many large organisations budget preparation will often extend over the six months prior to the budget period. The complex nature of budget preparation demands that a detailed timetable be produced to ensure that each component within the overall activity will be completed in time for input into other components of the system.

Budget timetables should be produced to meet a number of key dates which relate to divisional and group board meetings.

6. Budget training

If the budgeting system is to succeed it is important that the budget administration should include management training in the processes and techniques appropriate to a particular business. Such training should involve guided in-company instruction by staff familiar with the system and the specific responsibilities. It is not desirable to leave an individual with the manual and the responsibility – the training should precede the responsibility.

We have now set the scene for budgeting and budgetary control which is a vital area for all managers to understand. Budgeting is far more than simply working with numbers, as we have sought to illustrate with our review of key considerations within the budget environment, budgetary control and budget administration.

11.7 Preparation of a cash budget

From the following information, prepare a cash budget for the six months to 30th June 200X. The estimated cash balance at 1st January 200X is £4,000

	Revenues	Purchases	Wages
200X-1	£	£	£
November	40,600	24,500	
December	48,000	23,200	
200X			
January	34,200	16,600	5,600
February	36,400	18,900	6,200
March	38,500	20,300	6,350
April	42,500	22,100	6,500
May	43,400	24,400	6,650
June	47,100	27,200	6,800

a. Credit allowed to customers 60% pay in one month
                                                    40% pay in two months

b. Suppliers are paid one month in arrears

c. Other payments:

		£
January	Taxation	20,000
March	Equipment	40,000
June	Dividend	10,000

The steps to be taken in the preparation of a cash budget are shown below:

1   Enter the opening cash balance in January which is given, i.e. £4,000

2.   Calculate the receipts from trade receivables, 60% pay in one month, 40% pay in two months following the month of sale, therefore:

Cash Received	60% of Revenue in	40% of Revenue in
January	December	November
February	January	December
March	February	January
April	March	February
May	April	March
June	May	April

3. Trade payable are delayed by one month. Therefore, purchases in December will not be paid until January.

4. Complete the cash budget by entering the remaining figures, and then calculate the monthly and cumulative balances to establish the cash flow picture.

Table 11.3 *Monthly cash budget – for the six months ending 30th June 200X*

	Jan £'000	Feb £'000	Mar £'000	Apr £'000	May £'000	Jun £'000
Part A Receipts						
Revenues	45,040	39,720	35,520	37,660	40,900	43,040
Subtotal A	45,040	39,720	35,520	37,660	40,900	43,040
Part B Payments						
Purchases	23,200	16,600	18,900	20,300	22,100	24,400
Wages	5,600	6,200	6,350	6,500	6,650	6,800
Taxation	20,000					
Equipment			40,000			
Dividend						10,000
Subtotal B	48,800	22,800	65,250	26,800	28,750	41,200
Part C						
Cash flow (A–B)	–3,760	16,920	–29,730	10,860	12,150	1,840
Part D						
Balance b/f	4,000	240	17,160	–12,570	–1,710	10,440
Balance c/f (C+D)	240	17,160	–12,570	–1,710	10,440	12,280

In this case, there will be a shortage of cash in March and April, and we can use the statement to help identify the problem areas and possible courses of action. The main problem is the purchase of the capital equipment in March. As an alternative we could:

❑ delay the purchase of the capital equipment;

❑ negotiate terms for delayed payment;

❑ negotiate finance for the capital equipment;

❑ arrange hire or lease;

❑ obtain additional bank finance;

❑ reduce credit period allowed to customers; and/or,

❑ increase credit period taken (allowed) from suppliers.

Each course of action involves the consideration of an additional set of variables before arriving at a decision. For example, the last two items on the list above both affect the trading environment. If a company attempts either, it could lose customers and/or suppliers.

In February, May and June the statement shows that there will be a surplus of cash. In this case, a company should take steps to transfer funds into other activities which will generate interest. These include:

❑ bank deposit or building society;

❑ short-term money market. (Many large companies have departments whose function is to forecast closing cash positions on a daily basis and then negotiate terms on the overnight market).

11.8   Mechanics of budgeting

In this example we start with an opening balance sheet and a number of budget assumptions and show the preparation of monthly trading accounts, monthly cash budget, budgeted income statement for the period and a closing balance sheet.

Estimated balance sheet as at 30th June 200X

	£'000 Cost	£'000 Depn	£'000
NON-CURRENT ASSETS			
Land and buildings	650		650
Plant and machinery	1,760	500	1,260
	2,410	500	1,910
CURRENT ASSETS			
Inventory		950	
Accounts receivable		1,650	
Cash and cash equivalents		70	
			2,670
Total assets			4,580
CURRENT LIABILITIES			
Accounts payable		650	
Bank overdraft		1,100	
		1,750	
NON-CURRENT LIABILITIES			
Loan-term loan (12% per annum)		1,500	
Total liabilities			3,250
Net assets			1,330
EQUITY			
Issued share capital			400
Retained earnings			930
Total equity			1,330

The executives of *Rusty and Dusty Musty Ltd* are preparing budgets for the six months July to December 200X. They have produced two financial objectives as guidelines for the assessment of the budget:

1. To increase working capital by £150,000;

2. To reduce borrowings (overdraft and long-term loans) by £300,000.

The following transactions should be incorporated:

a. The board has approved the purchase of a new machine in August 200X costing £250,000.

b. Wages, assumed to be 10% of monthly revenues.

   Fixed costs estimated at £60,000 per month (all cash payments).

c. Depreciation to be charged at £24,000 per month.

d. Interim dividend of £50,000 payable 15th July 200X.

e. Revenues and closing inventory estimates:

	July £'000	Aug £'000	Sept £'000	Oct £'000	Nov £'000	Dec £'000
Revenues	600	760	840	1,000	680	520
Closing inventory	1,000	900	800	800	700	650

f. Trade payables at 30th June 200X are for purchases:

May	£270,000
June	£380,000

   Trade receivables at 30th June 200X are for revenues:

April	£500,000
May	£600,000
June	£550,000

   Assume the same credit periods will continue, i.e. two months for trade payables and three months for trade receivables.

g. Gross profit to revenues is budgeted at 30%.

h. Assume purchases to be the balancing figure for the preparation of the monthly trading accounts.

1. Monthly trading accounts

The monthly trading accounts record the physical transactions and balances. In this example we have been given a gross profit percentage and monthly forecast of closing inventories. Purchases are the balancing figure. Later we will use the summary when preparing the budgeted income statement.

The following steps should be taken during preparation of the monthly trading accounts. You can check the results in *Table 11.4*.

Step

1. Enter the revenues and closing inventories from note (e), then calculate the gross profit, i.e. 30% of revenues (30% of £600,000 in July).

2. Enter the opening inventories for July (£950,000) which is taken from the opening balance sheet, then enter the remaining opening inventory figures, i.e. previous month's closing inventories.

3. Cost of sales is the sum of revenues less gross profit, e.g. for July:

   (£600,000 − £180,000) = £420,000.

4. Purchases will be the balancing figures and calculated as follows:

   Cost of sales + Closing inventories − Opening inventories, e.g. for July:
   (£420,000 + £1,000,000 − £950,000) = £470,000.

Table 11.4   Monthly trading accounts for the six months ending 31st December 200X

	July £000	Aug £000	Sept £000	Oct £000	Nov £000	Dec £000	Summary £000
Revenues	600	760	840	1,000	680	520	4,400
Opening inventory	950	1,000	900	800	800	700	950
Purchases	470	432	488	700	376	314	2,780
	1,420	1,432	1,388	1,500	1,176	1,014	3,730
Closing inventory	1,000	900	800	800	700	650	650
Cost of sales	420	532	588	700	476	364	3,080
Gross profit	**180**	**228**	**252**	**300**	**204**	**156**	**1,320**

2. Monthly cash budget

At each stage, check the figures against *Table 11.5.*

Step

1. Enter the opening cash balance which is taken from the opening balance sheet.

2. Income from accounts receivable. The example states a three month delay, therefore:

Sales	Cash received
April	July
May	August
June	September
July	October
August	November
September	December
October	
November	Closing trade receivables figure
December	

3. Trade payables are delayed for two months. Therefore purchases from May to October will be paid for in July through to December. November and December purchases will remain unpaid and represent the closing trade payables figure.

4. Complete the cash budget by entering the remaining figures, then extract the monthly balances.

Table 11.5 Monthly cash budget – for the six months ending 31st December 200X

	July £'000	Aug £'000	Sept £'000	Oct £'000	Nov £'000	Dec £'000	Total £'000
Part A Receipts							
Revenues	500	600	550	600	760	840	3,850
Subtotal A	500	600	550	600	760	840	3,850
Part B Payments							
Purchases	270	380	470	432	488	700	2,740
Wages	60	76	84	100	68	52	440
Dividend	50						50
Machines		250				250	
Fixed Costs	60	60	60	60	60	60	360
Subtotal B	440	766	614	592	616	812	3,840
Part C							
Cash Flow (A–B)	60	–166	–64	8	144	28	10
Part D							
Balance b/f	70	130	–36	–100	–92	52	70
Balance c/f (C+D)	130	–36	–100	–92	52	80	80

3. Budgeted income statement

Key points:

1. The figures for the first section of the income statement (from revenues down to gross profit) are taken from the summary column of the monthly trading accounts, *Table 11.4*.

2. There is no delay in the payment of wages or fixed costs therefore, the totals can be taken from the total column of the monthly cash budget, *Table 11.5*.

3. Calculate the loan interest due for the six months,

   i.e. (£1,500,000 x 12% ÷ 2).

4. Enter depreciation, then add salaries, fixed costs, interest payable and depreciation; the sum of which should be deducted from gross profit to find the profit for the period, i.e. (£1,320,000 – £1,034,000 = £286,000).

Table 11.6   Budgeted income statement for the six months ending 31st December 200X

	£'000	£'000
Revenues		4,400
Opening inventory	950	
Purchases	2,780	
	3,730	
Closing inventory	650	
Cost of sales		3,080
Gross profit		1,320
Wages	440	
Fixed costs	360	
Interest payable	90	
Depreciation	144	
		1034
Profit for the period		286
Dividend		50
Retained profit		236

4. Budgeted closing balance sheet

The simplest way to prepare the closing balance sheet is to take each figure in turn from the opening balance sheet and,

if no change has occurred then enter the same figure in the closing balance sheet; or

if change has occurred, make the necessary adjustment then, enter the revised figure in the closing balance sheet.

You will find that the preparation of the closing balance sheet helps to 'tie up' a number of figures which, until now, had apparently been forgotten. At each stage, check the source of all figures and the end result in the closing balance sheet as illustrated in *Table 11.7*. The figures included there were calculated as follows:

Table 11.7   Budgeted closing balance sheet as at 31st December 200X

	£'000 Cost	£'000 Depn	£'000
NON-CURRENT ASSETS			
Land and buildings	650		650
Plant and machinery	2,010	644	1,366
	2,660	644	2,016
CURRENT ASSETS			
Inventories		650	
Trade and other receivables		2,200	
Cash and cash equivalents		80	
			2,930
Total assets			4,946
CURRENT LIABILITIES			
Trade and other payables		690	
Bank overdraft		1,100	
Interest payable		90	
		1,880	
NON-CURRENT LIABILITIES			
Loan-term loan (12% per annum)		1,500	
Total liabilities			3,380
Net assets			1,566
EQUITY			
Issued share capital			400
Retained earnings			1,166
Total equity			1,566

Key points:

1. Land and buildings: No change.

2. Plant and machinery: In this case, additional capital has been spent and the provision for depreciation increased. Therefore, the calculation is (£1,260,000 + £250,000 − £144,000 = £1,366,000).

3. Inventories: This is the closing inventories at December, i.e. £650,000.

4. Trade and other payables: Sales for October, November and December will remain unpaid at the end of the period, therefore (£1,000,000 + £680,000 + £520,000 = £2,200,000).

5. Cash: This is the closing cash position at December, i.e. £80,000.

6. Trade and other payables: Purchases for November and December will remain unpaid at the end of the period, therefore (£376,000 + £314,000 = £690,000).

7. Bank overdraft: No change.

8. Interest payable: We calculated the interest payable and entered £90,000 into the income statement. A similar entry is required in the closing balance sheet to recognise the liability.

9. Share capital: No change.

10. Retained earnings: This is found by taking the figure from the opening balance sheet and adding the profit for the period (£930,000 + £236,000 = £1,166,000).

11. Loan-term loan: No change.

5.   Interpretation of budget statements

The cash budget, shown in *Table 11.5*, produces a satisfactory result if taken for the whole six month period. However, there is a period in the middle when the company will not be able to meet its cash commitments. The main problem is the purchase of capital equipment in August and we considered possible courses of action when reviewing the cash budget.

6.   What about the two financial objectives set?

a. **To increase working capital by £150,000**

An examination of the net working capital position between the opening and closing balance sheets clearly shows an increase in working capital of £130,000 which does not meet this particular budget objective.

b. **Reduce borrowing by £300,000**

The assumptions contained in this budget revision do not meet this budget objective. There is no change in short-term or long-term debt financing.

As a consequence, the likely result in practice would be at least another round of budgeting to meet the objectives set.

11.9   Other budgeting techniques

1. Incremental/Zero-Base budgeting (ZBB)

In preparing a budget it is important to establish the base or starting point. One way, incremental budgeting, is to take the current levels as base data and to adjust for changes expected to occur during the budget period. For example, if salaries of a department are currently £100,000, with no increase in numbers expected, inflation is anticipated at 3%, the new budget figure would be £103,000. Although this may be an appropriate way of proceeding in such situations, the disadvantage of this approach is that it may allow past inefficiencies to become part of the new period's budget.

An alternative approach is the use of zero-base budgeting, which is also sometimes known as priority-based budgeting (PBB). The essence of a zero-base approach is to allow an organisation to actively search for, learn from and adapt to changing environments. *The Chartered Institute of Management Accountants'* Official Terminology defines Zero-Base budgeting as:

> *A method of budgeting whereby all activities are re-evaluated each time a budget is set. Discrete levels of each activity are valued and a combination chosen to match funds available.*

In practice this would mean that each manager has to budget ignoring the past, acting as though he were preparing a budget for the first time, and preparing a justification for the proposed spend. A decision package is prepared for each activity showing costs, purposes, alternatives, performance measurements and benefits. These packages are then screened and judged in a review process to determine benefits and the allocation of resources and funding. Advocates of this method claim that allocation of resources are more closely linked to need and benefit and it encourages an attitude which questions the status quo. However, it has to be said that it can take significant resourcing to undertake the activity, and as with all such areas of management there is a need to consider cost-benefit.

2. Activity-based budgeting

In *Chapter 8*, the development of activity–based costing (ABC) was considered. Organisations that have adopted this approach may well extend their use of the activity–based concepts, combining them with elements of priority–based budgeting to budget on an 'activity–base'. Such a budget will involve a form of matrix calculation of costs for major activities and the resource inputs (e.g. salaries, telecoms.) for each activity, with identification of the cost driver activity.

Exercise 11.1

E. Tee Ltd. prepares cash budgets on a monthly basis. The following forecasts are available for the four months ending 31st March 200X.

	Purchases	Revenues	Overhead expense	Wages
	£'000	£'000	£'000	£'000
December 200X-1	90	270	33	57
January 200X	60	180	31	60
February	120	165	36	51
March	30	150	30	52

Other information is available as follows:

a All purchases are on monthly credit terms – the suppliers being paid, less 2.5% cash discount, in the month following purchase.

b 20% of all revenues are made on a cash basis, the remainder being sold to credit customers who pay the month after the month of sale.

c Overhead expenses include depreciation amounting to £4,500 each month. Payments are made the month after the month the expenses were incurred.

d Wages are paid for in the month that they are incurred.

e A new computer installation, costing £37,500, is to be paid for in February 200X. During March 200X, old fixtures and fittings, which originally cost £27,000 are to be sold for £1,500 cash.

f The bank balance at 1st January 200X is expected to be £30,000.

REQUIRED

1. Produce a cash budget in tabular form for the quarter ending 31st March 200X showing the bank balance at each month end.

2. Comment on the results of your analysis, and suggest ways to deal with cash shortages and cash excesses.

Exercise 11.2

On 1st January 200X, *Dream Ltd.* is planning to open a new factory to manufacture tables.

Estimates for the first six months are as follows:

a   Revenues will be £40,000 per month for the first three months and £60,000 per month thereafter. Payment for one half of these revenues will be received in the month following the sale, the remainder will be received two months after the sale.

b   Production each month will equal that month's revenues, i.e. no inventories.

c   Raw materials will cost 30% of revenues and will be paid for in the month following the purchase.

d   Wages and salaries will cost 20% of revenues and will be paid in the month they occur.

e   Rent will be £40,000 per year, payable quarterly in advance.

f   Heat and light will cost £20,000 per year, payable at the end of each quarter.

g   Other expenses will cost £10,000 per month and will be paid at the end of each month.

h   Plant and machinery for the factory will be purchased on 1st January 200X at a cost of £50,000, and will be paid in ten equal instalments.

i   The company's rate of depreciation for plant and machinery is 25% per year.

j   The new factory will be provided with a bank balance of £25,000 at 1st January 200X.

REQUIRED

1.   Prepare a monthly cash budget for the factory for the six months ending 30th June 200X.

2.   Prepare a budgeted income statement for the six months ending 30th June 200X and a balance sheet as at that date.

3.   Advise management on any action which might be required from the information disclosed by the cash budget.

Exercise 11.3

Alastair Dryant is planning to commence business as a manufacturer on the 1st January 200X. The business is to be financed from capital of £25,000 provided by Dryant on the 1st January 200X and an overdraft limit of £15,000 agreed with the bank. Estimates of costs and revenues for the first six months are as follows:

a   Revenues: January £9,000; February £12,000; March £18,00; and £20,000 per month thereafter. Half of the revenues are expected to be for cash, the balance will be on one month's credit.

b   Production will take place during the month of sale, but raw materials are to be purchased in the month before production, except for the first month when two months inventories will be obtained. Raw materials are 40% of revenues value. Payment is made for raw materials in the second month following their purchase.

c   Direct wages and other direct expenses are expected to be a further 30% of revenues per month, they will be paid for in the month they are incurred.

d   Fixed expenses are budgeted at £2,200 per month, paid for in the month they are incurred.

e   During December 200X-1 machinery will be delivered, the cost of which has been quoted at £48,000. It has been decided to depreciate this machinery at 10% per annum on cost, and allowance for depreciation has been included in fixed expenses. Payment for the machinery will be in four equal monthly instalments commencing February 200X.

f   Dryant will draw a managers salary of £2,000 per month.

REQUIRED

1.   A cash budget for the first four months.

2.   Comment on the situation revealed by the cash budget.

Exercise 11.4

The executives of *P.C Ltd* are preparing budgets for the six months July to December 200X.

The budgeted balance sheet as at the 30th June 200X

Non-current assets		Equity	
Land and buildings	100,000	Share capital (£1 shares)	50,000
Plant and machinery	160,000	Retained earnings	115,000
		Loan loans at 12%	250,000
Current assets		**Current liabilities**	
Inventories	220,000	Trade and other payables	65,000
Trade and other receivables	150,000	Bank overdraft	150,000
	630,000		630,000

a   The board has approved the purchase of a new machine in August 200X costing £40,000.

b   Wages, assume 10% of monthly revenues.

 Fixed costs estimated at £5,000 per month (all cash payments).

c   Depreciation is to be charged at £3,000 per month.

d   Interim dividend of 20p per share, payable 15th July 200X.

e

	Jul	Aug	Sep	Oct	Nov	Dec
	£'000	£'000	£'000	£'000	£'000	£'000
Revenues	50	70	80	100	60	40
Closing inventories	200	190	180	170	170	160

f   Trade and other payables at 30th June 200X are for purchases: May £40,000 and June £25,000. Trade and other receivables at 30th June 200X are for revenues: April £70,000, May £40,000 and June £40,000.

 Credit periods are expected to be the same during the second half of 200X, i.e. two months for suppliers, and three months for customers.

g   Gross profit to revenues is budgeted at 30%. Assume purchases to be the balancing figure.

REQUIRED

1.   Prepare a cash budget for the six months to 31st December 200X.

2.   Describe the principle purposes of a cash budget.

Exercise 11.5

The executives of *Thrust Limited* are concerned about possible cash shortages arising from a number of large payments due in the third quarter of 200X.

a   The cash balance on 1st July 200X is forecast to be £30,000.

b   A new machine is to be installed in August 200X costing £40,000 and will be paid for in September 200X.

c   A sales commission of 2% on revenues is to be paid in the month following the sale.

d   Taxation of £110,000 is to be paid in August 200X.

e   In July 200X an interim dividend of £50,000 is to be paid to ordinary shareholders (ignore taxation).

f   Production costs are paid as incurred. The average delay in paying administration costs is one month.

g   The average delay in paying wages is one week, with research and development costs averaging two weeks.

h   To encourage payment of invoices, the company allows a cash discount of 5% if payment is made within the month of the sale, and 2% if payment is made in the month following the sale. It is estimated that 20% of the trade receivables pay within the month of the sale, and a further 50% of the trade receivables pay in the month following the sale. The remaining trade receivables are expected to pay their invoices in full, within two months.

i   The period of credit allowed by suppliers averages three months.

j   An issue of loan stock is expected to be made in August 200X which will result in £30,000 being received during that month.

A forecast of costs and revenues produced the following:

	Apr	May	Jun	Jul	Aug	Sep
				£'000		
Revenues	190	240	290	245	180	170
Purchases	60	55	80	50	40	45
Labour	50	45	65	40	30	35
Production costs	20	18	20	25	20	18
Administration costs	20	20	25	30	25	20
Research and development	6	7	8	10	15	12

REQUIRED

Prepare a cash budget for the three months to 30th September 200X.

Exercise 11.6

Findings Ltd are about to negotiate with the bank the short-term financing of a new venture until it has concluded arrangements for permanent finance. Budgeted income statement to 30th April 200X.

	Jan £'000	Feb £'000	Mar £'000	Apr £'000
Credit revenues	120	130	84	132
Materials	40	42	28	46
Labour	34	34	26	36
Production costs	7	8	7	8
Administrative costs	8	8	8	8
Selling and distribution costs	8	9	6	10
Net profit	23	29	9	24

The following additional information is available:

a.   There are no inventories of finished goods.

b.   Cost of materials has been arrived at as follows:

	Jan £'000	Feb £'000	Mar £'000	Apr £'000
Opening inventories	0	22	30	42
Purchases	62	50	40	50
less Closing inventories	22	30	42	46
Cost of raw materials	40	42	28	46

c.   The period of credit allowed by suppliers of materials is one month.

d.   To encourage early payment of invoices, *Findings Ltd.* allows a cash discount of 10% if payment is made within the month of sale. It is estimated that 10% of the trade receivables each month will take this discount, and a further 50% of the trade receivables of each month will pay in the following month. The remaining 40% are expected to pay their invoices in full, two months after the month of sale.

e.   The overhead costs include the following items which have been allocated on an equal monthly charge but which are payable as follows:

Costs	Monthly charge	Amount and date of payment
Production	£1,000	£4,000 in January
Administration	£800	£2,000 in January
Selling and distribution	£500	£1,500 in March

f.   Depreciation has been charged and included in production overhead at £1,500 per month.

g.   The capital budget indicates that capital payments will be made as follows:

   January £180,000   March £20,000.

h.   Unless stated otherwise, items can be treated on a cash basis.

REQUIRED

1.   Prepare a monthly cash budget to determine the finance required.

2.   Discuss the importance of cash budgets in a system of budgetary control.

STANDARD COSTING

When you have finished studying this chapter and completed the exercises, you should be able to:

❑ Understand who would set the standards for materials and labour in a standard costing system.

❑ Describe, calculate and interpret:

- Labour variances including, cost, efficiency and rate.
- Material variances including, cost, usage and price.
- Revenue variances including, total, volume and price.
- Variable overhead variances including, cost, efficiency and expenditure.

12.1   Introduction

An early CIMA definition for standard costing states:

> "A standard cost is a predetermined cost calculated in relation to a prescribed set of working conditions, correlating technical specification and scientific measurement of materials and labour to the prices and wage rates expected to apply during the period to which the standard cost is expected to relate with an addition of an appropriate share of budgeted overhead."

That being said, we all practice the basic techniques of standard costing in our daily lives. For example, driving to work – we normally have a standard time in mind that can be used to compare our actual time taken, the difference being the variance from the standard time (allowed). When setting our standard time we would have to take into account, the likely road conditions, the performance of the car and the abilities of the driver. If we completed the journey in less time (or more time) we could explain the reason(s) why.

Driving to work is a repetitive activity, therefore, it lends itself to the development of a standard. In business, standard costing is applied to the planning and control of direct materials and direct labour, although it can be used to develop a full standard cost and price for a product or service.

12.2   Setting the standards and variance analysis

1.   Who would set the standards for materials?

An engineer, designer, chemist or similar person would prepare a specification of material required, both quality and quantity. The recipe in a cookery book is a good example. It not only gives a listing of the ingredients and quantities but also specifies the method to be used.

The method to be used would dictate the prescribed set of working conditions (the driving to work example), in terms of location, equipment and people.

Standard prices are determined for each material. These will be prepared by the appropriate purchasing specialist and will apply throughout the period to which the standards have been developed, normally in line with the budget period.

2.   Who would set the standards for labour?

An industrial engineer will determine the best working method (using method study) and will then carry out timings to find out the time taken to complete each part of the process including the number of people and their grades.

It is important to recognise that should the working method change then the standard times will change. Often the labour standards have been reduced in the standard costs, in anticipation of the revision to the working method – normally a saving in labour through increased mechanisation.

Standard labour rates are determined for each grade of labour. The Personnel Director would be responsible for setting a base labour rate from which all other rates would be adjusted. When setting standard labour rates it is important to take into account holiday pay, normal bonus payments, normal overtime working and the mix of labour grades for each process.

3. What is a normal standard?

A normal standard is one that considers normal working conditions and a normal (achievable) level of activity. It is a standard that a worker can achieve without resorting to changes in working methods. If a standard is set too tight, and is not achievable, it is unlikely that the workforce will recognise the standard and will not produce the desired result.

4. Variance analysis

In budgeting systems, budget holders develop their budgets for the coming year. Once approved, these are used to compare actual expenditure and identify variances from budget. The same principle applies in standard costing systems where standard costs are developed for each product or service. Once approved, these are used to compare actual costs and identify variances from standard costs.

In standard costing, variances are used to determine who is responsible for each variance. For example, the material cost variance is split into a material usage variance and a material price variance. The former would be the responsibility of the production manager/supervisor, while the latter would be the responsibility of the purchasing specialist.

12.3 Example - Labour, material and revenue variances

1. Calculation of labour variances

A company manufactures a component with the following specification for direct labour:

Standard direct labour hours   20 hours

Standard direct labour rate   £5.00 per hour

During the month 250 components were produced, and the actual wages paid amounted to £30,800 for 5,600 hours worked.

Table 12.1   Calculation of standard costing variances – Labour

Column A Standard hours times standard rate			Column B Actual hours times standard rate			Column C Actual hours times actual rate		
Hours	Rate	£	Hours	Rate	£	Hours	Rate	£
5,000	5.00	25,000	5,600	5.00	28,000	5,600	5.50	30,800

£3,000 adverse
Labour efficiency variance

£2,800 adverse
Labour rate variance

£5,800 adverse
Labour cost variance

The steps to be taken in the calculation of the labour variances are shown below:

1.   Enter actual hours and actual wages paid in Column C, i.e. 5,600 hours and £30,800. Optional, divide the actual wages paid by the actual hours to arrive at the actual rate, i.e. £30,800 ÷ 5,600 hours = £5.50. *We will use this actual rate when interpreting the labour rate variance, see page 331.*

2. Enter actual hours in Column B.

3. Enter standard labour rate in Column B, then multiply the actual hours by the standard rate, i.e. 5,600 hours x £5.00 = £28,000.

4. Calculate the standard labour hours (number of components multiplied by the standard hour per component), i.e. 250 components x 20 hours = 5,000 hours. Enter the result in Column A.

5. Multiply the standard hours by the standard rate, i.e. 5,000 hours x £5.00 = £25,000. Enter the result in Column A.

6. Calculate and interpret the variances:

Labour cost variance. This is the total variance and is calculated by taking Column A minus Column C, i.e. £25,000 – £30,800 = £5,800 adverse.

Interpretation; we were 'allowed' £25,000 to produce the 250 components. We actually paid £30,800 in wages, therefore, the adverse variance of £5,800. Interpretation; it is not possible to say much about this variance other than in this case it is adverse. We must look at the two subsidiary variances, labour efficiency and labour rate, to find out the causes.

Labour efficiency variance. This is a sub-variance of the labour cost variance and is found by taking Column A minus Column B, i.e. £25,000 – £28,000 = £3,000 adverse.

Interpretation; we were 'allowed' 5,000 hours to produce the 250 components. We actually took 5,600 hours, i.e. 600 hours more at the standard labour rate of £5.00 per hour = 600 hours x £5.00 = £3,000 adverse. Consider reasons for the labour efficiency variance between the standard hours 'allowed' and the actual hours taken; could be caused by using a different skill of labour.

Labour rate variance. This is a sub-variance of the labour cost variance and is found by taking Column B minus Column C, i.e. £28,000 – £30,800 = £2,800 adverse.

Interpretation; for 5,600 hours worked, we were 'allowed' £28,000 at the standard labour rate. The actual wages paid were £30,800. This can be checked by taking the actual hours worked and multiplying by the difference between the standard labour hour rate and the actual labour hour rate, i.e. 5,600 hours x (£5.00 – £5.50) = £2,800 adverse. Consider reasons for the labour rate variance; an increase in the actual labour rate above those incorporated into the standard labour rate, similar with overtime rates, or simply have used a different (more expensive) grade of labour.

2. Calculation of material variances

A company manufactures a unit with the following specification for direct material:

Standard quantity of material   8 kgs.

Standard material price   £4.00 per kg

During the month 2,000 units were produced, and the value of the actual materials issued from stores was £65,520 for a quantity of 15,600 kgs.

Table 12.2 Calculation of standard costing variances – Material

Column A Standard quantity times standard price			Column B Actual quantity times standard price			Column C Actual quantity times actual price		
Qty.	Price	£	Qty.	Price	£	Qty.	Price	£
16,000	4.00	64,000	15,600	4.00	62,400	15,600	4.20	65,520

£1,600 favourable
Material usage variance

£3,120 adverse
Material price variance

£1,520 adverse
Material cost variance

The steps to be taken in the calculation of the material variances are shown below:

1. Enter actual quantity and actual value of materials issued from stores in Column C, i.e. 15,600 kgs and £65,520. Optional, divide the actual value of materials by the actual quantity to arrive at the actual price, i.e. £65,520 ÷ 15,600 kgs = £4.20 per kg. *We will use this actual price when interpreting the material price variance, see page 333.*

2. Enter actual quantity of materials issued from stores in Column B.

3. Enter standard material price in Column B, then multiply the actual quantity by the standard price, i.e. 15,600 hours x £4.00 = £62,400.

4. Calculate the standard quantity of materials allowed (actual units produced multiplied by the standard quantity), i.e. 2,000 x 8 kgs = 16,000 kgs. Enter the result in Column A.

5. Multiply the standard quantity by the standard price, i.e. 16,000 kgs x £4.00 = £64,000. Enter the result in Column A.

6. Calculate and interpret the variances:

    Material cost variance. This is the total variance and is calculated by taking Column A minus Column C, i.e. £64,000 – £65,520 = £1,520 adverse.

    Interpretation; we were 'allowed' £64,000 to produce the 2,000 units. We actually issued £65,520 worth of materials from stores, therefore, the adverse variance of £1,520. Interpretation; it is not possible to say much about this variance other than in this case it is adverse. We must look at the two subsidiary variances; material usage and material price, to find out the causes.

    Material usage variance. This is a sub-variance of the material cost variance and is found by taking Column A minus Column B, i.e. £64,000 – £62,400 = £1,600 favourable.

    Interpretation; we were 'allowed' 16,000 kgs to produce the 2,000 units. We actually used 15,600 kgs, i.e. 400 kgs less at the standard material price of £4.00 per kg = 400 hours x £4.00 = £1,600 favourable. Consider reasons for the material usage variance between the standard quantity 'allowed' and the actual quantity used; possible reasons for the favourable variance could be difference in batch sizes and/or less waste.

    Material price variance. This is a sub-variance of the material cost variance and is found by taking Column B minus Column C, i.e. £62,400 – £65,520 = £3,120 adverse.

    Interpretation; for 15,600 kgs issued from stores, we were 'allowed' £62,400 at the standard material price while the actual value of the materials issued from stores was £65,520. This can be checked by taking the actual quantity and multiplying by the difference between the standard material price per kg and the actual material price per kg, i.e. 15,600 kgs x (£4.00 – £4.20) = £3,120 adverse. Consider reasons for the material price variance; could be due to change in supplier, lower trade discounts, higher delivery costs or higher grade of material.

3. Calculation of revenues variances

A company sells a component and has achieved the following results for the month of March:

Budgeted volume   6,000 components

Budgeted selling price   £6.00 per component

During the month 8,000 components were sold at an actual price of £5.00 per component.

Table 12.3   Calculation of standard costing variances – Revenues

Column A Standard volume times standard price			Column B Actual volume times standard price			Column C Actual volume times actual price		
Vol.	Rate	£	Vol.	Rate	£	Vol.	Rate	£
6,000	6.00	36,000	8,000	6.00	48,000	8,000	5.00	40,000

£12,000 favourable
Revenues volume variance

£8,000 adverse
Selling price variance

£4,000 favourable
Total revenues variance

The steps to be taken in the calculation of the revenue variances are shown below:

1. Enter actual revenue volume and actual selling price in Column C, i.e. 8,000 hours and actual selling price, i.e. £5.00 per component. Multiply to give actual revenues.

2. Enter actual revenue volume in Column B.

3. Enter budgeted selling price in Column B. Multiply the actual revenues volume by the budgeted selling price, i.e. 8,000 components x £6.00 = £48,000.

4. Enter the budgeted revenues volume in Column A together with the budgeted selling price.

5. Multiply the budgeted revenues volume by the budgeted selling price, i.e. 6,000 components x £6.00 = £36,000. Enter the result in Column A.

6. Calculate and interpret the variances:

    Total revenues variance. This is the total variance and is calculated by taking Column C minus Column A, i.e. £40,000 – £36,000 = £4,000 favourable.

    Interpretation; the budgeted revenues were set at £36,000 while the actual revenues were £40,000. The company has achieved a higher level of revenues. Interpretation; it is not possible to say much about this variance other than it is favourable. We must look at the two subsidiary variance, revenue volume and selling price, to find out the reason(s).

    Revenues volume variance. This is a sub-variance of the total revenues variance and is found by taking Column B minus Column A, i.e. £48,000 – £36,000 = £12,000 favourable.

    Interpretation; the budgeted revenues were set at 6,000 components at £6.00 per component. The actual revenues were 8,000 components. The revenue volume variance is the difference in the revenues volume times the standard selling price, i.e. (8,000 – 6,000) x £6.00 = £12,000 favourable. Possible reason for this variance could be that the company has decided to reduce its selling price in order to obtain an increase in volume (and market share).

    Selling price variance. This is a sub-variance of the total revenues variance and is found by taking Column C minus Column B, i.e. £40,000 – £48,000 = £8,000 adverse.

    Interpretation; the actual revenues were 8,000 components at £5.00 per component while the budgeted selling price was set at £6.00 per component. The selling price variance is the actual components times the difference between the actual selling price less the budgeted selling price, i.e. 8,000 components x (£5.00 – £6.00) = £8,000 adverse. One possible reason for this variance is given in the revenues volume variance above. Also, it might be that the company cannot achieve £6.00 per component or that the trade discounts have had to be increased.

12.4 Comprehensive example

In this example we will produce the following:

1. A flexible budget

2. Variance analysis covering:

   Revenues variances

   Material variances

   Labour variances

   Variable overhead variances

3. A statement showing revenue and costs for the period together with a summary of variances.

Budget and actual data is given below

Budget	Units	Price/Rate	
Revenues	8,000	22.00	176,000
Direct materials	11,000	5.50	60,500
Direct labour	5,000	8.00	40,000
Variable overhead	5,000	3.00	15,000
Contribution margin			60,500

Actual	Units	Price/Rate	
Revenues	7,400	24.00	177,600
Direct materials	9,500	6.00	57,000
Direct labour	5,500	7.60	41,800
Variable overhead	5,250	2.80	14,700
Contribution margin			64,100

It would not be appropriate to calculate variances based on the difference between budget and actual. For example, the actual volume is 600 units less than budgeted, therefore, the costs in the budget are for 8,000 units while the costs in the actual relate to 7,400 units. In order to compare like with like we adjust the costs to take into account the differences in volume as shown in *Table 12.4* below. The selling prices per unit and costs are at budgeted levels. The result in *Table 12.4* shows the budget contribution margin to be £55,962.

Table 12.4 Flexible budget on actual volume (i.e. 8,000 to 7,400 units)

	Volume	Price/Rate	£
Revenues	7,400	22.00	162,800
Direct materials [(1)]	10,175	5.50	55,963
Direct labour [(2)]	4,625	8.00	37,000
Variable overhead [(3)]	4,625	3.00	13,875
Contribution margin			55,962

Notes:

[(1)] Budgeted direct materials x actual volume divided by budgeted volume, i.e. 11,000 x 7,400 ÷ 8,000 = 10,175.

[(2)] Budgeted direct labour x actual volume divided by budgeted volume, i.e. 5,000 x 7,400 ÷ 8,000 = 4,625.

[(3)] Budgeted variable overhead x actual volume divided by budgeted volume, i.e. 5,000 x 7,400 ÷ 8,000 = 4,625.

It is now possible to see the result of preparing the flexible budget. In *Table 12.5* we show the total variances, revenues £14,800 favourable while the costs are £6,662 adverse (i.e. 1,037 + 4,800 + 825). We will now calculate the variances for revenues, materials, labour and variable overheads.

Table 12.5 Flexible budget, actual and variance

	Flexible budget	Actual	Variance
Revenues (after volume)	162,800	177,600	14,800
Direct materials	55,963	57,000	– 1,037
Direct labour	37,000	41,800	– 4,800
Variable overhead	13,875	14,700	– 825
Contribution margin	55,962	64,100	8,138

Calculation of variances

In this example we will use an alternative method to calculate the variances. In the earlier examples we used a tabular form which is widely used. Here we are using a simple list method which again, is widely used. Check this alternative approach with the previous examples.

Revenues variances

We will calculate the total revenues variance then two subsidiary variances as shown in *Figure 12.1*.

Figure 12.1 Standard costing revenues variances

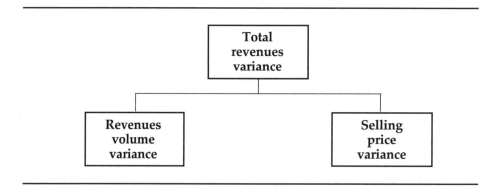

Table 12.6   Calculation of standard costing variances – Revenues

Total revenues variance

Actual revenues x actual price	(7,400 x £24.00)	177,600
Budgeted revenues x budgeted price	(8,000 x £22.00)	176,000
		1,600

Revenues volume variance

Actual revenues x budgeted price	(7,400 x £22.00)	162,800
Budgeted revenues x budgeted price	(8,000 x £22.00)	176,000
		– 13,200

Revenues **price variance**

Actual revenues x actual price	(7,400 x £24.00)	177,600
Actual revenues x budgeted price	(7,400 x £22.00)	162,800
		14,800

Interpretation of revenues variances

The total revenues variance is the difference between the actual revenues less the budgeted revenues. In this example we have a favourable variance of £1,600. The reasons for the difference can be found by an examination of the two subsidiary variances.

The first is the revenues volume variance which is the difference between the actual revenues less the budgeted volume times the budgeted selling price. In this example the difference between the actual and budget revenues is 600 units (adverse) times £22.00 per unit that gives − £13,200.

The second is the revenues price variance which is the actual revenues volume times the difference between the actual price less the budgeted selling price. In this example the actual revenues volume is 7,400 units times (the actual price of £24.00 less the budgeted price of £22.00) that gives £14,800 favourable.

Reasons for revenues variances could be:

Revenues volume   Better/worse economic conditions

Higher/lower selling price

Changes in competitive advantage

Selling price   Competition

Economic conditions

Increase/decrease in costs; hence selling price

Material variances

We will calculate the material cost variance then two subsidiary variances as shown in *Figure 12.2*.

Figure 12.2 Standard costing material variances

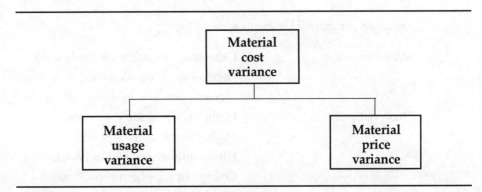

Table 12.7   Calculation of standard costing variances – Material

Material cost variance		
Standard quantity x standard price	(10,175 x £5.50)	55,963
Actual quantity x actual price	(9,500 x £6.00)	57,000
		– 1,037
Material usage variance		
Standard quantity x standard price	(10,175 x £5.50)	55,962
Actual quantity x standard price	(9,500 x £5.50)	52,250
		3,713
Material price variance		
Actual quantity x standard price	(9,500 x £5.50)	52,250
Actual quantity x actual price	(9,500 x £6.00)	57,000
		– 4,750

Interpretation of material variances

The material cost variance is the difference between the standard quantity (allowed) at the standard price less the actual materials (issued from stores) at actual prices. In this example we have an adverse variance of £1,037. The reasons for the difference can be found by an examination of the two subsidiary variances.

The first is the material usage variance which is the difference between the standard quantity (allowed) times the standard material price less the actual materials (issued from stores). In this example the difference between the actual and budget quantities is 675 units (favourable) times £5.50 per unit that gives £3,713.

The second is the material price variance which is the actual materials (issued from stores) times the difference between the standard price less the actual material price. In this example the actual materials is 9,500 units times (the standard price of £5.50 less the actual price of £6.00) that gives £4,750 adverse.

Reasons for material variances could be:

Material usage	Difference in quality or batch sizes
	Deterioration, obsolescence, loss, theft
	Increase/decrease in waste allowance
Material price	Higher/lower trade discounts
	Higher/lower delivery costs
	Higher/lower grade of materials
	Change in supplier/procedures

Labour variances

We will calculate the labour cost variance then two subsidiary variances as shown in *Figure 12.3*.

Figure 12.3 Standard costing labour variances

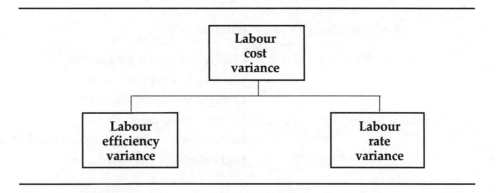

Table 12.8   Calculation of standard costing variances – Labour

Labour cost variance		
Standard hours x standard rate	(4,625 x £8.00)	37,000
Actual hours x actual rate	(5,500 x £7.60)	41,800
		– 4,800
Labour efficiency variance		
Standard hours x standard rate	(4,625 x £8.00)	37,000
Actual hours x standard rate	(5,500 x £8.00)	44,000
		– 7,000
Labour rate variance		
Actual hours x standard rate	(5,500 x £8.00)	44,000
Actual hours x actual rate	(5,500 x £7.60)	41,800
		2,200

Interpretation of labour variances

The labour cost variance is the difference between the actual wages paid less the budgeted wages. In this example we have an adverse variance of £4,800. The reasons for the difference can be found by an examination of the two subsidiary variances.

The first is the labour efficiency variance which is the difference between the standard hours (allowed) less the actual hours times the standard rate. In this example the difference between the budget and actual hours is 875 (adverse) times £8.00 per hour that gives £7,000 adverse.

The second is the labour rate variance which is the actual hours times the difference between the standard rate less the actual rate per hour. In this example the actual hours (worked) is 5,500 hours times (the standard rate of £8.00 less the actual rate of £7.60) that gives £2,200 favourable.

Reasons for labour variances could be:

Labour efficiency	Changes in working conditions
	Changes in grade of labour
	Changes in supervision
Labour rate	Changes in grade of labour
	Higher/lower overtime, productivity bonuses
	Higher/lower wage negotiations

Variable overhead variances

We will calculate the variable overhead cost variance then two subsidiary variances as shown in *Figure 12.4*.

Figure 12.4 Standard costing variable overhead variances

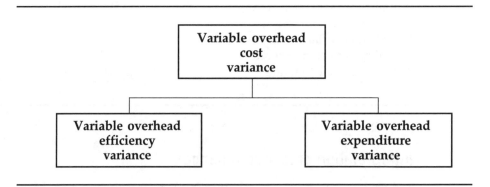

Table 12.9   Calculation of standard costing variances – Variable overheads

Variable overhead cost variance

Standard hours allowed x standard cost per hour	(4,625 x £3.00)	13,875
Actual hours worked x actual cost per hour	(5,250 x £2.80)	14,700
		– 825

Efficiency variance

Standard hours allowed x standard cost per hour	(4,625 x £3.00)	13,875
Actual hours worked x standard cost per hour	(5,250 x £3.00)	15,750
		– 1,875

Expenditure variance

Actual hours worked x standard cost per hour	(5,250 x £3.00)	15,750
Actual hours worked x actual cost per hour	(5,250 x £2.80)	14,700
		1,050

Interpretation of variable overhead variances

The variable overhead cost variance is the difference between the standard hours allowed less the actual hours worked. In this example we have an adverse variance of £825. The reasons for the difference can be found by an examination of the two subsidiary variances.

The first is the variable overhead efficiency variance which is the difference between the standard hours allowed less the actual hours worked times the standard rate. In this example the difference between the standard hours allowed and actual hours worked is 625 hours (adverse) times £3.00 per hour that gives – £1,875.

The second is the variable overhead expenditure variance which is the actual hours worked times the difference between the standard rate less the actual rate. In this example the actual hours worked is 5,250 hours times (the standard rate of £3.00 less the actual rate of £2.80) that gives £1,050 favourable.

Reasons for variable overhead variances could be:

Efficiency	Changes in working conditions
	Changes in equipment
Expenditure	Higher/lower variable costs
	Changes in suppliers/rates

Summary of standard costing variances

In *Table 12.10* we now show a summary of the standard costing variances. There are many different possibilities for the layout of such a summary. Here we have chosen to start with the budgeted revenues, adjust for the revenue variances to arrive at the actual revenues then deduct the standard cost of production to give the actual revenues at budgeted costs. Finally, a listing of the production cost variances is deducted from the actual revenues at budgeted costs to give the actual revenues at actual costs.

Table 12.10   Summary of standard costing variances

Budgeted revenues			176,000
Revenues volume variance	(7,400 – 8,000) x £22		– 13,200
Actual revenues at budget prices			162,800
Revenues price variance	7,400 x (£24 – £22)		14,800
Actual revenues			177,600
less Standard cost of production	(55,963 + 37,000 + 13,875)		106,838
Actual revenues at budgeted costs		(A)	70,762
Production cost variances:			
Material usage variance			
(Standard quantity – actual quantity) x standard price			
	(10,175 – 9,500) x £5.50		3,713
Material price variance			
Actual quantity x (standard price – actual price)			
	9,500 x (£5.50 – £6.00)		– 4,750
Labour efficiency variance			
(Standard hours – actual hours) x standard rate			
	(4,625 – 5,500) x £8		– 7,000
Labour rate variance			
Actual hours x (standard rate – actual rate)			
	5,500 x (£8.00 – £7.60)		2,200
Variable overhead expenditure			
Actual hours worked x (standard rate – actual rate)			
	5,250 x (£3.00 – £2.80)		1,050
Variable overhead efficiency			
(Standard hours allowed – actual hours worked) x standard rate			
	(4,625 – 5,250) x £3.00		– 1,875
Total production variances		(B)	– 6,662
Actual revenues at actual costs		(A – B)	64,100

To finish this example we now show a brief summary of the variances. This time we start at the actual revenues at budget prices and costs, £55,962 – *Table 12.4*, (which is already adjusted for the adverse revenue volume variance. We add the sales price variance then add the total of the production cost variances to give the actual revenues at actual costs of £64,100.

Table 12.11   Flexible budget to actual contribution margin

	£
Actual revenues at budget prices and costs	55,962
add Revenues price variance	14,800
Actual revenues at budget costs	70,762
add Production cost variances	– 6,662
Actual revenues at actual costs	64,100

12.5 Final example

To complete this chapter we will consider a problem where we are given certain variances and some of the data, then required to determine other pieces of data.

Given that the standard labour rate is £8.00 per hour, the actual hours (worked) are 350 hours, the total labour cost variance is £400 adverse and that the labour rate variance is £800 adverse, calculate the actual wage rate and the standard hours (allowed).

To answer this question we will use the columnar layout described earlier in this chapter and shown in *Table 12.12.*

Table 12.12 Standard costing variances – Labour

Column A Standard hours times standard rate			Column B Actual hours times standard rate			Column C Actual hours times actual rate		
Hours	Rate	£	Hours	Rate	£	Hours	Rate	£
400	**8.00**	**3,200**	350	8.00	**2,800**	350	**10.29**	**3,600**

£400 favourable   £800 adverse

Labour efficiency variance   Labour rate variance

£400 adverse

Labour cost variance

Notes:

1. Determine the labour efficiency variance, i.e. £400 favourable.

2. Calculate Column B, i.e. 350 x £8.00 = £2,800.

3. If Column B is £2,800 and the labour rate variance is £800 adverse then the total of Column C is £2,800 + £800 = £3,600.

4. The actual wage rate is £3,600 ÷ 350 hours = £10.29 per hour

5. If Column B is £2,800 and the labour efficiency variance is £400 favourable then the total of Column A is £2,800 + £400 = £3,200.

6. The standard hours allowed = £3,200 ÷ £8.00 = 400 hours.

Exercise 12.1

A company manufactures a component with the following standard specification for direct labour:

Grade 1   3 hours at £4.00 per hour
Grade 2   2 hours at £4.50 per hour
Grade 3   2 hours at £6.00 per hour

During the period 3,000 components were produced, and the direct labour recorded and paid was as follows:

Grade 1   6,000 hours   £26,400
Grade 2   7,000 hours   £34,650
Grade 3   7,000 hours   £46,200

REQUIRED

Calculate the labour variances

Exercise 12.2

The standard raw material mix for one batch of finished product is:

Material   A   770 lbs   at   £0.70 per lb
           B   200 lbs   at   £0.28 per lb
           C   500 lbs   at   £0.49 per lb
           D   60 lbs   at   £2.80 per lb

Material issued from stores for the week ending 30th November 200X was as follows:

Material   A   5,200 lbs   at   £0.84 per lb
           B   1,300 lbs   at   £0.35 per lb
           C   3,700 lbs   at   £0.42 per lb
           D   450 lbs   at   £2.50 per lb

Seven batches were produced during the period.

REQUIRED

Calculate the material variances

Exercise 12.3

Fairway Limited uses a standard costing system to control material and labour costs.

Details of the standard specification for materials and labour for one of its products, Fairway 300, is as follows:

Materials:	Inventory code	Standard quantity	Standard price
	A708	4 units	£3.00
	A022	6 units	£7.50

Labour:	Cost centre	Standard hours	Standard rate
	Turning	2 hours	£8.00
	Finishing	1 hour	£10.00

Material A708 is used only in the turning cost centre and Material A022 only in the finishing cost centre. Details of the materials and labour used to produce 60 units of product Fairway 300 during the period ended 30th June was as follows:

Materials:	Inventory code	Actual quantity	Actual price
	A708	230 units	£2.50
	A022	370 units	£7.00

Labour:	Cost centre	Actual hours	Actual rate
	Turning	130 hours	£975.00
	Finishing	58 hours	£580.00

REQUIRED

1. Prepare an analysis of the standard cost variances arising from the production for the month of June.

2. Indicate which variances the purchasing manager and the manager of each cost centre might be held responsible for and explain how the variances might have arisen.

Exercise 12.4

The plant manager of JR Components arranged a meeting with the supervisor from the Mixing Department to discuss the standard cost variances for the four weeks ending 30th November 200X.

The plant manager gave the supervisor the following details:

Standard material cost	£52,500
Actual materials issued from store	£54,400
Standard material cost variance	£1,900 adverse

The supervisor then went to the costing department and asked for further details of the variance. It was shown that 2,000 units had been produced for the period and that the materials issued from stores were as follows:

Material A   32,000 lbs   at   £0.80 per lb

Material B   16,000 lbs   at   £1.80 per lb

The standard materials required to produce one unit of finished product were as follows:

Material A   15 lbs   at   £0.75 per lb

Material B   10 lbs   at   £1.50 per lb

REQUIRED

From the information available, evaluate further variances and draft a memorandum to the plant manager explaining the results for the period.

Exercise 12.5

You are required to calculate the labour efficiency variance and the labour rate variance given the following:

Standard labour hours (allowed) to produce one unit   3 hours

Standard labour rate   £6.00 per hour

During the period, 100 units were produced.

Actual wages paid   £1,800

Actual hours worked   360 hours

Exercise 12.6

Standard quantity of materials required to make one batch is 300 kg, with a standard price of £3.00 per kg. The actual materials issued from stores for one batch was 250 kg with an actual cost of £1,000.

a.   Material usage variance is

b.   Material price variance is

Exercise 12.7

The standard quantity of materials required to make one batch is 250 kg, with a standard price of £5.00 per kg. During the period, the actual materials issued from stores for five batches was 1,100 kg with an actual cost of £5,720.

a.   The material usage variance is:

a.   The material price variance is:

Exercise 12.8

Concern has been expressed about the standard costing variances for the month of April.

The plant manager has given the supervisor the following details:

Standard material cost	£262,500
Actual materials issued	£272,000
Standard material cost variance	£9,500 adverse

The supervisor then went to the costing department and asked for further details of the variance. It was shown that 2,000 units had been produced for the month and that the materials issued from stores were as follows:

Material A   32,000 lbs at £4.00 per lb

Material B   16,000 lbs at £9.00 per lb

The supervisor also obtained details of the standard materials required to produce one unit of finished product:

Material A   15 lbs at £3.75 per lb

Material B   10 lbs at £7.50 per lb

REQUIRED

From the above information evaluate further variances and draft a memorandum to the plant manager explaining the results.

CAPITAL INVESTMENT APPRAISAL (1)

When you have finished studying this chapter and completed the exercises, you should be able to:

❑ Understand the need of organisations to identify and invest in high quality capital projects;

❑ Prepare a list of the main financial variables required for project appraisal;

❑ Identify the main points to consider when assessing the quality of input data;

❑ Evaluate capital projects using traditional methods of investment appraisal such as:

Simple Payback and Accounting Rate of Return (ARR);

Net Present Value (NPV) and Profitability Index (PI);

Internal Rate of Return (IRR).

13.1   Introduction

Growing a business by internal development, as opposed to external investment in other organisations, requires sound commercial judgement. Such growth only occurs when the future returns from internal investment exceed the present costs; this means that managers must test their judgement against the difficulties presented by a highly unpredictable and uncertain future.

In considering this problem we ask:

o   Are there any tools or techniques available from the realms of accounting and finance to help assess the desirability of particular investments?

o   What are the differences between these tools and techniques?

We will consider these questions and other important issues in this chapter in relation to the evaluation of investments within the business. Such evaluations are similar to those made by private individuals when say, buying a car. The decision needs first to be weighed against other spending priorities. Various models would then be considered evaluating the costs and benefits of each before the actual choice is made. After the purchase a conscious or perhaps subconscious evaluation would be undertaken on the quality of the decision.

The process is roughly the same for commercial decisions except that the financing of capital expenditure projects is treated separately.

13.2   Organising investment decisions

A major stimulus for much investment is often the concern about the future performance of the business if investment does not take place. However, in practice many businesses actually consider investment requirements according to the particular needs to be addressed. Let us consider such needs with reference to the following four categories of investment:

1.   Asset replacement;

2.   Cost saving;

3.   Expansion;

4.   Reactive investment.

1. Asset replacement

If a company fails to replace those assets which currently generate its cash flow and profit, then in the absence of any other investment, its performance will decline, whether quickly or slowly. If the current profile of activities are appropriate to future long-term plans then, in order to continue to generate adequate cash flows and profit, the business must replace assets as they become worn out or obsolete.

2. Cost saving

Cost saving projects are critical to companies which have products or services where revenues have reached the maximum level that can be sustained by the market. Irrespective of whether this maximum is temporary because of depressed economic conditions, or more permanent because the maximum achievable share of a mature market has been reached, a reduction in the firm's costs is possible by improving the efficiency of existing asset use. Revenues generation ratios (described in *Chapter 6*) can be used to identify possible areas for improvement, such as the automation of a previously labour intensive production system. This usually involves the substitution of an avoidable variable cost with an unavoidable fixed cost in order to secure forecast savings.

Finally, cost saving projects may be important to the not-for-profit organisation in which there may be no revenues associated with a project. The analysis of cost savings enables comparisons to be made with existing practice and between alternatives.

3. Expansion

Business growth can result from internal or organic expansion or by focusing upon external targets via an acquisitive strategy. Much investment activity can be related to the desire to achieve growth which many organisations (particularly smaller ones) will attempt to achieve internally. Successful internal growth will eventually permit an organisation to contemplate external expansion, particularly where its shares may be traded publicly. However, even companies with a successful track record of acquisitions will undertake internal investment resulting in business expansion to achieve growth.

4. Reactive investment

Reactive investment covers two particular types of capital expenditure. The first is that which is required as a defensive response to threatening changes in the commercial environment. For example, some of the changes which can be observed in the major U.K. clearing banks services, are the result of substantial investment caused by threats from previously dormant players in the financial services sector, such as Building Societies, in recent years. The second embraces that imposed upon the business because of legislative or other reasons where the benefits of the expenditure are not always readily measurable. It is perhaps, best illustrated by the following examples;

o   As a result of new legislation, the U.K. furniture industry was required to undertake substantial investment in fire resistant foam filling.

o   Following the Piper Alpha disaster, North Sea Oil companies have been required to undertake safety modifications to offshore installations estimated to cost hundreds of millions of pounds.

5. Managerial responsibility for investment

In larger organisations managerial responsibility for investment is usually delegated from top management to lower levels of management. This delegation will usually exclude the raising of finance other than from short-term sources. Decisions about sources of finance with long-term implications are usually taken by top management who will try to balance proportions of debt and equity so as to minimise the cost of capital to the business.

The delegation of managerial responsibility for the evaluation of capital expenditure can be achieved by specifying cut-off levels, the amount of which corresponds with given levels of seniority. For example, senior divisional management may be responsible for capital expenditure up to an agreed cut-off sum, and approval would have to be obtained from top management for capital expenditure above the agreed cut-off. In addition, such senior divisional management may also be required to approve submissions for capital expenditure from its divisional management, where the capital expenditure required exceeds the level of delegated responsibility.

13.3   Appraising investment opportunities

In this section we provide a background to the financial appraisal of potential investment opportunities. In common with many areas of accounting and finance, numerous terms are used to describe the financial appraisal process of which investment appraisal, project appraisal and capital budgeting are common. To avoid confusion and to reinforce the point that our concern is not with investing in securities of other organisations, we will adopt the term *project appraisal* to refer to the evaluation of capital projects.

You may find it easy to become lost in the detail of the financial issues associated with project appraisal, so let us take stock of the key financial requirements to be met:

❑   Only those projects which meet the objectives of the business should be selected, i.e. those which provide what the business regards as a satisfactory return for the risks involved;

❑   The return to be expected from a project must exceed the financing cost that the capital expenditure will necessitate, and;

❑   The most financially desirable project must be selected from the range of opportunities available (assuming, as is normally the case, that resources are limited and that not all projects can be undertaken).

In addition to these financial requirements, it is important to stress that for many investments non-financial factors may be very important. Therefore, account must also be taken of these so that both financial and non-financial considerations are given appropriate weight.

With these points in mind, and before we consider individual techniques for gauging the financial benefit, let us consider the main financial variables of a project appraisal. A definitive list is impossible, but the following items will usually occur in one form or another:

❏ The initial capital outlay including the cost of non-current assets, working capital and, if appropriate, deliberate start-up losses;

❏ The expected useful economic life of the project;

❏ An estimate of the residual value of assets remaining at the end of the project's useful economic life;

❏ The amounts and timing of all cost and revenue components associated with the project;

❏ Expected price level changes for each cost and revenue component;

❏ Taxation assumptions and any regional grants likely to affect the corporate position;

❏ The relevant cost of financing the project (cost of capital);

❏ Likely estimates of variation for each of the above variables.

Many of these financial variables will be discussed in the next section outlining the major project appraisal techniques. It is all to easy to focus upon the mechanics of the techniques themselves whilst losing sight of their limitations in the absence of good quality input data. It cannot be over-stressed that the benefit to be derived from any technique used for appraising a project can be no better than the quality of the input data employed.

13.4   Assessing the quality of input data

The main points to consider in assessing the quality of input data are:

1. Future orientation

The only capital outlay, operating costs and revenues relevant to a proposed capital project are those that concern the future. Sunk, i.e. past costs are irrelevant even though there may be a temptation to treat them otherwise, as are costs to be found in a company's cost or management accounting system. This is the case whether they are past or present and they are useful only as a guide in forecasting future cost levels.

It is not only the costs themselves that are irrelevant but also the patterns of cost behaviour. Such patterns may be appropriate to the routine accounting functions of budgeting and variance analysis, but may not be suitable for decisions where the relevant time span is longer than that required for effective control. Assumptions which ordinarily permit different costs to be described as fixed, variable or semi-variable in their behaviour may need to be adapted when five or ten year time scales are involved, since at the time a capital project decision is being made all costs relevant to the decision are variable. It is only when the project is accepted and implemented that project associated costs become fixed.

2. Attributable costs and revenues

The costs and revenues relevant to a capital project are only those which can be legitimately attributed to it rather than any other source. Whilst this notion is simple and manageable in principle at the level of the individual project, difficulties can be encountered in practice when the cumulative effects of several proposed capital projects need to be anticipated.

3. Differential costs and revenues

Where decisions require more than one course of action to be examined, the only costs and revenues to be considered are those that will differ under the alternative courses of action. Common costs and revenues may be ignored, provided they are expected to behave identically in each of the alternatives under consideration.

4.   Opportunity costs and benefits

These costs and benefits are usually the most difficult of all to deal with. Nevertheless, opportunity costs and benefits must be included in any project decision. For example, if a consequence of introducing a new model of a product currently sold at a profit is that revenues of the existing product will be lost, then the lost contribution on the existing product is an opportunity cost of the new model which must be included in the appraisal.

5. Financing costs

It is often tempting, but incorrect, during a project appraisal to include the financing costs associated with a proposal within the estimated operating costs. As we will show in the next section the financing costs do vary according to the appraisal techniques used, but they should not be included with the estimated operating costs.

6. Uncertainty and inflation

It is important that the risk and uncertainty associated with projects is incorporated within any appraisal, together with expectations about changes in costs and prices. Any failure to make appropriate allowances for risk, uncertainty and inflation can result in an appraisal of questionable value.

7. Qualitative issues

A serious limitation of conventional project appraisal is the omission of non-financial issues, such as improvements in product quality for corporate image, or a lower susceptibility to adverse social pressures. Whilst such benefits are often extremely difficult to assess, they should not be ignored.

13.5   Project appraisal techniques

We have now set the scene for project appraisal in our discussions of the financial variables required and important issues associated with the quality of cost and revenue inputs. The important issue for consideration now is how such data is organised for purposes of appraising a project. This we will illustrate with reference to the four main project appraisal techniques. We will deal with such issues as inflation, taxation and sensitivity analysis in the next chapter.

1. Payback period.

2. Accounting rate of return.

3. Net present value (NPV) and Profitability index (PI).

4. Internal rate of return (IRR).

The distinguishing characteristics of these four project appraisal techniques and their respective advantages and disadvantages are best illustrated with financial data. Accordingly we will use data for an imaginary organisation contemplating the following four alternative projects which are summarised in *Table 13.1* below.

Table 13.1 Basic data for four projects

	Project A £'000	Project B £'000	Project C £'000	Project D £'000
Capital outlay	−15,000	−18,000	−10,000	−18,000
Net cash inflows:				
Year 1	7,000	6,000	5,000	4,000
Year 2	4,000	6,000	5,000	5,000
Year 3	3,000	6,000		6,000
Year 4	2,000	6,000		7,000
Year 5	1,000	6,000		8,000

1. Payback period

The payback period is calculated with reference to cash flow data. It is expressed in terms of the period of time it takes for the net cash inflows (i.e. cash savings) to equal the capital outlay. For example, for Project B which has a capital outlay of £18 million and cash inflows of £6 million for each year of its five year expected economic life, the payback is exactly three years:

$$\frac{\text{Capital outlay}}{\text{Net cash inflow}} = \frac{£18 \text{ million}}{£ 6 \text{ million}} = 3 \text{ years}$$

Project B is straightforward because the payback period occurs exactly at the end of year three, but this is not usually the case. For example, if you try to calculate the payback period for projects A and D you will find that it does not occur at the end of a single year. Let us see how this can be dealt with using the data for Project A. The first step is to accumulate the cash flows as follows:

Table 13.2   Calculation of payback period – Project A

	£'000		
Capital outlay	−15,000		
Net cash inflows:	(i)	(ii)	(iii)
	Annual	Annual to payback	Cumulative to payback
	£'000	£'000	£'000
Year 1	7,000	7,000	7,000
Year 2	4,000	4,000	11,000
Year 3	3,000	3,000	14,000
Year 4	2,000	1,000	15,000

The figures in column (iii) show that in each of the first three years the whole of the net cash inflows are used to accumulate to £14 million. In the fourth year, only £1 million of the net cash inflows are required to make the accumulated net cash inflows equal to the capital outlay. Therefore, the payback period takes place in three and one half years, i.e. three years, plus £1 million out of £2 million.

The results for all four projects may be summarised as:

	Project A	Project B	Project C	Project D
Payback period (years)	3.5	3.0	2.0	3.4

The main aim in using any project appraisal technique is to find out which project should be selected from a number of competing projects. A simple ranking, in this case based on the project offering the shortest payback period, would reveal that Project C is the best project. However, some companies will evaluate the payback period in relation to the project's useful economic life. This means that Project B which pays back after three years of its estimated five year life may be viewed far more favourably than Project C, which pays back at the end of its useful economic life. The relationship between the payback period and the useful economic life for each of the projects may be summarised as:

	Project A	Project B	Project C	Project D
Payback period (years)	3.5	3.0	2.0	3.4
Useful economic life (years)	5	5	2	5
Payback ÷ economic life	0.70	0.60	1.00	0.68

Payback period has a major advantage over other methods because it is simple to calculate, understand and implement. Against this, the payback period focuses upon time taken to recover the capital outlay but cash flows generated after the payback period may not be taken into consideration. One other major shortcoming, the substance and importance of which will become evident shortly in our discussion of the discounting principle, is that unless the cash flows are specifically adjusted, the time value of money is ignored.

2. Accounting rate of return

The accounting rate of return differs from the payback period since its calculation draws on data relating to the whole life of a project. You must be aware, however, that it is calculated using a project's profit, rather than cash flows and thus suffers, as we saw earlier, from the ambiguity of the definition of profit. Once profit is defined the accounting rate of return is relatively straightforward to calculate. Take note that different users may arrive at different accounting rates of return using the same input data, and what is even more confusing is that none of the resulting calculations are necessarily incorrect!

The first step in calculating the rate of return is to add the estimated annual profit flows to establish the total profit of the proposed project. If only cash flow information is available then the annual cash flows must be added together to find the total cash flows, which in our example are £17 million, £30 million, £10 million and £30 million for Projects A, B, C and D, respectively. From this total, the capital outlay (i.e. the total depreciation) is deducted to give the total profit. The average annual profit required for the calculation is found by dividing the total profit by the life of the project. This is illustrated for our four example projects in *Table 13.3*.

Table 13.3 Calculation of accounting rate of return

		Project A £'000	Project B £'000	Project C £'000	Project D £'000
Total net cash inflow	(A)	17,000	30,000	10,000	30,000
less Capital outlay	(B)	15,000	18,000	10,000	18,000
Total profit	(C)=(A)–(B)	£2,000	£12,000	0	£12,000
Life (years)	(D)	5	5	2	5
Average annual profit	(C)÷(D)	£400	£2,400	0	£2,400

The accounting rate of return is then calculated by dividing the average annual profit by the capital outlay. For Project A, the calculation is:

$$\text{Accounting rate of return (\%)} = \frac{\text{Average annual profit}}{\text{Capital outlay}} \times 100$$

$$= \frac{\text{£0.4 million}}{\text{£15 million}} \times 100$$

$$= 2.7\%$$

Similar calculations for Projects B, C and D produce accounting rates of return of 13.3%, 0% and 13.3% respectively. A simple ranking from highest to lowest rate of return shows that Projects B and D are ranked equal.

	Project A	Project B	Project C	Project D
Accounting rate of return %	2.7	13.3	0	13.3
Ranking	3	1 =	4	1 =

It was indicated earlier that using the same input data, different accounting rates of return can be produced. How can this happen? It is conceivable that one might use some notion of average capital outlay rather than the total capital outlay adopted in our example and, indeed, some organisations do just this. As you will appreciate, anything which has the effect of reducing the capital outlay in the calculation will increase the accounting rate of return. Consider for example the effect on Project B if the average capital outlay was calculated as being £9 million. The rate of return percentage would double!

The potential ambiguity in accounting rate of return results is often presented as being a shortcoming. Nevertheless, the technique is used and with some success particularly where manuals of capital expenditure procedure provide a specific definition of the items to be used in accounting rate of return calculations. However, just like the simple payback technique, the accounting rate of return fails to take into account of the time value of money.

3. The principle of discounting

The two remaining techniques for discussion, the net present value (NPV), and the internal rate of return (IRR), are both reliant upon a principle which involves discounting, or scaling-down, future cash flows. In order to appreciate the principle involved we will compare discounting with the more familiar but related technique of compounding.

Compounding is applied to a sum of money so that its value in future may be calculated given a required rate of interest. Discounting is the reverse. Future cash inflows are discounted at a given rate of interest so that they may be directly compared to the present outlay of cash.

Figure 13.1 Compounding and Discounting cash flows

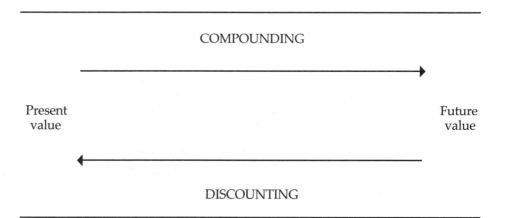

How is this discounting achieved? Cash flows can be discounted using factors which are readily available in statistical tables. The basis for their calculation is similar to the principles used in calculating compound interest. We will use the information in *Table 13.4* to show the relationship between compounding and discounting. There we make specific reference to the factors used to compound and discount cash at a 10% rate.

Table 13.4   Compound interest and discounted cash flow factors

	Compound interest factors 10%	Discounted cash flow factors (DCF) 10%
Year 0	1.000	1.000
Year 1	1.100	0.909
Year 2	1.210	0.826
Year 3	1.331	0.751
Year 4	1.464	0.683
Year 5	1.611	0.621

Using the factors in *Table 13.4*, £1,000 invested today at 10% compound interest would yield £1,210 at the end of year two, i.e. £1,000 x 1.21. The reverse can be seen if we assume a forecast cash flow of £1,210 at the end of year two, discounted at 10% back to a present value would produce £1,000, i.e. £1,210 x 0.826. The principle of discounting operates by scaling down future cash flows to produce a present value. In this way future cash flows can be readily compared with the present value of capital outlays. The reduction in the value of future cash flows using the discounting process is dependent upon the rate of interest. The higher the rate of interest, the more severely the cash flows will be scaled down. The technique of adjusting cash flows might seem tedious but discount factor tables are readily available at the end of the book. In these tables the present value of £1 has been calculated for a wide range of interest rates.

4. Determining the relevant discount rate

In order to calculate the net present value technique (and other discounting techniques such as, the profitability index, or the discounted payback period that we will discuss), the relevant discount factor must be known. This discount factor should be the company's required rate of return (sometimes known as the *hurdle* rate from the sporting analogy where hurdles have to be jumped to even stand a chance of being successful). This rate, as represented by the company's cost of capital, is the projects' break-even point. Projects undertaken yielding a return above this *hurdle* rate will increase the value of the business whilst those below will decrease value.

The components involved in the determination of a company's cost of capital have been the subject of much academic research and debate. However, there does seem to be some agreement that the appropriate rate should comprise the weighted average of the after tax cost of debt capital and the equity cost of capital. In the case of debt capital the after tax cost is used because interest is deductible before tax thus providing a reduced real cost. This is unlike dividend payments which have to be met from after tax profits. How this cost of capital is arrived at is best understood from the following example: *A* company has an after tax cost of debt of 6 per cent, an estimated cost of equity of 16 per cent and future gearing comprising 20 per cent debt and 80 per cent equity. In this simple case, the company's weighted average cost of capital is 14%, and the basis for the calculation is illustrated in *Table 13.5*.

Table 13.5   Weighted average cost of capital   (WACC)

	Weight A (%)	Cost B (%)	Weighted cost A x B % (%)
Debt	20	6	1.2
Equity	80	16	12.8
			14.0

This cost of capital includes the returns demanded by both debt-holders and shareholders because pre-interest cash flows are those to be discounted. Given that both debt-holders and shareholders have claims against these, the appropriate cost of capital will be one that incorporates the relative capital contribution of each group. Thus, total pre-interest cash flows which are attributable to both lenders and shareholders are discounted by a weighted cost of capital to yield a value to the business.

It is important to realise that the relative weights attached to debt and equity within the calculation should be based on the relative proportions of each estimated for the future. This is because the concern of a capital project appraisal is with the future and not with the past. Thus, the present or previous debt to equity proportions are irrelevant, unless they apply to the future. There is also a useful analogy with the matching principle introduced in relation to accounting in *Chapter 1*. The objective is to compare like with like, hence the use of a future orientated gearing ratio for establishing the cost of capital at which to discount future cash flows.

5. Net present value   (NPV)

We will now illustrate the application of the net present value (NPV) technique, where for a given rate of interest, future cash flows are discounted using the principle discussed in the previous section. The sum total of these discounted future cash flows is compared with the capital outlay and where it is greater than the outlay, the NPV is said to be positive and the project is acceptable on economic grounds. Conversely, if a negative NPV results (capital outlay is greater than the sum of discounted future cash flows) the project is not acceptable on economic grounds.

Using basic data for the four proposed projects illustrated earlier, and assuming a 10% cost of capital, the following NPV analysis can be carried out for Project B.

Table 13.6   Calculation of net present value – Project B

Year	Column 1 Net cash inflows 10%	Column 2 Discount factor £000	Column 3 (Col. 1 x Col. 2) Present Value £000
1	6,000	0.909	5,454
2	6,000	0.826	4,956
3	6,000	0.751	4,506
4	6,000	0.683	4,098
5	6,000	0.621	3,726
Present value of cash inflows			22,740
less Capital outlay			18,000
Net present value			£4,740

The annual net cash inflows shown in column 1 are multiplied by the discount factors at 10% shown in column 2 to produce the annual present value of the cash inflows in column 3. These annual present values are then added together to give the total present value of the cash inflows of £22.740 million. The net present value is calculated by deducting the capital outlay from the total present values of the cash inflows (i.e. £22.740 million – £18.000 million) giving £4.740 million. The effect of discounting the cash flows is also illustrated in *Figure 13.2*.

Figure 13.2   Comparison of cash flows – Project B

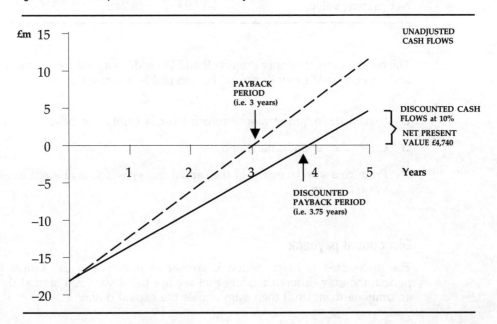

The capital outlay of £18 million is the starting point of the upper diagonal which is constructed from accumulating the annual net cash inflows of £6 million. The result is a cumulative cash inflow of £30 million at the end of year five. When these annual cash inflows of £6 million are discounted at 10% and plotted in the diagram, the lower diagonal results. The application of the 10% discount factor can be seen to cause a scaling-down which results in a net present value of £4.740 million. Raising the discount factor would scale-down the cash flows even further, thereby resulting in a lower net present value. One other observation from the diagram is the effect upon the payback period when discounted rather than undiscounted annual net cash inflows are used. You will see from the diagram that the *discounted payback period* is 3.75 years rather than the original three years when the net cash inflows are discounted at 10%. Furthermore, should the discount factor be increased resulting in a greater scaling down of cash flows, the discounted payback period becomes even longer.

We will consider the discounted payback and profitability index once we have reviewed the net present value calculations for all four projects.

Table 13.7 *Comparison of net present values*

	Project A £000	Project B £000	Project C £000	Project D £000
Present value of cash inflows	13,907	22,740	8,675	22,021
Capital outlay	15,000	18,000	10,000	18,000
Net present value	£–1,093	£4,740	£–1,325	£4,021

The results show that only Projects B and D produce a positive net present value and on economic grounds would be acceptable because they:

❑ Exceed the required rate of return (cost of capital) of 10%;

❑ Cover the capital outlay; and,

❑ Produce a sum in excess of the capital outlay which is referred to as the net present value.

Discounted payback

The discounted payback period is similar in principle to the simple payback period, the only difference being that we use the discounted annual flows, and accumulate them until their sum equals the capital outlay.

In *Figure 13.2*, we illustrated the discounted payback period for Project B of 3.75 years, but how is this calculated? Using the discounted annual cash flows for Project B, the discounted payback period can be calculated in a similar manner to simple payback:

Table 13.8   Calculation of discounted payback – Project B

	£'000		
Capital outlay	–18,000		
Discounted cash inflows:	**(i)**	**(ii)**	**(iii)**
	Annual	**Annual to payback**	**Cumulative to payback**
	£'000	**£'000**	**£'000**
Year 1	5,454	5,454	5,454
Year 2	4,956	4,956	10,410
Year 3	4,506	4,506	14,916
Year 4	4,098	3,084	18,000

Note.   The adjusted cash flows shown in column (i) have been extracted from Table 13.6

The discounted cash flows to achieve the £18 million capital outlay can be monitored from column (iii). At the end of Year three £14.916 million will be recovered, leaving £3.084 million to be recovered in Year four. Given that £4.098 million will be recovered from Year four, the proportion of a year represented by £3.084 million can be readily calculated. Thus discounted payback is achieved in three years plus £3.084 million divided by £4.098 million, which equals approximately 3.75 years.

Similar calculations for the discounted payback can be performed for Projects A, C and D to produce the following results:

Table 13.9   Comparison of discounted payback

	Project A	Project B	Project C	Project D
Discounted payback (years)	n/a	3.75	n/a	4.19

Profitability index (PI)

Where the capital outlay differs from project to project the profitability index is calculated and provides useful information to assist in the decision making process. The profitability index is a ratio which relates the present value of the cash inflows from a project to its capital outlay. For Project A this would be £13.907 million divided by £15 million which gives 0.93, and for Projects B, C and D it is 1.26, 0.87 and 1.22, respectively. It is now possible to rank all projects competing for limited funds using the profitability index – all other things being equal, the higher the profitability index the better.

Table 13.10 Calculation of profitability index

		Project A £000	Project B £000	Project C £000	Project D £000
Present value of net cash inflows	(A)	13,907	22,740	8,675	22,021
Capital outlay	(B)	15,000	18,000	10,000	18,000
Profitability index	(A) ÷ (B)	0.93	1.26	0.87	1.22

The index of 1.26 for Project B means that the capital outlay is covered once plus an additional 26% and where capital is restricted, should be preferred to the other alternatives on economic grounds. Where the profitability index is less than 1, e.g. Project A, this means that the project does not cover its capital outlay, therefore, does not provide the minimum return, i.e. company's cost of capital. However, before drawing any further conclusions let us consider the internal rate of return.

6.   Internal rate of return (IRR)

The net present value, the profitability index and the discounted payback calculations require knowledge of the company's cost of capital as necessary data input for their calculation, but internal rate of return (IRR) does not.

The IRR is a discounted cash flow method which seeks to find the discount rate at which the present value of net cash inflows from a capital project exactly equal the capital outlay, in other words at the IRR the net present value is zero.

The IRR can best be understood with reference to *Figure 13.3* where you can see that the lowest line corresponds with a NPV of £0. This is achieved by scaling–down the net cash inflows by applying a discount factor corresponding with the IRR percentage. Thus the percentage, which when converted to a discount factor and multiplied by the net cash inflows, gives a present value equal to the capital outlay, is the internal rate of return.

Figure 13.3   Graph showing internal rate of return (IRR)

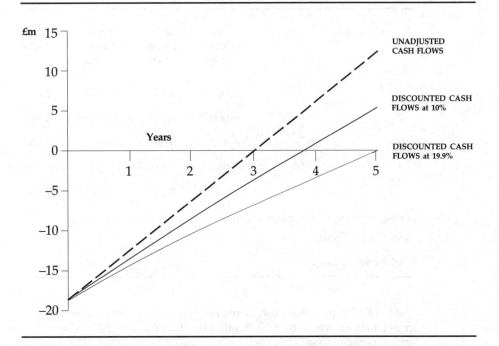

Once determined, the IRR percentage should then be compared with the company's cost of capital in order to establish the economic acceptability of a project. The principle is, that if the IRR exceeds the cost of capital then a project is acceptable on economic grounds. On the other hand, if the IRR from a project is lower than the cost of capital the project is not acceptable on economic grounds.

The calculation of the IRR is based on trial and error to find the discount rate corresponding to a zero net present value. As such, several calculations may need to be made and are best facilitated with the aid of a computer. The calculations necessary to find the IRR for Project B are based upon data summarised in *Table 13.11.*

Table 13.11   Trial and error calculation of internal rate of return (IRR) – Project B

Year	Cash inflows £'000	DCF factor 18%	Present value £'000	DCF factor 21%	Present value £'000
1	6,000	0.847	5,082	0.826	4,956
2	6,000	0.718	4,308	0.683	4,098
3	6,000	0.609	3,654	0.564	3,384
4	6,000	0.516	3,096	0.467	2,802
5	6,000	0.437	2,622	0.386	2,316
Present value of net cash inflows			18,762		17,556
less Capital outlay			18,000		18,000
Net present value			£762		£–444

Table 13.11 shows that cash flows for Project B, when discounted at 18% provide a net present value of £0.762 million. To find the IRR (where the net present value is zero), in this case, a higher discount is required. The result of increasing the rate to 21% shows that the net present value is negative at £–0.444 million. The internal rate of return must, therefore, fall between 18% and 21% and can be found approximately by linear interpolation.

$$IRR = d_1 + [n_1 \div (n_1 + n_2) \quad x \quad s]$$

Where: d_1 = lower dcf; d_2 = higher dcf; n_1 = NPV at lower dcf;
  n_2 = NPV at higher dcf; $s = d_2 - d_1$

Therefore, the IRR for Project B is calculated as follows:

$$IRR = 18 + (762 \div 1,206 \quad x \quad 3)$$

$$= 18 + 1.9$$

$$= 19.9\%$$

Similar calculations carried out for Projects A, C and D produce the following results shown alongside that for Project B:

	Project A	Project B	Project C	Project D
Internal rate of return %	6.1	19.9	0	17.5

The approximations of the IRR% in this case are fairly accurate and in fact those obtained from using a spreadsheet were 6%, 19.9%, 0% and 17.4% for Projects A, B, C and D respectively.

The results achieved from using manual calculations for the IRR can produce satisfactory results provided that the difference between the two discount rates is not too large (e.g. not greater than 5%). However, it is preferable to use a computer which allow the user to change any of the figures with relative ease.

One major problem with the IRR is that it may be impossible to provide a clear cut solution to projects that have irregular cash flows. In such a situation there may not be an internal rate of return, or if there is, it may not be unique.

13.6   Using annuity tables

In addition to the arithmetical tables which provide a stream of discount factors it is also possible to obtain arithmetical tables which give cumulative discount factors over a specific period of time. These tables, which are included in *pages 433 and 434*, are referred to as annuity tables because they convert a lump sum into a stream of equal annual payments. To find out the total present value of £100 over 10 years we could undertake 10 individual calculations in a similar manner to that illustrated in *Table 13.6*. Alternatively, we can achieve the same result from a single calculation by multiplying £100 by the cumulative discount factor found from the annuity tables.

Before we go any further it might help to consider the benefit of using cumulative discount factors in appraising potential investment opportunities. From *Table 13.12* we can identify the cumulative discount factors at 10% for any period between one and five years. If we return to Project B we can calculate the present value of the net cash inflows at 10% in one operation:

$$£6 \text{ million} \quad \times \quad 3.790 \quad = \quad £22.740 \text{ million}$$

This is a quicker method than the one used before, see *Table 13.6*, where five multiplications were required! However, this method can only be used where the annual cash flows are equal.

Table 13.12 Discount factors at 10%

Period	Discount factors at 10%	Cumulative discount factors at 10%
1	0.909	0.909
2	0.826	1.735
3	0.751	2.486
4	0.683	3.169
5	0.621	3.790

A final point regarding the cumulative discount factors. Compare the figures we have just used in *Table 13.12* above, with the corresponding figures in *Appendix A*. The slight difference is due to rounding and for the calculation of further examples we will use the figures from *Appendix A*, page 433.

Example – using annuity tables

We will continue to make use of Project B, (as we already know the answer) and use the cumulative discount factors to calculate the following:

1. The internal rate of return given a capital outlay of £18 million, annual savings of £6 million and a five year life.

2. The minimum annual savings for the project to be acceptable on economic grounds, given a cost of capital (discount rate) of 20%, a capital outlay of £18 million and a five year life.

3. The maximum capital outlay worth expending on such a project, given only that the cost of capital is 20%, annual savings are £6 million, and the expected life is five years.

1. Calculate the internal rate of return

First, we calculate the cumulative discount factor as follows:

Capital outlay ÷ annual savings

£18 million ÷ £6 million = 3.000

Second, we use the table in *Appendix A* and check the cumulative discount factors on the line for a five year life until we obtain a value which is close to the 3.000. In this case we will see that a figure of 2.991 is the closest and this represents the cumulative discount factors at 20%. With the use of interpolation, say between 19% and 20%, it is possible to arrive at rates correct to one decimal place, for example:

	19%	20%	
Annuity factors	3.058	2.991	
Difference		67	(ignore the decimal place)

Internal rate of return = 19 + (58 ÷ 67 x 1) = 19.9%

2. Calculate the minimum annual savings

We are given a cost of capital and the life of the project, therefore, we refer to *Appendix A* and extract the cumulative discount factors at 20% for a period of five years which give 2.991. The minimum annual savings is found from:

Capital outlay   ÷   cumulative discount factor

£18 million   ÷   2.991   =   £6.018 million

In this case, we conclude that if the capital outlay is expected to be £18 million and the company's cost of capital is 20% then the project will need to provide a minimum annual savings of £6.018 million for five years.

3. Calculate the maximum capital outlay

We follow the same procedure as in 2. above, and obtain a cumulative discount factor of 2.991. The maximum capital outlay is found from:

Annual savings   x   the cumulative discount factor

£6 million   x   2.991   =   £17.946 million

Here, we conclude that if the annual savings for five years are expected to be £6 million and the company's cost of capital is 20% then a maximum capital outlay of £17.946 million can be spent.

13.7 Project appraisal in practice

Many studies of project appraisal practice have been undertaken. Most have been orientated towards the practices of large organisations to which the following general observations apply:

1 The most frequently used technique is the payback period. This is often in conjunction with other techniques, but it may be used on its own for smaller projects.

2 The accounting rate of return is used despite potential ambiguities in definition.

3 When a discounted cash flow technique is used, it is more likely to be the internal rate of return method rather than the net present value method.

4 The use of techniques is guided by standard procedures, usually in the form of a capital budgeting manual of practice.

5 Qualitative judgement is regarded as important.

In addition to these five observations relating to the techniques, three others are noteworthy, however, they are outside the scope of this book:

o Inflation adjustments are made in appraising projects using rates applicable to specific inputs although the use of a single general rate is also practised.

o Adjustments for taxation are made to take account of the tax benefits, i.e. allowances on capital projects and the tax liabilities, i.e. payments due on any savings (profits).

o A formal analysis of risk is a standard pre-decision control procedure in many organisations, most often in the form of testing the sensitivity of key inputs and underlying economic assumptions.

One important question which emerges from the observations from the studies of practice is – 'Why the IRR is far more popular than the theoretically preferred NPV technique'? This has been attributed to a number of reasons, such as the appeal of a percentage to managers who, apparently, would be far less comfortable with interpreting a NPV calculation.

When using IRR calculations a ranking of projects can be obtained without the need for knowledge of the company's required rate of return although, as indicated in the last section, this ranking may be inferior to that provided by NPV calculations.

Associated with there being no need for a predetermined cut-off rate is the political appeal of the IRR. One recognised feature of the appraisal process is the potential for playing the system by ensuring that projects which have acquired the personal commitment of management always meet or exceed the prescribed hurdle rate. If the hurdle is not formally communicated then perhaps this problem can be removed. Certainly our observations of practice have found some confirmation of this view in some organisations. In such cases, the IRR usually in conjunction with other techniques, is prescribed for use below corporate level. At corporate level, however, where the desired hurdle is known the NPV technique may play a more significant role.

13.1   The management team of U. Dunnit Limited have four projects for consideration. In the past, they have evaluated projects against simple payback. The following information is available:

	Project A £	Project B £	Project C £	Project D £
Capital outlay	65,000	140,000	30,000	160,000
Net cash inflows:				
Year 1	30,000	45,000	20,000	35,000
Year 2	20,000	45,000	10,000	35,000
Year 3	15,000	45,000	10,000	55,000
Year 4	10,000	45,000		55,000
Year 5	10,000	45,000		65,000

REQUIRED

1.   Evaluate the projects using each of the following methods:

a   Simple payback.

b   Accounting rate of return.

c   Net present value and profitability index. Assuming a cost of capital of 6%.

d   Internal rate of return for the project with the best profitability index.

2.   Write a report to the Chairperson of the management team explaining each of the evaluation methods. You are also required to make a recommendation on the method(s) which should be used by the company for future project evaluation.

13.2   A company is considering the purchase of a new machine to extend its range of products and have obtained the following information:

Capital outlay   £390,000

Profit forecast:–   £

Year 1   60,000

Year 2   45,000

Year 3   21,000

Year 4   12,000

Year 5   12,000

The profit before taxation figures are stated after charging £24,000 per annum of factory overheads allocated to the project.

The scrap value of the machine at the end of the fifth year will be £60,000.

The management of the company will approve the project provided that it will result in a minimum return of 10% per annum.

REQUIRED

1. Advise the management of the company whether they should proceed with the project on the basis of the above figures.

2. Suggest what other factors should be taken into consideration before a final decision is made.

13.3   The senior engineer of *Maxifly Limited* has submitted a project to install equipment to manufacture a new type of fishing rod. The following information is available:–

Capital outlay	£480,000
Life of project	5 years
Profit forecast:	£
Year 1	32,000
Year 2	48,000
Year 3	60,000
Year 4	120,000
Year 5	48,000

The scrap value of the equipment is estimated to be £80,000 and will be received at the end of year five.

The company uses the straight-line method of depreciation. The company's cost of capital is 14 per cent.

REQUIRED

1. Calculate the net present value and the simple payback period for the project.

2. Although discounted cash flow is widely considered to be a superior method of investment appraisal, the simple payback method has still been shown to be the most popular method in practice. Suggest reasons why this may be the case.

13.4   Given a capital outlay of £90,000, the forecast savings (i.e. net cash inflows) over five years are as follows:

Year 1	£40,000
Year 2	£35,000
Year 3	£30,000
Year 4	£25,000
Year 5	£20,000

1.   Calculate simple payback.

2.   Calculate accounting rate of return.

13.5   A capital project has the following data:

Capital outlay	£130,000
Savings:	
Year 1	£60,000
Year 2	£50,000
Year 3	£40,000
Year 4	£30,000
Year 5	£20,000
Cost of capital	12%

1.   Calculate simple payback.

2.   Calculate net present value.

13.6   A project requires a capital outlay of £150 million.

The project is expected to have a useful economic life of five years and the organisation's cost of capital is 10%. The present costs incurred are £150 million per year. If the project were implemented it is estimated that future costs would be £100 million per year. (ignore inflation and taxation)

Calculate the net present value.

13.7   A machine with a purchase price of £70,000 is estimated to eliminate manual operations costing £20,000 per year. The machine will last five years and have no residual value at the end of its life.

REQUIRED

1.   Calculate the internal rate of return.

2.   Calculate the annual saving necessary to achieve a 12% internal rate of return.

3.   Calculate the net present value and the profitability index if the company's cost of capital is 10%.

CAPITAL INVESTMENT APPRAISAL (2)

When you have finished studying this chapter and completed the exercises, you should be able to:

❏ Illustrate the important differences which can arise in evaluating projects when using net present value (NPV) and internal rate of return (IRR).

❏ Apply inflation and taxation adjustments to capital projects.

❏ Undertake sensitivity analysis on capital projects.

❏ Put together a business case for a project.

14.1 Introduction

The successful introduction of a new product will attract competing products. This competition may force a reduction in price to a level which renders further investment non-economic. Although first entrants to a market may establish competitive advantage through the experience curve or product protection by trade marks or patents, cash flow projections should recognise market developments and competitor reactions.

To make an assessment of competitor reactions, existing managerial knowledge and judgement needs to be used in conjunction with expert systems specially designed to model cash flows in a dynamic environment. This will avoid an over–reliance on projections of revenues and cost of sales which, although internally consistent, do not reflect the real world.

In summary, sound financial management of capital projects should ensure that:

❑ Individual requests are in harmony with the plan for corporate growth and development, and the risks of accepting 'no hope' capital projects should be minimised;

❑ An appropriate hierarchical structure exists for authorising capital expenditure, which should encourage all good projects, even those proposed at low levels of authority;

❑ The numbers used in appraisal calculations are complete and valid in light of the circumstances surrounding a project request;

❑ Any method used to provide a measure of the relative desirability of projects is valid;

❑ Actual expenditures are compared to planned capital outlays, and that there is an appropriate control system to prevent a waste of resources;

❑ A post completion audit of selected major projects should be conducted to identify both good practice and mistakes to feed forward into new projects;

❑ A balance is maintained between those projects acquired on economic grounds and those which are a matter of necessity;

❑ A balance is maintained between high risk/high return projects and low risk/low return projects in order to prevent suffering the consequences of being at either end of the scale.

With the developments in personal computers and pre-programmable calculators, no technical barrier should exist to the widespread use of discounting procedures for evaluating proposed capital projects. However, in spite of the extensive experience of many companies with the techniques, problems still arise with the use and interpretation of project appraisal techniques. These problems arise when:

1. Payback is required over time periods far too short for certain types of capital projects;

2. Inappropriately high discount rates are used;

3. New capital projects are compared with unrealistic alternatives;

4. Capital projects selected are biased towards incremental opportunities;

5. Evaluations ignore important capital project costs and benefits.

1. Payback is required over time periods far too short for certain types of capital projects

Considerable judgement is required in appraising certain types of capital projects, particularly those in new untested process technologies. Many companies have been known to impose very short payback periods, such as two or three years, on all types of capital projects.

Some types of capital projects, particularly those involving process technology like Flexible Manufacturing Systems (FMS) or Computer-Integrated-Manufacturing (CIM) are difficult to justify when subjected to such payback criteria in the face of more traditional alternative projects. Given that the benefits from such projects will arise several years in the future, when major renovation or replacement of traditional automated machines would be required, discounted cash flow analysis is far more appropriate. However, there are problems associated with quantifying the costs and benefits of such projects which makes the practical use of discounted cash flow techniques very difficult.

2. Inappropriately high discount rates are used

It is not uncommon to find companies using excessive discount rates for appraising capital projects. The use of an excessively high discount rate in appraising a long-lived capital project has as many drawbacks as using an arbitrarily short appraisal time. This is because discount rates compound geometrically every time period, penalising cash flows received five or more years in the future.

3. New capital projects are compared with unrealistic alternatives

We indicated earlier in *Chapter 13* that making a decision may require a comparison to be made against an alternative involving doing nothing. Where an evaluation is made with the status quo, it is quite incorrect to assume that present cash flows can be maintained.

When a new technology becomes available and requires a substantial investment of funds, it will probably also be available to others. This means that a likely alternative to adopting the technology will be vulnerable market share and gross margins, with the possible consequence of declining cash flows in the future.

4. Capital projects selected are biased towards incremental opportunities

The project approval process for many companies specifies different levels of authorisation for different levels of management. Such a procedure can create an incentive for managers to propose a sequence of small projects that fall just below the cut-off point for higher level approval.

A consequence of this approach is that the company can become less efficient because a division never receives the full benefit from a completely redesigned and re-equipped plant that can exploit the latest technology.

5. Evaluations ignore important capital project costs and benefits

It is not uncommon for capital project proposals to underestimate costs quite significantly. This is particularly the case for projects that embody revolutionary new technological features. Computer software and training staff may be significant costs associated with the project which can be easily overlooked.

While some costs are readily identified, but overlooked, others are more difficult to measure. Innovative technologies provide benefits in reduced stocks, improved quality and reduced floor space which can be estimated but other returns such as improved flexibility, faster response times to changing market conditions, reductions in lead times and opportunities to learn, innovate, and grow from new technology will be much more difficult to quantify.

The inadequacy of the information provided by costing systems in relation to the complex characteristics of new processes is a major source of the problem. Very simply, procedures used within companies may not be updated to respond to such complexities in the required time-frame.

Shorter product life cycles and more flexible technologies mean that plant is now being installed which may last for several product life cycles, and may also be used to produce several products simultaneously. The result is that the relationship between plant life and product life has changed, with the consequence that the basis for investment must also be changed, as must the costing systems to permit an allocation of capital and running costs over a range of products.

Thus, the key problem with the conventional application of project appraisal techniques is that they are unable to quantify the technological benefits of a new investment, many of which are seen as being unquantifiable and intangible. Such intangible benefits (apparently) almost invariably appear in a different department from where the investment is made. Furthermore, because they were not forecast or quantified, when they do appear they are recorded as an unplanned variance which is not attributed to the project.

There are no simple solutions to these problems. Current experience with such new technologies is limited such that the benefits of flexibility, reduced throughput time and lead time, organisational learning, and technology options are difficult to estimate. This does not mean however that they need, necessarily, to be assigned a zero value when conducting a financial appraisal. As with all projects, there will be those factors difficult to quantify but which must be taken into consideration if a real view is to be formed. These are no exception.

14.2   Differences between NPV and IRR

IRR seems to be preferred by non-financial managers. One reason for its appeal is that it is simple because the output from its calculation produces a percentage figure which can be compared against a company's hurdle rate. If the IRR is above the hurdle rate then the project is acceptable. If the IRR is below the hurdle rate the project is not acceptable.

NPV and IRR will provide the same accept/reject for the majority of capital projects. However, there are a number of situations where this is not the case and it will be seen that the use of IRR will produce an incorrect decision. These are because:

1. The output from an IRR calculation is a percentage return rather than the physical size of the earnings;

2. There are differences in the reinvestment assumptions;

3. The IRR can give more than one rate of return;

4. The IRR can incorrectly rank mutually exclusive projects.

1. The output from an IRR calculation is a percentage

This is best understood with reference to the following example:

	Project X	Project Y
Capital outlay	£18,000	£60,000
Annual savings (5 years)	£ 8,000	£20,000
IRR	34.2%	19.9%
NPV (at 10% cost of capital)	£12,328	£15,820
Profitability index	1.80	1.26

Project X has an IRR of 34.2% compared to only 19.9% for Project Y, but this does not take into account the difference in the absolute size of the earnings. Project Y is clearly preferable to Project X in terms of the NPV it generates despite its lower IRR. However, in this case, where the capital outlays are substantially different we should make the decision based on the higher profitability index, i.e. Project X with a value of 1.80.

2. Differences in the reinvestment assumptions

In using the NPV and IRR approaches there is an assumption that future cash flows from projects are available for reinvestment. However, there are major differences in the way in which these reinvestment assumptions are made.

NPV assumes that annual cash flows are reinvested at the company's cost of capital. On the other hand, IRR assumes that annual cash flows are reinvested at the percentage IRR obtained from each project.

For Project X, NPV assumes that the £8,000 annual cash flow is reinvested at the cost of capital of 10%. IRR assumes that it is reinvested at 34.2%.

The reality is that the company has determined that the return it expects from reinvestment is its stated cost of capital. IRR requires that the reinvestment is often much higher and as such is not theoretically correct.

One method that seeks to remove the issues regarding the reinvestment assumption in the IRR calculation is the development of the modified IRR (MIRR). This requires that the cash inflows are adjusted to a terminal or future value. The result is then divided into the capital outlay. This produces a decimal figure that can be "read" using present value tables, i.e. if a project has a five year life, read along the five year row until a value fits the decimal figure calculated above. From the column heading this will give the MIRR percentage.

For the purpose of a worked example we will use the data for Project X on *page 387* and assume a cost of capital at 10%. Previously, the results for Project X gave a NPV of £12,328 and an IRR of 34.2%.

Table 14.1 Calculation of terminal value and MIRR for Project X

Terminal value of cash inflows: 8,000 x 6.105 [1] = £48,840

[1] Sum of compound interest factors for five years at 10%

MIRR = £18,000 ÷ £48,840 = 0.3686 [2]

[2] Consult the present value tables for a five year life

MIRR = 22%

In this example cash flows have been compounded at the company's cost of capital, then a calculation, or reading from present value tables to produce a result. Where Project X had an IRR of 34.2%, the MIRR now shows 22%.

In most cases the MIRR will provide a satisfactory result based on cash inflows compounded at the company's cost of capital to produce a terminal or future value. This is in line with the NPV calculations. However, MIRR does have its critics who will produce figures to show its shortcomings. In many of these cases the MIRR examples are often dealing with extreme cash flows.

3.   IRR can produce more than one rate of return

In capital projects where the cash flows are irregular, i.e. not consistently positive, it is possible to find that the IRR method produces more than one rate of return.

		Project Z
Capital outlay		£5,387
Cash inflows	Year 1	£7,575
	Year 2	£5,353
	Year 3	–£8,000

Figure 14.1   Calculation of NPV's from 14 to 28%

Discount factor %	14	16	18	20	22	24	26	28
Net present value £000's	−27	−8	0	6	14	6	0	−22

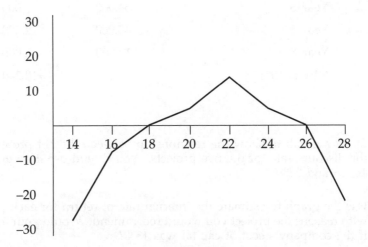

Note: We have used discount factors correct to three decimal places.

4. IRR can incorrectly rank mutually exclusive projects

Mutually exclusive projects exist where there are two or more projects, any of which is acceptable in technical terms, but only one is required to perform the task demanded. In this case, the decision rule is that the most acceptable in economic terms should be selected first. The question is what decision rule do we use? Should we use internal rate of return (IRR), or net present value (NPV)? Does the IRR and NPV methods always produce the same results? To answer these questions we will use the following example.

A company is considering which of two mutually exclusive projects it should undertake. The company anticipates a cost of capital of 10% and the net cash inflows for the projects are as follows:

	Project X £	Project Y £
Capital outlay	120,000	120,000
Net cash inflows:		
Year 1	21,000	130,000
Year 2	48,000	6,000
Year 3	54,000	6,000
Year 4	45,000	2,000
Year 5	12,000	2,000
NPV at 10%	+17,478	+10,240

1. Draw a graph to show the relationship between the net present value and the discount rate for the two projects. You should use discount rates at 10, 14, 18 and 22%.

2. Use the graph to estimate the internal rate of return for each project. State with reasons the project you would recommend. Would your advice change if the company's cost of capital was 15%?

The first stage is to calculate the net present value for each project. These are shown in *Table 14.2*.

Table 14.2   Net present value for Project X and Y

	Discount rate %	Project X NPV £	Project Y NPV £	Incremental NPV (X–Y)
(a)	10	+17,478	+10,240	+7,238
(b)	14	+4,647	+4,896	−249
(c)	18	−6,399	−22	−6,377
(d)	22	−16,035	−4,420	−11,615

In the final column of *Table 14.2* we show the incremental net present values which are simply the net present value for Project X less the net present value for Project Y. We will return to the incremental approach in a later section.

Figure 14.2 Comparison of mutually exclusive projects

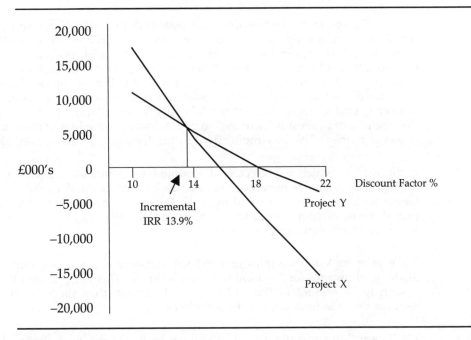

The second part of our example asks for an estimate of the IRR for each project. From the graph, we can see that the line for Project X cuts the horizontal axis at 15.5% approximately, while for Project Y the IRR is 18% approximately. We have also shown the incremental IRR (this shows the point where there is no preference for Project X or Project Y).

The decision rule is that we should choose the project with the highest net present value provided that the company's cost of capital is less than the incremental IRR. In this case if the cost of capital is less than the incremental IRR (i.e. between 0 to 13.9%) then we would choose Project X. If the cost of capital was greater than 13.9% but less than 18% we would choose Project Y provided that it produced a positive net present value.

A summary of the results produces the following:

	Project X	Project Y	Incremental
NPV at 10%	+17,478	+10,240	
IRR	15.5%	18.0%	13.9%

14.3   Effect of inflation

In our discussion of discounting, we assumed that the discounting process simply reflects the opportunity cost of money. Perhaps the easiest way to understand this opportunity cost is that in a world with no change in prices, individuals would still have preference for cash now versus cash later. This is understood by considering whether if you sought to borrow money from a bank in a world with zero inflation it would still require you to pay interest. The answer is undoubtedly, yes! What happens in an inflationary environment is that the rate of interest is increased to compensate for the loss of the purchasing power of money. This has implications for undertaking an investment appraisal.

If the rate at which a project is discounted incorporates expectations about inflation, then similar expectations need to be incorporated in the cash flows. Please remember that any resulting cash flows, (or in this case adjustments to cash flows or discount rates) should be based on inflation assumptions relating to future levels and not past levels.

If we refer back to examples in previous sections, you will see that we have made no allowance for inflation in the cash flows. This is a problem if inflation is seen to be present in the cost of capital. If not, then there is no problem because the rule in dealing with inflation is:

1.   If cash flows and the cost of capital are in real terms, such that no inflation expectations have been built into either, then the real cash flows can be discounted to reflect the real cost of capital.

2.   If inflation expectations are present in either the cash flows or the cost of capital, then an adjustment must be made to ensure that the two are matched. In other words, inflated cash flows should be discounted by a cost of capital which includes inflationary expectations.

An adjustment can be made for inflation in the discount rate by rearranging the formula which is shown in the following example:

$(1+m) = (1+i)\ (1+r)$.

where

m = the money or nominal rate

i = the expected rate of inflation, and

r = the real rate

Using this formula, we can adjust the cost of capital expressed in real terms to one that incorporates inflation, and vice versa. For example, if the cost of capital in real terms (r) is 10% and the expected rate of inflation (i) is 10%, then the money rate (m) is 21%, i.e.

(1+m) = (1.10) (1.10) = 1.21, and

m = 1.21 − 1 = 0.21, or 21%

Or, if we know that the money rate quoted by a financial institution like a bank is 21%, and the expected rate of inflation is 10%, then we can find the real rate of 10% by rearranging the formula, i.e. (1 + r) = (1 + m) ÷ (1 + i).

Alternatively, as we will illustrate, if the cost of capital available incorporates the expected rate of inflation then this can be left and adjustments can be made to the cash flows. The advantage of this approach is that inflation does not necessarily impact on all sectors of the economy evenly and it may, therefore, be necessary to take into account the differential effects of inflation. For example, we know that on occasion retail prices and wage rates have moved at differential rates.

An example

Consider the following example where there is a capital outlay of £90,000 which will result in annual savings of £30,000 for five years and a cost of capital of 10%.

We will now show the effect of inflation on a capital project where no adjustments have been made for inflation (i.e. *Table 14.3*). In what follows we will illustrate how:

❑ Adjustments are made to the cash flows and the discount rate to allow for inflation at 6%;

❑ Different inflation factors are applied to revenues, costs and the discount rate.

Table 14.3 Net present value of capital project with no Inflation

		£
Present value of cash inflows	(£30,000 x 3.791)	113,730
less Capital outlay		90,000
Net present value (NPV)		23,730

1. Adjustments to cash inflows and discount rate.

First, we must adjust the cash flows to increase them by 6% per annum, compound.

Table 14.4   Adjustment of cash inflows/savings

Year	£	Factor	Adjusted cash flows £
1	30,000	1.06	31,800
2	31,800	1.06	33,708
3	33,708	1.06	35,730
4	35,730	1.06	37,874
5	37,874	1.06	40,146

Next, we adjust the discount rate to include 6% inflation, as follows:

$$(1 + \text{rate}) \quad \text{x} \quad (1 + \text{inflation})$$

$$1.10 \quad \text{x} \quad 1.06 \quad = \quad 1.166\%$$

Therefore, the new discount rate is 16.6%. To obtain discount factors at 16.6% you could take a point between 16% and 17%. However, it is possible to obtain discount factors with the aid of a calculator. In simple terms, we need to divide 1 by 1.166 which will give 0.858 for year 1. We then carry out successive divisions by 1.166 until we have the required number of factors. Test your calculator to find out how the constant works. For example, on many calculators you can enter say 1.166 then press divide divide (yes twice), then equals equals; this should give 0.858 rounded to three decimal places. For the remaining factors keep pressing the equals button. The long method is now shown in *Table 14.5*:

Table 14.5   Calculation of discount factors at 16.6%

1	1.00000 ÷ 1.166	=	0.85763	0.858
2.	0.85763 ÷ 1.166	=	0.73553	0.736
3.	0.73553 ÷ 1.166	=	0.63081	0.631
4.	0.63081 ÷ 1.166	=	0.54100	0.541
5.	0.54100 ÷ 1.166	=	0.46400	0.464

Table 14.6   Net present value – with inflation

	A Cash flow	B DCF factor 16.6%	C Present value
Year	£		£
1	31,800	0.858	27,284
2	33,708	0.736	24,809
3	35,730	0.631	22,546
4	37,874	0.541	20,490
5	40,146	0.464	18,628
Present value of net cash inflows			113,757
less Capital outlay			90,000
Net present value (NPV)			£23,757

You will notice that the net present value is the same in *Table 14.3 and 14.6*. (the slight difference is due to rounding). This result shows that if inflation is ignored, or that inflation is applied equally to the cash flows and the discount factors, the result is the same. In this case, *Table 14.6*, we have increased the cash flows by 6% and increased the discount factors by 6% – therefore, we are discounting higher cash flows at higher discount rates.

2. Differential inflation

Differential inflation adjustments need to be made where the cash inflows and the cash outflows inflate at different rates. Different inflation assumptions need to be incorporated in each of the components which make up the total cash flow and within the discount rate.

In this example, we will assume that the discount rate includes expected inflation of 6% per annum, while the components making up the annual cash flows are affected as follows:

Cash inflows   £130,000   +   5% per annum

Cash outflows   £100,000   +   7% per annum.

Table 14.7   Adjusting revenues and costs for inflation

Year	Cash inflows 1.05 £	Cash outflows 1.07 £	Net cash inflows £
0	130,000	100,000	n/a
1	136,500	107,000	29,500
2	143,325	114,490	28,835
3	150,491	122,504	27,987
4	158,016	131,079	26,937
5	165,917	140,255	25,662

In *Table 14.7*, we have adjusted the revenues by 5% per annum and the costs by 7% per annum. The third column shows the net cash flows which now show a decline over the lifetime of the project.

Table 14.8   Net present value – with differential inflation

Year	A Cash inflows £	B DCF factor 16.6%	C Present value £
1	29,500	0.858	25,311
2	28,835	0.736	21,223
3	27,987	0.631	17,660
4	26,937	0.541	14,573
5	25,662	0.464	11,907
Present value of net cash inflows			90,674
less Capital outlay			90,000
Net present value (NPV)			£674

In *Table 14.6*, with a single inflation rate applied to the individual cash flows and the discount rate, the net present value was +£23,757. This meant that the project was viable and could be considered for selection.

However, in *Table 14.8*, with differential inflation, the net present value is now £674. This shows the effect of a small change in the inflation assumptions; in this case, we reduced the revenue inflation from 6% to 5% while we increased the cost of inflation from 6% to 7%.

It is possible to show that the arithmetic effect of applying the same inflation rate to the individual cash flows and to the discount rate produces the same net present value. It is tempting to conclude that it is possible to ignore inflation in the cash flows and the discount rate. The application of different inflation assumptions to individual components of the cash flows and to the discount rate, however, can have a significant effect on the accept/reject of a project. You will also find that the issue becomes even more complex when both taxation and inflation have to be taken into consideration.

14.4   The treatment of taxation

Taxation will have an impact on both cash and profit streams used in project appraisal. Although taxation is beyond the scope of this book the general principle to follow in project appraisal is similar to that of inflation discussed earlier in this chapter. This means that in addition to cash flows being discounted using an interest rate allowing for inflation, the discount rate must also allow for taxation.

In reality, the detail of taxation as applied to project appraisal is beyond the concern of most non-financial managers. Provided you have understood the principle of comparing 'like' cash flows with a 'like' discount rate discussed with regard to inflation, that is sufficient. It is then time to involve a taxation specialist!

1. The effect of taxation on cash flows

In this section, it is assumed that the capital projects that are being appraised relate to companies which operate in a profit making environment, and that these companies purchase capital assets which qualify for capital allowances and are subject to the payment of corporation tax.

There are three areas for consideration when applying tax adjustments to capital project cash flows. These are:

❑   The timing of tax receipts/payments; *

❑   Tax payable on project savings;

❑   Capital allowance.

---

*   Please note, the timing of tax receipts and payments will reflect the tax laws of a specific country. For example, in the UK, companies whose profits exceed £1.5 million will have to pay their corporation tax, quarterly, in advance.

The timing of tax receipts/payments

When appraising capital projects, companies assume that:

❑ Tax will be paid in the year following the one in which taxable profits (i.e. project savings/revenues) are made;

❑ Tax will be recovered in the year following the one in which tax allowances are available.

Tax payable on project savings

It is often not appreciated that any financial benefits (i.e. savings) resulting from a capital project will have tax consequences. All things being equal, greater savings will produce higher profits, not all of which will be of benefit to the project initiator – the tax authorities will demand their share less, of course, any capital allowances (discussed in the next section).

Capital allowances

In certain circumstances, the expenditure incurred on the capital outlay for a project can be deducted from the profit generated by a company in the form of a capital allowance.

These capital allowances reduce future tax payments according to the amount of allowance available, the tax rate in operation and the economic life of each project.

Capital allowances can be likened to a personal tax allowance in so far as they reduce the amount of earnings subject to assessment for tax. A company can normally reduce its taxable profits by the amount of capital allowances available.

2. An example *

If we take the same example we used for inflation, where there is a capital outlay of £90,000 which will result in annual savings of £30,000 for five years. We will now assume:

1. A cost of capital of 10%;

2. Capital allowances, calculated on a 25% reducing balance, apply;

3. Corporation tax at the rate of 35%;

4. A one year delay in the effect of taxation on receipts and payments;

5. Sufficient profits available to offset capital allowances.

---

* This example is provided to show how tax can be incorporated into cash flows and assumes companies in the UK with annual profits less than £1.5 million.

Table 14.9   *Calculation of after tax capital allowances*

Year	A Reducing balance £	B Capital allowance (at 25%) £	C Tax saved using capital allowance £
1	90,000	22,500	7,875
2	67,500	16,875	5,906
3	50,625	12,656	4,430
4	37,969	9,492	3,322
5	28,477	7,119	2,492
6	21,358	21,358	7,475

The £90,000 shown in year 1 is the original capital outlay. The availability of the 25% capital allowance means that we are allowed 25% of this amount that can be offset against taxable profits, hence the £22,500 in column B. However, the net tax effect is 35% of the £22,500 which equals £7,875.

In year 2, the reduced balance (i.e. from £90,000) is £67,500 (£90,000 − £22,500), and the process continues.

In year 6, the reduced balance is £21,358.

We have assumed that the project ends in year 5, therefore, the whole of the remaining balance is taken and offset against our taxable profits.

The tax payable on the annual savings is simply 35% of £30,000 which equals £10,500. For project appraisal, we assume that tax will be payable one year later, i.e. from year 2 through to year 6.

A full appraisal incorporating tax is given in *Table 14.10*.

Table 14.10 Project appraisal incorporating taxation

Year	A Tax saved using capital allowances £	B Savings £	C Tax on savings at 35% £	D Cash flow (A+B+C) £	E DCF 10 % factor	F Net present value £
1	7,875	30,000		37,875	0.909	34,428
2	5,906	30,000	−10,500	25,406	0.826	20,985
3	4,430	30,000	−10,500	23,930	0.751	17,971
4	3,322	30,000	−10,500	22,822	0.683	15,587
5	2,492	30,000	−10,500	21,992	0.621	13,657
6	7,475		−10,500	−3,025	0.564	−1,706
Present value of net cash inflows						100,922
less Capital outlay						90,000
Net present value (NPV)						£10,922

The tax saved by claiming capital allowances, column A, is shown above in *Table 14.10.* The savings for the project are shown from year 1 through to 5, whilst the tax due on the savings is shown in column C. This is delayed one year with the final tax being due in year 6. The cash flow in column D is the sum of columns A plus B plus C.

The individual cash flows can then be adjusted by the company's cost of capital to find their present value. Finally, these are aggregated and the capital outlay is deducted to give the net present value (NPV) of £10,922.

Compare this with the result of the project without any adjustment for taxation, *i.e. Table 14.3,* that shows a net present value (NPV) of £23,757. In *Table 14.10* it can be seen in Column D that the cash flows are greater in year 1 but decline steadily over the life of the project, compared to the without tax cash flows which were £30,000 per year.

14.5   Sensitivity analysis

One important management tool available for questioning both potential benefits and risks associated with a project is sensitivity analysis. In essence, the assumptions surrounding a project can be input to a computer spreadsheet to produce a base case net present value (NPV) and internal rate of return (IRR), from which changes in assumption can easily be made to gauge the effect upon them. The mechanics of such an application are now considered within the context of a simple example. The data to be used in our example concerns a project with the following features:

Capital outlay	£5,000,000
Life	10 years
Revenues volume	80,000 units
Selling price	£85 per unit
Labour costs	£22 per unit
Material costs	£40 per unit
Fixed costs	£660,000 per annum
Cost of capital	12%

In practice, the data would be far more detailed, and important factors like taxation and inflation should be included if the resulting net present value (NPV) is to be calculated at a company cost of capital. However, we have deliberately made the example as simple as possible to show the advantages of such an application.

Steps:

1. Determine the cash flow and calculate the net present value (NPV) before making any adjustments to the input variables;

2. Adjust each of the input variables adversely by a fixed percentage, in this case we will use 10%;

3. Determine the alternative cash flows and calculate revised net present values (NPVs);

4. Rank each of the input variables according to the sensitivity of the net present value (NPV).

1. Determine the cash flow and calculate net present value (NPV)

a. Determine the cash flow

(Revenues volume x contribution per unit) – specific fixed costs

=   (80,000 x £23.00) – £660,000

=   £1,180,000

Calculation of contribution per unit:

	£
Selling price	85.00
– Labour cost	22.00
– Material cost	40.00
= Contribution per unit	23.00

b. Calculate the net present value (NPV)

(Cash flow x annuity factor) – capital cost

=   (£1,180,000 x 5.630) – £5,000,000

=   £1,667,000

2. Adjust the input variables adversely by 10%

Table 14.11   Input variables varied adversely by 10%

	Original estimate	Factor	Varied adversely by 10%
Capital outlay	£5,000,000	x 1.10	£5,500,000
Life (years)	10	less 1	9
Revenues volume (units)	80,000	÷ 1.10	72,727
Selling price	£85.00	÷ 1.10	£77.27
Labour costs per unit	£22.00	x 1.10	£24.20
Material costs per unit	£40.00	x 1.10	£44.00
Fixed costs per annum	£660,000	x 1.10	£726,000
Cost of capital	12%	x 1.10	13.2%

Calculation of the revenues volume and selling price is as follows:

a.   Vary the revenues volume adversely by 10%:

   80,000 units divided by (1 plus 0.10) = 72,727 units

b.   Vary the selling price adversely by 10%:

   £85.00 divided by (1 plus 0.10) = £77.27

Alternative calculation of revenues volume and selling price:

For simplicity, it is possible to take 10% of the revenues volume, i.e. 80,000 times 10% which equals 8,000 units. The net figure would be 72,000 units. Similarly, the selling price would be reduced by £8.50 to give a net of £76.50. It is important to realise that this method is not technically correct and will not produce a consistent movement in each of the variables.

3. Determine alternative cash flows and calculate revised NPVs

Table 14.12   Determine the alternative cash flows

	A Revenues volume units	B Contri- bution per unit £	C Fixed costs £	D Cash flow (A x B – C) £
Capital outlay	80,000	23.00	660,000	1,180,000
Life (years)	80,000	23.00	660,000	1,180,000
Revenues volume (units)	72,727	23.00	660,000	1,012,721
Selling price	80,000	15.27	660,000	561,600
Labour costs per unit	80,000	20.80	660,000	1,004,000
Material costs per unit	80,000	19.00	660,000	860,000
Fixed costs per annum	80,000	23.00	726,000	1,114,000

Calculation of contribution per unit:

	Selling price £	Labour cost £	Material cost £
Selling price	77.27	85.00	85.00
– Labour cost	22.00	24.20	22.00
– Material cost	40.00	40.00	44.00
= Contribution per unit	15.27	20.80	19.00

Notes for calculations in *Table 14.12*.

1. Column A.   For each variable we must determine the volume; these are all at 80,000 units except for the reduction in revenue volume to 72,727 units.

2. Column B.   For each variable we must determine the contribution per unit. These are all at £23.00 per unit except for the adverse changes in selling price, labour costs and material costs; revised calculations are shown on *page 403*, i.e. £15.27, £20.80 and £19.00.

3. Column C.   These are the fixed costs and are all at £660,000 per annum except for the increase in fixed costs line to £726,000.

4. Column D.   Shows the revised cash flows for each of the elements within the project. The calculation is (Column A x Column B - Column C).

In *Table 14.13*, we calculate the revised net present values (NPVs) using annuity tables, (see *pages 433 to 434*).

Table 14.13   Calculate NPVs (using annuity tables)

	A Cash flow £	B Annuity factor	C Present value of cash flow (A x B) £	D Capital outlay £	E Net present value (C – D) £
Capital outlay	1,180,000	5.650	6,667,000	5,500,000	1,167,000
Life (years)	1,180,000	5.328	6,287,040	5,000,000	1,287,040
Revenue volume	1,012,721	5.650	5,721,874	5,000,000	721,874
Selling price	561,600	5.650	3,173,040	5,000,000	–1,826,960
Labour costs p.u.	1,004,000	5.650	5,672,600	5,000,000	672,600
Material costs p.u.	860,000	5.650	4,859,000	5,000,000	–141,000
Fixed costs p.a.	1,114,000	5.650	6,294,100	5,000,000	1,294,100
Cost of capital	1,180,000	5.382	6,351,940	5,000,000	1,351,940

Notes for calculations in *Table 14.13*.

1. Column A. We take the revised cash flows from *Table 14.12*, Column D.

2. Column B. For ease of calculation we are using annuity factors to arrive at the present value of the cash flows. For most of the elements we will use the annuity factor for a 10 year life, at 12%, i.e. 5.650. The second element, the life, we use the annuity factor for a 9 year life, at 12%, i.e. 5.328. The last element, the cost of capital, we use the annuity factor for a 10 year life, at 13.2%, i.e. 5.382. For this last annuity factor we used a standard spreadsheet program to determine the value of 5.382.

3. Column C. Column A (revised cash flow) times Column B (annuity factor).

4. Column D. This is the capital outlay. For most of the elements, the capital outlay is £5,000,000. The only exception is the capital outlay element which is adversely adjusted by 10% to £5,500,000.

5. Column E. Column C (present value of cash flows) - Column D (capital outlay).

4. Rank each of the input variables

The final stage in the sensitivity analysis is to rank each of the elements of the project in descending order based on the revised net present values (NPVs). Here we take the output from *Table 14.13*, Column E, starting with the selling price with a negative net present value (NPV) of –£1,826,960 through to fixed costs with a net present value (NPV) of £1,294,100.

Table 14.14   *Input variables in decreasing order of sensitivity*

	NPV £
Selling price	–1,826,960
Material costs	–141,000
Labour costs	672,600
Revenues volume	721,874
Capital outlay	1,167,000
Life	1,287,000
Fixed costs	1,294,100
Cost of capital	1,351,940

The analysis highlights the variables which will have the greatest impact on the net present values (NPVs) of a project. By amending the original data by 10% negative, two sensitive variables to the project are found, i.e. the selling price and the material costs. If the selling price were not £85.00 per unit but only achieved £77.27 per unit, then the project would generate a negative NPV of £1,826,960, while a 10% increase in material costs would generate a negative NPV of £141,000.

Given that the company's cost of capital is 12%, then a £7.73 reduction in selling price could be a potential disaster. With knowledge of this potential problem area, an investigation could be undertaken by the marketing department to establish whether difficulties in achieving a selling price of £85.00 are likely. If so, then despite the initially favourable NPV, the project is not acceptable on economic grounds. This, of course, assumes there to be no revenue volume/ selling price relationship such that a reduction in price to £77.27 might well be associated with an increase in revenue volume. This is one other area of investigation readily considered by using a computerised model.

In summary, such analysis permits project proposals to be evaluated and the analysis can be used to identify sensitive variables without having to input any additional data. In practice, the analysis would be extended much further than in the example so as to explore changes in a number of variables and any interrelationships between them.

Exercise 14.1

D.R. Afty Ltd., make a range of wooden doors for the building industry. The production engineer has investigated replacing three existing machines with either the latest models, or a multi-purpose model.

The following data has been collected:

Machine type	Existing machines		Proposed models	
	Original capital outlay	Operating expenses per year	Capital outlay	Operating expenses per year
	£	£	£	£
Cutting	20,000	15,000	27,000	9,000
Planing	30,000	25,000	35,000	17,000
Sanding	10,000	5,000	12,000	2,000
Multi-purpose model			132,000	16,000

Assume all machines to have a 10 year life.
The cost of capital within the company is 15%. (Tip: use annuity tables)
Ignore taxation

REQUIRED

Which proposal should be accepted, and why?

Exercise 14.2

A company is considering two mutually exclusive investment projects, A and B, each of which involves an initial cash outlay of £190,000 for A, and £300,000 for B. The estimated net cash inflows from each project are:

	A	B
Year 1	87,500	75,000
Year 2	87,500	150,000
Year 3	87,500	195,000
IRR	18.1%	16.2%

REQUIRED

1. Draw a graph to show the relationship between the net present value (NPV) and discount rate for the two projects, using rates of 10, 14, 18 and 22%.

2. Use the graph to estimate the internal rate of return (IRR) for each project. If the company adopts a criterion rate of 10%. Which project would you recommend?

3. Briefly summarise the relative merits of the net present value (NPV) and internal rate of return (IRR) as methods of investment appraisal.

Exercise 14.3

A company is considering which of two mutually exclusive projects it should undertake. The finance director thinks the project with the higher NPV should be chosen whereas the managing director thinks that the one with the higher IRR should be undertaken especially as both projects have the same initial outlay and length of life. The company anticipates a cost of capital of 10% and the net after cash flows of the projects to be as follows:

	Project RUF £	Project TUF £
Year 0	−115,000	−110,000
Year 1	35,000	75,000
Year 2	35,000	20,000
Year 3	35,000	20,000
Year 4	35,000	20,000
Year 5	35,000	20,000
IRR	15.9	17.5

REQUIRED

1. Calculate the net present value (NPV) and profitability index (PI) for each project.
2. Recommend, with reasons, which project if any you would undertake.
3. Explain the inconsistency in ranking of the two projects in view of the remarks of the directors.

Exercise 14.4

It is your company's policy to apply inflation rates to all capital projects, these are:

Revenue	+7% per annum
Costs	+4% per annum
Cost of capital	+5%

The following information is available for a capital project:

Capital outlay	£200,000
Revenue	£250,000 per year
Costs	£180,000 per year
Life	5 years
Cost of capital	12% (real)

REQUIRED

1. Calculate the NPV without inflation adjustments
2. Calculate the NPV with inflation adjustments

Exercise 14.5

It is your company's policy to apply inflation rates to all capital projects, these are:

Selling price +4% per annum; Material costs +3% per annum; Labour costs +8% per annum; Fixed costs +2% per annum.

The following information is available for a capital project:

Capital outlay	£7,000,000
Volume	600,000 units per year
Selling price	£12.00 per unit
Material costs	£2.25 per unit
Labour costs	£5.25 per unit
Fixed costs	£1,000,000 per year
Life	10 years
Cost of capital	14%

REQUIRED

Calculate the NPV with inflation adjustments

Exercise 14.6

The following data refers to proposed capital project number 327:

Capital outlay	£180,000
Life	5 years
Annual savings	£72,000
Capital allowance	25%
Corporation tax	30%
Cost of capital	12%

REQUIRED

Prepare a suitable financial evaluation and advise your board of directors whether or not they should acquire the machine.

Exercise 14.7

The following data refers to proposed capital project number 106:

Capital outlay	£250,000
Life	6 years
Annual savings	£70,000
Capital allowance	25%
Corporation tax	30%
Cost of capital	10%

REQUIRED

Prepare a suitable financial evaluation and advise your board of directors whether or not they should acquire the machine.

Exercise 14.8

The following data relates to a proposed capital project:

Capital outlay	£7,000,000
Life	10 years
Revenues volume	900,000 units
Selling price	£8.00 per unit
Material costs	£1.50 per unit
Labour costs	£3.50 per unit
Fixed costs	£1,000,000 per annum
Cost of capital	14%

REQUIRED

1. Calculate the project's net present value (NPV).

2. Undertake a sensitivity analysis (adjust each variable adversely by 10%).

3. Comment on the results.

Exercise 14.9

The following data relates to a proposed capital project:

Capital outlay	£500,000
Life	5 years
Revenues volume	50,000 units
Selling price	£25.00 per unit
Material costs	£12.00 per unit
Labour costs	£8.00 per unit
Fixed costs	£75,000 per annum
Cost of capital	10%

REQUIRED

1. Calculate the project's net present value (NPV).

2. Undertake a sensitivity analysis (you will find that some of the variables are extremely sensitive).

3. Comment on the results.

References

Bliss, J.H., 'The story told by the financial and operating statements', *Management and Administration*, Vol. 7, No. 1, January, pp.25–30, 1924.

B.I.M. Study Group, 'Accounting Ratios', *Accountancy*, July, pp.267–271, 1956.

Cadbury Report, Financial Aspects of Corporate Governance, 1992.

Dobson, R.W., 'Return on capital', *Management Accounting*, November, pp.438–447, 1967.

Horngren, C.T., *Accounting for management contol*, Second Edition, Prentice Hall, 1970.

Parker, R.H., *Understanding company financial statements*, Pelican Books, 1975.

% Period	1	2	3	4	5	6	7	8	9	10
1	0.990	0.980	0.971	0.962	0.952	0.943	0.935	0.926	0.917	0.909
2	0.980	0.961	0.943	0.925	0.907	0.890	0.873	0.857	0.842	0.826
3	0.971	0.942	0.915	0.889	0.864	0.840	0.816	0.794	0.772	0.751
4	0.961	0.924	0.888	0.855	0.823	0.792	0.763	0.735	0.708	0.683
5	0.951	0.906	0.863	0.822	0.784	0.747	0.713	0.681	0.650	0.621
6	0.942	0.888	0.837	0.790	0.746	0.705	0.666	0.630	0.596	0.564
7	0.933	0.871	0.813	0.760	0.711	0.665	0.623	0.583	0.547	0.513
8	0.923	0.853	0.789	0.731	0.677	0.627	0.582	0.540	0.502	0.467
9	0.914	0.837	0.766	0.703	0.645	0.592	0.544	0.500	0.460	0.424
10	0.905	0.820	0.744	0.676	0.614	0.558	0.508	0.463	0.422	0.386
11	0.896	0.804	0.722	0.650	0.585	0.527	0.475	0.429	0.388	0.350
12	0.887	0.788	0.701	0.625	0.557	0.497	0.444	0.397	0.356	0.319
13	0.879	0.773	0.681	0.601	0.530	0.469	0.415	0.368	0.326	0.290
14	0.870	0.758	0.661	0.577	0.505	0.442	0.388	0.340	0.299	0.263
15	0.861	0.743	0.642	0.555	0.481	0.417	0.362	0.315	0.275	0.239
16	0.853	0.728	0.623	0.534	0.458	0.394	0.339	0.292	0.252	0.218
17	0.844	0.714	0.605	0.513	0.436	0.371	0.317	0.270	0.231	0.198
18	0.836	0.700	0.587	0.494	0.416	0.350	0.296	0.250	0.212	0.180
19	0.828	0.686	0.570	0.475	0.396	0.331	0.277	0.232	0.194	0.164
20	0.820	0.673	0.554	0.456	0.377	0.312	0.258	0.215	0.178	0.149

% Period	11	12	13	14	15	16	17	18	19	20
1	0.901	0.893	0.885	0.877	0.870	0.862	0.855	0.847	0.840	0.833
2	0.812	0.797	0.783	0.769	0.756	0.743	0.731	0.718	0.706	0.694
3	0.731	0.712	0.693	0.675	0.658	0.641	0.624	0.609	0.593	0.579
4	0.659	0.636	0.613	0.592	0.572	0.552	0.534	0.516	0.499	0.482
5	0.593	0.567	0.543	0.519	0.497	0.476	0.456	0.437	0.419	0.402
6	0.535	0.507	0.480	0.456	0.432	0.410	0.390	0.370	0.352	0.335
7	0.482	0.452	0.425	0.400	0.376	0.354	0.333	0.314	0.296	0.279
8	0.434	0.404	0.376	0.351	0.327	0.305	0.285	0.266	0.249	0.233
9	0.391	0.361	0.333	0.308	0.284	0.263	0.243	0.225	0.209	0.194
10	0.352	0.322	0.295	0.270	0.247	0.227	0.208	0.191	0.176	0.162
11	0.317	0.287	0.261	0.237	0.215	0.195	0.178	0.162	0.148	0.135
12	0.286	0.257	0.231	0.208	0.187	0.168	0.152	0.137	0.124	0.112
13	0.258	0.229	0.204	0.182	0.163	0.145	0.130	0.116	0.104	0.093
14	0.232	0.205	0.181	0.160	0.141	0.125	0.111	0.099	0.088	0.078
15	0.209	0.183	0.160	0.140	0.123	0.108	0.095	0.084	0.074	0.065
16	0.188	0.163	0.141	0.123	0.107	0.093	0.081	0.071	0.062	0.054
17	0.170	0.146	0.125	0.108	0.093	0.080	0.069	0.060	0.052	0.045
18	0.153	0.130	0.111	0.095	0.081	0.069	0.059	0.051	0.044	0.038
19	0.138	0.116	0.098	0.083	0.070	0.060	0.051	0.043	0.037	0.031
20	0.124	0.104	0.087	0.073	0.061	0.051	0.043	0.037	0.031	0.026

% Period	21	22	23	24	25	26	27	28	29	30
1	0.826	0.820	0.813	0.806	0.800	0.794	0.787	0.781	0.775	0.769
2	0.683	0.672	0.661	0.650	0.640	0.630	0.620	0.610	0.601	0.592
3	0.564	0.551	0.537	0.524	0.512	0.500	0.488	0.477	0.466	0.455
4	0.467	0.451	0.437	0.423	0.410	0.397	0.384	0.373	0.361	0.350
5	0.386	0.370	0.355	0.341	0.328	0.315	0.303	0.291	0.280	0.269
6	0.319	0.303	0.289	0.275	0.262	0.250	0.238	0.227	0.217	0.207
7	0.263	0.249	0.235	0.222	0.210	0.198	0.188	0.178	0.168	0.159
8	0.218	0.204	0.191	0.179	0.168	0.157	0.148	0.139	0.130	0.123
9	0.180	0.167	0.155	0.144	0.134	0.125	0.116	0.108	0.101	0.094
10	0.149	0.137	0.126	0.116	0.107	0.099	0.092	0.085	0.078	0.073
11	0.123	0.112	0.103	0.094	0.086	0.079	0.072	0.066	0.061	0.056
12	0.102	0.092	0.083	0.076	0.069	0.062	0.057	0.052	0.047	0.043
13	0.084	0.075	0.068	0.061	0.055	0.050	0.045	0.040	0.037	0.033
14	0.069	0.062	0.055	0.049	0.044	0.039	0.035	0.032	0.028	0.025
15	0.057	0.051	0.045	0.040	0.035	0.031	0.028	0.025	0.022	0.020
16	0.047	0.042	0.036	0.032	0.028	0.025	0.022	0.019	0.017	0.015
17	0.039	0.034	0.030	0.026	0.023	0.020	0.017	0.015	0.013	0.012
18	0.032	0.028	0.024	0.021	0.018	0.016	0.014	0.012	0.010	0.009
19	0.027	0.023	0.020	0.017	0.014	0.012	0.011	0.009	0.008	0.007
20	0.022	0.019	0.016	0.014	0.012	0.010	0.008	0.007	0.006	0.005

% Period	31	32	33	34	35	36	37	38	39	40
1	0.763	0.758	0.752	0.746	0.741	0.735	0.730	0.725	0.719	0.714
2	0.583	0.574	0.565	0.557	0.549	0.541	0.533	0.525	0.518	0.510
3	0.445	0.435	0.425	0.416	0.406	0.398	0.389	0.381	0.372	0.364
4	0.340	0.329	0.320	0.310	0.301	0.292	0.284	0.276	0.268	0.260
5	0.259	0.250	0.240	0.231	0.223	0.215	0.207	0.200	0.193	0.186
6	0.198	0.189	0.181	0.173	0.165	0.158	0.151	0.145	0.139	0.133
7	0.151	0.143	0.136	0.129	0.122	0.116	0.110	0.105	0.100	0.095
8	0.115	0.108	0.102	0.096	0.091	0.085	0.081	0.076	0.072	0.068
9	0.088	0.082	0.077	0.072	0.067	0.063	0.059	0.055	0.052	0.048
10	0.067	0.062	0.058	0.054	0.050	0.046	0.043	0.040	0.037	0.035
11	0.051	0.047	0.043	0.040	0.037	0.034	0.031	0.029	0.027	0.025
12	0.039	0.036	0.033	0.030	0.027	0.025	0.023	0.021	0.019	0.018
13	0.030	0.027	0.025	0.022	0.020	0.018	0.017	0.015	0.014	0.013
14	0.023	0.021	0.018	0.017	0.015	0.014	0.012	0.011	0.010	0.009
15	0.017	0.016	0.014	0.012	0.011	0.010	0.009	0.008	0.007	0.006
16	0.013	0.012	0.010	0.009	0.008	0.007	0.006	0.006	0.005	0.005
17	0.010	0.009	0.008	0.007	0.006	0.005	0.005	0.004	0.004	0.003
18	0.008	0.007	0.006	0.005	0.005	0.004	0.003	0.003	0.003	0.002
19	0.006	0.005	0.004	0.004	0.003	0.003	0.003	0.002	0.002	0.002
20	0.005	0.004	0.003	0.003	0.002	0.002	0.002	0.002	0.001	0.001

%	1	2	3	4	5	6	7	8	9	10
Period										
1	0.990	0.980	0.971	0.962	0.952	0.943	0.935	0.926	0.917	0.909
2	1.970	1.942	1.913	1.886	1.859	1.833	1.808	1.783	1.759	1.736
3	2.941	2.884	2.829	2.775	2.723	2.673	2.624	2.577	2.531	2.487
4	3.902	3.808	3.717	3.630	3.546	3.465	3.387	3.312	3.240	3.170
5	4.853	4.713	4.580	4.452	4.329	4.212	4.100	3.993	3.890	3.791
6	5.795	5.601	5.417	5.242	5.076	4.917	4.767	4.623	4.486	4.355
7	6.728	6.472	6.230	6.002	5.786	5.582	5.389	5.206	5.033	4.868
8	7.652	7.325	7.020	6.733	6.463	6.210	5.971	5.747	5.535	5.335
9	8.566	8.162	7.786	7.435	7.108	6.802	6.515	6.247	5.995	5.759
10	9.471	8.983	8.530	8.111	7.722	7.360	7.024	6.710	6.418	6.145
11	10.368	9.787	9.253	8.760	8.306	7.887	7.499	7.139	6.805	6.495
12	11.255	10.575	9.954	9.385	8.863	8.384	7.943	7.536	7.161	6.814
13	12.134	11.348	10.635	9.986	9.394	8.853	8.358	7.904	7.487	7.103
14	13.004	12.106	11.296	10.563	9.899	9.295	8.745	8.244	7.786	7.367
15	13.865	12.849	11.938	11.118	10.380	9.712	9.108	8.559	8.061	7.606
16	14.718	13.578	12.561	11.652	10.838	10.106	9.447	8.851	8.313	7.824
17	15.562	14.292	13.166	12.166	11.274	10.477	9.763	9.122	8.544	8.022
18	16.398	14.992	13.754	12.659	11.690	10.828	10.059	9.372	8.756	8.201
19	17.226	15.678	14.324	13.134	12.085	11.158	10.336	9.604	8.950	8.365
20	18.046	16.351	14.877	13.590	12.462	11.470	10.594	9.818	9.129	8.514

%	11	12	13	14	15	16	17	18	19	20
Period										
1	0.901	0.893	0.885	0.877	0.870	0.862	0.855	0.847	0.840	0.833
2	1.713	1.690	1.668	1.647	1.626	1.605	1.585	1.566	1.547	1.528
3	2.444	2.402	2.361	2.322	2.283	2.246	2.210	2.174	2.140	2.106
4	3.102	3.037	2.974	2.914	2.855	2.798	2.743	2.690	2.639	2.589
5	3.696	3.605	3.517	3.433	3.352	3.274	3.199	3.127	3.058	2.991
6	4.231	4.111	3.998	3.889	3.784	3.685	3.589	3.498	3.410	3.326
7	4.712	4.564	4.423	4.288	4.160	4.039	3.922	3.812	3.706	3.605
8	5.146	4.968	4.799	4.639	4.487	4.344	4.207	4.078	3.954	3.837
9	5.537	5.328	5.132	4.946	4.772	4.607	4.451	4.303	4.163	4.031
10	5.889	5.650	5.426	5.216	5.019	4.833	4.659	4.494	4.339	4.192
11	6.207	5.938	5.687	5.453	5.234	5.029	4.836	4.656	4.487	4.327
12	6.492	6.194	5.918	5.660	5.421	5.197	4.988	4.793	4.611	4.439
13	6.750	6.424	6.122	5.842	5.583	5.342	5.118	4.910	4.715	4.533
14	6.982	6.628	6.302	6.002	5.724	5.468	5.229	5.008	4.802	4.611
15	7.191	6.811	6.462	6.142	5.847	5.575	5.324	5.092	4.876	4.675
16	7.379	6.974	6.604	6.265	5.954	5.668	5.405	5.162	4.938	4.730
17	7.549	7.120	6.729	6.373	6.047	5.749	5.475	5.222	4.990	4.775
18	7.702	7.250	6.840	6.467	6.128	5.818	5.534	5.273	5.033	4.812
19	7.839	7.366	6.938	6.550	6.198	5.877	5.584	5.316	5.070	4.843
20	7.963	7.469	7.025	6.623	6.259	5.929	5.628	5.353	5.101	4.870

%	21	22	23	24	25	26	27	28	29	30
Period										
1	0.826	0.820	0.813	0.806	0.800	0.794	0.787	0.781	0.775	0.769
2	1.509	1.492	1.474	1.457	1.440	1.424	1.407	1.392	1.376	1.361
3	2.074	2.042	2.011	1.981	1.952	1.923	1.896	1.868	1.842	1.816
4	2.540	2.494	2.448	2.404	2.362	2.320	2.280	2.241	2.203	2.166
5	2.926	2.864	2.803	2.745	2.689	2.635	2.583	2.532	2.483	2.436
6	3.245	3.167	3.092	3.020	2.951	2.885	2.821	2.759	2.700	2.643
7	3.508	3.416	3.327	3.242	3.161	3.083	3.009	2.937	2.868	2.802
8	3.726	3.619	3.518	3.421	3.329	3.241	3.156	3.076	2.999	2.925
9	3.905	3.786	3.673	3.566	3.463	3.366	3.273	3.184	3.100	3.019
10	4.054	3.923	3.799	3.682	3.571	3.465	3.364	3.269	3.178	3.092
11	4.177	4.035	3.902	3.776	3.656	3.543	3.437	3.335	3.239	3.147
12	4.278	4.127	3.985	3.851	3.725	3.606	3.493	3.387	3.286	3.190
13	4.362	4.203	4.053	3.912	3.780	3.656	3.538	3.427	3.322	3.223
14	4.432	4.265	4.108	3.962	3.824	3.695	3.573	3.459	3.351	3.249
15	4.489	4.315	4.153	4.001	3.859	3.726	3.601	3.483	3.373	3.268
16	4.536	4.357	4.189	4.033	3.887	3.751	3.623	3.503	3.390	3.283
17	4.576	4.391	4.219	4.059	3.910	3.771	3.640	3.518	3.403	3.295
18	4.608	4.419	4.243	4.080	3.928	3.786	3.654	3.529	3.413	3.304
19	4.635	4.442	4.263	4.097	3.942	3.799	3.664	3.539	3.421	3.311
20	4.657	4.460	4.279	4.110	3.954	3.808	3.673	3.546	3.427	3.316

%	31	32	33	34	35	36	37	38	39	40
Period										
1	0.763	0.758	0.752	0.746	0.741	0.735	0.730	0.725	0.719	0.714
2	1.346	1.331	1.317	1.303	1.289	1.276	1.263	1.250	1.237	1.224
3	1.791	1.766	1.742	1.719	1.696	1.673	1.652	1.630	1.609	1.589
4	2.130	2.096	2.062	2.029	1.997	1.966	1.935	1.906	1.877	1.849
5	2.390	2.345	2.302	2.260	2.220	2.181	2.143	2.106	2.070	2.035
6	2.588	2.534	2.483	2.433	2.385	2.339	2.294	2.251	2.209	2.168
7	2.739	2.677	2.619	2.562	2.508	2.455	2.404	2.355	2.308	2.263
8	2.854	2.786	2.721	2.658	2.598	2.540	2.485	2.432	2.380	2.331
9	2.942	2.868	2.798	2.730	2.665	2.603	2.544	2.487	2.432	2.379
10	3.009	2.930	2.855	2.784	2.715	2.649	2.587	2.527	2.469	2.414
11	3.060	2.978	2.899	2.824	2.752	2.683	2.618	2.555	2.496	2.438
12	3.100	3.013	2.931	2.853	2.779	2.708	2.641	2.576	2.515	2.456
13	3.129	3.040	2.956	2.876	2.799	2.727	2.658	2.592	2.529	2.469
14	3.152	3.061	2.974	2.892	2.814	2.740	2.670	2.603	2.539	2.477
15	3.170	3.076	2.988	2.905	2.825	2.750	2.679	2.611	2.546	2.484
16	3.183	3.088	2.999	2.914	2.834	2.757	2.685	2.616	2.551	2.489
17	3.193	3.097	3.007	2.921	2.840	2.763	2.690	2.621	2.555	2.492
18	3.201	3.104	3.012	2.926	2.844	2.767	2.693	2.624	2.557	2.494
19	3.207	3.109	3.017	2.930	2.848	2.770	2.696	2.626	2.559	2.496
20	3.211	3.113	3.020	2.933	2.850	2.772	2.698	2.627	2.561	2.497

Appendix B

Polly Ester Holdings plc

(December 2003 to December 2006)

This case study was prepared by John Robertson using data from published sources. It is intended as a basis for assignment/class discussion and not as an illustration of good or bad management.

1. BUSINESS EXPANSION

During the year 2004, 72 new shops were added to the portfolio, including three *Pencosmo*, two *Green and Gillies,* and six shops in North America that related to a new venture which the chairperson believed was significant to the group's future direction. These were *Polly Ester* mother and daughter shops, selling a co-ordinated range of clothes and bedroom furnishing products for babies and daughters up to the age of 15, and dresses for their mothers.

In the year 2005, 76 new shops were added to the portfolio including 15 mother and daughter shops. The group envisage further expansion of the *Polly Ester* shops, particularly in North America, Europe and the Far East. Increasingly, however, the emphasis was to move towards the mother and daughter, and home concepts. Mother and daughter was a growing success in North America and the group tended to capitalise on the achievement by a rapid build up of the chain. *Polly Ester* home shops were launched in the UK in April 2006, in North America in January 2006 and opened in Europe and the Far East later in the year.

It appeared to be the groups' intention to build the home furnishings range to a point where they could offer a complete *Polly Ester* furnishings collection, while the introduction of cabinet furniture was seen as a significant step in the realisation of this aim.

The group actively planned to extend the sales of their home furnishing ranges outside the retail shops and mail order. Their plans included department store shop-in-shops in the UK and North America, and wholesaling of home furnishing ranges in Germany, North America and the Far East.

In the year 2006, the group were committed to launch their new *Polly Ester* home collection in the UK at a time when escalating interest rates were dampening consumer demand in the sector. In relative terms, the new furniture range sold well but sales of wallcovering and fabrics suffered a sharp decline. This in turn, led to reduced demand for print production at their plants in Belgium and Ireland.

2.   ACQUISITIONS

In 2005, the group acquired two small businesses which enjoyed a strong brand identification. These were *Green and Gillies*, a traditional outdoor clothing specialist wholesaler and retailer in the UK. Also *Pencosmo* in the UK, a long established perfumery business with five shops in the Birmingham area. It was intended to develop the product ranges of these two companies, and expand the shop outlets. The company appears to be actively seeking other acquisitions of brand names which will sit comfortably alongside *Polly Ester*.

A new textile plant was opened during 2004 in Ireland which, together with a vinyl wallcovering plant, were expected to provide substantial increases in volume and quality of products for the foreseeable future.

In February 2006, the group acquired *Nufurnishing Industries Inc.*, a company engaged in the sourcing and sale of designer bed linen mainly to department stores in North America and the Far East. The group also signed a franchise agreement with *Styleright Corporation of America*, a retail company in the US trading as units. The agreement gave the group exclusive right to operate units shops in the UK. It was a new concept in female attire and is enjoying tremendous success in North America.

3.   DISPOSALS

During the year 2006, the group disposed of *Green and Gillies* an outdoor clothing venture in North America. It was considered that the group resources would be better deployed supporting the *Polly Ester* brand business.

4.   EUROPE

Europe offers opportunities for UK business. *Polly Ester* opened its first shop in Florence in 1992. The group now has 65 shops in seven countries and expects to open in Portugal during the year 2007. Europe is not an easy market to operate in, each country having different requirements and tastes, but the group is now well established and can look forward to the benefits of harmonisation.

5.   DECLINE IN PROFITS

In 2005 and 2006, the major reason for the decline in profits were a loss of margin in the overseas core business, a substantial start-up loss, and subsequent venture in *Green and Gillies*, and a sharp increase in interest charges. Most of the reduction in margin can be attributed to the fact that, as sterling based manufacturers, the group has passed the point where they can raise prices to their customers to compensate for the effects of an overvalued pound, particularly in their most important market, North America.

6.   CHANGE IN ORGANISATION STRUCTURE

The group have taken action to reduce the cost base of the business and improve margins. As a preliminary step in this process, the group now operates as a number of strategic business units, rather than on a divisional basis.

The product division has now been divided into Brand management – the design, Sourcing and supply of the *Polly Ester* brand, and *Polly Ester* Manufacturing - which is subdivided into four business units; Garment manufacturing, Textiles and wallcovering, Soft furnishings manufacture, and Distribution.

The creation of strategic business units will give senior managers the freedom to take decisions within a framework which clearly defines their responsibilities. It will increase the level of financial awareness throughout the business and allow increased control over working capital and investment decisions.

7.   REORGANISATION and QUALITY

In 2006, the reorganisation of the Garment division led to the loss of 89 staff. Major cost–cutting and quality improvement initiatives leading to the adoption of BS 5750 introduced in the Garment and Textile factories are already showing results and will produce further significant benefits for the group over the next two years.

8.   OPERATIONS

The North America retail division is committed to improving operating systems to support business growth. During 2007 new wholesale, merchandising and point-of-sale systems are planned to be installed.

With an increasing proportion of the product range being sourced from outside the group, the brand management group has strengthened its international buying team, resulting in a more efficient and imaginative purchasing operation.

Improved quality assurance procedures have been introduced at the plants in Belgium and Ireland leading to the adoption of BS 5750.

9.   BORROWINGS

Despite the considerable achievements which have served to enhance the value and prospects for growth in the *Polly Ester* brand, the Board recognised that the group's borrowing levels remained high and that specific measures were needed to reduce them. The board has implemented a further reduction in overheads and a rationalisation programme which might include the disposal of certain businesses or assets, the reduction of stock and restrictions of new shop openings. The benefits of this rationalisation programme should be seen during the course of 2007.

The chairman announced that the Group has recently signed new credit facilities with its bankers to meet funding requirements.

In view of the level of Group borrowings and the results for the year, the directors have decided not to recommend a final dividend in respect of the year ended December 2006 and are unlikely to declare an interim dividend during the current year.

10.   MOVEMENT OF DIRECTORS

Mr. R.J. Somers resigned on 8th July 2004.

Mr. Philip Peters, who was the Group Finance Director resigned on 20th December 2005.

Mr. Adrian Moorhouse, who was the Managing Director Industries, resigned on 28th July 2005.

Mr. Harold Waterman was appointed as Finance Director by the Board on the 15th April 2007.

During the year 2006, Mr. Michael Smythe, who was Managing Director Retail, took over as Managing Director Industries.

POLLY ESTER HOLDINGS PLC

CONSOLIDATED INCOME STATEMENT

for the year ended 31st December

	2003	2004	2005	2006
	£'000	£'000	£'000	£'000
Revenues	512,676	604,431	757,293	889,824
Cost of sales	196,872	234,642	324,132	414,126
Gross profit	315,804	369,789	433,161	475,698
Other operating expenses	251,586	298,458	362,460	457,284
Operating profit	64,218	71,331	70,701	18,414
Profit/(Loss) related companies	261	-135	126	-531
Royalty income	4,689	5,127	4,830	3,273
Finance income	2,133	255	180	84
Finance expense	-3,951	-7,344	-15,069	-25,989
Profit before taxation	67,350	69,234	60,768	-4,749
Taxation	-23,979	-25,533	-21,405	-6,288
Profit attributable to shareholders	43,371	43,701	39,363	-11,037
Dividends	-13,473	-14,073	-14,073	-5,091
Retained profit for the year	29,898	29,628	25,290	-16,128
Earnings Per Share (pence)	7.24	7.3	6.57	-1.84

POLLY ESTER HOLDINGS PLC

CONSOLIDATED BALANCE SHEET

for the year ended 31st December

	2003 £'000	2004 £'000	2005 £'000	2006 £'000
NON-CURRENT ASSETS				
Tangible assets	171,876	210,723	239,202	242,352
Investments	1,515	1,404	1,380	2,046
CURRENT ASSETS				
Inventory	136,563	200,472	227,370	314,412
Trade and other receivables	36,444	46,020	62,910	82,650
Cash and cash equivalent	16,521	13,344	13,008	5,841
	189,528	259,836	303,288	402,903
TOTAL ASSETS	362,919	471,963	543,870	647,301
CURRENT LIABILITIES				
Trade and other payables	54,876	74,946	108,366	149,337
Borrowings	23,592	102,720	24,465	257,223
Bills of exchange	2,235	3,384	6,978	0
Taxation and social security	33,042	36,399	15,144	2,934
Proposed dividend	8,982	8,982	8,982	0
	122,727	226,431	163,905	409,494
NON-CURRENT LIABILITIES				
Accounts payable	3,159	6,186	4,908	1,602
Borrowings	26,010	19,665	126,336	8,574
Taxation	4,182	1,635	2,847	18
Provisions	1,536	-3,357	6,516	8,559
	34,887	24,129	140,607	19,053
EQUITY				
Called up share capital	29,940	29,940	29,940	29,940
Share premium	64,320	64,320	64,320	64,320
Retained earnings	111,045	127,143	145,098	124,494
Total equity	205,305	221,403	239,358	218,754
TOTAL LIABILITIES	362,919	471,963	543,870	647,301

POLLY ESTER HOLDINGS PLC

NOTES TO THE ACCOUNTS

	2003 £'000	2004 £'000	2005 £'000	2006 £'000
1. GEOGRAPHIC ANALYSIS OF REVENUE				
United Kingdom	231,732	282,741	377,793	409,236
North America	199,590	224,580	270,429	355,053
Continental Europe	64,818	78,426	85,527	91,734
Other	16,536	18,684	23,544	33,801
	512,676	604,431	757,293	889,824
2. GEOGRAPHIC ANALYSIS: RETAIL OPERATIONS				
Revenue:				
U.K. and Eire		285,000	377,700	406,200
North America		224,400	270,600	309,900
Europe		74,400	85,500	83,700
Number of shops:				
U.K. and Eire		140	164	184
North America		140	172	185
Europe		61	66	65
Retail Space: (square feet)				
U.K. and Eire		302,700	344,200	393,700
North America		197,700	235,600	255,600
Europe		95,400	100,700	99,000
3. OTHER OPERATING EXPENSES				
Retail and distribution costs	168,366	203,574	255,918	309,855
Administrative expenses	83,220	94,884	106,542	147,429
4. PROFIT BEFORE TAX is stated after charging				
Depreciation of assets	21,426	34,341	41,124	49,146
Directors' emoluments	2,766	3,312	3,279	3,117
Auditors' remuneration	936	1,005	894	963
Operating lease/hire charges	30,222	39,678	45,138	60,246
Interest payable	3,951	7,344	15,069	25,989

POLLY ESTER HOLDINGS PLC

NOTES TO THE ACCOUNTS

	2003 £'000	2004 £'000	2005 £'000	2006 £'000
5. EARNINGS PER SHARE				
Profit attributable to shareholders	43,371	43,371	39,363	-11,037
Number of ordinary shares	598,800	598,800	598,800	598,800
Earnings per ordinary share	7.24	7.30	6.57	–1.84
6. EMPLOYEES				
Average weekly number:				
Manufacturing	2,218	2,384	2,839	2,838
Retail	2,538	3,425	3,289	3,636
Administration	993	1,132	1,296	1,470
Employee costs:				
Wages and salaries	140,181	168,396	195,273	224,394
Social security costs	14,133	16,686	18,639	22,053
Other pension costs	2,052	4,416	4,653	7,434
Over £30,000: Number of employees				
100,001 – 105,000	4	2	10	2
115,001 – 120,000	6	7	7	7
130,001 – 135,000	7	6	9	4
145,001 – 150,000		2	2	13
160,001 – 165,000			2	3
175,001 – 180,000				1
190,001 – 195,000			2	2
235,001 – 240,000				1
250,001 – 255,000				1
7. DIRECTORS' EMOLUMENTS				
60,001 – 65,000	1			
90,001 – 95,000		1	1	1
135,001 – 140,000		1		1
150,001 – 155,000	1		1	
180,001 – 185,000			2	
195,001 – 200,000	1			
210,001 – 215,000	1			
225,001 – 230,000		2		
285,001 – 290,000	1		1	
300,001 – 305,000				1
345,001 – 350,000				1
450,001 – 455,000	1			
735,001 – 740,000			1	1
765,001 – 770,000		1		

POLLY ESTER HOLDINGS PLC

NOTES TO THE ACCOUNTS

	2003 £'000	2004 £'000	2005 £'000	2006 £'000
8. NON-CURRENT ASSETS				
Cost at beginning of year		241,179	304,035	365,868
Translation difference		-10,350	-3,876	12,699
Additions		85,578	75,501	51,057
Disposals		-12,372	-9,792	-20,004
		304,035	365,868	409,620
Depreciation at beginning of year		69,303	93,312	126,666
Translation difference		-2,991	-1,539	5,235
Depreciation charge for year		34,341	41,124	49,146
Disposals		-7,341	-6,231	-13,779
		93,312	126,666	167,268
Net book value at end of year		210,723	239,202	242,352
Net book value at start of year		171,876	210,723	239,202
9. RETAINED EARNINGS				
Balance at beginning of year		111,045	127,143	145,098
Exchange differences		-8,970	-5,754	11,514
Profit retained for the year		29,634	25,290	-29,511
Goodwill on acquisitions		-4,560	-1,641	-2,607
Balance at end of year		127,143	145,098	124,494

Glossary of terms

Absorption costing

The practice of charging all costs, both variable and fixed, to operations, processes or products.

Accounting period

The period of time between two reporting dates.

Accounting policies

These are disclosed in the annual reports published by quoted companies and represent the interpretation of accounting principles and requirements adopted by the board of directors.

Accounting principles

A number of generally accepted accounting principles are used in preparing financial statements. They are only generally accepted and do not have the force of law. You should note that sometimes they are referred to as accounting concepts and conventions.

Accounting rate of return (ARR)

A method used to evaluate an investment opportunity that ignores the time value of money. The return generated by an investment opportunity is expressed as a percentage of the capital outlay.

Activity based costing (ABC)

The practice that measures the cost and performance of activities, resources and the things that consume them.

Age analysis

A statement analysing the transactions that make up debtor/creditor balance into discreet 'ageing' periods.

Amortisation

The writing-off of a non-current asset over a time period. It is often used in conjunction with intangible assets, e.g. goodwill.

Annual report

A report issued to shareholders and other interested parties which normally includes a chairman's statement, report of the directors, review of operations, financial statements and associated notes.

Annuity

A series of payments of an equal, or constant, amount of money at fixed intervals for a specified number of periods.

Balance sheet

A statement showing the financial position of a company in terms of its assets and liabilities at a specified point in time.

Bank borrowings

Includes bank overdraft and bank loans.

Budget
A financial and/or quantitative statement, prepared and approved prior to a defined period of time, of the policy to be pursued during that period for the purpose of attaining a given objective.

Capital investment appraisal
The evaluation of proposed capital projects. Sometimes referred to as project appraisal.

Capital structure
The composition of a company's sources of long-term funds, e.g. equity and debt.

Cash flow statement
A statement that UK and US companies are required to include in their published accounts. Such statements analyse cash flows under three types of activity:

Investing activities;

Financial activities;

Operating activities.

Chairperson's statement
A statement by the chairman of a company, normally included as part of the annual report, which contains reference to important events.

Common–size analysis
A method of analysis where data in the income statement, and the balance sheet are expressed as a percentage of some key figure.

Compounding
A technique for determining a future value given that a present value, a time period and an interest rate are known.

Contribution
The difference between revenues and the marginal cost of sales.

Contribution per unit
The difference between the selling price and the marginal cost per unit.

Cost allocation
Where an item of cost can be allocated directly to a cost centre.

Cost apportionment
Where an item of cost cannot be allocated directly to a cost centre. Apportionment requires that a range of bases are used which is fair across all cost centres, e.g. floor area, machine hours, plant value.

Cost centre
A location, person or item(s) of equipment that costs may be ascertained, apportioned to, and used for the purpose of cost control.

Cost of capital
The cost of long-term funds to a company.

Cost of sales

The costs that are attributable to the revenues made. It is usually before the deduction of selling, distribution and administration costs.

Cost unit

A normal unit of quantity of a product, service or time in relation to which costs may be ascertained or expressed, e.g. per 100, per tonne.

Current assets

Those assets of a company that are reasonably expected to be realised in cash, or sold, or consumed during the normal operating cycle of the business. They include inventories, trade receivables, short-term investments, bank and cash balances.

Current liabilities

Those liabilities which a company may rely upon to finance short-term activities. They include trade payables, bank overdraft, proposed final dividend, and current taxation.

Current ratio

A measure of short-term solvency. It is calculated as current assets divided by current liabilities. It gives an indication of a company's ability to pay its way within one year.

Depreciation

An accounting adjustment to take account of the diminution in value of a non-current asset over its economic life.

Discounted cash flow (DCF)

A technique for calculating whether a sum receivable at some time in the future is worthwhile in terms of value today. It involves discounting, or scaling-down, future cash flows.

Dividend

The proportion of the profits of a company distributed to shareholders.

Earnings per share (EPS)

Profit before taxation divided by the weighted average number of ordinary shares in issue during the period. The calculation and result is shown by way of note in a company's annual report.

Equity

The sum of issued share capital, capital reserves and revenue reserves which is also known as shareholders' funds, or net worth.

Equity share capital

The share capital of a company attributable to ordinary shareholders.

First In first out (FIFO)

The price paid for the material first taken into stock. Issues from stores are priced based on the oldest material taken into stock.

Fixed costs

A cost that tends not to vary with the level of activity. Fixed costs are often determined by management decisions to invest in plant and equipment; once undertaken these result in period/time related costs and often bear little resemblance to activity.

Flexible budget

A budget which, by recognising the differences in variable, semi-variable and fixed costs, changes in relation to the level of activity attained.

Finance expense (or interest payable)

Money payable (but not necessary paid) on interest bearing debt.

Floating charge

A charge against assets as security for a debt. It is a general claim against any available asset of the company.

Gearing

Expresses the relationship between some measure of interest-bearing capital and some measure of equity capital or the total capital employed.

Goodwill

The difference between the amount paid for a company as a whole and the net value of the assets and liabilities acquired.

Income statement

A statement showing what profit has been made over a period and the uses to which the profit has been put.

Intangible assets

Assets the value of which do not relate to their physical properties, e.g. goodwill and brands.

Internal rate of return (IRR)

The rate of discount at which the present value of the future cash flows is equal to the initial outlay, i.e. at the IRR the net present value is zero.

Key ratio

A term sometimes given to the profitability ratio. In the UK this is usually defined as profit before tax plus interest payable expressed as a percentage of net capital employed.

Labour cost variance

The difference between the standard cost of labour allowed for the actual output less the actual wages paid.

Labour efficiency variance

The difference between the standard hours of labour allowed less the actual hours at the standard price.

Labour rate variance

The actual hours at the difference between the standard rate less the actual rate.

Labour hour rate

An actual or predetermined rate. Calculated by dividing the cost apportioned (to a cost centre) by the actual or forecast labour hours for the period.

Last In first out (LIFO)

The price paid for the material last taken into stock. Issues from stores are priced based on the most recent material taken into stock.

Liabilities

The financial obligations owed by a company. These can be to shareholders, other providers of debt, trade and other payables.

Liquid assets (or acid test)

The difference between current assets and inventories.

Liquid ratio

Liquid assets divided by current liabilities. It attempts to show a company's ability to pay its way in the short-term.

Loan capital

Finance that has been borrowed and not obtained from the shareholders.

Machine hour rate

An actual or predetermined rate. Calculated by dividing the cost apportioned (to a cost centre) by the actual or forecast machine hours for the period.

Material cost variance

The difference between the standard cost of materials allowed for the actual output less the actual cost of materials used.

Material price variance

The actual quantity at the difference between the standard price less the actual price.

Material usage variance

The difference between the standard materials allowed less the actual quantity at the standard price.

Minority interest

The proportion of shares in subsidiary companies which is not held by a holding company. Profit attributable to minority interests and accumulated balances are shown in the consolidated financial statements.

Net assets

Total assets minus current liabilities minus non-current liabilities.

Net capital employed

The sum of non-current assets, investments, current assets minus current liabilities.

Net present value (NPV)

The difference between the discounted value of future net cash inflows and the initial outlay..

Non-current assets

Those assets which an organisation holds for use within the business and not for resale. They consist of tangible assets, like land and buildings, plant and machinery, vehicles, fixtures and fittings; and intangible assets like goodwill.

Non-current liabilities

Liabilities which are not due for repayment within one year.

Ordinary shares

Shares which attract the remaining profits after all other claims, and, in liquidation, which attract the remaining assets of a company after trade payables and other charges have been satisfied.

Payback period

How long it will take to recover the outlay involved in a potential investment opportunity from net cash inflows.

Price earnings ratio (PE)

One of the most significant indicators of corporate performance which it is widely quoted in the financial press. It is calculated by dividing the market price of a share by the earnings per share (or the total market value by the total profit attributable to shareholders).

Quoted investments

Investments in another company which has its shares quoted on a stock exchange..

Reducing balance depreciation

A method of depreciation whereby the periodic amount written off is a percentage of the reduced balance. (cost less accumulated depreciation).

Relevant data

Relevant data for decision making is *future oriented* – that is *yet to be incurred*.

Residual value

Value generated beyond the planning period

Retained earnings

Profits accumulated over a period of time and retained in the business.

Revenues (sales or turnover)

Income derived from the principal activities of a company, net of value added tax (VAT).

Share capital (issued)

The product of the total number of shares issued and the nominal value of the shares.

Shareholder's funds

Another name for equity.

Share premium

The excess paid for a share, to a company, over its nominal value.

Short-termism

A term associated with managing for today rather than tomorrow and beyond.

Straight line depreciation

A method of depreciation whereby an equal amount is written off the value of a non-current asset over its estimated economic life.

Standard cost

A cost prepared prior to a defined period of time; calculated in relation to a prescribed set of working conditions in respect to material quantities and prices, labour hours and rates with an appropriate share of overheads.

Standard costing

The preparation and use of standard costs, their comparison with actual costs and the analysis of variances.

Standard price

A predetermined price on the basis of a specification of all the factors affecting that price.

Tangible assets

An asset having a physical identity such as land and buildings, plant and machinery, vehicles, etc.

Time value of money

A concept which is an integral part of the discounted cash flow technique used in capital investment appraisal. It recognises that cash flows in the later years of an investment opportunity cannot be compared with cash flows in the earlier years.

Total assets

The sum of non-current assets, investments and current assets.

Trade and other receivables

Amounts owed to a company by its customers.

Trade and other payables

Amounts owing by a company by its suppliers.

Variable cost

A cost that tends to vary directly with the level of activity.

Weighted average cost of capital (WACC)

A term associated with the view that there is an optimal or ideal capital structure. It is calculated as follows:

Weighted average cost of capital = %Debt (K_d) + %Equity (K_e)

where K_d = Cost of debt K_e = Cost of equity

Working capital

The excess of current assets (inventories, trade and other receivables, and cash) over current liabilities (trade and other payables, bank overdraft etc.).

Exercise 2.1

Cash

Dr.			Cr.		
Mar 1	Capital	10,000	Mar 7	Equipment	3,500
Mar 9	Revenues	3,000			

Capital

Dr.			Cr.		
			Mar 1	Cash	10,000

Purchases

Dr.			Cr.
Mar 6	R. Matthews	2,500	

R. Matthews & Sons

Dr.			Cr.		
			Mar 6	Purchases	2,500

Equipment

Dr.			Cr.
Mar 7	Cash	3,500	

Revenues

Dr.			Cr.		
			Mar 9	Cash	3,000

Exercise 2.2

Bank

Dr.					Cr.
Oct 1	Capital	20,000	Oct 5	Motor van	2,500

Capital

Dr.					Cr.
			Oct 1	Bank	20,000

Purchases

Dr.				Cr.
Oct 2	F. Ewart & Co	3,200		

F. Ewart & Co

Dr.					Cr.
Oct 8	Returns outwards	300	Oct 2	Purchases	3,200

Motor van

Dr.				Cr.
Oct 5	Bank	2,500		

Returns outwards

Dr.					Cr.
			Oct 8	F. Ewart & Co	300

Exercise 2.3

Bank

May 1	Capital	3,000	May 5	Cash (contra)	500
May 15	U. Candoit	2,500	May 8	Motor van	1,500
			May 31	DottyCom Ltd	2,000

Capital

		May 1	Bank	3,000

Purchases

May 4	DottyCom Ltd	3,000

DottyCom Ltd

May 14	Returns outwards	500	May 4	Purchases	3,000
May 31	Bank	2,000			

Cash

May 5	Bank (contra)	500

Motor van

May 8	Bank	1,500

Revenues

		May 11	U. Candoit	2,500

U. Candoit

May 11	Revenues	2,500	May 15	Bank	2,500

Returns outwards

		May 14	DottyCom Ltd	500

Furniture

May 22	B. Wise Ltd	1,500

B. Wise Ltd

		May 22	Furniture	1,500

Exercise 2.4

Bank

Aug 1	Capital	8,000	Aug 4	Cash (contra)	2,000
Aug 28	M. Istaken Ltd	4,500	Aug 31	I.T. Digital & Co	4,000

Capital

			Aug 1	Bank	8,000

Purchases

Aug 3	I.T. Digital & Co	6,000	
Aug 30	U.N. Wise Ltd	1,500	

I.T. Digital & Co

Aug 21	Returns outwards	300	Aug 3	Purchases	6,000
Aug 31	Bank	4,000			

Cash

Aug 4	Bank (contra)	2,000	Aug 7	Furniture	1,500

Furniture

Aug 7	Cash	1,500	

Revenues

			Aug 10	M. Istaken Ltd	4,500

Returns Outwards

			Aug 21	I.T. Digital & Co	300

M. Istaken Ltd

Aug 10	Revenues	4,500	Aug 28	Bank	4,500

U.N. Wise Ltd

			Aug 30	Purchases	1,500

Exercise 2.5

Bank

Dr.					Cr.
Nov 1	Balance b/d	20,000	Nov 13	Cash (contra)	1,000
Nov 5	Interest received	450	Nov 16	Insurance	1,200

Capital

Dr.				Cr.
		Nov 1	Balance b/d	28,000

Cash

Dr.					Cr.
Nov 1	Balance b/d	2,000	Nov 1	Rent	800
Nov 13	Bank (contra)	1,000	Nov 13	Wages	1,400

Motor van

Dr.			Cr.
Nov 1	Balance b/d	6,000	

Rent

Dr.			Cr.
Nov 1	Cash	800	

Interest received

Dr.				Cr.
		Nov 5	Bank	450

Wages

Dr.			Cr.
Nov 13	Cash	1,400	

Insurance

Dr.			Cr.
Nov 16	Bank	1,200	

Exercise 2.6

Bank

Dr.					Cr.
Aug 1	Balance b/d	8,000	Aug 10	Telephone	300

Capital

Dr.					Cr.
			Aug 1	Balance b/d	16,400

Cash

Dr.					Cr.
Aug 1	Balance b/d	1,400	Aug 1	Wages	600
Aug 3	Rent received	300	Aug 6	Motor expenses	500

Motor van

Dr.				Cr.
Aug 1	Balance b/d	7,000		

Wages

Dr.				Cr.
Aug 1	Cash	600		

Rent received

Dr.				Cr.
		Aug 3	Cash	300

Motor expenses

Dr.				Cr.
Aug 6	Cash	500		

Telephone

Dr.				Cr.
Aug 10	Bank	300		

Exercise 2.7

Bank

Dr.				Cr.
Aug 1	Capital	50,000	Aug 10 L. Last Ltd	11,400
Aug 14	K. Krankie	18,500	Aug 10 C. Cooke & C0	20,900
Aug 14	N. Nettle	25,000	Aug 21 Betta-Build	8,000
			Aug 31 Motor van	15,000

Capital

Dr.			Cr.
	Aug 1	Balance b/d	50,000

Purchases

Dr.			Cr.
Aug 2	R.E. Turn Ltd	30,000	
Aug 2	L. Last Ltd	12,000	
Aug 2	C. Cooke & Co	22,000	
Aug 9	Cash	18,000	

R.E. Turn Ltd

Dr.			Cr.
Aug 18 Returns outwards	5,000	Aug 2 Purchases	30,000

L. Last Ltd

Dr.			Cr.
Aug 10 Bank	11,400	Aug 2 Purchases	12,000
Aug 10 Discount received	600		

C. Cooke & Co

Dr.			Cr.
Aug 10 Bank	20,900	Aug 2 Purchases	22,000
Aug 10 Discount received	1,100		

Revenues

Dr.			Cr.
	Aug 5	Cash	32,000
	Aug 7	Sid Spice	14,000
	Aug 7	K. Krankie	19,000
	Aug 7	N. Nettle	30,000

Cash

Dr.					Cr.
Aug 5	Revenues	32,000	Aug 6	Wages	4,400
Aug 30	J. Jones	12,000	Aug 9	Purchases	18,000
			Aug 13	Wages	4,400

Wages

Dr.				Cr.
Aug 6	Cash	4,400		
Aug 13	Cash	4,400		

Sid Spice

Dr.					Cr.
Aug 7	Revenues	14,000	Aug 27	Returns inwards	1,200

K. Krankie

Dr.					Cr.
Aug 7	Revenues	19,000	Aug 14	Bank	18,500
			Aug 14	Discount allowed	500

N. Nettle

Dr.					Cr.
Aug 7	Revenues	30,000	Aug 14	Bank	25,000
			Aug 14	Discount allowed	800

Discount received

Dr.					Cr.
			Aug 10	L. Last Ltd	600
			Aug 10	C. Cooke & Co	1,100

Discount allowed

Dr.				Cr.
Aug 14	K. Krankie	500		
Aug 14	N. Nettle	800		

Shop fixtures

Dr.				Cr.
Aug 15	Betta-Build	8,000		

Betta Build

Dr.					Cr.
Aug 21 Bank	8,000	Aug 15	Shop Fixtures		8,000

Returns outwards

Dr.					Cr.
		Aug 18	R. E. Turn Ltd		5,000

Returns inwards

Dr.			Cr.
Aug 27 Sid Spice	1,200		

J. Jones

Dr.					Cr.
		Aug 30	Cash		12,000

Motor van

Dr.			Cr.
Aug 31 Bank	15,000		

Trial balance as at 31st August

	Dr.	Cr.
Bank	38,200	
Purchases	82,000	
Cash	17,200	
Wages	8,800	
Sid Spice	12,800	
N. Nettle	4,200	
Discount allowed	1,300	
Shop fixtures	8,000	
Returns inwards	1,200	
Motor van	15,000	
Capital		50,000
R.E. Turn Ltd		25,000
Revenues		95,000
Discount received		1,700
Returns outwards		5,000
J. Jones		12,000
	188,700	188,700

Exercise 2.8

Bank

Dr.						Cr.
Jun 1	Capital	60,000	Jun 5	Motor van	8,000
Jun 25	P. Mickelson	4,300	Jun 7	Motor expenses	120
			Jun 21	E. Els	5,500
			Jun 21	G. Norman	4,000

Cash

Dr.						Cr.
Jun 1	Capital	5,000	Jun 4	Purchases	2,300
Jun 23	T. Woods	6,200	Jun 15	Motor expenses	50
Jun 26	Revenues	3,400	Jun 20	Drawings	1,000
			Jun 27	Drawings	2,400
			Jun 29	Postage stamps	40

Capital

Dr.					Cr.
		Jun 1	Bank	60,000
		Jun 1	Cash	5,000

Purchases

Dr.				Cr.
Jun 2	D. Duval	50,000	
Jun 4	Cash	2,300	
Jun 11	N. Price	24,000	
Jun 11	E. Els	6,200	
Jun 11	G. Norman	4,600	

D. Duval

Dr.					Cr.
		Jun 2	Purchases	50,000

Revenues

Dr.			Cr.
	Jun 3	T. Woods	6,600
	Jun 3	F. Couples	2,500
	Jun 3	P. Mickleson	4,300
	Jun 9	C. Montgomerie	2,400
	Jun 9	L. Westwood	2,600
	Jun 9	D. Clarke	6,500
	Jun 26	Cash	3,400
	Jun 30	F. Couples	4,300
	Jun 30	P. Mickleson	6,700
	Jun 30	L. Westwood	4,500

T. Woods

Dr.				Cr.
Jun 3	Revenues	6,600	Jun 23 Cash	6,200
			Jun 23 Discount allowed	400

F. Couples

Dr.				Cr.
Jun 3	Revenues	2,500	Jun 19 Returns inwards	1,100
Jun 30	Revenues	4,300		

P. Mickleson

Dr.				Cr.
Jun 3	Revenues	4,300	Jun 25 Bank	4,300
Jun 30	Revenues	6,700		

Motor van

Dr.			Cr.
Jun 5	Bank	8,000	

Motor expenses

Dr.			Cr.
Jun 7	Bank	120	
Jun 15	Cash	50	

C. Montgomerie

Dr.			Cr.
Jun 9	Revenues	2,400	

L. Westwood

Dr.						Cr.
Jun 9	Revenues	2,600				
Jun 30	Revenues	4,500				

D. Clarke

Dr.						Cr.
Jun 9	Revenues	6,500				

N. Price

Dr.						Cr.
Jun 13	Returns outwards	2,500	Jun 11	Purchases	24,000
Jun 28	Returns outwards	4,200			

E. Els

Dr.						Cr.
Jun 21	Bank	5,500	Jun 11	Purchases	6,200
Jun 21	Discount received	700			

G. Norman

Dr.						Cr.
Jun 21	Bank	4,000	Jun 11	Purchases	4,600
Jun 21	Discount received	600			

Returns outwards

Dr.						Cr.
			Jun 13	N. Price	2,500
			Jun 28	N. Price	4,200

Returns inwards

Dr.						Cr.
Jun 19	F. Couples	1,100				

Drawings

Dr.						Cr.
Jun 20	Cash	1,000				
Jun 27	Cash	2,400				

Discount received

Dr.			Cr.
	Jun 21	E. Els	700
	Jun 21	G. Norman	600

Discount allowed

Dr.		Cr.
Jun 23 T. Woods	400	

Postage stamps

Dr.		Cr.
Jun 29 Cash	40	

Trial balance as at 30th June

	Dr.	Cr.
Bank	46,680	
Cash	8,810	
Purchases	87,100	
F. Couples	5,700	
P. Mickleson	6,700	
Motor van	8,000	
Motor expenses	170	
C. Montgomerie	2,400	
L. Westwood	7,100	
D. Clarke	6,500	
Returns inwards	1,100	
Drawings	3,400	
Discount allowed	400	
Postage stamps	40	
Capital		65,000
D. Duval		50,000
Revenues		43,800
N. Price		17,300
Returns outwards		6,700
Discount received		1,300
	184,100	184,100

Exercise 3.1

Equipment

Dr.					Cr.
Jan 1	Balance b/d	500,000			

Provision for depreciation – Equipment

Dr.			2004		Cr.
2004					
Dec 31	Balance c/d	115,000	Dec 31	Income statement	115,000
2005			2005		
Dec 31	Balance c/d	230,000	Jan 1	Balance b/d	115,000
			Dec 31	Income statement	115,000
		230,000			230,000
2006			2006		
Dec 31	Balance c/d	345,000	Jan 1	Balance b/d	230,000
			Dec 31	Income statement	115,000
		345,000			345,000
2007			2007		
			Jan 1	Balance b/d	345,000

Income statement for the year ended 31st December

Dr.			Cr.
2004/2005/2006			
Depreciation of equipment	115,000		

Balance sheet as at 31 December 2006

ASSETS		LIABILITIES
Non-current assets:		
Equipment at cost	500,000	
less Depreciation	345,000	
Net book value	155,000	

Exercise 3.2

Equipment

Dr.			Cr.
Jan 1	Balance b/d	500,000	

Provision for depreciation – Equipment

Dr.					Cr.
2004			2004		
Dec 31	Balance c/d	200,000	Dec 31	Income statement	200,000
2005			2005		
Dec 31	Balance c/d	320,000	Jan 1	Balance b/d	200,000
			Dec 31	Income statement	120,000
		320,000			320,000
2006			2006		
Dec 31	Balance c/d	392,000	Jan 1	Balance b/d	320,000
			Dec 31	Income statement	72,000
		392,000			392,000
2007			2007		
			Jan 1	Balance b/d	392,000

Income statement for the year ended 31st December

Dr.		Cr.
2004		
Depreciation of equipment	200,000	
2005		
Depreciation of equipment	120,000	
2006		
Depreciation of equipment	72,000	

Balance sheet as at 31 December 2006

ASSETS		*LIABILITIES*
Non-current assets:		
Equipment at cost	500,000	
less Depreciation	392,000	
Net book value	108,000	

Exercise 3.3

Albert Doe & Sons

Dr.					Cr.
Mar 1	Balance b/d	900	Mar 4	Bad debts a/c	900

Barney Brothers

Dr.					Cr.
Aug 1	Balance b/d	3,500	Aug 18	Bad debts a/c	3,500

Jim Cunning

Dr.					Cr.
Oct 1	Balance b/d	1,700	Oct 7	Bad debts a/c	1,700

Bad debts account

Dr.					Cr.
Mar 4	A. Doe & Sons	900	Dec 31	Income statement	6,100
Aug 18	Barney Brothers	3,500			
Oct 7	Jim Cunning	1,700			
		6,100			6,100

Income statement for the year ended 31st December

Dr.		Cr.
Bad debts account	6,100	

Exercise 3.4

Blight & Co

Dr.						Cr.
Feb 1	Balance b/d	3,300	Feb 19	Bad debts a/c		3,300

B. Dreadenough

Dr.						Cr.
May 1	Balance b/d	800	May 6	Bad debts a/c		800

H. Hardup Ltd

Dr.						Cr.
Sept 1	Balance b/d	6,000	Sept 15	Bad debts a/c		6,000

Bad debts account

Dr.					Cr.
Feb 19	Blight & Co	3,300	Dec 31	Income statement	10,100
May 6	B. Dreadenough	800			
Sept 15	H. Hardup Ltd	6,000			
		10,100			10,100

Income statement for the year ended 31st December

Dr.				Cr.
Bad debts account	10,100			

Exercise 3.5

Provision for doubtful debts account

Dr.					Cr.
2005			2005		
Dec 31	Balance c/d	9,500	Jan 1	Balance b/d	8,000
			Dec 31	Income statement	1,500
		9,500			9,500
2006			2006		
Dec 31	Balance c/d	11,500	Jan 1	Balance b/d	9,500
			Dec 31	Income statement	2,000
		11,500			11,500
2007			2007		
			Jan 1	Balance b/d	11,500

Income statement for the year ended 31st December

Dr.		Cr.
2005		
Provision for doubtful debts	1,500	
2006		
Provision for doubtful debts	2,000	

Balance sheet as at 31 December 2006

ASSETS		LIABILITIES
Current assets:		
Trade receivables	1,150,000	
less Provision	11,500	
	1,138,500	

Exercise 3.6

Provision for doubtful debts account

Dr.						Cr.
2005				2005		
Dec 31	Balance c/d	1,200		Jan 1	Balance b/d	1,600
Dec 31	Income statement	400				
		1,600				1,600
2006				2006		
Dec 31	Balance c/d	1,500		Jan 1	Balance b/d	1,200
				Dec 31	Income statement	300
		1,500				1,500
2007				2007		
				Jan 1	Balance b/d	1,500

Income statement for the year ended 31st December

Dr.				Cr.
2005			2005	
			Provision for doubtful debts	400
2006			2006	
Provision for doubtful debts	300			

Balance sheet as at 31 December 2006

ASSETS			LIABILITIES
Current assets:			
Trade receivables	180,000		
less Provision	1,500		
	178,500		

Exercise 3.7

Wages account

Dr.					Cr.
Oct 7	Bank	25,000	Oct 31	Income statement	109,500
Oct 14	Bank	25,000			
Oct 21	Bank	25,000			
Oct 28	Bank	25,000			
Oct 31	Balance c/d	9,500			
		109,500			109,500
Nov 4	Bank	26,000	Nov 1	Balance b/d	9,500
Nov 11	Bank	26,000	Nov 30	Income statement	117,000
Nov 18	Bank	26,000			
Nov 25	Bank	26,000			
Nov 30	Balance c/d	22,500			
		126,500			126,500
			Dec 1	Balance b/d	22,500

Income statement for the period ended

Dr.		Cr.
31st October		
Wages	109,500	
31st November		
Wages	117,000	

Balance sheet as at 31st October

ASSETS		LIABILITIES	
		Current liabilities:	
		Accruals (wages due)	9,500

Exercise 3.8

Rent account

Dr.					Cr.
Jan 1	Balance b/d	2,000	Dec 31	Income statement	8,400
Apr 1	Bank	4,200	Dec 31	Balance c/d	2,200
Oct 1	Bank	4,400			
		10,600			10,600
Jan 1	Balance b/d	2,200			

Income statement for the period ended 31st October

Dr.		Cr.
Rent	8,400	

Balance sheet as at 31st October

ASSETS		LIABILITIES
Current assets:		
Prepayments (rent)	2,200	

Exercise 4.1

Trading account

Opening inventories	67,700	Revenues	536,300
Purchases	300,000		
	367,700		
− Closing inventories	99,200		
= Cost of sales	268,500		
Gross profit c/d	267,800		
	536,300		536,300

Income statement

General expenses	4,700	Gross profit b/d	267,800
Rent	8,000		
Motor expenses	14,700		
Salaries	71,200		
Insurance	7,800		
Depn. of motor vehicle	11,200		
Net profit for period	150,200		
	267,800		267,800

Balance sheet

Non-current assets:			Owners capital	464,500
Premises		400,000	add Profit for period	150,200
Vehicles	56,000		less Drawings	87,000
less Depreciation	33,600	22,400	Closing capital	527,700
Current assets:			Current liabilities:	
Inventories	99,200		Trade payables	103,200
Trade receivables	81,800		General expenses due	500
Bank	28,000			103,700
		209,000		
		631,400		631,400

Exercise 4.2

Trading account

Opening inventories	30,000	Revenues	300,000
Purchases	200,000		
	230,000		
− Closing inventories	40,000		
= Cost of sales	190,000		
Gross profit c/d	110,000		
	300,000		300,000

Income statement

Administrative costs	62,000	Gross profit b/d	110,000
Selling costs	19,000	Income from investments	2,000
Audit fee	1,000		
Interest paid	1,000		
Prov. for doubtful debts	300		
Net profit for period	28,700		
	112,000		112,000

Balance sheet

Non-current assets:			Owners capital	138,300
Land and buildings		100,000	add Profit for period	28,700
Vehicles		20,000	less Drawings	15,000
Trade investments		20,000	Closing capital	152,000
Current assets:			Current liabilities:	
Inventories		40,000	Trade payables	40,000
Trade receivables	30,000		Bank overdraft	20,000	
less provision	1,000	29,000	Admin costs due	2,000	22,000
Cash		5,000		62,000
		74,000		
		214,000		214,000

Exercise 4.3

Trading account

Opening inventories	219,400	Revenues	712,000
Purchases	400,000		
	619,400		
− Closing inventories	199,200		
= Cost of sales	420,200		
Gross profit c/d	291,800		
	712,000		712,000

Income statement

Rent	31,200	Gross profit b/d	291,800
Insurance	5,500		
Lighting and heating	10,320		
Motor expenses	39,200		
Salaries and wages	97,000		
Sundry expenses	16,120		
Interest payable	15,000		
Bad debts written off	6,000		
Net profit for period	71,460		
	291,800		291,800

Balance sheet

Non-current assets:			Owners capital	685,980
Buildings		545,000	add Profit for period	71,460
Motor vehicles		70,000	less Drawings	125,560
Furniture and fittings		79,200	Closing capital	631,880
Current assets:			Current liabilities:	
Inventories		199,200	Trade payables	165,000
Trade receivables	136,200		Bank overdraft	250,000
less Bad debts	6,000	130,200		415,000
Insurance prepaid		600		
Cash		22,680		
		352,680		
		1,046,880		1,046,880

Exercise 4.4

Trading account

Opening inventories	40,000	Revenues	350,000
Purchases	190,000		
	230,000		
– Closing inventories	20,000		
= Cost of sales	210,000		
Gross profit c/d	140,000		
	350,000		350,000

Income statement

Rates	4,000	Gross profit b/d	140,000
General expenses	30,000		
Wages and salaries	40,000		
Bad debts written off	1,000		
Distribution costs	25,000		
Loan interest	10,000		
Depn. of machinery	11,000		
Net profit for period	19,000		
	140,000		140,000

Balance sheet

Non-current assets:		Owners capital	86,000
Land and buildings	100,000	add Profit for period	19,000
Machinery 110,000		less Drawings	17,000
less Depreciation 44,000	66,000	Closing capital	88,000
		Loan at 10%	100,000
Current assets:		Current liabilities:	
Inventories	20,000	Trade payables	38,000
Trade receivables	25,000	Loan interest due	5,000
Bank	20,000		43,000
	65,000		
	231,000		231,000

Exercise 4.5

Trading account

Opening inventories	27,600	Revenues	103,200
Purchases	86,400		
	114,000		
− Closing inventories	31,200		
= Cost of sales	82,800		
Gross profit c/d	20,400		
	103,200		103,200

Income statement

Discount allowed	1,800	Gross profit b/d	20,400
Bad debts	1,800		
General expenses	5,100		
Repairs to premises	1,800		
Depreciation of fix & fitt	540		
Net profit for the period	9,360		
	20,400		20,400

Partnership appropriation accounts

	Smith	Jones	Total
Interest on capital	600	270	870
Salaries		3,000	3,000
Balance	3,660	1,830	5,490
	4,260	5,100	9,360

Partnership capital accounts

	Smith	Jones
Opening capital	12,000	5,400
add Profit appropriation	4,260	5,100
less Drawings	1,800	4,800
Closing capital	14,460	5,700

Balance sheet

Non-current assets:			Capital accounts:	
Freehold premises		30,000	Smith	14,460
Fixtures and fittings	5,400		Jones	5,700
less Depreciation	1,440	3,960		20,160
Current assets:			Current liabilities:	
Inventories		31,200	Trade payables	34,800
Trade receivables		37,200	Bank overdraft	48,600
Insurance prepaid		300		
Cash		900		
		103,560		103,560

Exercise 4.6

Trading account

Opening inventories	56,000	Revenues	516,000
Purchases	268,000		
	324,000		
– Closing inventories	44,000		
= Cost of sales	280,000		
Gross profit c/d	236,000		
	516,000		516,000

Income statement

Overheads	60,000	Gross profit b/d	236,000
Depreciation of equipment	46,000		
Net profit c/d	130,000		
	236,000		236,000

Partnership appropriation accounts

	Jim	Dougal	Rosie	Total
Interest on capital	7,200	4,800	3,840	15,840
Salaries		24,000	20,000	44,000
Balance	35,080	23,387	11,693	70,160
	42,280	52,187	35,533	130,000

Partnership capital accounts

	Jim	Dougal	Rosie
Opening capital	60,000	40,000	32,000
add Profit appropriation	42,280	52,187	35,533
less Drawings	36,000	28,000	20,000
Closing capital	66,280	64,187	47,533

Balance sheet

Non-current assets:			Capital accounts:	
Equipment	220,000		Jim	66,280
less Depreciation	82,000	138,000	Dougal	64,187
			Rosie	47,533
				178,000
Current assets:			Current liabilities:	
Inventories		44,000	Trade payables	64,000
Trade receivables		48,000		
Bank		12,000		
		242,000		242,000

Exercise 4.7

Income and expenditure account

Wages	63,750	Subscriptions	74,250
General expenses	3,750	Social takings	23,750
Insurance	2,500		
Rates	3,750		
Printing and stationery	2,500		
Depn. of furn. & equip.	9,375		
Surplus to capital a/c	12,375		
	98,000		98,000

Balance sheet

Non-current assets:			Opening capital fund		125,000
Premises		75,000	add Surplus for period		12,375
Equipment	37,500		Closing capital fund		137,375
less Depreciation	9,375	28,125			
Current assets:			Current liabilities:		
Subs in arrears	1,250		Trade payables	2,500	
Cash	36,250		Subs paid in advance	750	
		37,500			3,250
		140,625			140,625

Exercise 4.8

Bar trading account

Opening inventories	5,400	Revenues	58,800
Purchases	46,500		
	51,900		
– Closing inventories	3,600		
= Cost of sales	48,300		
Wages – bar attendant	3,000		
Sundry bar expenses	720		
Profit from bar	6,780		
	58,800		58,800

Income and expenditure account

Wages	69,000	Profit from bar	6,780
Insurance	2,880	Subscriptions	90,600
Rates	2,100	Locker rents	3,600
Printing and stationery	1,200		
Depreciation of equipment	840		
Surplus to capital a/c	24,960		
	100,980		100,980

Balance sheet

Non-current assets:			Opening capital fund		128,100
Premises		108,000	add Surplus for period		24,960
Equipment	22,750		Closing capital fund		153,060
less depreciation	6,790	15,960			
Current assets:			Current liabilities:		
Stock – bar	3,600		Creditors – bar pur.	1,500	
Subs in arrears	1,500		Subs paid in adv.	2,100	
Insurance in adv	1,320		Sundry bar expenses	420	
Cash	26,700				4,020
		33,120			
		157,080			157,080

In order to reduce the space required for vertical layouts, we have provided these answers using two sided Trading account, Income statement, Appropriation Account and Balance sheet.

Exercise 5.1

Trading account

Opening inventories	54,000	Revenues	540,000
Purchases	360,000		
	414,000		
− Closing inventories	72,000		
= Cost of sales	342,000		
Gross profit c/d	198,000		
	540,000		540,000

Income statement

Administrative costs	108,000	Gross profit b/d	198,000
Selling costs	34,200	Rent received	2,000
Audit fee	1,800	Income from investments	3,600
Interest paid	2,160	Prov. for doubtful debts	300
Depreciation of vehicles	5,000		
Net Profit for the period	52,740		
	203,900		203,900

Balance sheet

Non-current assets:			Equity:		
Land and buildings		234,000	Issued share capital		180,000
Vehicles	36,000		Retained earnings		147,140
less Depreciation	5,000	31,000	Total equity		327,140
Trade investments		36,000			
Current assets:			Current liabilities:		
Inventories		72,000	Trade payables		72,000
Trade receivables	54,000		Bank overdraft		36,000
less Provision	500	53,500	Interest due		360
Cash		9,000			108,360
		134,500			
		435,500			435,500

Exercise 5.2

Trading account

Opening inventories	189,000	Revenues	1,890,000
Purchases	1,260,000		
	1,449,000		
− Closing inventories	252,000		
= Cost of sales	1,197,000		
Gross profit c/d	693,000		
	1,890,000		1,890,000

Income statement

Interest paid	6,300	Gross profit b/d	693,000
Discount allowed	12,200	Income from investments	12,600
Selling costs	119,700	Discount received	22,200
Audit fee	6,100		
Bad debts written off	4,400		
Administration costs	380,900		
Net profit for the period	198,200		
	727,800		727,800

Balance sheet

Non-current assets:			Equity:	
Land and buildings		819,000	Issued share capital	630,000
Vehicles		126,000	Retained earnings	516,200
Trade investments		114,000	Total equity	1,146,200
Current assets:			Current liabilities:	
Inventories		252,000	Trade payables	252,000
Trade receivables	185,400		Bank overdraft	126,000
less Bad debt	800	184,600	Admin costs due	2,900
Cash		31,500		380,900
		468,100		
		1,527,100		1,527,100

Exercise 5.3

Trading account

Opening inventories	281,400	Revenues	4,410,000
Purchases	2,604,000		
	2,885,400		
− Closing inventories	325,500		
= Cost of sales	2,559,900		
Gross profit c/d	1,850,100		
	4,410,000		4,410,000

Income statement

Rent and rates	151,200	Gross Profit b/d	1,850,100
Directors remuneration	115,500	Income from investments	8,400
Office expenses	102,900		
Heating and lighting	58,800		
Sales expenses	114,800		
Insurance	35,700		
Wages and salaries	700,200		
Auditors remuneration	25,000		
Depn. of equipment	176,400		
Depn. of vehicles	42,000		
Provision for doubtful debts	31,500		
Interest on loan at 10%	14,700		
	1,551,900		
Net Profit c/d	306,600		
	1,858,500		1,858,500

Appropriation account

Corporation tax	126,000	Net profit b/d	306,600
Ordinary dividend	40,000	Retained earnings	277,200
Preference dividend	8,400		
Retained earnings	409,400		
	583,800		583,800

Balance sheet

Non-current assets:			Equity:		
Equipment	882,000		Issued share capital		420,000
less Depreciation	495,600	386,400	Retained earnings		409,400
Vehicles	168,000		Preference share capital		105,000
less Depreciation	126,000	42,000	Total equity		934,400
Investments quoted		58,800	Long-term loan at 10%		147,000
Current assets:			Current liabilities:		
Inventories		325,500	Trade payables		144,900
Trade receivables	630,000		Wages due		25,200
less Provision	31,500	598,500	Interest on loan due		14,700
Rates paid in advance		6,300	Corporation tax		126,000
Bank		14,700	Dividend proposed		40,000
		945,000			350,800
		1,432,200			1,432,200

Exercise 5.4

Trading account

Opening inventories	1,206,000	Revenues	18,900,000
Purchases	11,160,000		
	12,366,000		
− Closing inventories	1,395,000		
= Cost of sales	10,971,000		
Gross profit c/d	7,929,000		
	18,900,000		18,900,000

Income statement

Administrative expenses	441,000	Gross profit b/d	7,929,000
Bad debts written off	98,000	Income from investments	36,000
Directors remuneration	495,000		
Heating and lighting	252,000		
Insurance	126,000		
Marketing and selling	270,000		
Rent and rates	675,000		
Wages and salaries	3,150,000		
Depn. of equipment	756,000		
Depn. of vehicles	180,000		
Provision for doubtful debts	63,000		
Interest on loan at 10%	75,600		
Net profit c/d	1,383,400		
	7,965,000		7,965,000

Appropriation account

Corporation tax	540,000	Net profit b/d	1,383,400
Interim dividend	36,000	Retained earnings	1,188,000
Final dividend	135,000		
Retained earnings	1,860,400		
	2,571,400		2,571,400

Balance sheet

Non-current assets:			Equity:		
Equipment	3,780,000		Issued share capital		2,250,000
less Depreciation	2,124,000	1,656,000	Retained earnings		1,860,400
Vehicles	720,000		Total equity		4,110,400
less Depreciation	540,000	180,000			
Investments quoted		252,000	Long-term loan at 12%		630,000
Current assets:			Current liabilities:		
Inventories		1,395,000	Trade payables		621,000
Trade receivables	2,700,000		Interest on loan due		75,600
less Bad debt	26,000		Corporation tax		540,000
less Provision	135,000	2,539,000	Final dividend		135,000
Insurance prepaid		27,000			1,371,600
Bank		63,000			
		4,024,000			
		6,112,000			6,112,000

Exercise 5.5

Trading account

Opening inventories	270,000	Revenues	2,700,000
Purchases	1,710,000		
	1,980,000		
− Closing inventories	360,000		
= Cost of sales	1,620,000		
Gross profit c/d	1,080,000		
	2,700,000		2,700,000

Income statement

Marketing & selling costs	540,000	Gross profit b/d	1,080,000
Administration costs	203,400	Rent received	18,000
Audit fee	9,000		
Rates	9,000		
Depn. of equipment	36,000		
Depn. of vehicles	18,000		
Bad debts write off	9,000		
Provision for doubtful debts	1,800		
Net profit c/d	271,800		
	1,098,000		1,098,000

Appropriation account

Corporation tax	58,500	Net profit b/d	271,800
Dividend at 8%	21,744	Retained earnings	387,000
Retained earnings	578,556		
	658,800		658,800

Balance sheet

Non-current assets:			Equity:	
Land and buildings		1,080,000	Issued share capital	855,000
Equipment	360,000		Retained earnings	578,556
less Depreciation	72,000	288,000	Total equity	1,433,556
Vehicles	180,000			
less Depreciation	108,000	72,000		
Current assets:			Current liabilities:	
Inventories		360,000	Trade payables	360,000
Trade receivables	270,000		Bank overdraft	180,000
less Bad debts	9,000		Administration costs due	32,400
less Provision	19,800	241,200	Corporation tax	58,500
Cash		45,000	Dividend proposed	21,744
		646,200		652,644
		2,086,200		2,086,200

Exercise 5.6

Trading account

Opening inventories	402,000	Revenues	6,300,000
Purchases	3,720,000		
	4,122,000		
− Closing inventories	465,000		
= Cost of Sales	3,657,000		
Gross profit c/d	2,643,000		
	6,300,000		6,300,000

Income statement

Advertising	90,000	Gross profit b/d	2,643,000
Directors remuneration	165,000	Income from investments	12,000
Electricity	84,000		
Insurance	42,000		
Office expenses	147,000		
Rent and rates	225,000		
Wages and salaries	1,074,000		
Depn. of equipment	252,000		
Depn. of vehicles	60,000		
Auditors fees	36,000		
Provision for doubtful debts	21,000		
Interest on loan at 10%	21,000		
Net profit c/d	438,000		
	2,655,000		2,655,000

Appropriation account

Corporation tax	180,000	Net profit b/d	438,000
Interim dividend	12,000	Retained earnings	396,000
Final dividend	75,000		
Retained earnings	567,000		
	834,000		834,000

Balance sheet

Non-current assets:			Equity:	
Equipment	1,260,000		Issued share capital	750,000
less Depreciation	708,000	552,000	Retained earnings	567,000
Vehicles	240,000		Total equity	1,317,000
less Depreciation	180,000	60,000		
Investments quoted		84,000	Long-term loan at 10%	210,000
Current assets:			Current liabilities:	
Inventories		465,000	Trade payables	207,000
Trade receivables	900,000		Auditors fee	36,000
less Provision	45,000	855,000	Interest on loan due	21,000
Insurance prepaid		9,000	Corporation tax	180,000
Bank		21,000	Final dividend	75,000
		1,350,000		519,000
		2,046,000		2,046,000

Exercise 6.1

Non-current assets	?	Issued share capital	110,000
		Retained earnings	140,000
		Equity	250,000
		Long-term loans	?
Current assets:		Current liabilities:	
Inventories	210,000	Trade payables	170,000
Trade receivables	105,000	Bank overdraft	70,000
Cash	45,000		
	360,000		240,000

a. Total borrowings = £250,000 x 0.72 = £180,000
    Long-term loans = £180,000 − £70,000 = **£110,000**

b. Total liabilities = £250,000 + £110,000 + £240,000 = £600,000
    Non-current assets = £600,000 − £360,000 = **£240,000**

c. Current ratio = £360,000 ÷ £240,000 = **1.50 to 1**

d. Return on net assets = £48,000 ÷ (£240,000 + £360,000 − £240,000) x 100 = **13.3%**

Exercise 6.2

Premises	9,000	Issued share capital	1,000
Vehicle	6,000	Retained earnings	9,000
		Equity	10,000
		Long-term loans	9,000
Current Assets:		Current liabilities:	
Inventories	16,000	Trade payables	16,000
Trade receivables	9,000	Bank overdraft	6,000
Cash	1,000		
	26,000		22,000

1. Profitability, key ratio = (£500 + £3,500) ÷ (£15,000 + £26,000 − £22,000) x 100 = **21.1%**

2. Profit margin ratio = (£500 + £3,500) ÷ £25,500 x 100 = **15.7%**

3. Revenue generation ratio = £25,500 ÷ (£15,000 + £26,000 − £22,000) = **1.34 to 1**

4. Current ratio = £26,000 ÷ £22,000 = **1.18 to 1**

5. Liquid (or acid test) ratio = (£26,000 − £16,000) ÷ £22,000 = **0.45 to 1**

6. Inventory turn = £20,000 ÷ £16,000 = **1.25 times**

7. Trade receivable weeks = £9,000 ÷ (£25,500 ÷ 52) = **18.4 weeks**

8. Borrowings ratio = (£9,000 + £6,000) ÷ £10,000 = **1.50 to 1**

9. Income gearing = £3,500 ÷ (£500 + £3,500) x 100 = **87.5%**

Exercise 6.3

Non current assets	90,000	Issued share capital	50,000
		Retained earnings	20,000
		Equity	70,000
		Long-term loans	50,000
Current assets:		Current liabilities:	
Inventories	50,000	Trade payables	40,000
Trade receivables	30,000	Bank overdraft	20,000
Cash	10,000		
	90,000		60,000

1. Profitability, key ratio = (£22,000 + £8,000) ÷ (£90,000 + £90,000 − £60,000) x 100 = **25%**
2. Profit margin ratio = (£22,000 + £8,000) ÷ £700,000 x 100 = **4.3%**
3. Revenue generation ratio = £700,000 ÷ (£90,000 + £90,000 − £60,000) = **5,83 to 1**
4. Current ratio = £90,000 ÷ £60,000 = **1.50 to 1**
5. Liquid (or acid test) ratio = (£90,000 − £50,000) ÷ £60,000 = **0.67 to 1**
6. Inventory turn = £480,000 ÷ £50,000 = **9.6 times**
7. Trade receivable weeks = £30,000 ÷ (£700,000 ÷ 52) = **2.2 weeks**
8. Borrowings ratio = (£50,000 + £20,000) ÷ £70,000 = **1.00 to 1**
9. Income gearing = £8,000 ÷ (£22,000 + £8,000) x 100 = **26.7%**

Exercise 6.4

Premises	3,000	Issued share capital	200
Vehicle	1,500	Retained earnings	2,800
	4,500	Equity	3,000
		Long-term loans	1,800
Current assets:		Current liabilities:	
Inventories	4,500	Trade payables	5,000
Trade receivables	2,500	Bank overdraft	2,000
Cash	300		
	7,300		7,000

1. Profitability, key ratio = (£200 + £700) ÷ (£4,500 + £7,300 − £7,000) x 100 = **18.8%**
2. Profit margin ratio = (£200 + £700) ÷ £8,000 x 100 = **11.3%**
3. Revenue generation ratio = £8,000 ÷ (£4,500 + £7,300 − £7,000) = **1.67 to 1**
4. Current ratio = £7,300 ÷ £7,000 = **1.04 to 1**
5. Liquid (or acid test) ratio = (£7,300 − £4,500) ÷ £7,000 = **0.40 to 1**
6. Inventory turn = £6,300 ÷ £4,500 = **1.4 times**
7. Trade receivable weeks = £2,500 ÷ (£8,000 ÷ 52) = **16.3 weeks**
8. Borrowings ratio = (£1,800 + £2,000) ÷ £3,000 = **1.27 to 1**
9. Income gearing = £700 ÷ (£200 + £700) x 100 = **77.8%**

Exercise 6.5

Land and buildings		Issued share capital	100,000
Equipment	110,000	Retained earnings	50,000
		Equity	150,000
		Long-term loans	160,000
Current assets:		Current liabilities:	
Inventories	150,000	Trade payables	220,000
Trade receivables	250,000	Bank overdraft	80,000
Cash	20,000	Accruals (wages)	20,000
	420,000		320,000

a.   Total liabilities = £150,000 + £160,000 + £320,000 = £630,000
     Land and buildings = £630,000 − £420,000 − £110,000 = **£100,000**

b.   Gearing ratio = (£160,000 + £80,000) ÷ £150,000 = **1.60 to 1**

c.   Current ratio = £420,000 ÷ £320,000 = **1.31 to 1**

d.   Return on net assets = (£210,000 + £420,000 − £320,000) x 15 ÷ 100 = **£46,500**

Exercise 6.6 (suggestions for possible movements)

General points:

❏   This is not an answer to a specific question, it is simply suggestions/pointers to help with interpretation;

❏   List all the ratios in a table showing the annual results side by side;

❏   Interpret each ratio in turn. Then provide a summary for each group of ratios, e.g. profitability;

❏   Where you have three years or more, look at the overall movement, i.e. from the earliest to the latest year;

❏   Alternatively, where there is a substantial change in one year, interpret that movement;

❏   Your aim in interpretation is to show the examiner that you understand these ratios;

❏   Tip for interpretation, use the ratio to help you. Has the numerator increased or decreased? Has the denominator increased or decreased? What might have caused the numerator and/or denominator to increase or decrease?

Key profitability ratio
Profit as a percentage of capital employed.
Profit can be taken either as profit before taxation or profit before taxation plus interest payable.
Capital employed can be taken either as total assets less current liabilities or simply total assets.

❏   An absolute ratio, the higher the better;

❏   Shows whether a company has achieved higher or lower profits than in previous year(s), and/or against competitors. Does not give any indication why there is a movement in the ratio. Must interpret profit margin and revenue generation ratios to identify reason(s) for movements.

Average profit margin ratio
Profit as a percentage of revenues.
Profit can be taken either as Profit before Taxation or Profit before Taxation plus Interest Payable.

❏   Shows the average profit generated by a companY;

❏   Can hide high profit and loss making parts of a company;

❏   Try to identify reasons for any change;

❏   For example, should a company increase its profit margins on its products, the ratio should increase. If a company reduced its costs the profit margin ratio increase. If a company increased its selling prices the profit margin ratio would increase;

❏   An increase in the profit margin ratio could also be due to a change in the mix of products making up the total revenues. For example, a company could be selling more higher margin lines and less of lower margin lines. This could be a redistribution of their own products and/or products that it had acquired when purchasing new businesses.

Revenue generation ratio
Revenues divided by capital employed.
Capital employed can be taken either as total assets less current liabilities or simply total assets.

❏   Known as the asset utilisation or revenue generation ratio;

❏   Shows the amount of revenue in £'s generated by each £ of capital employed;

❏   An increase in the ratio could be due to an increase in revenues and/or a reduction in the capital employed. For example, if a company reduced it profit margins in order to try to obtain additional market share; revenues should increase, therefore, given that the capital employed remained constant there would be an increase in the ratio;

❏   Similarly, if a company disposed of under-utilised assets, given that revenues remained constant there would be an increase in the ratio;

❏   Should a company pursue an expansion policy, capital employed should increase and revenues should also increase. However, revenues might lag behind the increases in capital employed.

Current ratio
Current assets divided by current liabilities.

❏   Gives an indication how a company might be able to pay its way in the short to medium term, i.e. three months to one year;

❏   Does not consider a company's ability to generate or attract finance;

❏   Interpretation should be against industry averages and/or historic trends for the ratio;

❏   A ratio of 1.50 to 1 means that the current liabilities are covered once plus an additional 50%;

❏   Movement in a ratio from 1.50 to 1.25 should be interpreted without the 1.00 (i.e. unity). Therefore, the additional cover has fallen from 50% down to 25%.

Liquid ratio (or acid test)
Liquid assets divided by current liabilities.
Liquid assets exclude inventory.

❑   Gives an indication how a company might be able to meet its short-term obligations;

❑   Can be influenced by movements in bank overdrafts;

❑   Interpretation should be against industry averages and/or historic trends for the ratio;

❑   When trying to decide an appropriate level for this ratio you should take into account, the average movement in the working capital cycle, how profitable or loss making and the level of gearing. For example, if the movement in the working capital cycle is say 6 weeks, the company is making higher than average profits for the industry and it is low geared then a low ratio might be in order.

Inventory turn
Cost of sales divided by inventory.

❑   The average number of times in a year that a company turns over its inventory, e.g. a inventory turn of 5 times means that a company holds approximately 10 weeks inventory;

❑   Interpretation should be against industry averages and/or historic trends for the ratio;

❑   Movements in the ratio should be confirmed by undertaking a similar analysis within product groups;

❑   Too much of a company's resources tied up in inventory means idle facilities in the working capital cycle, also the physical cost of holding inventory and the possibility of obsolescence.

Trade receivable weeks
Trade receivables divided by average weekly (or daily) revenues.

❑   The trade receivable collection period;

❑   The length of time it takes in weeks (or days) for a company to collect its debts.

❑   This is linked to a company's ability to generate revenues;

❑   The aim is to achieve a balance between revenues and bad debts;

❑   Interpretation should be against industry averages and/or historic trends for the ratio;

❑   Too much of a company's resources tied up in trade receivables means idle facilities in the working capital cycle including the possibility of increases in bad debts.

Borrowings ratio
Total borrowings divided by equity.
Total borrowings include both long-term debt and bank overdraft (i.e. all interest bearing debt).

m   Shows the number of times total borrowings (or interest bearing debt) exceeds equity;

m   A ratio of < 0.5 would be considered low gearing, while > 1.0 is considered to be in the high gearing region;

m   It is important to achieve an appropriate level of gearing. For example, a company that is low geared might not be making best use of debt finance (if it is cheaper than equity finance);

m   Movement in this ratio is an important factor.

Income gearing ratio
Interest payable as a percentage of (profit before tax + interest payable).

m   The previous ratio showed the level of gearing. This ratio shows whether a company can afford its level of gearing;

m   Profit before tax plus interest payable represents the available profits;

m   A level of 25% is considered ideal. This shows that a company's interest payments are covered four times.

Exercise 6.7

Premises	300	Issued share capital	400
Vehicle	200	Retained earnings	800
	500	Equity	1,200
Current assets:		Current liabilities:	
Inventories	2,100	Trade payables	2,000
Trade receivables	1,200	Bank overdraft	800
Cash	200		
	3,500		2,800
	4,000		4,000

1. Profitability, key ratio = (£200 + £100) ÷ (£500 + £3,500 − £2,800) x 100 = **25%**

2. Profit margin ratio = (£200 + £100) ÷ £3,500 x 100 = **8.6%**

3. Revenue generation ratio = £3,500 ÷ (£500 + £3,500 − £2,800) = **2.92 to 1**

4. Current ratio = £3,500 ÷ £2,800 = **1.25 to 1**

5. Liquid (or acid test) ratio = (£3,500 − £2,100) ÷ £2,800 = **0.50 to 1**

6. Inventory turn = £2,000 ÷ £2,100 = **0.95 times**

7. Trade receivable weeks = £1,200 ÷ (£3,500 ÷ 52) = **17.8 weeks**

Exercise 6.8

1. Profitability ratios

	2002 £'000	2003 £'000	2004 £'000	2005 £'000	2006 £'000
PBIT	12,000	15,000	19,500	28,600	35,000
Net assets	37,000	83,000	93,000	109,000	125,000
Total assets	102,000	147,000	160,000	179,000	225,000
Revenues	90,000	118,000	124,000	140,000	170,000
PBIT ÷ Net assets %	32.43	18.07	20.97	26.24	28.00
PBIT ÷ Revenues %	13.33	12.71	15.73	20.43	20.59
Revenues ÷ Net assets (times)	2.43	1.42	1.33	1.28	1.36
PBIT ÷ Total assets %	11.76	10.20	12.19	15.98	15.56
PBIT ÷ Revenues %	13.33	12.71	15.73	20.43	20.59
Revenues ÷ Total assets (times)	0.88	0.80	0.78	0.78	0.76

2. Liquidity ratios

	2002 £'000	2003 £'000	2004 £'000	2005 £'000	2006 £'000
Current assets	76,000	77,000	80,000	83,000	90,000
Current liabilities	65,000	64,000	67,000	70,000	100,000
Inventories	50,000	50,000	51,000	52,000	58,000
Trade receivables	24,000	25,000	26,000	28,000	24,000
Revenues	90,000	118,000	124,000	140,000	170,000
Cost of sales	78,000	103,000	104,500	111,400	135,000
Current ratio (times)	1.17	1.20	1.19	1.19	0.90
Liquid ratio (times)	0.40	0.42	0.43	0.44	0.32
Cost of sales ÷ Inventory (times)	1.56	2.06	2.05	2.14	2.33
Trade receivable ÷ A.W.R. (weeks)	13.9	11.0	10.9	10.4	7.3

3. Gearing ratios

	2002 £'000	2003 £'000	2004 £'000	2005 £'000	2006 £'000
Total borrowing	30,000	38,000	38,000	41,000	65,000
Equity	18,000	57,000	67,000	80,000	92,000
Interest payable	3,000	3,000	3,500	3,600	10,000
P.B.I.T.	12,000	15,000	19,500	28,600	35,000
Total borrowing ÷ Equity	1.67	0.67	0.57	0.51	0.71
Interest payable ÷ PBIT %	25.0	20.0	17.9	12.6	28.6

Exercise 6.9

Preparatory work:

Current assets	=	1.75 x £125,000	=	£218,750
Liquid assets	=	1.05 x £125,000	=	£131,250
Inventory (CA – LA)	=	£218,750 – £131,250	=	£87,500
Non-current assets (TA – CA)	=	£258,750 – £218,750	=	£50,000
Net assets (TA – CL)	=	£258,750 – £125,000	=	£133,750
Net current assets (CA – CL)	=	£218,750 – £125,000	=	£93,750
Net profit	=	£93,750 x 20%	=	£18,750
Gross profit	=	£18,750 + £33,250	=	£52,000
Revenues	=	£52,000 ÷ 20 x 100	=	£260,000
Cost of sales	=	£260,000 – £52,000	=	£208,000
Trade receivables	=	£260,000 ÷ 52 x 12	=	£60,000

H.O. Ratio Limited
Income statement for the year ended 31st October 200X

	£
Revenues	260,000
Cost of sales	–208,000
Gross profit	52,000
Expenses	–33,250
Net profit	18,750

H.O. Ratio Limited
Balance sheet as at 31st October 200X

	£			£
Non-current assets	50,000	Issued share capital		125,000
		Retained earnings		18,750
		Equity		143,750
Current assets:		Current liabilities:		125,000
Inventories	87,500			
Trade receivables	60,000			
Cash	71,250			
	218,750			
	268,750			268,750

Exercise 7.1

Preliminary calculations:

		2005	2006
A.	Total assets	120,000	123,000
B.	Total borrowings	33,000	38,000
C.	Revenues - Total assets	35,000	52,000
D.	Total debt	61,000	68,000
E.	Current assets - Total debt	17,000	11,000
F.	Equity - Total borrowings	26,000	17,000
G.	Liquid assets	38,000	34,000
H.	Liquid assets - Bank Overdraft	30,000	8,000

Robertson's 1983 ratio model:

		Weight	2005	2006
R_1	C ÷ Revenues	0.3	0.07	0.09
R_2	Profit before tax ÷ A	3.0	0.15	0.10
R_3	E ÷ Current liabilities	0.6	0.28	0.12
R_4	F ÷ D	0.3	0.13	0.08
R_5	H ÷ Trade payables	0.3	0.36	0.08
	Total score		0.99	0.47

Exercise 8.1

A. Overhead analysis sheet

Works overhead	Basis for apportionment	Total	Shop 1	Shop 2
Indirect labour	Direct labour	8,400	3,360	5,040
Salaries	Direct labour	42,000	16,800	25,200
Depreciation	Plant value	18,900	7,560	11,340
Maintenance	Technical estimate	19,600	12,000	7,600
Rent and rates	Floor area	32,200	16,100	16,100
Totals		121,100	55,820	65,280

B. Overhead absorption rates

Shop 1: $\dfrac{\text{Overheads}}{\text{Labour hours}} = \dfrac{£55,820}{6,000 \text{ hours}} = £9.3 \text{ per labour hour}$

Shop 2: $\dfrac{\text{Overheads}}{\text{Labour hours}} = \dfrac{£65,280}{9,000 \text{ hours}} = £7.25 \text{ per labour hour}$

C. Estimated product cost

		JOBS	
		A1127	A1131
Direct materials		184.00	262.00
Direct labour Shop 1 (11hrs x £10.00 = £110.00)		90.00	110.00
Direct labour Shop 2		0	98.00
Outwork		99.00	55.00
Prime cost		373.00	525.00
Overheads Shop 1 (11hrs x £9.30 = £102.30)		83.70	102.30
Shop 2		0	50.75
Product cost		456.70	678.05

Exercise 8.2

A. Overhead analysis sheet

Works overhead	Basis for apportionment	Total	Shop 1	Shop 2
Indirect labour	Direct labour	12,000	3,000	9,000
Salaries	Direct labour	30,000	7,500	22,500
Depreciation	Plant value	16,600	6,200	10,400
Maintenance	Technical estimate	14,000	4,400	9,600
Rent and rates	Floor area	20,000	6,667	13,333
Totals		92,600	27,767	64,833

B. Overhead absorption rates

Shop 1: $\dfrac{\text{Overheads}}{\text{Labour hours}} = \dfrac{£27,767}{5,000 \text{ hours}} = £5.55$ per labour hour

Shop 2: $\dfrac{\text{Overheads}}{\text{Labour hours}} = \dfrac{£64,833}{15,000 \text{ hours}} = £4.32$ per labour hour

C. Estimated product cost

		JOBS	
		E102	E110
Direct materials		71.80	228.04
Direct labour	Shop 1 (12hrs x £7.50 = £90.00)	120.00	90.00
Direct labour	Shop 2	0	84.00
Outwork		65.00	40.00
Prime cost		256.80	442.04
Overheads	Shop 1 (12hrs x £5.55 = £66.60)	88.80	66.60
	Shop 2	0	34.56
Product cost		345.60	543.20

Exercise 8.3

Direct materials	544	£5.00	2,720
Direct labour	220	£15.00	3,300
Variable overhead	220	£9.00	1,980
Total variable cost			8,000
Fixed overhead		50%	4,000
Total cost			12,000
Profit		30%	3,600
Quote price			£15,600

Exercise 8.4

Direct materials						200.00
Direct labour	Shop 1	5 hrs	x	£14.00	70.00	
Direct labour	Shop 2	3 hrs	x	£10.00	30.00	100.00
Overheads	Shop 1	10 hrs	x	£42.00	420.00	
Overheads	Shop 2	3 hrs	x	£2 0.00	60.00	480.00
Manufacturing cost						780.00
Administration costs				30%		234.00
Total costs						1,014.00
Profit				20%		202.80
						£1,216.80

Exercise 8.5

Basis of apportionment	*Methods of absorption*
Floor area	Percentage of materials
Plant value	Percentage of labour
Machine hours	Labour hour rate
Number of employees	Machine hour rate
Labour hours	
Technical estimate	

Exercise 8.6

Direct materials	550	£4.00	2,200
Direct labour	220	£14.00	3,080
Variable overhead	220	£11.00	2,420
Total variable cost			7,700
Fixed overhead		66.7%	5,136
Total cost			12,836
Profit		30%	3,851
Quote price			£16,687

Exercise 8.7

Direct materials						144.00
Direct labour	Machine shop	3 hrs	x	£12.00	36.00	
Direct Labour	Assembly	5 hrs	x	£7.50	37.50	73.50
Overheads	Machine shop	4 hrs	x	£36.00	144.00	
Overheads	Assembly	5 hrs	x	£15.00	75.00	219.00
Manufacturing cost						436.50
Administration costs				25%		109.13
Delivery charges						30.00
Total costs						575.63
Profit				15%		86.34
						£661.97

Exercise 8.8

a. Traditional overhead apportionment

Fixed factory overheads ÷ total machine hours

£525,000 ÷ 120,000 = £4.375 per machine hour

	A1123		A1139
Cost per component (£4.375 x 4hrs)	£17.50	(£4.375 x 4hrs) £17.50	

Overhead costs absorbed

		A1123		A1139
	(5,000 x £17.50)	**£87,500**	(25,000 x £17.50)	**£437,500**

b. ABC method of apportionment

Volume related rate:

£250,000 ÷ 120,000 machine hours = £2.08333 per machine hour

Purchasing related rate:

£125,000 ÷ 500 purchase orders = £250 per purchase order

Setup related rate:

£150,000 ÷ 190 setups = £789.474 per setup

		A1123		A1139
Volume costs	(20,000 x £2.08333)	41,667	(100,000 x £2.08333)	208,333
Purchasing costs	(150 x £250)	37,500	(350 x £250)	87,500
Setup costs	(70 x £789.474)	55,263	(120 x £789.474)	94,737
		134,430		**390,570**

Exercise 9.1

Revenues (70,000 units)	210,000	30.00	30.00	31.20
less Variable costs	140,000	20.00	21.00	20.00
= Contribution	70,000	10.00	9.00	11.20
less Fixed costs	40,000			
= Profit	£30,000			

1. BEP units £40,000 ÷ £10.00 = **4,000 units**

2a. BEP fixed costs increase by 10%
£44,000 ÷ £10.00 = **4,400 units**

2b. BEP variable costs increase by 5%
£40,000 ÷ £9.00 = **4,444 units**

2c. BEP selling price increase by 4%
£40,000 ÷ £11.20 = **3,571 units**

2d. No change, break-even as 1. above, i.e. **4,000 units**

Exercise 9.2

Revenues (30,000 units)	750,000	25.00	25.00	23.00
less Variable costs	450,000	15.00	16.00	15.00
= Contribution	300,000	10.00	9.00	8.00
less Fixed costs	200,000			
= Profit	£100,000			

1. BEP units £200,000 ÷ £10.00 = **20,000 units**
BEP sterling 20,000 x £25.00 = **£500,000**

2. BEP variable costs increase to £16.00
£200,000 ÷ £9.00 = **22,222 units**

3. BEP units £235,000 ÷ £10.00 = 23,500 units
BEP sterling 23,500 x £25.00 = **£587,500**

4. Minimum selling price (refer to formula sheet)
[(£200,000 + £70,000) ÷ 30,000] + £15.00 = **£24.00**

5. Volume of sales (refer to formula sheet)
   (£200,000 + £100,000) ÷ £8.00 = **37,500 units**

6. BEP Units £40,000 ÷ £10.00 = **4,000 units**

Exercise 9.3

Revenues		6,000,000	300.00	280.00	280.00
Materials	2,200,000				
Labour	640,000				
Variable prod. costs	160,000				
Total variable costs		3,000,000	150.00	150.00	156.00
Contribution		3,000,000	150.00	130.00	124.00
Fixed prod. costs	1,440,000				
Selling and admin.	1,960,000				
Total fixed costs		3,400,000			
Profit		– 400,000			

1. BEP units £3,400,000 ÷ £150.00 = **22,667 units**

2. BEP units £3,400,000 ÷ £130.00 = **26,154 units**

3. Contribution   (60,000 ÷ 2) x £130.00   3,900,000
   Fixed costs   3,400,000
   Profit   **500,000**

4. Contribution   (60,000 x £124.00)   7,440,000
   Fixed costs   (2 x £3,400,000 x 1.10)   7,480,000
   Profit / loss   **– 40,000**

   $$\text{Break-even point (units)} \quad = \quad \frac{£7,480,000}{£124.00}$$

   $$= \quad \textbf{60,323 units}$$

9.4

a.

Revenues (5,500 units)	462,000	84.00	84.00
less Variable costs	220,000	40.00	44.00
= Contribution	242,000	44.00	40.00
less Fixed costs	195,000		
= Profit	**£47,000**		

b. BEP units £195,000 ÷ £44.00 = 4,432 units
BEP sterling4,432 x £84.00 = **£372,288**

c. BEP variable costs + 10%
£195,000 ÷ £40.00 = **4,875 units**

9.5

1.	Standard £	Super £	Deluxe £	Total £
Selling price	300.00	375.00	550.00	
Direct material	90.00	120.00	160.00	
Direct labour	45.00	45.00	90.00	
Variable overhead	20.00	30.00	50.00	
Variable costs	155.00	195.00	300.00	
Contribution per unit	145.00	180.00	250.00	
Revenue volume (units)	4,000	3,000	1,000	
Contribution margin	580,000	540,000	250,000	1,370,000
Fixed costs				1,000,000
Profit				370,000

2. Choice – reduce selling price of Deluxe by £75.00

Contribution per unit	£250.00 – £75.00	=	£175.00
Volume change	1,000 x 1.50	=	1,500 units
Contribution margin	1,500 x £175.00	=	£262,500
Profit increase	£262,500 – £250,000	=	**£12,500**

Choice – drop Deluxe, increase production of Super (i.e. highest contribution)

	Standard	Super	Total
Extra volume Super [1]		2,000	
Contribution per unit		£180.00	
	£	£	£
Extra contribution		360,000	360,000
Contribution margin	580,000	540,000	1,120,000
			1,480,000
Fixed costs [2]			1,000,000
Profit			480,000

[1] £90.00 x 1,000 units ÷ £45.00 = 2,000 units

Profit increase   £480,000 – £370,000 = **£110,000**

Exercise 9.6

a.				
Sales (25,000 units)	625,000	25.00	25.00
less Variable costs	375,000	15.00	15.00
= Contribution	250,000	10.00	10.00
less Fixed costs	200,000		260,000
= Profit	**£50,000**		

b. BEP units £200,000 ÷ £10.00 = 20,000 units
BEP sterling 20,000 x £25.00 = **£500,000**

c. Minimum selling price
[(£260,000 + £50,000) ÷ 25,000] + £15.00 = **£27.40**

Exercise 9.7

Sales (5,500 units)	1,750,000	35.00	35.00	35.00	38.00
less Variable costs	1,300,000	26.00	23.00	26.00	26.00
= Contribution	450,000	9.00	12.00	9.00	12.00
less Fixed costs	350,000				
= Profit	£100,000				

a. BEP units £350,000 ÷ £9.00 = 38,889 units
    BEP sterling 38,889 x £35.00 = **£1,361,115**

b. BEP variable costs decrease to £23.00
    £350,000 ÷ £12.00 = **29,167 units**

c. BEP units £370,000 ÷ £9.00 = 41,111 units
    BEP sterling 41,111 x £35.00 = **£1,438,885**

d. Minimum selling price
    [(£350,000 + £120,000) ÷ 50,000] + £26.00 = **£35.40**

e. Volume of revenues
    (£350,000 + £100,000) ÷ £12.00 = **37,500 units**

f. BEP units £60,000 ÷ £9.00 = **6,667 units**

Exercise 9.8

a.	Sales (35,000 units)	840,000	24.00		24.00
	less Variable costs	560,000	16.00		16.00
	= Contribution	280,000	8.00		8.00
	less Fixed costs	200,000			260,000
	= Profit	**£80,000**			

b. BEP units £200,000 ÷ £8.00 = 25,000 units
    BEP sterling 25,000 x £24.00 = **£600,000**

c. Minimum selling price
    [(£260,000 + £80,000) ÷ 35,000] + £16.00 = **£25.71**

Exercise 9.9

Sales (70,000 units)	2,940,000	42.00	42.00	42.00	45.00
less Variable costs	2,310,000	33.00	30.00	33.00	33.00
= Contribution	630,000	9.00	12.00	9.00	12.00
less Fixed costs	490,000				
= Profit	£140,000				

a. BEP units £490,000 ÷ £9.00 = 54,444 units
    BEP sterling 54,444 x £42.00 = **£2,286,648**

b. BEP variable costs decrease to £30.00
    £490,000 ÷ £12.00 = **40,834 units**

c. BEP units £550,000 ÷ £9.00 = 61,111 units
    BEP sterling 61,111 x £42.00 = **£2,566,662**

d. Minimum selling price
    [(£490,000 + £180,000) ÷ 70,000] + £33.00 = **£42.57**

e. Volume of revenues
    (£490,000 + £140,000) ÷ £12.00 = **52,500 units**

f. BEP units £72,000 ÷ £9.00 = **8,000 units**

Exercise 10.1

1. Statement showing Bristol and Reading depots making losses

		Swindon	Bristol	Reading	Total
Revenue volume		67,000	22,000	10,000	99,000
	£	£	£	£	£
Revenues	22.00	1,474,000	484,000	220,000	2,178,000
Direct material	6.50	435,500	143,000	65,000	643,500
Direct labour	3.40	227,800	74,800	34,000	336,600
Variable overhead	5.10	341,700	112,200	51,000	504,900
Selling and distribution:					
Variable		117,920	48,400	26,400	192,720
Fixed		70,000	60,000	60,000	190,000
Factory fixed costs		169,192	55,556	25,252	250,000
Total costs		1,362,112	493,956	261,652	2,117,720
Profit / Loss		111,888	– 9,956	– 41,652	60,280

2a. Statement showing effect of closure of Bristol and Reading depots

		Swindon	Total
Revenue volume		67,000	67,000
	£	£	£
Revenues	22.00	1,474,000	1,474,000
Direct material	6.50	435,500	435,500
Direct labour	3.40	227,800	227,800
Variable overhead	5.10	341,700	341,700
Selling and distribution:			
Variable		117,920	117,920
Fixed		70,000	70,000
Contribution to factory fixed		281,080	281,080
Factory fixed costs			250,000
Profit / Loss			31,080

2b. Statement showing effect of closure of the Reading depot

		Swindon	Bristol	Total
Revenue volume		67,000	22,000	89,000
	£	£	£	£
Revenues	22.00	1,474,000	484,000	1,958,000
Direct material	6.50	435,500	143,000	578,500
Direct labour	3.40	227,800	74,800	302,600
Variable overhead	5.10	341,700	112,200	453,900
Selling and distribution:				
Variable		117,920	48,400	166,320
Fixed		70,000	60,000	130,000
Contribution to factory fixed		281,080	45,600	326,680
Factory fixed costs				250,000
Profit / Loss				76,680

Exercise 10.2

1. Best use of scarce resources – ranking

	A	B	C	D	E	F	G
Revenues	7,000	2,000	2,000	4,000	6,000	2,000	4,000
Variable costs	6,000	1,400	1,700	3,500	4,000	1,200	2,600
Contribution	1,000	600	300	500	2,000	800	1,400
Machine hours	40	20	20	60	80	20	120
Contribution per machine hour	25.00	30.00	15.00	8.33	25.00	40.00	11.67
Ranking	3=	2	5	7	3=	1	6

2. Product income statement (for a single week)

	F	B	A	E	Total
Machine hours	20	20	40	80	160
	£	£	£	£	£
Revenues	2,000	2,000	7,000	6,000	17,000
Materials	600	800	4,000	3,000	8,400
Labour	600	600	2,000	1,000	4,200
Variable costs	1,200	1,400	6,000	4,000	12,600
Contribution	800	600	1,000	2,000	4,400
Fixed costs (£115,440 ÷ 52)					2,220
Profit					2,180

Exercise 10.3

1. Order from regular customer

			£
Direct materials	100	£40.00	4,000
Direct labour	240	£5.00	1,200
Variable overhead	240	£15.00	3,600
Total variable cost			8,800
Fixed overhead		62.5%	5,500
Total cost			14,300
Profit		20%	2,860
Quote price			£17,160

2. Labour in short supply

   Contribution per labour hour (£780,000 – £400,000) ÷ 10,000 = £38.00

Total variable cost	£8,800
Contribution to fixed and profit (240 hrs x £38.00)	£9,120
Quote price	£17,920

3. Check the considerations (in the text) when arriving at a price for a special order.

   In this case we could quote any figure above total variable cost, i.e. £8,801. The assumption being that the company has covered its fixed costs from the existing customer base and any amount above total variable cost will go straight to profit.

Exercise 10.4

1.   Variable costs of making cartons:

		£ p.a.
Direct materials		84,000
Direct labour		18,000
Electricity (power costs)		4,500
Repairs to plant		3,000
		109,500
Cost of buying in cartons:		
360,000 cartons at £325 per 1,000		117,000
additional storage costs		9,000
		126,000

The variable costs of making the cartons is less than the cost of buying in the cartons, therefore *Simply Packers Ltd* should continue to produce their own cartons.

Exercise 10.5

	A	B	C	D
Revenues	14,000	4,000	4,000	8,000
Variable costs	12,000	2,800	3,400	6,400
Contribution	2,000	1,200	600	1,600
Labour hours	80	40	40	80
Contribution per labour hr.	25	30	15	20
Ranking	2	1	4	3

Exercise 10.6

Relevant costs which would be eliminated if electric motors were bought-in.

	£
Direct materials	16,000
Direct labour	24,000
Variable production overhead	16,000
Fixed production overhead	12,000
	£68,000
Cost of buying in cartons:	
32,000 motors at £2.50 per unit	80,000
less Rent received	8,000
	£72,000

The relevant costs of manufacture are less than the cost of buying the electric motors from *Wedge Ltd*, therefore the company should continue to produce their own motors.

Exercise 10.7

Production capacity 240,000 ÷ 0.60 = 400,000 units

Therefore, increase in capacity/sales = 160,000 units

	Total p.a.	Per unit
	£	£
Revenues		9.60
Variable costs		7.80
Contribution	288,000	1.80
Additional fixed costs	150,000	
Increase in profit	138,000	

Exercise 10.8

Best use of scarce resources – determine labour hours

	A	B	C	D	E	F
Units	400	1,000	300	800	500	300
Labour cost per unit	40.00	90.00	90.00	50.00	70.00	90.00
Labour cost	16,000	90,000	27,000	40,000	35,000	27,000
Labour hours [1]	2,000	11,250	3,375	5,000	4,375	3,375

[1] labour cost divided by £8.00 per hour

Best use of scarce resources – ranking

	A	B	C	D	E	F
Units	400	1,000	300	800	500	300
Contribution per unit	140.00	295.00	265.00	185.00	195.00	275.00
Contribution	56,000	295,000	79,500	148,000	97,500	82,500
Labour hours	2,000	11,250	3,375	5,000	4,375	3,375
Contribution per Labour hour	28.00	26.22	23.56	29.60	22.29	24.44
Ranking	2	3	5	1	6	4

Product income statement

	D	A	B	F	C	Total
Labour hours	5,000	2,000	11,250	3,375	3,375	25,000
	£	£	£	£	£	£
Revenues	384,000	168,000	570,000	171,000	153,000	
Materials	164,000	76,000	160,000	45,000	39,000	
Labour	40,000	16,000	90,000	27,000	27,000	
Variable overhead	32,000	20,000	25,000	16,500	7,500	
Total variable costs	236,000	112,000	275,000	88,500	73,500	
Contribution	148,000	56,000	295,000	82,500	79,500	661,000
Fixed overheads [2]						300,000
Profit						361,000

[2] Fixed overheads = Labour rate x hours x 1.50
= £8.00 x 25,000 x 1.5
= £300,000

Exercise 10.10

	A	B	C	D
Revenues	16,000	6,000	6,000	10,000
Variable costs	13,000	3,800	4,400	7,400
Contribution	3,000	2,200	1,600	2,600
Labour hours	80	40	40	80
Contribution per labour hr	37.5	55	40	32.5
Ranking	3	1	2	4

Exercise 10.11

WITHOUT RESTRICTION

	A	B	C	D	Total
AMILL (Kgs) [1]	2,700	5,184	3,240	11,520	
Selling price (£)	3.24	4.92	4.62	6.00	
Variable costs (£)	1.80	2.76	2.28	4.20	
Contribution Per kg (£)	1.44	2.16	2.34	1.80	
Volume	18,000	21,600	18,000	28,800	
	£	£	£	£	£
Contribution	25,920	46,656	42,120	51,840	166,536
Fixed costs					30,000
Profit					136,536

[1]   Calculation to find the amount of AMILL used for Product A

£0.90 ÷ £6.00 x 18,000 = 2,700 kgs

CONTRIBUTION PER UNIT OF LIMITING FACTOR

	A	B	C	D
Contribution (£)	25,920	46,656	42,120	51,840
AMILL (kgs)	2,700	5,184	3,240	11,520
Contribution per gg of Limiting factor	9.60	9.00	13.00	4.50
Ranking	2	3	1	4

WITH RESTRICTION

	C	A	B	D	Total
Contribution per kg (£)	2.34	1.44	2.16	1.80	
Volume (2)	18,000	18,000	21,600	2,190	
	£	£	£	£	£
Contribution £	42,120	25,920	46,656	3,942	118,638
Fixed costs					30,000
Profit					88,638

(2) Calculation to determine the balance of AMILL to produce/sell Product D.

Product	C	3,240
	A	2,700
	B	5,184
		11,124
Product	D	876
		12,000

Kgs of Product D = 876 ÷ 11,520 x 28,800 = 2,190

Exercise 10.12

Budget forecast and special order

	Price/Rate	£	£
Revenues (125,000 units)	25.00		3,125,000
Revenues (35,000 units)	18.00		630,000
Total revenues			3,755,000
Direct materials	4.00	640,000	
Direct labour	7.00	1,120,000	
Variable overhead	2.00	320,000	
Fixed overhead		420,000	
Total production cost			2,500,000
= Gross margin			1,255,000
Selling costs			200,000
			1,055,000

Differential

	Price/Rate	£	£
Revenues (35,000 units)	18.00		630,000
Direct materials	4.00	140,000	
Direct labour	7.00	245,000	
Variable overhead	2.00	70,000	
Total production costs			455,000
= Gross margin			175,000

Exercise 10.13

Marginal cost of production

	£	Jan £	£	Feb £
Revenues volume		160,000		195,000
Production volume		190,000		175,000
Closing inventories volume		30,000		10,000
Revenues		10,816,000		13,182,000
Opening inventories	0		1,092,000	
Factory costs	6,916,000		6,370,000	
	6,916,000		7,462,000	
less Closing inventories	1,092,000		364,000	
		5,824,000		7,098,000
Contribution		4,992,000		6,084,000
less Factory overheads		975,000		975,000
		4,017,000		5,109,000

Absorption cost of production

	£	Jan £	£	Feb £
Revenues volume		160,000		195,000
Production volume		190,000		175,000
Closing inventories volume		30,000		10,000
Revenues		10,816,000		13,182,000
Opening inventories	0		1,242,000	
Variable costs	7,866,000		7,245,000	
	7,866,000		8,487,000	
less Closing inventories	1,242,000		414,000	
		6,624,000		8,073,000
Gross profit		4,192,000		5,109,000

Exercise 11.1

E. TEE Ltd
CASH BUDGET
for the quarter ending 31st March 200X

	Jan £	Feb £	Mar £
Part A			
Receipts:			
Revenues	216,000	144,000	132,000
Cash sales	36,000	33,000	30,000
Fixtures and fittings			1,500
Sub total A	252,000	177,000	163,500
Part B			
Payments:			
Trade and other payables	87,750	58,500	117,000
Overhead expense	28,500	26,500	31,500
Wages	60,000	51,000	52,000
Computer		37,500	
Sub total B	176,250	173,500	200,500
Part C			
Balance (A–B)	75,750	3,500	– 37,000
Part D			
Balance b/f	30,000	105,750	109,250
Balance c/f	105,750	109,250	72,250

Exercise 11.2

DREAM Ltd

CASH BUDGET

for the six months ending 30th June 200X

	Jan	Feb	Mar	Apr	May	Jun
	£	£	£	£	£	£
Part A Receipts:						
Revenues	0	20,000	40,000	40,000	50,000	60,000
Sub total A	0	20,000	40,000	40,000	50,000	60,000
Part B Payments:						
Raw materials	0	12,000	12,000	12,000	18,000	18,000
Wages	8,000	8,000	8,000	12,000	12,000	12,000
Rent	10,000			10,000		
Heat and light			5,000			5,000
Other expenses	10,000	10,000	10,000	10,000	10,000	10,000
Capital equipment	5,000	5,000	5,000	5,000	5,000	5,000
Sub total B	33,000	35,000	40,000	49,000	45,000	50,000
Part C						
Balance (A–B)	–33,000	–15,000	0	–9,000	5,000	10,000
Part D						
Balance b/f	25,000	–8,000	–23,000	–23,000	–32,000	–27,000
Balance c/f	–8,000	–23,000	–23,000	–32,000	–27,000	–17,000

DREAM Ltd
BUDGETED INCOME STATEMENT
for the six months ended 30th June 200X

	£	£
Revenues		300,000
Raw materials	90,000	
Wages and salaries	60,000	
Rent	20,000	
Heat and light	10,000	
Other expenses	60,000	
Depreciation (50,000 x 25% ÷ 2)	6,250	
		246,250
Net profit		53,750

DREAM Ltd
BUDGETED BALANCE SHEET
as at   30th June 2000X

	£	£	£
Non-current assets:	Cost	Depn.	N.B.V.
Plant and machinery	50,000	6,250	43,750
Current assets:			
Trade and other receivables		90,000	
Cash and cash equivalent		0	
		90,000	
less Current liabilities:			
Trade and other payables	38,000		
Bank overdraft	17,000	55,000	35,000
			78,750
Equity:			
Issued share capital			25,000
Retained earnings			53,750
			78,750

Exercise 11.3

ALASTAIR DRYANT
CASH BUDGET
for the four months ending 30th April 200X

	Jan	Feb	Mar	Apr
	£	£	£	£
Part A Receipts:				
Revenues		4,500	6,000	9,000
Cash sales	4,500	6,000	9,000	10,000
Sub total A	4,500	10,500	15,000	19,000
Part B Payments:				
Raw materials	0	0	8,400	7,200
Wages and expenses	2,700	3,600	5,400	6,000
Fixed expenses	1,800	1,800	1,800	1,800
Managers salary	2,000	2,000	2,000	2,000
Machinery	0	12,000	12,000	12,000
Sub total B	6,500	19,400	29,600	29,000
Part C				
Balance (A–B)	–2,000	–8,900	–14,600	–10,000
Part D				
Balance b/f	25,000	23,000	14,100	–500
Balance c/f	23,000	14,100	–500	–10,500

Calculation of purchases and and trade payables:

	Jan	Feb	Mar	Apr
	£	£	£	£
Revenues	9,000	12,000	18,000	20,000
Materials: 40%	3,600	4,800	7,200	8,000
Purchases				
January	3,600			
February	4,800			
March		7,200		
April			8,000	
May				8,000

Calculation of expenses:
Fixed expenses of £2,200 less £400 per month depreciation.

Exercise 11.4

P.C. Ltd
CASH BUDGET
for the six months to 31st December 200X

	Jul £	Aug £	Sep £	Oct £	Nov £	Dec £
Part A Receipts:						
Revenues	70,000	40,000	40,000	50,000	70,000	80,000
Sub total A	70,000	40,000	40,000	50,000	70,000	80,000
Part B Payments:						
Trade payables	40,000	25,000	15,000	39,000	46,000	60,000
Wages	5,000	7,000	8,000	10,000	6,000	4,000
Capital equipment		40,000				
Fixed costs	5,000	5,000	5,000	5,000	5,000	5,000
Dividend	10,000					
Sub total B	60,000	77,000	28,000	54,000	57,000	69,000
Part C						
Balance (A–B)	10,000	–37,000	12,000	–4,000	13,000	11,000
Part D						
Balance b/f	0	10,000	–27,000	–15,000	–19,000	–6,000
Balance c/f	10,000	–27,000	–15,000	–19,000	–6,000	5,000

Calculation to determine purchases:

	Jul £000	Aug £000	Sep £000	Oct £000	Nov £000	Dec £000
Revenues	50	70	80	100	60	40
– Gross profit	15	21	24	30	18	12
= Cost of sales	35	49	56	70	42	28
+ Closing inventories	200	190	180	170	170	160
	235	239	236	240	212	188
– Opening inventories	220	200	190	180	170	170
= Purchases	15	39	46	60	42	18

Exercise 11.5

Thrust Limited – Cash budget, for the quarter ending 30th September 200X

	July £	Aug. £	Sept. £
Part A Receipts:			
Revenues	260,650	241,250	194,000
Loan stock		30,000	
Sub total A	260,650	271,250	194,000
Part B Payments:			
Purchases	60,000	55,000	80,000
Wages	46,250	32,500	33,750
Research and development	9,000	12,500	13,500
Administration costs	25,000	30,000	25,000
Production costs	25,000	20,000	18,000
Taxation		110,000	
Dividend	50,000		
Capital expenditure			40,000
Commissions	5,800	4,900	3,600
Sub total B	221,050	264,900	213,850
Part C: Balance (A–B)	39,600	6,350	–19,850
Part D			
Balance b/f	30,000	69,600	75,950
Balance c/f	69,600	75,950	56,100

Calculation of revenues:

	May	June	July	Aug.	Sept.
Revenues (£)	240,000	290,000	245,000	180,000	170,000
In month 20%			49,000	36,000	34,000
1 month 50%			145,000	122,500	90,000
2 months 30%			72,000	87,000	73,500
			266,000	245,500	197,500
less cash discount 5%			–2,450	–1,800	–1,700
cash discount 2%			–2,900	–2,450	–1,800
			260,650	241,250	194,000

Exercise 11.6

FINDINGS Ltd
CASH BUDGET
for the quarter ending 30th April 200X

	Jan £	Feb £	Mar £	Apr £
Part A Receipts:				
Revenues [1]	10,800	71,700	120,560	105,880
Sub total A	10,800	71,700	120,560	105,880
Part B Payments:				
Purchases	–	62,000	50,000	40,000
Labour	34,000	34,000	26,000	36,000
Capital expenditure	180,000		20,000	
Production expenses [2]	8,500	5,500	4,500	5,500
Administration expenses	9,200	7,200	7,200	7,200
Selling and distribution	7,500	8,500	7,000	9,500
Sub total B	239,200	117,200	114,700	98,200
Part C				
Balance (A–B)	–228,400	–45,500	5,860	7,680
Part D				
Balance b/f	0	–228,400	–273,900	–268,040
Balance c/f	–228,400	–273,900	–268,040	–260,360

[1] Calculation of revenues:

	Jan £	Feb £	Mar £	Apr £
Revenues	120,000	130,000	84,000	132,000
10%	12,000	13,000	8,400	13,200
1 month 50%	–	60,000	65,000	42,000
2 months 40%	–	–	48,000	52,000
	12,000	73,000	121,400	107,200
less cash discount 10%	– 1,200	– 1,300	– 840	– 1,320
	10,800	71,700	120,560	105,880

(2) Calculation of production costs

	Jan	Feb	Mar	Apr
	£	£	£	£
Production costs	7,000	8,000	7,000	8,000
deduct Depreciation	–1,500	–1,500	–1,500	–1,500
deduct Monthly charge	–1,000	–1,000	–1,000	–1,000
add Cash payment	4,000			
	8,500	5,500	4,500	5,500

Exercise 12.1

	Standard hours times standard rate			Actual hours times standard rate			Actual hours times actual rate		
	Hrs	Rate	£	Hrs	Rate	£	Hrs	Rate	£
1	9,000	4.00	36,000	6,000	4.00	24,000	6,000		26,400
2	6,000	4.50	27,000	7,000	4.50	31,500	7,000		34,650
3	6,000	6.00	36,000	7,000	6.00	42,000	7,000		46,200
			99,000			97,500			107,250

Labour efficiency variance   Labour rate variance

£1,500   – £9,750

Labour cost variance

– £8,250

Exercise 12.2

	Standard quantity times standard price			Actual quantity times standard price			Actual quantity times actual price		
	Qty	Price	£	Qty	Price	£	Qty	Price	£
A	5,390	0.70	3,773	5,200	0.70	3,640	5,200	0.84	4,368
B	1,400	0.28	392	1,300	0.28	364	1,300	0.35	455
C	3,500	0.49	1,715	3,700	0.49	1,813	3,700	0.42	1,554
D	420	2.80	1,176	450	2.80	1,260	450	2.50	1,125
			7,056			7,077			7,502

Material usage variance   Material price variance

– £21   – £425

Material cost variance

– £446

Exercise 12.3a

	Standard quantity times standard price			Actual quantity times standard price			Actual quantity times actual price		
	Qty	Price	£	Qty	Price	£	Qty	Price	£
A	240	3.00	720	230	3.00	690	230	2.50	575
B	360	7.50	2,700	370	7.50	2,775	370	7.00	2,590
			3,420			3,465			3,165

Material usage variance   Material price variance

– £45   £300

Material cost variance

£255

Exercise 12.3b

	Standard hours times standard rate			Actual hours times standard rate			Actual hours times actual rate		
	Hrs	Rate	£	Hrs	Rate	£	Hrs	Rate	£
1	120	8.00	960	130	8.00	1,040	130	*7.50*	975
2	60	10.00	600	58	10.00	580	58	*10.00*	580
			1,560			1,620			1,555

Labour efficiency variance   Labour rate variance

– £60   £65

Labour cost variance

£5

Exercise 12.4

	Standard quantity times standard price			Actual quantity times standard price			Actual quantity times actual price		
	Qty	Price	£	Qty	Price	£	Qty	Price	£
A	30,000	0.75	22,500	32,000	0.75	24,000	32,000	0.80	25,600
B	20,000	1.50	30,000	16,000	1.50	24,000	16,000	1.80	28,800
			52,500			48,000			54,400

Material usage variance Material price variance

£4,500 −£6,400

Material cost variance

−£1,900

Exercise 12.5

	Standard hours times standard rate			Actual hours times standard rate			Actual hours times actual rate		
	Hrs	Rate	£	Hrs	Rate	£	Hrs	Rate	£
	300	6.00	1,800	360	6.00	2,160	360	5.00	1,800

Labour efficiency variance Labour rate variance

− £360 £360

Labour cost variance

£0

Exercise 12.6

	Standard quantity times standard price			Actual quantity times standard price			Actual quantity times actual price		
	Qty	Price	£	Qty	Price	£	Qty	Price	£
	300	3.00	900	250	3.00	750	250	4.00	1,000

Material usage variance Material price variance

£150 − £250

Material cost variance

− £100

Exercise 12.7

Standard quantity times standard price			Actual quantity times standard price			Actual quantity times actual price		
Qty	Price	£	Qty	Price	£	Qty	Price	£
1,250	5.00	6,250	1,100	5.00	5,500	1,100	5.20	5,720

Material usage variance   Material price variance

£750   – £220

Material cost variance

£530

Exercise 12.8

	Standard quantity times standard price			Actual quantity times standard price			Actual quantity times actual price		
	Qty	Price	£	Qty	Price	£	Qty	Price	£
A	30,000	3.75	112,500	32,000	3.75	120,000	32,000	4.00	128,000
B	20,000	7.50	150,000	16,000	7.50	120,000	16,000	9.00	144,000
			262,500			240,000			272,000

Material usage variance   Material price variance

£22,500   –£32,000

Material cost variance

–£9,500

Exercise 13.1

Payback period – Project A = 3 years

	£	Annual to payback £	Cumulative to payback £
Capital outlay	− 65,000		
Cash inflows:	Annual		
	£		
Year 1	30,000	30,000	30,000
Year 2	20,000	20,000	50,000
Year 3	15,000	15,000	65,000

Payback period – Project B = 3.1 years

	£	Annual to payback £	Cumulative to payback £
Capital outlay	− 18,000		
Cash inflows:	Annual		
	£		
Year 1	45,000	45,000	45,000
Year 2	45,000	45,000	90,000
Year 3	45,000	45,000	135,000
Year 4	45,000	5,000	140,000

Payback period – Project C = 2 years

	£	Annual to payback £	Cumulative to payback £
Capital outlay	− 30,000		
Cash inflows:	Annual		
	£		
Year 1	20,000	20,000	20,000
Year 2	10,000	10,000	30,000

Payback period – Project D = 3.6 years

	£	Annual to payback £	Cumulative to payback £
Capital outlay	− 160,000		
Cash inflows:	Annual		
	£		
Year 1	35,000	35,000	35,000
Year 2	35,000	35,000	70,000
Year 3	55,000	55,000	125,000
Year 4	55,000	35,000	160,000

Accounting rate of return

	A £	B £	C £	D £
Net cash inflows	85,000	225,000	40,000	245,000
less capital outlay	65,000	140,000	30,000	160,000
Profit over the life of each project	20,000	85,000	10,000	85,000
Life (years)	5	5	2	5
Average annual profit	4,000	17,000	5,000	17,000
Accounting rate of return	6.2%	12.1%	16.7%	10.6%

Accounting rate of return: calculations for Project A

Project A = 4,000 ÷ 65,000 x 100 = 6.2%

Net present value – Project A   **Profitability index = 1.14**

Year	Cash flows £	DCF factor 6.0%	Present value £
1	30,000	0.943	28,290
2	20,000	0.890	17,800
3	15,000	0.840	12,600
4	10,000	0.792	7,920
5	10,000	0.747	7,470
Present value of cash inflows			74,080
less Capital outlay			65,000
Net present value			9,080

Net present value – Project B   **Profitability index = 1.35**

Year	Cash flows £	DCF factor 6.0%	Present value £
1	45,000	0.943	42,435
2	45,000	0.890	40,050
3	45,000	0.840	37,800
4	45,000	0.792	35,640
5	45,000	0.747	33,615
Present value of cash inflows			189,540
less Capital outlay			140,000
Net present value			49,540

Net present value – Project C   **Profitability index = 1.21**

Year	Cash flows £	DCF factor 6.0%	Present value £
1	20,000	0.943	18,860
2	10,000	0.890	8,900
3	10,000	0.840	8,400
Present value of cash inflows			36,160
less Capital outlay			30,000
Net present value			6,160

Net present value – Project D   **Profitability index = 1.27**

Year	Cash flows £	DCF factor 6.0%	Present value £
1	35,000	0.943	33,005
2	35,000	0.890	31,150
3	55,000	0.840	46,200
4	55,000	0.792	43,560
5	65,000	0.747	48,555
Present value of cash inflows			202,470
less Capital outlay			160,000
Net present value			42,470

Internal rate of return – Project B only

Year	Cash flows £	DCF factor 17%	Present value £	DCF factor 19%	Present value £
1	45,000	0.855	38,475	0.840	37,800
2	45,000	0.731	32,895	0.706	31,770
3	45,000	0.624	28,080	0.593	26,685
4	45,000	0.534	24,030	0.499	22,455
5	45,000	0.456	20,520	0.419	18,855
Present value of cash inflows			144,000		137,565
less Capital outlay			140,000		140,000
Net present value			+ 4,000		– 2,435

$$\text{Internal rate of return} \quad = \quad 17 + \frac{4{,}000}{(4{,}000 + 2{,}435)} \times 2$$

$$= \quad 17 + 1.2$$

$$= \quad 18.2\%$$

Exercise 13.2

Convert profit to cash flows:

Year	Profit £		Overhead £		Depn [1] £		Cash flow £
1	60,000	+	24,000	+	66,000	=	150,000
2	45,000	+	24,000	+	66,000	=	135,000
3	21,000	+	24,000	+	66,000	=	111,000
4	12,000	+	24,000	+	66,000	=	102,000
5	12,000	+	24,000	+	66,000	=	102,000

$$\text{[1] Depreciation} \quad = \quad \frac{(\text{Capital outlay} - \text{Residual value})}{\text{Life}}$$

Year	Cash flows [2] £	DCF factor 10 %	Present value £
1	150,000	0.909	136,350
2	135,000	0.826	111,510
3	111,000	0.751	83,361
4	102,000	0.683	69,666
5	162,000	0.621	100,602
Present value of cash inflows			501,489
less Capital outlay			390,000
Net present value			111,489

[2]   The residual value of £60,000 is added to the cash flow for year 5 to give £162,000.

Exercise 13.3

Convert profit to cash flows:

Year	Profit £		Depn (1) £		Cash flow £
1	32,000	+	80,000	=	112,000
2	48,000	+	80,000	=	128,000
3	60,000	+	80,000	=	140,000
4	120,000	+	80,000	=	200,000
5	48,000	+	80,000	=	128,000

(1) Depreciation = £400,000 ÷ 5 = £80,000

Net present value:

Year	Cash flows (2) £	DCF factor 14 %	Present value £
1	112,000	0.877	98,224
2	128,000	0.769	98,432
3	140,000	0.675	94,500
4	200,000	0.592	118,400
5	208,000	0.519	107,952
Present value of cash inflows			517,508
less Capital outlay			480,000
Net present value			37,508

(2) The residual value of £80,000 is added to the cash flow for year 5 to give £208,000.

Payback period:

	£		
Capital outlay	– 480,000		
Cash inflows:	Annual	Annual to payback	Cumulative to payback
	£	£	£
Year 1	112,000	112,000	112,000
Year 2	128,000	128,000	240,000
Year 3	140,000	140,000	380,000
Year 4	200,000	100,000	480,000

Payback period = 3.5 years

Exercise 13.4

1. Payback period:

	£'000	Annual to payback	Cumulative to payback
Capital outlay	− 90,000		
Cash inflows:	Annual		
	£'000	£'000	£'000
Year 1	40,000	40,000	40,000
Year 2	35,000	35,000	75,000
Year 3	30,000	15,000	90,000

Payback period   =   2 years 6 months

2. Accounting rate of return:

	£
Net cash inflows	150,000
less Capital outlay	90,000
Profit over the life of Project	60,000
Life (years)	5
Average annual profit	12,000

Accounting rate of return   =   12,000 ÷ 90,000 x 100   =   13.3%

Exercise 13.5

1. Payback period

	£'000	Annual to payback	Cumulative to payback
Capital outlay	− 130,000		
Cash inflows:	Annual		
	£'000	£'000	£'000
Year 1	60,000	60,000	60,000
Year 2	50,000	50,000	110,000
Year 3	40,000	20,000	130,000

Payback period   =   2 years 6 months

2.   **Net present value**

Year	Cash flows £000	DCF factor 12 %	Present value £000
1	60,000	0.893	53,580
2	50,000	0.797	39,850
3	40,000	0.712	28,480
4	30,000	0.636	19,080
5	20,000	0.567	11,340
Present value of cash inflows			152,330
less Capital outlay			130,000
Net present value			22,330

Exercise 13.6

			£m
Present value of cash inflows	(£50m x 3.791)	=	189.55
less Capital outlay			150.00
Net present value			39.55
Profitability index	(189.55 ÷ 150.00)		1.26

Exercise 13.7

This answer uses annuity tables

1.   Internal rate of return

Capital outlay ÷ Annual savings = £70,000 ÷ £20,000 = 3.500

Consult annuity tables for a 5 year life. 3.517 is equal to 13%, therefore internal rate of return is approximately **13%**.

2.   Annual savings to achieve a 12% internal rate of return

Capital outlay ÷ Annuity at 12% = £70,000 ÷ 3.605 = **£19,417**

3. **Net present value and profitability index**

		£
Present value of cash inflows	(£20,000 x 3.791) =	75,820
less Capital outlay		70,000
Net present value		5,820
Profitability index	(£75,820 ÷ £70,000)	1.08

Exercise 14.1

Replace existing machines:

	Outlay £	Annual savings £
Cutting machine	27,000	6,000
Planing machine	35,000	8,000
Sanding machine	12,000	3,000
	74,000	17,000

		£
Present value of cash inflows	(£17,000 x 5.019) =	85,323
less Capital outlay		74,000
Net present value		11,323
Profitability index	(85,323 ÷ 74,000)	1.15

Replace existing machines with a multipurpose machine:

Annual savings £45,000 – £16,000 = £29,000

		£
Present value of cash inflows	(£29,000 x 5.019) =	145,551
less Capital outlay		132,000
Net present value		13,551
Profitability index	(145,551 ÷ 132,000)	1.10

Choose the option with the highest profitability index, i.e. 1.15

Exercise 14.2

Calculate NPVs for Project A - using annuity tables:

At 10% discount rate: £
Present value of cash inflows £87,500 x 2.487   =   217,613
less Capital outlay   190,000
                                                              ─────────
Net present value (NPV)   27,613

At 14% discount rate: £
Present value of cash inflows £87,500 x 2.322   =   203,175
less Capital outlay   190,000
                                                              ─────────
Net present value (NPV)   13,175

At 18% discount rate: £
Present value of cash inflows £87,500 x 2.174   = 190,225
less Capital outlay   190,000
                                                          ─────────
Net present value (NPV)   225

At 22% discount rate: £
Present value of cash inflows £87,500 x 2.042   = 178,675
less Capital outlay   190,000
                                                          ─────────
Net present value (NPV)   -11,325

Calculate NPVs for Project B:

Year	Cash flows £	DCF factor 10 %	Present value £
1	75,000	0.909	68,175
2	150,000	0.826	123,900
3	195,000	0.751	146,445

Present value of cash inflows   338,520
less Capital outlay   300,000
                                                          ─────────
Net present value (NPV)   38,520

Year	Cash flows £	DCF factor 14 %	Present value £
1	75,000	0.877	65,775
2	150,000	0.769	115,350
3	195,000	0.675	131,625

Present Value of Cash Inflows		312,750
less Capital Outlay		300,000
Net Present Value		12,750

Year	Cash flows £	DCF factor 18 %	Present value £
1	75,000	0.847	63,525
2	150,000	0.718	107,700
3	195,000	0.609	118,755

Present value of cash inflows		289,980
less Capital outlay		300,000
Net present value (NPV)		-10,020

Year	Cash flows £	DCF factor 22 %	Present value £
1	75,000	0.820	61,500
2	150,000	0.672	100,800
3	195,000	0.551	107,445

Present value of cash inflows		269,745
less Capital outlay		300,000
Net present value (NPV)		-30,255

Summary of NPVs and incremental NPVs

Discount rate	Project B £	Project A £	Incremental NPV (B - A) £
10%	38,520	27,613	10,907
14%	12,750	13,175	-425
18%	-10,020	225	-10,245
22%	-30,255	-11,325	-18,930

Exercise 14.3

1.

Year	Cash flows £	DCF factor 10 %	Present value £
1	35,000	0.909	31,815
2	35,000	0.826	28,910
3	35,000	0.751	26,285
4	35,000	0.683	23,905
5	35,000	0.621	21,735

Present value of cash inflows   132,650
less Capital outlay   115,000

Net present value   17,650

$$P.I. = \frac{132,650}{115,000} = 1.15$$

Year	Cash flows £	DCF factor 10%	Present value £
1	75,000	0.909	68,175
2	20,000	0.826	16,520
3	20,000	0.751	15,020
4	20,000	0.683	13,660
5	20,000	0.621	12,420

Present value of cash inflows   125,795
less Capital outlay   110,000

Net present value   15,795

$$P.I. = \frac{125,795}{110,000} = 1.14$$

Exercise 14.4

1.   **No adjustments for inflation**

Net present value with no inflation

(£250,000 - £180,000) x   3.605   =   £252,350
less Capital outlay   £200,000
                                                    ─────────
Net present value   £52,350

2.   **Adjusting revenues and costs for inflation**

Year	Revenues 1.07 £	Costs 1.04 £	Net cash flows £
0	250,000	180,000	
1	267,500	187,200	80,300
2	286,225	194,688	91,537
3	306,261	202,476	103,785
4	327,699	210,575	117,124
5	350,638	218,998	131,640

Adjusting the cost of capital:
1.12 x 1.05 = 1.176   therefore 17.6%

3.   **Net present value - with differential inflation**

Year	Savings £	DFC 17.6%	Present value £
1	80,300	0.850	68,255
2	91,537	0.723	66,181
3	103,785	0.615	63,828
4	117,124	0.523	61,256
5	131,640	0.445	58,580

Present value of cash inflows   318,100
Capital outlay   200,000
                                                    ─────────
Net present value (NPV)   118,100

Exercise 14.5

Adjusting revenues and costs for inflation:

Year	Revenues 1.04 £000	Material costs 1.03 £000	Labour costs 1.08 £000	Specific fixed costs 1.02 £000	Net cash flows £000
0	7,200	1,350	3,150	1,000	
1	7,488	1,391	3,402	1,020	1,675
2	7,788	1,432	3,674	1,040	1,642
3	8,099	1,475	3,968	1,061	1,595
4	8,423	1,519	4,286	1,082	1,536
5	8,760	1,565	4,628	1,104	1,463
6	9,110	1,612	4,999	1,126	1,373
7	9,475	1,660	5,399	1,149	1,267
8	9,854	1,710	5,830	1,172	1,142
9	10,248	1,761	6,297	1,195	995
10	10,658	1,814	6,801	1,219	824

Net present value - with differential inflation

Year	Savings £000	DCF 14.0%	Present value £000
1	1,675	0.877	1,469
2	1,642	0.769	1,263
3	1,595	0.675	1,077
4	1,536	0.592	909
5	1,463	0.519	759
6	1,373	0.456	626
7	1,267	0.400	507
8	1,142	0.351	401
9	995	0.308	306
10	824	0.270	222

Present value of cash inflows		7,539
Capital outlay		7,000
Net present value (NPV)		539

Exercise 14.6

Calculation of after tax capital allowance

Year	A Reducing balance	B Capital allowance (at 25%)	C Tax saved using capital allowance (at 35%)
	£	£	£
1	180,000	45,000	15,750
2	135,000	33,750	11,813
3	101,250	25,313	8,860
4	75,937	18,984	6,644
5	56,953	14,238	4,983
6	42,715	42,715	14,950

(1) *In the final year the capital allowance if any balance remaining, i.e. £42,715*

Project appraisal incorporating tax

Year	C Tax saved using cap allowance £	D Operating cash inflow (2) £	E Tax on cash inflow £	G Cash flow £	H DCF 12 %	I Present value £
1	15,750	72,000		87,750	0.893	78,361
2	11,813	72,000	-25,200	58,613	0.797	46,715
3	8,860	72,000	-25,200	55,660	0.712	39,630
4	6,644	72,000	-25,200	53,444	0.636	33,990
5	4,983	72,000	-25,200	51,783	0.567	29,361
6	14,950		-25,200	-10,250	0.507	-5,197

Present value of cash inflows	222,860
Capital outlay	180,000
Net present value (NPV)	42,860

Exercise 14.7

Calculation of after tax capital allowances

	A	B	C
Year	Reducing balance	Capital allowance	Tax saved using capital allowance
		(at 25%)	(at 35%)
	£	£	£
1	250,000	62,500	21,875
2	187,500	46,875	16,406
3	140,625	35,156	12,305
4	105,469	26,367	9,228
5	79,102	19,776	6,922
6	59,326	14,832	5,191
7	44,494	44,494	15,573

[1] *In the final year the capital allowances is any balance remaining, i.e. £44,494.*

Project appraisal incorporating tax

	C	D	E	F	G	H
	Tax saved using cap allowance	Operating cash inflow	Tax on cash inflow	Cash flow	DCF 10 %	Present value
Year	£	£	£	£		£
1	21,875	70,000		91,875	0.909	83,514
2	16,406	70,000	-24,500	61,906	0.826	51,134
3	12,305	70,000	-24,500	57,805	0.751	43,412
4	9,228	70,000	-24,500	54,728	0.683	37,379
5	6,922	70,000	-24,500	52,422	0.621	32,554
6	5,191	70,000	-24,500	50,691	0.564	28,590
7	15,573		-24,500	-8,927	0.513	-4,580

Present value of cash inflows	272,003
Capital outlay	250,000
Net present value (NPV)	22,003

Exercise 14.8

1. **Determine the annual net cash flow**

    (Revenues volume x Contribution per unit) - Specific fixed costs

    = (900,000 x £3.00) - £1,000,000

    = £1,700,000

2. **Calculate the project's NPV:**

    (Annual net cash flow x Annuity factor) - Capital cutlay

    = (£1,700,000 x 5.216) - £7,000,000

    = £1,867,200

3. **Adjust the input variables adversely by 10%**

Input variables adversely affected by 10%

	Original estimate	Varied adversely by 10%
Capital outlay	£7,000,000	£7,700,000
Life	10	9.091 (say 9)
Revenues volume	900,000	818,182
Selling price	£8.00	£7.27
Material cost	£1.50	£1.65
Labour cost	£3.50	£3.85
Specific fixed costs	£1,000,000	£1,100,000
Cost of capital	14	15.4

4. **Determine alternative cash flows and calculate revised NPV's**

	A Revenues volume	B Contri- bution p.unit	C Fixed costs	D Cash flow (A*B)-C
	Units	£	£	£
Capital Outlay	900,000	3.00	1,000,000	1,700,000 '
Life (years)	900,000	3.00	1,000,000	1,700,000
Revenues volume	818,182	3.00	1,000,000	1,454,546
Selling price	900,000	2.27	1,000,000	1,043,000
Material cost	900,000	2.85	1,000,000	1,565,000
Labour cost	900,000	2.65	1,000,000	1,385,000
Specific fixed costs	900,000	3.00	1,100,000	1,600,000

5. Calculate NPV's using annuity tables

	A Cash flow	B Annuity factor	C Present value of cash flow	D Capital outlay	E Net Present value
	£		£	£	£
Capital outlay	1,700,000	5.216	8,867,200	7,700,000	1,167,200
Life	1,700,000	4.946	8,408,200	7,000,000	1,408,200
Revenues volume	1,454,546	5.216	7,586,912	7,000,000	586,912
Selling price	1,043,000	5.216	5,440,288	7,000,000	-1,559,712
Material cost	1,565,000	5.216	8,163,040	7,000,000	1,163,040
Labour cost	1,385,000	5.216	7,224,160	7,000,000	224,160
Specific fixed cost	1,600,000	5.216	8,345,600	7,000,000	1,345,600
Cost of capital	1,700,000	4.943	8,403,100	7,000,000	1,403,100

6. Rank input variables according to sensitivity of NPV's

NPV	£
Selling price	-1,559,712
Labour cost	224,160
Revenues Volume	586,912
Material cost	1,163,040
Capital outlay	1,167,200
Specific fixed costs	1,345,600
Cost of capital	1,403,100
Life	1,408,200

Exercise 14.9

1. Determine the annual net cash flow:

(Revenues volume x Contribution per unit) - Specific fixed costs

=   (50,000   x   £5.00) -   £75,000

=   £175,000

2. Calculate the project's NPV:

(Annual net cash flow   x   Annuity factor) - Capital outlay

=   (£175,000   x   3.791) -   £500,000

=   £163,425

3. **Adjust the input variables adversely by 5%**

	Original estimate	Varied adversely by 5%
Capital outlay	£500,000	£525,000
Life (years)	5	4.76 (say 5)
Revenues volume (units)	50,000	47,619
Selling price	£25.00	£23.81
Material cost	£12.00	£12.60
Labour cost	£8.00	£8.40
Specific fixed costs	£75,000	£78,750
Cost of capital	10	10.5

4. **Determine alternative cash flows and calculate revised NPVs**

	A Revenues volume	B Contribution p.unit	C Fixed cost	D Cash flow (A*B)-C
	Units	£	£	£
Capital outlay	50,000	5.00	75,000	175,000
Life	50,000	5.00	75,000	175,000
Revenues volume	47,619	5.00	75,000	163,095
Selling price	50,000	3.81	75,000	115,500
Material cost	50,000	4.40	75,000	145,000
Labour cost	50,000	4.60	75,000	155,000
Specific fixed costs	50,000	5.00	78,750	171,250

5. **Calculate NPV's using annuity tables**

	A Cash flow	B Annuity factor	C Present value of cash flow	D Capital outlay	E Net present value
	£		£	£	£
Capital outlay	175,000	3.791	663,425	525,000	138,425
Life	175,000	3.791	663,425	500,000	163,425
Revenues volume	163,095	3.791	618,293	500,000	118,293
Selling price	115,500	3.791	437,861	500,000	-62,139
Material cost	145,000	3.791	549,695	500,000	49,695
Labour cost	155,000	3.791	587,605	500,000	87,605
Specific fixed costs	171,250	3.791	649,209	500,000	149,209
Cost of capital	175,000	3.743	655,025	500,000	155,025

6. **Rank input variables according to sensitivity of NPVs**

NPV	£
Selling price	-62,139
Material cost	49,695
Labour cost	87,605
Revenues volume	118,293
Capital outlay	138,425
Specific fixed costs	149,209
Cost of capital	155,025
Life	163,425

Index

A

B

C